SHAKESPEARE BEYOND D(

Did Shakespeare write Shakespeare? The authorship question has been much treated in works of fiction, film and television, provoking interest all over the world. Sceptics have proposed many candidates as the author of Shakespeare's works, including Francis Bacon, Christopher Marlowe and Edward de Vere, the seventeenth Earl of Oxford. But why and how did the authorship question arise and what does surviving evidence offer in answer to it? This authoritative, accessible and frequently entertaining book sets the debate in its historical context and provides an account of its main protagonists and their theories. Presenting the authorship of Shakespeare's works in relation to historiography, psychology and literary theory, twenty-two distinguished scholars reposition and develop the discussion. The book explores the issues in the light of biographical, textual and bibliographical evidence to bring fresh perspectives to an intriguing cultural phenomenon.

PAUL EDMONDSON is Head of Research and Knowledge and Director of the Stratford-upon-Avon Poetry Festival for The Shakespeare Birthplace Trust. His publications include: *Twelfth Night: A Guide to the Text and Its Theatrical Life* and (co-authored with Stanley Wells) *Shakespeare's Sonnets, Coffee with Shakespeare* and *Shakespeare Bites Back* (an e-book about the Shakespeare Authorship Discussion, published in October 2011). His other publications include work on Shakespeare and the Brontës, the poetry of Shakespeare and Christopher Marlowe and the musicality of Shakespeare's words. He is curator of *6minuteswithShakespeare.com*, The Shakespeare Birthplace Trust's response to the authorship debate. He is also a priest in The Church of England.

STANLEY WELLS, CBE, is Honorary President and Former Chairman of the Trustees of Shakespeare's Birthplace, Emeritus Professor of Shakespeare Studies of the University of Birmingham and Honorary Emeritus Governor of the Royal Shakespeare Theatre, of which he was for many years Vice-Chairman. He was for nearly twenty years the editor of the annual *Shakespeare Survey*, and writes for the *New York Review of Books* and many other publications. He has edited *The New Cambridge Companion to Shakespeare Studies* and is General Editor (with Gary Taylor) of *The Complete Oxford Shakespeare*. His most recent books are *Shakespeare For All Time; Looking for Sex in Shakespeare; Shakespeare & Co.*; and *Is It True What they Say About Shakespeare? His Shakespeare, Sex, and Love* was published in 2010.

Frontispiece. *William Shakespeare, his method of work*, 1904, by Max Beerbohm.
Photo: The Shakespeare Birthplace Trust. © The Estate of Max Beerbohm.
Reproduced by permission of Berlin Associates Ltd.

SHAKESPEARE BEYOND DOUBT

Evidence, Argument, Controversy

EDITED BY

PAUL EDMONDSON AND STANLEY WELLS

CAMBRIDGE
UNIVERSITY PRESS

CAMBRIDGE UNIVERSITY PRESS
Cambridge, New York, Melbourne, Madrid, Cape Town,
Singapore, São Paulo, Delhi, Mexico City

Cambridge University Press
The Edinburgh Building, Cambridge CB2 8RU, UK

Published in the United States of America by Cambridge University Press, New York

www.cambridge.org
Information on this title: www.cambridge.org/9781107017597

© Cambridge University Press 2013

First published 2013
Reprinted 2013

Printed and bound in the United Kingdom by Bell and Bain Ltd

A catalogue record for this publication is available from the British Library

Library of Congress Cataloguing in Publication data
Shakespeare beyond doubt : evidence, argument, controversy / edited by Paul Edmondson
and Stanley Wells.
pages   cm
Includes bibliographical references and index.
ISBN 978-1-107-01759-7
I. Shakespeare, William, 1564–1616 – Authorship.   I. Edmondson, Paul, editor of compilation.
II. Wells, Stanley, 1930– editor of compilation.
PR2937.S445   2013
822.3′3 – dc23   2012040135

ISBN 978-1-107-01759-7 Hardback
ISBN 978-1-107-60328-8 Paperback

Contents

Illustrations

Contributors

HARDY M. COOK, Bowie State University

PAUL EDMONDSON, The Shakespeare Birthplace Trust

BARBARA EVERETT, Somerville College, Oxford

PAUL FRANSSEN, University of Utrecht

ANDREW HADFIELD, University of Sussex

STUART HAMPTON-REEVES, University of Central Lancashire

GRAHAM HOLDERNESS, University of Hertfordshire

MACDONALD P. JACKSON, University of Auckland

JOHN JOWETT, The Shakespeare Institute, University of Birmingham

DAVID KATHMAN, independent scholar

MATT KUBUS, The Shakespeare Institute, University of Birmingham

DOUGLAS M. LANIER, University of New Hampshire

JAMES MARDOCK, University of Nevada

KATHLEEN E. MCLUSKIE, The Shakespeare Institute, University of Birmingham

ANDREW MURPHY, University of St Andrews

ALAN H. NELSON, University of California

CHARLES NICHOLL, independent scholar

ERIC RASMUSSEN, University of Nevada

CAROL CHILLINGTON RUTTER, University of Warwick

JAMES SHAPIRO, Columbia University, New York

ALAN STEWART, Columbia University, New York

STANLEY WELLS, The Shakespeare Birthplace Trust

General introduction

Paul Edmondson and Stanley Wells

In August 1856, a 45-year-old American lady by the name of Delia Bacon paid a visit to Stratford-upon-Avon, where she lodged initially at 15 College Street, not far from Holy Trinity Church. She met with the vicar, George Granville, who allowed her access outside normal visiting hours to Shakespeare's grave, which she wished to investigate in the hope that it concealed solutions to an imagined code which would demonstrate that there were reasons to question received ideas about the authorship of Shakespeare's works. "'If I only had the proper tools", she complained to herself, "I could lift the stone myself, weak as I am, with no one to help" ... A strange weariness overcame her. She left, her mission unaccomplished.'[1]

We can relate these events around Shakespeare's grave to numerous aspects of the intellectual and cultural climate of the time which occupied the popular imagination: Gothic fiction and drama with their tales of subterranean passages and arcane messages; the questioning of religious orthodoxy; geological discoveries; the authorship of the Homeric poems; archaeological investigations; and the search for the origins of life. Charles Darwin's *The Origin of Species* was to be published three years later, in 1859. Detective fiction with its emphases on the solving of mysteries and the imposing of an all-controlling pattern on a world uncertain of itself was beginning to appear. One of its earliest exponents was Edgar Allan Poe, whom Bacon herself had beaten to the prize in a short story competition.

Delia Bacon published her disintegrationist work *The Philosophy of the Plays of Shakspere Unfolded* in 1857. Her doubts about Shakespeare's authorship had been anticipated by an eccentric New York lawyer, Colonel Joseph C. Hart in a curious and highly derivative book called *The Romance of Yachting* published in 1848.[2] Credulous of John Payne Collier's Henslowe forgeries, Hart was influenced also by a denigratory 'Life of Shakespeare' in Dionysus Lardner's *Cabinet Cyclopaedia*, which found that the plays 'absolutely teem with the grossest impurities, – more gross by far than can be found in any contemporary dramatist'.[3] Hart ramblingly and rantingly fantasized that Shakespeare, who 'grew up in ignorance and viciousness, and became a common poacher ... purchased or obtained surreptitiously' other men's plays which he then 'spiced with obscenity, blackguardism, and impurities'. He did not identify the original author or authors. We cannot tell whether Bacon knew Hart's book. It is her work that has proved to be seminal, and her name will recur frequently throughout the rest of this volume. Doubting that someone with Shakespeare's educational background could have written the works, she proposed that they were produced by a committee led by the philosopher, scientist and statesman, Sir Francis Bacon. A significant cultural foothold had become established. In early years, interest centred on Francis Bacon. An American Bacon Society, dedicated to propagating the theory that he wrote Shakespeare's works, was founded in 1885 and an English one in the following year. Since that time the proposition that the works were written by anyone else apart from Shakespeare has found expression in many forms.

Throughout this book we use the term 'anti-Shakespearian' to describe those who propagate any theory which disputes Shakespeare's authorship and co-authorship of the works attributed to him. In the past the term has been 'anti-Stratfordian', which allows the work attributed to Shakespeare to be separated from the social and cultural context of its author. But to deny Shakespeare of Stratford's connection to the work attributed to him is to deny the essence of, in part, what made that work possible. Michelangelo cannot be separated from Florence and Rome; Charles Dickens would not be Charles Dickens without London. Shakespeare was formed by both Stratford-upon-Avon and London. The phrases 'the Stratford man', 'actor from Stratford' and even 'anti-Stratfordian' perpetuate this kind of divide. These terms concede that it is possible to separate an artist from his or her background and cultural context. 'Anti-Shakespearian' seems to us to be a more accurate and honest term to use, even when we are referring to great Shakespeare writers and actors of the past and present.

Since Delia Bacon's time, thousands of books and articles have been published questioning Shakespeare's authorship and putting forward an extraordinary range of alternative nominees. An online search for 'Shakespeare's authorship' will reveal an abundance of proponents of anti-Shakespearian theories, and they are by no means confined to Britain and America. Some emanate, for example, from France, Germany, Italy, Norway, Russia and Sweden. And though some of them are amateurs, others are persons of high intellectual ability fully conversant with the techniques of academic scholarship.

Some of the candidates proposed over the decades were more or less contemporary with Shakespeare (most of them university educated or aristocratic, such as Sir Walter Ralegh and the Earls of Southampton, Rutland and Derby, and even including both Queen Elizabeth I and King James I. Others (such as Sir Philip Sidney) were dead by the time some of Shakespeare's plays and poems were written, and at least one (Daniel Defoe, born around 1659) lived long after Shakespeare's time. Fashions in candidature constantly fluctuate; beyond Francis Bacon, the most popular have been Christopher Marlowe and, currently, Edward de Vere, the seventeenth Earl of Oxford. Over the years, authorship has figured in innumerable newspaper reports, prominent public discussions, debates, radio and television broadcasts and in several mock trials, most notably in Washington, DC, in 1987 (with three Supreme Court justices) and in London in 1988 at the Inner Temple (with three Lord Justices) – the Shakespearian cause prevailed on both occasions. Many works of fiction have taken the topic as a point of departure. During the first decade of the twenty-first century the doubters began to achieve a higher profile through, especially, the proponents of the online 'Declaration of Reasonable Doubt' (see Chapter 17) which is proud to put to the fore various famous people who have signed it, including leading actors such as Sir Derek Jacobi, Jeremy Irons, Mark Rylance and Michael York. At least two universities actively encourage doubts about Shakespeare's authorship (see Chapters 17 and 19). The discussion achieved a high public profile in consequence of the prominent Hollywood film *Anonymous* (Sony Pictures, 2011, directed by Roland Emmerich) in which Shakespeare is portrayed as a drunken, inarticulate buffoon, acting as a front-man for the Earl of Oxford whom the film depicts as the covert author of Shakespeare's plays (as well as the illegitimate son of Queen Elizabeth I and illegitimate father, with Queen Elizabeth, of the Earl of Southampton, Shakespeare's patron). The poster advertising the film portrays a figure representing Shakespeare with his back to the viewer accompanied by the question 'Was Shakespeare a Fraud?' The film's distributors circulated educational materials designed to encourage teachers to doubt Shakespeare's authorship and to spread that doubt among their pupils.

At least until the end of the twentieth century the subject was the province of amateurs (that is, people with no professional commitment to literary or historical studies). What became known as 'the Shakespeare Authorship Debate' was largely ignored by many Shakespeare scholars who stood aloof from it, regarding it as a topic unworthy of their attention, even as a supreme expression of human folly. Shakespeare organizations

PAUL EDMONDSON AND STANLEY WELLS

and scholars are accustomed to being slandered with the accusation that they are defending Shakespeare's authorship, and what is often slightingly referred to as 'the Shakespeare industry', for selfish, commercial reasons.

Nevertheless the authorship discussion is a complex intellectual phenomenon well worthy of objective consideration. It raises questions about the nature of historical evidence, the moral responsibility of academic enquiry, the place of artists' works in relation to their lives, the cultural and intellectual formation of Shakespeare and his contemporaries, the status of scholarly and expert authority, the relationship between the professional scholar and the general public, the psychology of conspiracy theories and the practice of collaborative playwriting in Shakespeare's time.

It is partly in response to these developments that The Shakespeare Birthplace Trust felt the time had come to take a more active part in discussion of a topic which is of central importance not only to its activities but to those of innumerable other organizations world-wide and indeed to anyone interested in the works of the world's best-known and most influential writer (see Chapter 19).

This collection of essays is divided into three parts. Part I is concerned with some of the most conspicuous alternative nominees for Shakespeare's authorship and with the history of the claims that have been made for them. Part II examines various aspects of Shakespeare's authorship including his collaboration with other professional writers. Part III engages with ways in which the Shakespeare Authorship Discussion has found expression in the popular imagination. It is our hope that the collection will both illuminate the phenomenon and shine a Shakespearian light on a too-long-established heresy.

PART I

Sceptics

This first part of our book offers essays about claims that have been made on behalf of various individuals as alternative authors of the works more generally attributed to Shakespeare. Until the early years of the twenty-first century such claims were thought to have originated around 1785, over 150 years after Shakespeare died, in the work of a Warwickshire clergyman named James Wilmot (1726–1828). This belief originated in an article by Professor Allardyce Nicoll published in 1932 in the *Times Literary Supplement* entitled 'The First Baconian' which describes two lectures reportedly given before the Ipswich Philosophical Society by one James Corton Cowell in 1805. They claim that Wilmot amused himself in his retirement by trying to write a life of Shakespeare and tell how, losing faith in Shakespeare, he constructed a theory that the true author of the works was Francis Bacon. But in old age, Cowell reported, Wilmot instructed his housekeeper to burn his papers. His story would have been lost to posterity had he not previously confided it to Cowell, whose lectures were preserved in the University of London Library. But James Shapiro, in his invaluable book *Contested Will*, follows up suspicions about the authenticity of the documents first expressed in the anti-Shakespearian journal *Shakespeare Matters* 2 (Summer 2003) which show that the lectures draw on information, and even vocabulary, which was not available in Cowell's time. Nor is there any other evidence that Cowell, or the Ipswich Philosophical Society, ever existed. Only one conclusion is possible: the lectures are forgeries, and Nicoll was deceived by them. Even Shapiro doesn't know who perpetrated the fraud, or why. He guesses that it may have been done for money or have originated in 'the desire on the part of a Baconian to stave off the challenge posed by

1

supporters of the Earl of Oxford'. Furthermore, the deception 'reassigned the discovery of Francis Bacon's authorship from a "mad" American woman to' – and here Shapiro silently quotes *Richard II* 1.3.272 – 'a true-born Englishman'. As a result of these discoveries, the anti-Shakespearian movement must now be pushed forward to the middle of the nineteenth century. As Shapiro intriguingly remarks, 'the authorship question and the "whodunit" emerged at the same historical moment'.[1] In preparing this book Stanley Wells also examined the lectures, which remain unpublished, and was impressed by their plausible appearance of authenticity. There is no wonder that Nicoll was taken in by them. They warrant further investigation.

As we remark in our general introduction, the anti-Shakespearian movement must now be seen as finding its first thorough expression in the work of the American Delia Bacon, and especially in her long book, *The Philosophy of the Plays of Shakspere Unfolded*, of 1857, often described by those who have not read it as unreadable. One person who has worked his way through the book's intellectually contorted prose is Graham Holderness (Chapter 1), who writes of it and of its author with rare sympathy and understanding, demonstrating that, for all her wrong-headedness, if she were to be 'Delivered from her fruitless crusade to liberate the Shakespearian oeuvre from an allegedly false authorial ascription, Delia Bacon could become a founding mother of political Shakespeare criticism, ideological critique and collaborationist bibliography.'

Delia Bacon believed that the plays were written by a consortium of writers including Francis Bacon. Since her time it has been more common for single authors to be proposed, and one of them is Francis Bacon himself. Alan Stewart, distinguished as a biographer and editor of Bacon, tells the complex and often entertaining story of efforts to establish him as the author of Shakespeare, many of which depend on attempts to identify secret codes and hidden messages in the works such as Delia Bacon hoped to discover by opening Shakespeare's grave (Chapter 2).

One of the more absurd candidates, but one who has attracted and continues to attract many supporters, is Christopher Marlowe, whose death in 1593, early in Shakespeare's career, is one of the best recorded events in English literary history, and who is actually quoted and referred to as a 'dead shepherd' in *As You Like It* (3.5.82–3). Charles Nicholl, author of the immensely successful study of Marlowe's last hours, *The Reckoning* (1992), recounts how early attempts to identify him as the author of Shakespeare survived Leslie Hotson's discovery of the documentary evidence establishing conclusively, to anyone with a respect for historical evidence, that Marlowe died before most of Shakespeare's works were written (Chapter 3).

During the later part of the twentieth century Bacon and Marlowe were overtaken in the authorship stakes by Edward de Vere, seventeenth Earl of Oxford, whose candidature had first been propounded in 1920 by Thomas Looney. Oxford died in 1604, so his adherents have to explain away the evidence relating to the dates of composition of Shakespeare's later plays. Oxford's candidature has also become associated with what has become known as the Tudor Prince theory, according to one version of which Oxford was Queen Elizabeth's secret lover, and the Earl of Southampton their son. Alan Nelson, author of a major biography of the Earl, *Monstrous Adversary: The Life of Edward de Vere, 17th Earl of Oxford*, examines the numerous fallacies and illogicalities in presentations of the case for his authorship of Shakespeare (Chapter 4).

Though Bacon, Marlowe and de Vere have become the most heavily supported claimants, over the years a plethora of other names have been proposed. As Matt Kubus observes in the final chapter of this section of our book, 'Mathematically, each time an additional candidate is suggested, the probability decreases that any given name is the true author.' This fact has not stemmed the flow of pretenders to the throne, which may well have increased even before this book reaches publication.

CHAPTER I

The unreadable Delia Bacon

Graham Holderness

By common consensus, among both her admirers and her detractors, Delia Bacon's pioneering book on Shakespeare authorship, *The Philosophy of the Plays of Shakspere Unfolded* (1857), is 'unreadable'.[1] The case she presents, for an alternative theory of Shakespeare authorship, remains unproven, since (as she herself came close to admitting) she could adduce no direct evidence whatsoever to support it. Her work cannot truly be described as comprehensively influential, even within 'Shakespeare Authorship studies', as her hypothesis was one of collective and collaborative authorship, whereas virtually all alternative authorship claimants favour a particular individual. Her methodology, which was to elicit from the plays a 'philosophy' that could in her view have been understood and expounded only by writers other than William Shakespeare of Stratford, has in the present been superseded, in alternative candidature polemics, by largely biographical readings of the works.

So why should anyone bother to read the writings of Delia Bacon? Why attempt to read the unreadable?

The outlines of Delia Bacon's life have been thoroughly delineated in some key contemporary studies. I will confine myself to those biographical facts that are relevant to a study of her impact and influence. Born into a cultivated but poor New England background, daughter of a minister, Delia Bacon left school at the age of fourteen and became a schoolteacher. In due course she graduated to teaching adult women, and even lecturing to audiences of women and men in New York. Her initial ventures into writing were of a creative kind: she published some stories, beat Edgar Allan Poe in a newspaper short story competition, and then began writing a play, intended to feature the English star actress Ellen Tree. Bacon clearly felt a strong conflict between her Puritan background and her imaginative bent towards fiction and drama. Eventually the play was published as a work of drama rather than theatre – a 'dialogue', 'not a play', 'not intended for the stage'.[2] Around 1845 she began to pursue studies in Shakespeare authorship, driven by a conviction that Shakespeare was not the true author of the works, and that they were in reality written by others.

In America Bacon managed to interest such literary giants as Ralph Waldo Emerson and Nathaniel Hawthorne in her theories. In 1853 she journeyed to England in search of evidence to prove her case, and met with Thomas Carlyle, who dealt generously with her, though he found her ideas unpalatable. In England she pursued her research, and it was from England that she launched her authorship campaign, in an article 'William Shakespeare and his Plays: An Inquiry Concerning Them', published anonymously in *Putnam's Monthly Magazine* in 1856.[3] After the publication of her book the following year, Delia Bacon was afflicted by a psychological breakdown, repatriated to America, and spent her final years in a sanitorium.

In her *Putnam's* essay she systematically laid the foundations of Shakespearian doubt. She claimed, as all alternative authorship proponents claim, that William Shakespeare of Stratford could not possibly have written the plays and poems ascribed to him, for a number of reasons. One was that he apparently did not have the education and experience necessary for their composition, having never attended university, and never travelled abroad. The plays are informed by 'the highest literary culture of the age'[4] and Shakespeare of Stratford could not possibly have possessed it. She also found it impossible to believe that a man as devoted to financial and commercial acquisition as Shakespeare could have produced works of such political and philosophical significance.

How could the player's mercenary motive and the player's range of learning and experiment give us the key to this new application of the human reason to the human life? How could we understand, from such a source, this new, and strange, and persevering application of thought to life. . . .[5]

She found it incredible that the author of those works could have gone largely unrecognized and unacknowledged by the great intellectuals of the age; and that such an author could have shown so little concern to publish and preserve the works for posterity.

Hence it follows, not only that William Shakespeare was manifestly not the author of the works attributed to him, but that whoever was the true author, or authors, must have inhabited the higher echelons of Elizabethan and Jacobean society. In Delia Bacon's work, the aristocratic and courtly characters in Shakespeare's plays are regarded as the appropriate source for this new 'philosophy', which could not conceivably have been within the grasp of uneducated and proletarian actors. The 'courtly Hamlet' is contrasted with the group of strolling players he instructs in the third act of *Hamlet, Prince of Denmark*. Surely, Bacon argues, the author of *Hamlet* was more like the Prince than the players?

Condemned to refer the origin of these works to the vulgar, illiterate man who kept the theatre where they were first exhibited, a person of the most ordinary character and aims, compelled to regard them as the result merely of an extraordinary talent for pecuniary speculation in this man, how could we, how could any one, dare to see what is really in them?

... Condemned to look for the author of Hamlet himself – the subtle Hamlet of the university, the courtly Hamlet, 'the glass of fashion and the mould of form' – in that dirty, doggish group of players, who come into the scene summoned like a pack of hounds to his service ... how could we understand him – the enigmatical Hamlet, with the thought of ages in his foregone conclusions?[6]

Delia Bacon is commonly associated, perhaps simply because of the coincidence of names, with the claim that Lord Bacon was the true author of the Shakespearian œuvre. She did *not* however argue, as others later did, that the plays were solely the work of Lord Bacon. Indeed, at exactly the same time a separate, and perhaps independent case was being made for Bacon as the sole author, by William Henry Smith. Smith published his own book, *Bacon and Shakespeare*, the following year, thus coinciding with the publication of Delia Bacon's. But her argument was quite different from his.[7]

Her case was both more complex and correspondingly more difficult to prove. It was essentially that a 'school' of Renaissance intellectuals, including Francis Bacon and led by Sir Walter Ralegh, were responsible for the composition of the plays ascribed to Shakespeare, though their authorship remained cloaked in anonymity. Delia Bacon saw the Elizabethan monarchy, and its Jacobean successor, as a continuum of despotic tyranny, presided over by a paranoid monarch, supported by a repressive civil service and secured by a ruthless secret police. The monarchy and its court were instruments of violent coercion that could tolerate no disloyalty or dissent, and absolutely vetoed freedom of speech. Men such as Ralegh and Bacon, possessed of republican and libertarian ideas that in such conditions were dangerous even to espouse, still more to express, turned to writing plays as a means of covertly disseminating their opinions. Bacon described them as a 'little clique of disappointed and defeated politicians who undertook to head and organize a popular opposition against the government, and were compelled to retreat from that enterprise' (p. 15). The one historical juncture where this conspiracy found the courage to raise its head into public visibility was when followers of the Earl of Essex commissioned a performance of *Richard II* as a precursor of their attempted rebellion in 1601. Normally understood as an attempt by insurrectionists to use the old play, with its depiction of a monarch's forced abdication, as a rehearsal for the real deposition of Elizabeth I, Delia Bacon saw it rather as the direct programmatic expression of a conspiracy, involving both the aristocratic insurgents, and their intellectual supporters, who were themselves responsible for authorship of the play. But the rebellion was a failure. 'Driven from one field, they showed themselves in another. Driven from the open field, they fought in secret' (p. 37). Through the public medium of the theatre, incendiary political ideas could be promulgated to the people, while their true authors could remain protected by a cloak of anonymity. Had the true authorship of the plays become known to the government, both the plays and their authors would have been violently suppressed.

Delia Bacon found in the 'Shakespeare' plays (particularly in *King Lear*, *Julius Caesar* and *Coriolanus*) and in the minds of their putative authors – who are usually, frustratingly, alluded to, rather than explicitly named, in her writings – a sceptical scientific philosophy, an anti-monarchic republican politics and a proto-democratic vision of human and civil rights. The plays, like the minds and lives of their authors, exude that sceptical and progressive 'new philosophy' that, in John Donne's words, 'call[ed] all in doubt',[8] and that far transcended the limited intellectual horizons of the conservative monarchical culture these men sought to challenge. The plays expose the pretensions of kingly authority to divine prerogative, and demonstrate that the distinctions between monarchs and ordinary people are purely conventional and artificial. The plays offer a penetrating critique of the contradictions on which traditional monarchical authority rests, and for Delia Bacon this critique was indistinguishable from the inductive scientific reasoning pioneered by Francis Bacon. A true and abiding 'sovereignty' requires a different basis, though Delia Bacon stopped short of finding this authority in the 'masses', who in the sixteenth century were still 'ignorant' and unfit for 'rule' (p. 532). The plays ascribed to Shakespeare were circulated by Ralegh, Francis Bacon and others, in order both to educate these masses, and to establish a blueprint for a future society of intellectual freedom and political liberty.

In this hypothesis, those radical and liberating writings clearly did not have their desired effect. Had the enterprise succeeded, then England would presumably have become a republic, or a constitutional monarchy, decades before the Commonwealth and the 'Glorious Revolution'. The 'despotism' of Elizabeth, continued by her successor, James I, would have been over-thrown and replaced by political liberty and representative institutions. By a historical short-cut, England would have become something very much like America.

Just as Delia Bacon needed to exaggerate the educational poverty and cultural deficiency of Shakespeare the provincial player, in order to render it unthinkable that he could have been the true author, so she needed to caricature Elizabethan government as a violently coercive and despotic tyranny so as to make it plausible that some of the age's leading intellectuals should have resorted to a covert conspiracy to challenge the hegemonic culture via stage plays whose authorship they were obliged to disclaim. She comments on *Julius Caesar*:

Does not all the world know that scholars, men of reverence, men of world-wide renown, men of every accomplishment, were tortured, and mutilated, and hung, and beheaded, in both these two reigns, for writings wherein Caesar's ambition was infinitely more obscurely hinted at – writings unspeakably less offensive to majesty than this? (p. 360)

It is of course true that the leading exponents of her 'school', Ralegh and Bacon, were both imprisoned by James I, though for conspiracy and corruption respectively. Ralegh was executed, and Bacon pardoned. Other presumed members of the 'school' were not so treated: Edmund Spenser was honoured, and the Earl of Oxford alternately favoured and tolerated. But Bacon's hypothesis needed to establish a scenario, again redolent of the American Revolution, in which all good men were for liberty, and against the crown. She needed to portray them as so committed to their cause – 'determined to make their influence felt in that age, in spite of the want of encouragement which the conditions of that time offered to such an enterprise' (p. 30) – that they were prepared to participate in a dangerous conspiracy. At the same time she had to depict them as so fearful of the potential consequences that they cloaked their ambitions in secrecy, sought to conceal 'their lives as well as their works', and resolved to 'play this great game in secret' (p. 19).

Why should such men, who all wrote and published copiously in the literary fields of poetry, history, philosophy, find in the drama a congenial instrument for the transmission of those opinions they wished to avoid expressing in their own writings? The key to this problem lies in the fact that the Elizabethan drama was both a courtly and a popular cultural form. The same acting companies performed the same plays in the public theatres and in the milieu of the court. A successful Elizabethan or Jacobean dramatist was able to deploy a medium that could speak identically to courtier and apprentice, to monarch and citizen, to the patrician elite and to the plebeian masses. What this school of radical intellectuals needed was what Delia Bacon calls, in a prescient phrase, an 'organ of communication' that would address both the 'potent and resistless rulers' (p. 31) and their enslaved subjects; that would convert the court to the love of liberty, and enthuse the people with a dream of freedom.

It is clear from this proposition that Delia Bacon saw the Shakespeare plays not primarily as art, or entertainment, but more as a huge project of public education in political ethics and civic values. The hospitality afforded to this project by the theatre consisted, not in its capacity for stirring action and thrilling language, for complexity of characterization and poetic depth, but rather in the fact that, as an inclusive cultural form, the drama facilitated the transmission of ideas from the progressive elite to the uneducated masses. As James Shapiro points out, Delia Bacon's notion of a Tudor and Jacobean 'school' sometimes sounds less like an intellectual academy than a pedagogical fraternity offering courses in 'civics' in some anachronistic programme of adult education.[9]

Delia Bacon did not write to please, or to charm, or to entertain, but to prove a number of propositions. These are: that Shakespeare's works contain a prescient, progressive, libertarian philosophy, a republican politics and an emancipatory vision of the rights of man; that they could not have been written by William Shakespeare of Stratford; and that they were in fact written by several others, including Lord Bacon and Sir Walter Ralegh, as elaborated above.

Although Delia Bacon clearly managed to interest some of the truly great writers of her time – Emerson, Hawthorne, Carlyle – in her ideas, she did not persuade any of them to the truth of her convictions. Her work was instantly targeted as false prophecy by Shakespeare experts. The American Shakespearian Richard Grant White accomplished the suppression of further articles in *Putnam's Monthly Magazine*, and later stigmatized Bacon as a lunatic, implying that the mental collapse of her last years was already implicit in her campaign against Shakespeare as author.

To dismiss Delia Bacon as simply wrong, as White did, would seem today a less than satisfactory conclusion. But wrong she certainly was. Her argument that the Stratford Shakespeare was, through lack of education and cultural deficiency, in no way up to the job of writing the plays has been comprehensively refuted by generations of scholars, biographers and critics, and is reaffirmed in this volume. Her counter-claim, that the plays were the work of several other Elizabethan intellectuals, can hardly be considered an argument at all, since no direct evidence of any kind has ever been produced to endorse it, either by Delia Bacon or by any other Shakespeare authorship doubter. Stylistic similarities, verbal echoes, biographical correspondences between the works of these various writers can certainly be found, as they can for any other, to any degree homogeneous, culture. But the one single piece of evidence that would connect any of these alternative candidates to the works of Shakespeare has never, despite centuries of bardicidal searching and iconoclastic effort, been found.

On the other hand, Delia Bacon's remarkably innovative and insightful method of reading the plays, as politically incendiary critiques of power and as prescient visions of human liberty, has been repeatedly corroborated by generation after generation of critics and readers, and remains a powerful, if not dominant, perspective, in both criticism and the theatre. Her assault on the 'Golden Age' of Elizabeth I as, in reality, a cruel and violent despotism, maintained by illegal torture, arbitrary imprisonment and barbaric execution will seem to the liberal historian exaggerated and forced, but coincides exactly with that critique of power that became, via the influence of Michel Foucault, a constitutive element in both New Historicist and cultural materialist criticisms of Shakespeare. Likewise her theory that the plays, constituted as they seem to be from a comprehensive and historically influential world-view, were more likely written collectively and collaboratively than by a single, however gifted, person, has from time to time attracted critical favour, and is today becoming an influential paradigm in Shakespeare studies.

These separable features of Delia Bacon's work emerge from modern readings as inexplicable polarities, rather than as co-ordinated elements in a coherent and plausible argument. So much so, that contemporary thinkers are inclined to split the anti-Stratfordian and alternative authorship polemics from the historical and critical interpretations of the plays in Delia Bacon's work. As James Shapiro comments:

Delia Bacon's claim that the plays were politically radical was a century and a half ahead of its time. So, too, was her insistence that some of the plays should be read as collaborative. Had she limited her argument to these points instead of conjoining it to an argument about how Shakespeare couldn't have written them, there is little doubt that, instead of being dismissed as a crank and a madwoman, she would be hailed today as the precursor of New Historicism, and the first to argue that the plays anticipated the political upheavals England experienced in the mid-seventeenth century.[10]

Shapiro's tactic in this paragraph demonstrates one of the ways in which Delia Bacon can be reconstructed as 'readable'. She simply needs to be retrospectively rescued from herself, her good ideas uncoupled from her bad, her better wisdom disaggregated from her eccentricity. Delivered from her fruitless crusade to liberate the Shakespearian œuvre from an allegedly false authorial ascription, Delia Bacon could become a founding mother of political Shakespeare criticism, ideological critique and collaborationist bibliography.

Shapiro's kindness to Delia Bacon's memory is one of a number of strategies deployed in contemporary Shakespeare studies to recuperate her from the harsh judgments of history, notwithstanding the irreparable incorrectness of her driving beliefs. Delia Bacon was a remarkable woman, and modern writers have called for some measure of retrospective justice for a woman who, with little formal education and no independent means, acquired, by persevering auto-didacticism, sufficient knowledge and understanding to lay claims on the attention of some of the greatest writers of her day. She was an inspiring teacher, with a practical experience of pedagogy that gave her a formidable grasp of the principles of education. She was a powerful writer and speaker with a charismatic capability that probably persuaded some of her listeners, to some degree, beyond their better judgment. She was a dedicated fighter, and a tireless evangelist, for the cause she believed to be true. Her book, said Nathaniel Hawthorne, 'is the product of a most faithful and conscientious labour, and a truly heroic devotion of intellect and heart. No man or woman has ever thought or written more sincerely than the author of this book.'[11] Such characteristics, deployed as they were in an unwinnable campaign, may be considered as deserving of sympathy, if not of acceptance, from the present.

The rehabilitation of Delia Bacon has recuperated her as inspired but in error, a descriptor that could obviously be applied to many much more important thinkers of the past. Great intellectuals may be great but mistaken. Copernicus, Aristotle, Marx and Darwin are no less revered because time and scientific advances have proved them wrong in fundamentals as well as in particulars. Since Delia Bacon's time there have been immense changes in the position of women, a shift that facilitates reconsideration of her as a gifted woman struggling to be heard in a male-dominated environment.[12] Changes in our understanding of power and ideology have made it possible to see her retrospectively as a 'dissident', setting out to challenge established orthodoxies.[13] Although the 'Shakespeare authorship doubt' she pioneered remains a minority, though vocal, opinion, questions raised by a consideration of the complexities involved in mapping the space of relationship between a writer and his works make questions about authorship much more discussable than they were in Delia Bacon's day.[14] In addition the way in which she was treated by her contemporaries, particularly in respect of her mental illness, stands as a shameful chapter in intellectual history. While it was entirely reasonable to challenge Bacon's work as wrong and misguided, to undermine her credibility by characterizing her as a madwoman, whose opinions were merely the symptoms of a 'mental aberration',[15] was deeply uncharitable. There can be little doubt that such shabby treatment of an 'amateur' scholar by combative professionals helped to establish the environment of paranoia in which many modern authorship doubters tend to function.

Is it possible then, by the exercise of these strategies of rehabilitation, to have made the unreadable, readable? Can we exorcize the eccentric and deluded Delia Bacon from the gifted woman who impressed Nathaniel Hawthorne with her critical abilities, engaged her students with her methods of reading and, in spite of her errors, anticipated some of the most influential critical and theoretical movements in modern literary studies?

One of the obvious contributing factors to the reputation of Delia Bacon's writing for unreadability is her style. Most modern discussions of her work extract from her 623-page book the main points of her argument, illustrating them by selective quotation, in exactly the way I have done above. But there is something about her prose that is immediately daunting, obfuscating, disorientating to the modern reader. Let me offer a close reading of a representative passage to explore why this should be so. Here Bacon is introducing Sir Walter Ralegh as the primary intellectual stimulus for an accelerated revival of learning in Elizabeth's court:

The brave, bold genius of Raleigh flashed new life into that little nucleus of the Elizabethan development. The new '*Round Table*,' which that newly-beginning age of chivalry, with its new weapons and devices, and its new and more heroic adventure had created, was not yet 'full' till he came in. The Round Table grew rounder with this knight's presence. Over those dainty stories of the classic ages, over those quaint memorials of the elder chivalry, that were spread out on it, over the dead letter of the past, the brave Atlantic breeze came in, the breath of the great future blew, when the turn came for this knight's adventure; whether opened in the prose of its statistics, or set to its native music in the mystic melodies of the bard who was there to sing it. The Round Table grew spheral, as he sat talking by it; the Round Table dissolved, as he brought forth his lore, and unrolled his maps upon it; and instead of it, – with all its fresh yet living interests, tracked out by land

and sea, with the great battle-ground of the future outlined on it, – revolved the
round world. '*Universality*' was still the motto of these Paladins; but 'The Globe' –
the Globe, with its *two* hemispheres, became henceforth their device. (p. 42)

Two main threads of allusion run concurrently through this passage. One
is to scientific ideas, from 'nucleus' to 'hemispheres', and consists of the
assertion that Ralegh invigorated contemporary understanding with his
scientific perspective. The other, from 'brave' to 'device', is to the chivalric
mythology of King Arthur and the knights of the Round Table, and in
this paradigm Ralegh represents a rebirth and a transformation of the
chivalric ideal. The new man, who has travelled the globe, expanding his
own and humanity's horizons, comes to court informed by great advances
in geography and other discoveries, and takes his allotted place in an old
chivalric order. He completes the Round Table, as Sir Galahad completes
it in the Arthurian stories. But in place of the 'elder chivalry' represented
by those myths, the modern knight brings a new understanding of the
natural world. The 'brave Atlantic breeze' that comes in with him blows
away the 'dead letter' of the past. The round table becomes 'spheral', in
other words becomes an emblem of the round world on which Ralegh
unfolds his maps.

   The prose of this passage is heavily rhetorical, conveying the effect of
a loud public statement rather than the quiet conversation attempted by
a more orthodox literary criticism. In place of statement and evidence,
we have assertion and gesture, as in the piling up of subordinate clauses.
The language is heavily loaded with metaphors and images, so that the
symbolic dimension features more prominently than the historical: we are
more aware of what Delia Bacon believes all this to mean than of what it
was that actually happened.

   If we asked what is actually being communicated in this passage, the
answer would boil down to a fairly simple and uncontroversial assertion:
Ralegh was one of a number of free thinkers who stimulated the philosophical energies of the Elizabethan intelligentsia. But if we asked to what
genre of intellectual expression such a prose belongs, the answer would
be more difficult to find. This is not history, since its narrative enlists
no specific evidence in favour of its assertions. It is not literary criticism,
since it alludes to no textual source. It is in fact a kind of poetry, since
it operates by metaphor and simile, by rhythm and phrasing, rather than
by logical argument or evidenced demonstration. The attempt to define
this scientific school, which was also a chivalric order, a fraternity which
lay somewhere between the Royal Society and Camelot, is advanced by

poetic allusion, and persuades by quickening the imagination rather than by satisfying the intellect that a case has been made. This leaves the reader in some ambiguity about what is actually being said about the relationship between the contemporary and the past. The language and imagery of the Middle Ages is formulated here with some affection and nostalgia, as it was by Sir Walter Scott and Thomas Carlyle, although Delia Bacon's argument is a progressive narrative about its supersession by the philosophy of the future.

In other words, Delia Bacon wrote about Shakespeare authorship as a poet or novelist rather than as a literary or historical scholar. Her talents as a writer lay entirely in the direction of imaginative prose, and she unfortunately mistook her vocation in pursuing scholarly controversy and literary polemics. Her overheated imagination, Gothic sensibility and linguistic fertility, encountered as unreadable by students of Shakespeare, were all typical of her age. If she had concentrated her energies on writing fictional prose like Hawthorne's, or Gothic romance like Poe's, or poetic history like Carlyle's, she might have shaped for herself a very different reputation as a writer.

All of Delia Bacon's writings on Shakespeare authorship continually allude to some great discovery or revelation that would prove her case beyond all reasonable doubt. She genuinely believed such a discovery was possible, and clearly hoped that in England, in Stratford or St Albans, perhaps in the tombs of Shakespeare and Francis Bacon, she would find it: some definitive connection between the works and an alternative author. Her writing handles the absence of this evidence tentatively, uncertainly, with some ambiguity. At times she seems to be promising that the revelation is close at hand, at other times further off. Hawthorne opened his preface to her book by quoting an unpublished passage in which she suggests that her work is deliberately leaving the problem unsolved, either because the truth would be too hard for her readers to bear, or because she wanted them to share in the process of discovery and enlightenment.

If we were reading this prose as fiction, fantasy or romance, all those gestures towards an unrevealed truth, all those suggestions as to the true meaning of a hidden code, all those testimonies to the possession of an endlessly deferred Gnostic secret, might make for a remarkable literary experience. Delia Bacon could have been, if not a female Edgar Allan Poe, at least the Dan Brown of her age. But reading it as a scholarly treatise, an intellectual argument, a historical narrative, we can only conclude that it remains, in its anguished totality, a scholarship without content, an argument without conclusion and a history without evidence.

CHAPTER 2

The case for Bacon

Alan Stewart

In June 1853, Thomas Carlyle and his wife Jane Welsh Carlyle hosted a somewhat bizarre tea party at their Chelsea home on Cheyne Walk.[1] The guest of honour was a Connecticut lady referred to Carlyle by Ralph Waldo Emerson, Miss Delia Bacon.[2] On Emerson's suggestion, Carlyle had also invited James Spedding. Spedding and Miss Bacon had something in common – a passionate interest in the life and works of Francis Bacon. Spedding had in 1834 resolved to write a life of Bacon, and subsequently devoted his life to that pursuit.[3] Miss Bacon, by contrast, was devoting her life to claiming that Bacon had written the plays of William Shakespeare.[4]

In the mid-nineteenth century, Francis Bacon was widely regarded as one of Britain's most powerful intellects, a motor of progress and the father of modern science. Alexander Pope had notoriously dubbed him the 'brightest, wisest, meanest of mankind', and, although the question of Bacon's 'meanness' would continue to incite passionate debate – and lead men like Spedding to spend their lives defending his reputation – few would doubt the epithets of 'brightest, wisest'. In 1592, Bacon famously declared he had 'taken all Knowledge, to be my *Province*',[5] and his vast range of activities – lawyer, politician, parliamentarian, courtier, essayist, natural philosopher – bore out his claim. In later years, he embarked on a massive master-plan for the reworking of all knowledge, known as the Great Instauration. If Shakespeare's plays had to be attributed to a contemporary with almost superhuman ambition and range, then Bacon naturally led the field.

Delia Bacon took the opportunity to inform the world's leading Bacon specialist of her theory, as she relayed to her sister:

My visit to Mr. Carlyle was very rich. I wish you could have heard him laugh. Once or twice I thought he would have taken the roof off. And first, they were perfectly stunned – he and the gentleman [Spedding] he had invited to meet me. They turned black in the face at my presumption. 'Do you mean to say' so and so, said Mr. Carlyle, with his strong emphasis; and I said that I did; and they both looked at me with staring eyes, speechless for want of words in which to convey their sense of my audacity. At length, Mr. Carlyle came down upon me with such a volley; I did not mind it in the least. I told him he did not know what was in the Plays, if he said that, and no one *could* know who believed that that booby wrote them. It was then that he began to shriek. You could have heard him a mile.[6]

Although it is Carlyle's laugh that is remembered about this encounter, perhaps its most intriguing feature is the presence of James Spedding. By 1853, he was still a few years off publishing the first of seven edited volumes of Bacon's *Works*; he would not finish his project until the last of another seven volumes, of *Letters and the Life of Bacon*, appeared in 1874. In Delia Bacon's account, Spedding is silent, but the encounter certainly made an impression on him – in 1867 he recalled that 'I had an interview with Miss Delia Bacon when she first came over'[7] – and over the next three decades, James Spedding would remain intimately involved in what came to be known as the 'Baconian' theory. For although he was determined to rehabilitate Bacon for the Victorian age, Spedding was very much a modern scholar, with a flexible view of authorship. In 1850, Spedding had suggested in the *Gentleman's Magazine* that Shakespeare's *Henry VIII* was in fact the work of two men, Shakespeare and John Fletcher.[8] And he was keen to claim that Bacon had written more than the works that bore his name. But he had no idea how his edition would have the unexpected side effect of boosting the 'Baconian' cause at precisely the right moment.

The case for Bacon would elaborate itself in multifarious ways but the essential arguments were in place within thirty years of Spedding's meeting with Delia Bacon: Bacon had written the works attributed to Shakespeare, and the evidence for it was contained in a cipher, and obliquely hinted at in some letters; there were multiple 'parallelisms' between the writings of Bacon and the writings of Shakespeare; and further proof could be found in two manuscripts – Bacon's notebook and the scribbled cover of a miscellany. It was Delia Bacon's contribution to suggest the use of a cipher; but James Spedding played his part by bringing to light materials that fuelled the imaginations of Delia Bacon's successors. From that first meeting in the Carlyles' parlour, the histories of Bacon scholarship and Baconian scholarship would be inexorably linked. This chapter tells the story of the case for Bacon, and assesses the evidence that it forwarded.[9]

DELIA BACON, WILLIAM HENRY SMITH AND NATHANIEL HOLMES

In January 1856, *Putnam's Monthly Magazine* published an anonymous piece entitled 'William Shakespeare and His Plays: An Inquiry Concerning

Them'. Taking its lead from Friedrich August Wolf's debunking of the myth of 'Homer', the essay mocks the idea that 'the crowning glory of that great epoch', Renaissance England, can be explained by 'the story of the Stratford poacher'. Shakespeare – variously characterized as 'a mild, respectable, obliging man' or 'a stupid, ignorant, illiterate, third-actor play-actor' – had neither the genius nor the time to write the plays. But in Shakespeare's milieu of 'wits and poets', one might 'find the philosopher who writes, in his prose as well, and over his own name also, "In Nature's INFINITE BOOK OF SECRESY, / A little I can read" –'. The essayist goes on to write of 'the Philosopher who is only the Poet in disguise – the Philosopher who calls himself the New Magician – the Poet who was toiling and plotting to fill the globe with his Arts, and to make our common, everyday human life poetical'. One does not have to look far to find 'ONE, with learning broad enough, and deep enough, and subtle enough, and comprehensive enough, one with nobility of aim and philosophic and poetic genius enough, to be able to claim his own, his own immortal progeny'.[10] The philosopher was not named, but the essayist obligingly quotes from his *Advancement of Learning* – and the identity of that essayist as Delia Bacon would be obvious to those who had read the 'Our Weekly Gossip' column of the *Athenaeum* in March 1855.[11]

A more blunt approach was taken by one William Henry Smith, who in September 1856, published an open letter to Lord Ellesmere, a recent president of the Shakespeare Society, entitled *Was Lord Bacon the Author of Shakespeare's Plays?*,[12] following it in 1857 with a full book on *Bacon and Shakespeare*.[13] Smith's objections to Shakespeare's authorship were primarily biographical and class-inflected: Shakespeare was simply not the right kind of man to have written the plays. But at the end of his pamphlet, Smith printed a letter to Bacon from his friend Tobie Matthew, with a postscript that read: 'The most prodigious wit that ever I knew of my nation, and of this side of the sea, is your lordship's name, *though he be known by another*.'[14] As later Baconians elaborated, this meant that the 'most prodigious wit' was Bacon, but he was 'known by another' name, i.e. Shakespeare – although why Matthew should suddenly talk to and about his addressee in the third person is unexplained. In truth, the meaning is quite clear. Matthew (1577–1655), an English Catholic convert living on the Continent, was referring to another English member of his faith ('of my nation') also living abroad ('of this side of the sea') born as a Bacon ('of your lordship's name'), but living under an alias. The obvious candidate is Nathaniel Bacon (1598–1676), an expatriate Catholic who was highly learned ('most prodigious wit') and who went by the name of Nathaniel Southwell.

These early attempts are very different – Smith, accused of plagiarism, pointed out that 'the most casual reader must see that we have nothing in common. Miss Bacon seems a highly gifted poetical lady whilst I am a very commonplace matter of fact person.'[15] But they share a belief that Shakespeare cannot have written the plays attributed to him, that a philosopher with the scope of Francis Bacon can have done, and that Bacon's authorship was both known to some and disguised to others. But Delia Bacon had more complex ideas to reveal in her mammoth 1857 volume, *The Philosophy of the Plays of Shakspere Unfolded*,[16] or as its projected title put it, 'New Light on the Globe Theatre: The Advancement of Learning to its true Sphere as propounded by Francis Bacon and other Writers of the Globe School, including the Part of Sir Walter Ralegh'.[17] The work has inspired and baffled readers ever since. Nathaniel Hawthorne attempted to throw some light on it in a preface by quoting 'a manuscript of the author's, not intended for present publication' in which she characterized the age in which Shakespeare lived:

It was the time when the cipher, in which one could write '*omnia per omnia*,' was in such request . . . It was a time, too . . . when a '*nom de plume*' was required, when puns, and charades, and enigmas, and anagrams, and monograms, and ciphers, and puzzles, were not good for sport and child's play merely; when they had need to be close; when they had need to be solvable, at least, only to those who *should* solve them.[18]

The reference was clear enough: in his 1605 *Advancement of Learning*, Bacon identifies the three 'vertues' necessary to ciphers: 'that they be not laborious to write and reade; that they bee impossible to discypher; and in some cases, that they bee without suspition'. He briefly limns the perfect cipher: 'The highest Degree whereof, is to write OMNIA PER OMNIA; which is vndoubtedly possible, with a proportion Quintuple at most, of the writing infoulding, to the writing infoulded, and no other restraint whatsoeuer.'[19] In his 1623 *De augmentis scientiarum* Bacon gave a fuller treatment of this 'bi-literal cipher' in which the secret message ('the interior Letter') would be encoded in another message ('the exterior Letter'). Each character of the interior letter would be rendered in the exterior letter by five characters, so that the exterior letter will 'bear a quintuple proportion to' the interior letter. The content of these characters is irrelevant – but each character is to be *formed* in one of two ways, and it is in this binary differentiation that the true message will be encoded. Bacon realized that he had hit on something important with this binary rendering of information: 'Neither is it a small matter these *Cypher-Characters* have, and may perform: For by this *Art* a way is opened, whereby a man may express and signify the intentions of his mind, at any distance of place, by objects which may be presented to the eye, and accommodated to the ear: provided those objects be capable of a twofold difference only; as by Bells, by Trumpets, by Lights and Torches, by the report of Muskets, and any instruments of like Nature.'[20] Or the Morse Code, for that matter – and indeed Delia Bacon's interests in Baconian cipher had been stimulated in the 1830s by her friend Samuel F. B. Morse, then professor of painting and sculpture in the University of the City of New York (now New York University). Sailing home from Europe in 1832, Morse had conceived the idea of the telegraph, and the cipher needed to keep telegraphed state messages secret – and he shared with Delia Bacon his inspiration: 'Did Delia Bacon know that Francis Bacon had invented such a secret code, for diplomatic use?' Morse asked.[21]

Delia Bacon herself outlines the cipher in her book, and hints that the missing fourth part of Bacon's *Instauratio magna* is contained in ciphered words elsewhere.[22] But there is nothing in the *Philosophy* to suggest that she ever applied the workings of Bacon's bi-literal cipher – it acts here rather as a metaphor for Bacon's act of ciphering his philosophy in Shakespeare's plays – and it would be thirty years before her hint about the cipher would be fully exploited. The immediate boost to the Baconian cause would come from another source. In late January 1857, the first volume of the *Works* of Bacon, edited by Spedding with Robert Leslie Ellis and Douglas Denon Heath was published, to be followed by another six volumes by January 1859. Then, starting in 1861, Spedding went on to bring out – in another seven volumes – *The Letters and the Life*, a biography based on Bacon's letters and other writings. In these volumes, Spedding claimed as Bacon's many works that had circulated anonymously, as well as letters that Bacon ghost-wrote for his patron, Robert Devereux, second Earl of Essex, and entertainments that he penned for Essex – and thereby presented a Bacon who indeed wrote as someone else, and composed some dramatic works. Bacon's known writings thus increased exponentially, and before long these new materials were absorbed into the Baconian scholarship.

William Henry Smith, for example, pursued Spedding, who recalled 'a good deal of correspondence with Mr. W. H. Smith, who was much bent on making a convert of me'.[23] And then, in November 1866, Spedding received a letter from Nathaniel Holmes (1815–1901) in St Louis, a Judge of the Supreme Court of the State of Missouri.[24] Holmes opened by claiming: 'I have derived so much pleasure and help from your excellent edition of Lord Bacon's works (in the Boston republication of it) that I cannot refrain from acknowledging it to you personally.'[25] The letter was followed in early 1867 by a copy of his book, *The Authorship of Shakespeare*, in which Holmes contrasted Shakespeare's and Bacon's lives, drew attention to the dramatic works that the first volume of the *Letters and the Life* had brought to light, and produced multiple parallelisms between Shakespeare's and Bacon's writings.[26] Holmes implored Spedding for his opinion: 'there is no man in the world more capable than yourself of setting me right if I have fallen into any fatal mistake as to anything that relates to what is historically known of Bacon or his writings. Your opinion, that this Theory cannot be true, would go far to stagger me in my faith; and your concurrence would be to me "Confirmation strong / As proofs of Holy Writ".'[27]

In February 1867, Spedding sent a long response to Holmes, apologizing that 'I must declare myself not only unconvinced, but undisturbed. To ask me to believe that the man who was accepted by all the people of his own time, to many of whom he was personally known as the undoubted author of the best plays then going, was *not* the author of them, is like asking me to believe that Charles Dickens was not the author of "Pickwick".' While Bacon may have penned court entertainments, he 'was never suspected of wasting time in writing poetry, and is not known to have written a single blank verse in all his life'. Spedding did not rule out that Shakespeare knew Bacon's works: 'Shakespeare may have derived a good deal from Bacon: he had no doubt read the "Advancement of Learning" and the first edition of the "Essays"; and most likely had frequently heard him speak in the Star Chamber. But among all the parallelisms which you have collected with so much industry to prove the identity of the writers, I have not observed one in which I should not myself have inferred from the difference of style a difference of hand.'[28]

Spedding sent a copy of his riposte to William Henry Smith, in the hope – as he put it – that 'my answer will do for both'. Smith returned the letters, huffily claiming that 'I do it thus promptly that you may know where they are, should you desire to fulminate them against any fresh "perverts" to this American heresy.' He now saw Holmes as a more receptive audience for his ideas: 'I think that I should be more successful in an appeal to the American Bench than to the Anglican Bar.'[29] But the Holmes-Smith-Spedding correspondence somehow reached the hands of Shakespeare scholar Clement Mansfield Ingleby,[30] who addressed the Royal Society of Literature in January 1868 on the subject, claiming that 'I have looked over the collections of Messrs. W. H. Smith and Holmes, and I must confess I am astonished; but my astonishment has not been provoked by the quantity or closeness of the resemblances adduced, but by the spectacle of educated men attempting to found such an edifice on

such a foundation.'[31] Although it aimed some barbs at the Baconians –
'The critic has the same interest in the works of Miss Delia Bacon,
Mr. W. H. Smith, and Judge Holmes, as the physician has in morbid
anatomy. He reads them, not so much as for the light which they
throw on the question of authorship, as for their interest as examples
of wrong-headedness'[32] – Ingleby's lecture also served to bring together
these disparate figures, and give them a history and a coherence. (It also
no doubt spurred Ingleby to complete his *Shakspeare's Century of Prayse*
(1874), the register of evidence of early references to Shakespeare, later
revised as *The Shakspere Allusion-Book*.)[33] And soon the Baconians would
have more ammunition to fire back.

THE NORTHUMBERLAND MANUSCRIPT

In August 1867, Algernon Lloyd Percy, Earl Percy (1810–99) invited the
antiquary John Bruce (1802–69) to inspect and catalogue his archive at his
London residence on the Strand, Northumberland House.[34] Bruce there
found 'two black boxes of considerable size, presumed to contain papers,
but nobody knew of the boxes having ever been opened, or could give
any information respecting their history, or tell what kind of papers they
contained'. Of particular interest was 'a paper book, much damaged by fire
about the edges, though not so much as to make the contents generally
undecipherable'.[35]

Earl Percy contacted James Spedding, who examined the volume and
reported his findings in an 1870 publication, *The Conference of Pleasure*.[36]
Most of its contents were tracts written in the 1590s by Francis Bacon,
although not always credited to him, plus two older, non-Baconian pieces:
Philip Sidney's letter to Queen Elizabeth opposing her proposed marriage
to the duc d'Anjou (*c.* 1579), and part of the libel *Leicester's Commonwealth*
(1584). Spedding was particularly interested in four speeches of praise,
entitled 'Of tribute, or giving what is dew', two of which were previously
unknown. The volume's most striking page, however, was its cover: a
patchwork of scribbled words that appeared to include a contents list that
corresponded only roughly to what was in the volume. One portion read:

> Orations at Graie's Inne revels
> . . .   Queen's Ma[ts]
>   By Mr. Frauncis Bacon.
> Essaies by the same author.
> Richard the Second.

Richard the Third.
Asmund and Cornelia.
Isle of Dogs fr (?).
By Thomas Nashe, inferior places.[37]

This list appeared to put Bacon's *Essays* next to two Shakespeare plays, *Richard II* and *Richard III*. But Spedding also had to account for the fact that the cover contains not only the name 'Mr. Frauncis Bacon' repeated several times, but also the name 'William Shakespeare', 'being written eight or nine times over for no other reason that can be discerned'. Spedding speculated that 'the writer (or more probably another into whose possession the volume passed) has amused himself with writing down promiscuously the names and phrases that most ran in his head' (p. xxii); he felt this was interesting if the scribblings could be dated to the Elizabethan era, since they then constituted 'one of the earliest evidences of the growth of Shakespeare's *personal* fame as a dramatic author; the beginning of which cannot be dated much earlier than 1598' (p. xxiii).

But Spedding also knew that his explanation that this was random scribbling would not be enough for certain of his readers: 'What other inferences will be drawn from its appearance on the cover of this manuscript by those who start with the conviction that Bacon and not Shakespeare was the real author of Richard II. and Richard III., I cannot say' (p. xxiv). The answer was not long in coming. Spedding had included in his edition a facsimile of the cover, which allowed Nathaniel Holmes to peruse it at leisure. Holmes – who, since publishing *The Authorship of Shakespeare*, had been appointed Royall Professor of Law at Harvard in 1868, only to be forced to resign the post in 1872 – renewed his correspondence with Spedding,[38] and subsequently revised his book to take account of the discovery. In an appendix on the Northumberland manuscript,[39] he identified 'the leading facts that seem to bear upon the question of the authorship of these Shakespeare plays, – a question which Mr. Spedding seems not to have regarded as any part of his function to examine or consider' (p. 657). In addition to the *Richard II* and *Richard III* references, Holmes detected other Shakespeariana:

A line from the 'Rape of Lucrece' is written thus: '*Revealing day through every cranie peeps and,*' the writer taking *peeps* from the next couplet instead of *spies*. Three others (not noticed in Mr. Spedding's Introduction) are *Anthony comfrt. and consorte*, and *honorificabilitudino* and *plaies*. (pp. 658–9)

Holmes identifies 'Anthony' as Bacon's elder brother Anthony Bacon: 'it would be highly probable that an amanuensis or copyist in the employ of Francis would have the brother Anthony in mind also, while casually trying his pen' (p. 659). The word *honorificabilitudino* 'is not found in any dictionary that I know of' but Costard in *Love's Labour's Lost* uses the word *honorificabilitudinatibus*. Perhaps, as Spedding suggested, this implied that Shakespeare was becoming famous enough for a Bacon scribe to jot down his name, and the titles of his plays, but, Holmes argued,

> It is quite as easily and perhaps better explained by considering that if this scribbler were Bacon's amanuensis, and that he had been employed in copying plays from Bacon's own originals, he would know very well who was the real author of them, and, at the same time, would know (what Sir Tobie Matthew knew perfectly well) that the most prodigious wit of all England was of the name of Bacon, though he were known by another; and this singular fact might very readily pop into the head of a wicked amanuensis (even some years later than the completion of the volume), and draw the name of William Shakespeare from his idle pen. (p. 659)

There is a strong likelihood that the Northumberland manuscript dates from the 1590s, and derives from the household or the inner circle of Francis Bacon: no other known manuscript contains so many pieces by Bacon from this period. There is nothing in the *contents* of the manuscript that suggests Shakespeare. We are left with the cover. It is indeed possible that 'Richard II' and 'Richard III' refer to Shakespeare's plays, and that *honorificabilitudino* is an allusion to *Love's Labour's Lost*: but it is also true that all three plays were available in printed quartos by 1598, so that does not guarantee a close relationship between the manuscript and the author of the plays. Moreover, the repeated writing of 'William Shakespeare' follows the spelling of the playwright's name as it had appeared in print in 1593 and 1594. Even *Honorificabilitudino* is less specific than it seems: *honorificabilitudinatibus* is close to proverbial as a ridiculously long word. Dante refers to it, as does Rabelais, and it appears in the commentary on Erasmus's *Adagia* as part of one of the few Latin lines of verse that have only two or three words: 'Gaudet honorificabilitudinatibus Hermes, / Consuetudinibus, sollicitudinibus' (3.2.68). These, as a recent editor notes, are the stuff of 'schoolboy jokes, adult pen-trials'.[40] It seems highly likely that we are seeing here a classic example of the latter – and that, as Spedding pointed out, the most compelling evidence the cover might offer is that Shakespeare was relatively well known in the late 1590s.

THE *PROMUS*

In 1881, James Spedding died after being knocked down by a cab. With his death, the discovery of 'new' Bacon materials came to an end for almost a century.[41] But, unwittingly, Spedding had left a hostage to fortune. In volume VII of his edition (1859), he allowed the world a glimpse of another Bacon document – a notebook, of forty-eight folios, in Bacon's hand in the British Museum's Harleian collection, in which Bacon had collected a vast number of phrases, largely proverbial, in English, Latin, French, Greek, Spanish and Italian.[42] Spedding dubbed it the *Promus of formularies and elegancies*, after a phrase at the head of one of its lists; he found it 'chiefly interesting as an illustration of Bacon's manner of working' but opined that 'There is not much in it of his own' and that as a result 'this *Promus*, which is of considerable length, is not worth printing *in extenso*'. He therefore merely described it, and printed 'some extracts by way of specimen'.[43]

But the specimen extracts piqued the interest of a Baconian, Constance Mary Fearon Pott (1833–1915), who was drawn to what she excitedly described as '*50 pages, nearly all autograph*'[44] of unknown Bacon. Pott wrote that her 'attention became directed to these manuscripts of Bacon by some remarks upon them made by Mr. Spedding in his Works of Bacon. From the few specimens which are there given it appeared probable that in these notes corroborative evidence would be found to support some of the points which it was desired to establish, and as the subject then in hand was the vocabulary and style of Bacon, there was a hope of gleaning, perhaps, a few additional facts and evidences from this new field of inquiry. This hope has been fulfilled to a degree beyond expectation . . .'[45]

Under her married name, Mrs Henry Pott produced an edition of the notebook, presenting a transcription of the entire document, numbering each phrase, and then cross-referencing it to any parallels she detected in Shakespeare's work (and, where appropriate, its scriptural or classical source). One example will suffice. Phrase no. 2 reads 'Corni contra croci. Good means against badd, hornes to crosses.' Pott claims that this is echoed 'Thirty times' in Shakespeare, and gives a representative sampling:

> This it is that makes me bridle passion, | And bear with mildness my misfortune's cross. (*3 H. VI*. iv. 4.)
> I have given way unto this cross of fortune. (*M. Ado*, iv. 1.)
> We must do good against evil. (*All's W*. ii. 5)
> Fie, Cousin Percy! How you cross my father . . .
> He holds your temper in a high respect,
> And curbs himself even of his natural scope
> When you do cross his humour. (*1 Hen. IV*. iii. 2)
> I love not to be crossed,
> He speaks the mere contrary. Crosses love not him.
>
> (*L. L. L*. i. 2).[46]

Her method here is clear. The Italian phrase 'Corni contra croci' means literally 'Horns against crosses': it implies an opposition between the diabolic and the (Christian) holy, which Pott generalizes to encompass 'good against evil' as in the *All's Well* quotation. But she also takes the word 'crosses' out of grammatical context: although it is a plural noun in *croci*, Pott uses it to pick up Shakespearian uses of 'cross' as a verb ('How you cross my father', 'you do cross his humour', 'I love not to be crossed'). In other words, she is merely performing a word-search for 'cross', blithely ignoring the fact that it has multiple senses.

Pott scored something of a *coup* by obtaining a preface from the City of London headmaster Edwin A. Abbott, noted scholar of both Bacon and Shakespeare, and teacher of such future literary luminaries as Sidney Lee and Arthur H. Bullen.[47] Although 'not able to believe that Francis Bacon wrote Shakespeare', Abbott admitted that 'On one point... I must honestly confess that I am a convert to the author', namely 'that there is a very considerable similarity of phrase and thought between these two great authors', which Abbott took to imply that Bacon knew Shakespeare's plays. In particular, 'the *Promus* seems to render it highly probable, if not absolutely certain, that Francis Bacon in the year 1594 had either heard or read Shakespeare's *Romeo and Juliet*'. Abbott was struck by the phrases 'golden sleepe' and 'up-rouse' which formed part of Pott's phrases nos. 1207 and 1215. Both, Abbott pointed out, occurred in Friar Laurence's admonishment of Romeo: 'But where unbruised youth with unstuff'd brain / Doth couch his limbs, there *golden sleep* doth reign: / Therefore thy earliness doth me assure / Thou art *up-roused* by some distemperature' (2.3.40). '*One* of these entries would prove little or nothing; but anyone accustomed to evidence will perceive that *two* of these entries constitute a coincidence amounting almost to a demonstration that either (1) Bacon and Shakespeare borrowed from some common and at present unknown source; or (2) one of the two borrowed from the other.' Abbott however did not subscribe to Mrs Pott's theory: 'The author's belief is... that the play is indebted for these expressions to the *Promus*; mine is that the *Promus* borrowed them from the play.'[48] Here again, Pott's working methods destroy her own case. Pott had mistranscribed the second phrase in question. Where the manuscript has 'Cowrt howres. / Constant; abedd when yow are bedd; & vp when yow are vp', Pott had given 'Court howres. Court oures. Abedd-rose you – owt bed. Uprouse. You are upp': there is no 'uprouse' in Bacon's manuscript.[49]

More strikingly, Pott did not recognize (or refused to recognize) the nature of the manuscript. The *Promus* is a notebook of commonplace phrases, mainly proverbs. There are indeed *similar* ideas in the plays of Shakespeare, as there are in the works of every writer of the English Renaissance – this was a commonplace culture, and literary production was an endlessly inventive endeavour with commonplace materials. As Pott knew well, the English proverbs are derived from John Heywood's immensely popular print collection; recent research has shown that many of the Latin phrases come directly from a 1581 edition of an *Epitome* of Erasmus's *Adagia*, while the Italian phrases (including 'Corni contra croci') derive from John Florio's 1591 collection.[50] Contrary to Pott's assertions, very few of the *Promus*'s phrases appear in that form in Shakespeare's plays – and those that do are English proverbs, common precisely because they are proverbial. But a good number of the *Promus*'s entries appear verbatim in the works of Francis Bacon; and some are in fact working notes for what will later become 'De spe terrestri' and for Essex's Accession Day device of November 1595; while others are notes from Aristotle's *Rhetoric* that will be reworked as Bacon's *Colours of Good and Evil* and *Antitheta*.[51]

Her edition of the *Promus* gave Mrs Pott a pre-eminence among Baconians. On 18 December 1885, the Potts' London home, 81 Cornwall Gardens, hosted the first meeting of the Bacon Society, formed to 'afford . . . assistance' to 'the labours of Mrs. Pott'. Mr Henry Pott was appointed the Honorary Treasurer with Mr Francis Fearon (Mrs Pott's brother) as Honorary Secretary, and the President was named as William Henry Smith.[52] The following June, the first issue appeared of the *Journal of the Bacon Society* (later *Baconiana*) and the Society is still in business today (www.baconsocietyinc.org/). But there followed growing marginalization as Baconian theories, from the 1880s onwards, became increasingly bizarre. Republican Minnesota congressman Ignatius L. Donnelly temporarily abandoned his Atlantean theories to elaborate Delia Bacon's cipher suggestion into *The Great Cryptogram* in 1888.[53] The American physician Orville Ward Owen invented a 'cipher wheel' that revealed Bacon's true parents to be Elizabeth and her secret husband Robert Dudley, Earl of Leicester, and his brother to be the Earl of Essex – making Bacon the true heir to the throne.[54] The Michigan high school principal Elizabeth Wells Gallup discovered that Bacon had authored the works of Christopher Marlowe, George Peele and even Robert Burton;[55] while the American art collector Walter Conrad Arensberg found a secret Rosicrucian history.[56] It was not until 1957 that the cryptographers William and Elizebeth Friedman, who had worked with Gallup, demonstrated the unlikelihood that Bacon's cipher could ever have been employed.[57] But by the time the Friedmans debunked the cipher, as

Bacon's recent editor Graham Rees puts it, 'Bacon's stock, high for three centuries, had begun to collapse.' Not only did the cipher theories sound ridiculous to most, but Bacon – arch-representative of the 'progress' that had led to world wars and disaster – was no longer a suitable author for the plays.[58] It was time for a new William Shakespeare.

CHAPTER 3

The case for Marlowe

Charles Nicholl

Christopher Marlowe has been one of the more popular candidates put forward by 'anti-Stratfordians' as the true author of works attributed to William Shakespeare. He has one great advantage over other contenders in that he is a major poet and dramatist in his own right. Against this he has one pressing disadvantage, which is that he was killed in the year 1593, and was therefore dead when most of Shakespeare's plays were written. His proponents ('Marlovians') have continuously addressed these two aspects of his claim, seeking on the one hand to emphasize his poetic fitness for the role, and on the other to disprove, or anyway to challenge, the historical record of his inconveniently early death. Their default theory is that the apparent death of Marlowe was an elaborate hoax enabling him to disappear to the continent, thereby escaping charges of heresy then being levelled at him. They also note an apparent chronological neatness: the first publication bearing Shakespeare's name – the narrative poem *Venus and Adonis* – went on sale just a few weeks after Marlowe's death or disappearance.

The Marlovian claim has not been rewarded with any general acceptance, but its propagandists did score a notable victory when they persuaded the Dean and Chapter of Westminster Abbey to permit the inclusion of a question mark by Marlowe's death-date on a commemorative stained-glass window installed at Poets' Corner in 2002.

Of all the contenders Marlowe is the closest to Shakespeare in time, social class and professional activity. He was born in February 1564, just a couple of months before Shakespeare; he was the son of a Canterbury shoemaker, as Shakespeare was the son of a Stratford glover; he earned his living in the precarious world of the Elizabethan playhouses (though unlike Shakespeare he also had a sideline in political and intelligence work, which may well have bolstered his theatrical earnings). It can at least be said of the Marlovian claim that it is free of the snobbery underpinning the authorship controversy, which generally works from the premise that

Shakespeare's origins were too lowly to allow him to scale the upper peaks of Parnassus, and which tends to prefer blue-blooded earls and high-profile knights – even those with no proven literary ability – to mere professional scribblers. The true author of the plays, asserted the leading Oxfordian, J. Thomas Looney, was not 'the kind of man we should expect to rise from the lower middle-class population of the towns'.[1] As well as being objectionable, this is inaccurate in terms of literary history. Many Elizabethan and Jacobean playwrights sprang precisely from this industrious, aspiring artisan class: not just Marlowe and Shakespeare, but Robert Greene, Thomas Middleton and John Webster, the sons respectively of a saddler, a bricklayer and a coachmaker; and Ben Jonson, who claimed his father was a Protestant minister, but who was brought up from infancy in the home of his stepfather, a Westminster bricklayer, and who was apprenticed in that trade before turning to the theatre.

What distinguishes Marlowe from Shakespeare is his education. While biographers of Shakespeare can only muster some suppositious remarks about his education at Stratford grammar school (a reasonable assumption but not a demonstrable fact), Marlowe has a suitably upward trajectory from his relatively humble beginnings. From at least 1578 he was at King's School, Canterbury, and from 1580 he studied at Corpus Christi College, Cambridge, where he was the recipient of a scholarship endowed by a former Archbishop of Canterbury, Matthew Parker. He left university a Master of Arts in 1587, and became part of that loose grouping of writers in London known as the 'University Wits'. He was accounted by his contemporaries a man of scholarship – '[His] learning I reverence' (Henry Chettle); 'Cristofer Marly by his profession a scholar' (Sir Robert Sidney); one of 'my fellow scholars about this city' (Robert Greene).[2] This measurable quota of intellectual sophistication is stressed by Marlovians, on the debatable assumption that the writing of great literature requires a university degree.

Marlowe was one of the earliest contenders for the Shakespeare authorship, making his first appearance in this role in the 1890s. In chronological terms – the chronology, that is, of the authorship controversy – he stands second only to the original claimant, Sir Francis Bacon, whose authorship was first proposed by Delia Bacon in 1856. (I exclude from this computation the earliest and most plausible contender, William Shakespeare of Stratford, and the earliest expression of the Baconian theory, the so-called 'Cowell Lectures' of 1805, which are now thought to be a twentieth-century forgery.)

The first to put forward Marlowe's authorship of at least some of Shakespeare's plays was an American lawyer and part-time writer named Wilbur

Gleason Zeigler (1857–1935). In 1895 he published a novel, not very subtly titled *It was Marlowe*, in which he proposed that Marlowe's death in 1593 was a fabrication, and that the poet survived for a further five years during which he wrote such plays as *Titus Andronicus, Romeo and Juliet, Richard III* and *Hamlet*. It is presented in the guise of fiction, but is certainly intended as a serious historical enquiry. In a seven-page preface Zeigler supplies some background to his writing of it. In his youth, he tells us, he had read Marlowe's plays, particularly *Tamburlaine* and *Dr Faustus*:

There was something in them to excite more than the passing interest of a boy; and for a long time I mourned over the accepted account of the untimely and disgraceful ending of that unfortunate poet – 'our elder Shelley,' as Swinburne has termed him. Later the Bacon-Shakespere controversy attracted my attention; and while I became skeptical concerning the authorship by William Shakespere of the dramas that bear his name, I could not attribute them to the pen of Francis Bacon.[3]

He considered Bacon's extant writings – an 'enduring monument of law and philosophy' – too different from Shakespeare's, but thought Marlowe could certainly have written the latter 'had his life been prolonged' beyond the age of twenty-nine. The idea is part of its time, influenced not just by the 'skeptical' questions first raised by the Baconians, but by the whole nineteenth-century revival of Marlowe, after two centuries of comparative neglect. This was pioneered by William Hazlitt, but is most powerfully expressed by the late Victorian poet Algernon Swinburne, whom Zeigler frequently quotes. The book's epigraph is a stirring pronouncement by Swinburne: 'It is not for any man to measure, above all it is not for any workman in the field of tragic poetry lightly to take on himself the responsibility or the authority to pronounce, what it is that Christopher Marlowe could not have done.'[4]

Zeigler was writing at a time when knowledge of Marlowe's death was based on a few rather vague comments by contemporaries, and on an erroneous entry in the 1593 burial register of St Nicholas's, Deptford, which states that he had been killed by a certain 'Francis Frezer'. His storyline draws on the single-sentence account given by Francis Meres in *Palladis Tamia* (1598), an important repository of Elizabethan literary gossip: 'Marlowe was stabbed to death by a bawdy serving-man, a rival of his in his lewd love.'[5] This was expanded in the seventeenth century by Anthony à Wood, whose version of it begins: 'He being deeply in love with a certain woman . . . had for his rival a certain bawdy serving-man, one rather fit to be a pimp than an ingenious amoretto as Marlowe conceived himself to be.'[6] (This misses the probable hint of homosexuality in Meres's construction of 'lewd love' as the cause of the fatal quarrel: that Marlowe was gay was certainly one of the claims of his detractors, and is also arguable from some of his writing.) Zeigler's novel – subtitled 'A Story of the Secret of Three Centuries' – begins with Marlowe consorting with a former sweetheart called Anne, now unhappily married to the churlish and unattractive Francis Frazer. A fight ensues when Frazer catches them together, but – in what might be called the twist that launched a thousand theories – it is Frazer who is killed. To escape punishment Marlowe swaps clothes with the corpse, and with the help of fellow playwrights Shakespeare and George Peele, who testify that the body is his, he makes his getaway. Later he is pursued by the fanatical Puritan, Richard Bame – another name culled from a confusion, 'Bame' being a nineteenth-century misreading of the signature of Richard Baines, the informer (in fact a turned Catholic rather than a Puritan) who delivered evidence of Marlowe's blasphemies to the authorities. Marlowe writes *Titus Andronicus*, which Peele and Shakespeare pass off as their work, and so the deception begins.

Zeigler's idea that Marlowe actually died in 1598 draws on another bit of faulty anecdotal history – the statement by John Aubrey that Ben Jonson had 'killed Mr Marlow the poet on Bunhill, coming from the Green Curtain play-house'.[7] In his preface, employing the interrogative syntax much favoured in authorship literature, Zeigler wonders: 'Did Marlowe die in 1598, rather than 1593? Was Aubrey right?' The answer to both questions is 'No'. Aubrey was confusing another episode of literary violence: Jonson's killing of the actor Gabriel Spenser in a duel on Hoxton Fields. Zeigler probably knew this, but has succumbed to the lure of the counterfactual not just within his fictional narrative but also within his supposedly serious, non-fiction preface. This is an early paradigm of authorship controversialism, where invented evidence plays a determining role in what is presented as a genuine historical argument.

Further support for the Marlovian claim came a few years later from Dr Thomas Corwin Mendenhall (1841–1924). A distinguished physicist, a President of the American Association for the Advancement of Science and a meteorologist who had a valley and glacier in Alaska named after him, Mendenhall was also an early exponent of 'stylometry'. Applying the statistical principle of frequency distribution, he believed that the occurrence of different word-lengths in a writer's work formed a unique pattern, which could be used to identify that writer's authorship of other texts. His initial sampling of these 'word spectra' in Bacon and Shakespeare proved negative, but when he turned his attention to Marlowe and Shakespeare he discovered a similarity of distribution which he described as a 'sensation'. He published his findings in *Popular Science Monthly* in 1901, with graphs showing what appeared to be an almost exact correspondence. For instance, both writers used an average of 240 four-letter words per thousand, 130 five-letter words and 60 six-letter words, with other word-lengths close if not exact.[8]

The obvious fallacy in Mendenhall's method when applied to early modern texts is the fluidity of spelling in that period, and the extent to which printed copy has been prey to the vicissitudes of transmission. Spellings may be the author's, but are at least as likely to be those of copyists and compositors. In the case of compositors, their spelling choices are governed by extraneous factors such as lineation and availability of type. Thus these computations for Marlowe and Shakespeare are partly based on an ungovernable sample of anonymous orthographers. It has also been shown that word-length distributions vary according to genre: an analysis of the works of Sir Philip Sidney by C. B. Williams (1975) gives very different readings for his prose and his poetry.[9] This would also affect a comparison of Shakespeare's plays with those of Marlowe, which feature much less prose. Despite these caveats, current Marlovians such as Daryl Pinksen and Peter Farey have continued to elaborate on Mendenhall's stylometry.

In 1925 J. Leslie Hotson made his game-changing discovery of the coroner's inquest on Marlowe's death, which he unearthed among the bundles of Chancery miscellanea in the Public Records Office.[10] Here, after three centuries of rumour and misinformation, was the pristine record of Marlowe's last hours, as established by the Royal Coroner, William Danby, and sixteen jurors, assembled at Deptford on 1 June 1593, with the corpse of the poet laid out for examination. It was found that on 30 May Marlowe had met up with three men at a house in Deptford Strand owned by a widow named Eleanor Bull, and that after a day spent in their company he became involved in an argument over the 'reckoning': a 'sum of pence' owed for the day's food and drink. He was killed by a dagger-thrust which entered his right eye-socket and penetrated two inches into his brain. His killer was one Ingram Frizer, a shady businessman employed by Thomas Walsingham, at whose house near Chislehurst Marlowe had recently been staying. It was claimed by the other men present – Nicholas Skeres and Robert Poley – that Marlowe had attacked first. The coroner concluded that Frizer had acted in self-defence, and (as Hotson also found) he received a royal pardon four weeks later, on 28 June 1593.[11]

Though many have questioned the findings of the inquest, their doubts concern the reliability of the witnesses – a trio of very dodgy characters – and the account they gave of the circumstances and motives of the killing. What no one doubts (or no one except Marlovian controversialists) is that the inquest authentically records the fact of Marlowe's death at Deptford Strand in the early evening of Wednesday 30 May 1593. But the desire of anti-Stratfordians is always to create alternative narratives, with or without the backing of evidence, and despite this extensive scene-of-crime documentation Marlovians continue to claim that Marlowe's death was faked. They have to: it is a *sine qua non* of their belief that he wrote the works of Shakespeare, most of which were demonstrably written after 1593. Zeigler's original theory could not be right – Marlowe did not kill his antagonist in the fight – but the scenario of a body-switch remains central.

In the mid-1930s the case began to attract the attentions of Calvin Hoffman (real name Leo Hochman), a New York theatrical agent and publicist who would become the best-known and most doggedly persistent of all Marlovians. For twenty years he pursued this 'literary will o' the wisp that gave me no rest', until 'there grew to dominate my days and dreams an imposture unbelievable in magnitude'.[12] In 1955 he published *The Murder of the Man who was Shakespeare* (issued in Britain as *The Man who was Shakespeare*). His theory can be summed up as follows. In May 1593 Marlowe was under investigation for atheistic opinions revealed to the authorities by Richard Baines and others. The purpose of the meeting at Deptford was to engineer Marlowe's disappearance, thereby to protect him from imprisonment, torture and possible execution. This was arranged by Thomas Walsingham, who was Marlowe's homosexual lover, and who had known connections with at least two of the three men present at Deptford. A sailor from Deptford docks was lured down a dark alley by Frizer and Skeres and murdered. It was this body which was viewed by Coroner Danby and his jurors on 1 June, and hurriedly buried in an unmarked grave at Deptford churchyard. Walsingham bribed Danby to ensure everything passed off smoothly, and also used his influence so that Frizer was speedily exonerated. Marlowe meanwhile was spirited away to the continent, probably to Italy, there to spend the next twenty years penning plays and poems under the borrowed name of a dull-witted but usefully compliant actor called William Shakespeare.

Only two links in this circumstantial chain have any evidential backing. It is true that Marlowe was in a parlous situation at this time, having been summoned before the Privy Council on 18 May, and ordered to report to them daily; and it is true that Walsingham had prior connections with

Robert Poley, a career spy who had worked with him in the 1580s, and with Frizer.[13] These are genuinely part of the backdrop of the Deptford meeting, and can indeed be interpreted as deepening or complicating the nature of the meeting. But all the rest – the homosexual relationship, the waylaid sailor, the body switch, the suborned coroner, even the unmarked grave – is mere invention.

Hoffman was nothing if not thorough, and a great many minor discoveries are drawn into the force-field of this theory. For instance, he finds that among the small bequests of Walsingham's will (5 May 1630) is one of 40 shillings to a scrivener named Thomas Smith. It was he, obviously, who 'copied the Marlowe documents (i.e. the Shakespeare plays) for Walsingham to distribute to the London theatres'.[14] There are others who must also have been in on the scam, such as the publisher of Shakespeare's Sonnets, Thomas Thorpe, whose famously riddling dedication of the book to 'Mr W. H.' is solved to Hoffman's satisfaction as a reference to Thomas 'Walsing-Ham'.[15] Thorpe had earlier published the first edition of Marlowe's translation of Lucan (*Lucan's First Book translated Line for Line by Chr. Marlow*, 1600). His playful dedication to fellow-publisher Edward Blount refers to the poet's ghost returning to haunt St Paul's Churchyard: 'Blount: I purpose to be blunt with you, and out of my dullness to encounter you with a dedication in the memory of that pure elemental wit, Chr. Marlow; whose ghost or genius is to be seen walk the Churchyard in (at the least) three or four sheets.' This is taken by Hoffman as an intentional hint that Marlowe was actually still alive.[16] Such literal readings are also foisted on the commendatory verses in front of the First Folio, particularly the poem signed 'I. M.', probably the minor poet and translator James Mabbe:

> We wondered (Shakespeare) that thou went'st so soon
> From the world's stage to the grave's tiring-room.
> We thought thee dead, but this thy printed worth
> Tells thy spectators that thou went'st but forth
> To enter with applause . . . [17]

And then there is the prologue of *The Jew of Malta*, spoken in the guise of 'Machevil' (or Machiavelli). This dark Marlovian tragicomedy was staged in 1592, but Hoffman insists that the prologue is a late addition, and that a simple key (Machiavel = Marlowe) decodes its message to the cognoscenti:

> Albeit the world think Machevil is dead,
> Yet was his soul but flown beyond the Alps . . .
> To some perhaps my name is odious,

But such as love me guard me from their tongues,
And let them know that I am Machevil,
And weigh not men, and therefore not men's words.
Admir'd I am of those that hate me most:
Though some speak openly against my books,
Yet will they read me . . .
I count religion but a childish toy,
And hold there is no sin but ignorance.
Birds of the air will tell of murders past!
I am asham'd to hear such fooleries![18]

At the end of his book Hoffman has a thirty-page appendix listing hundreds of 'parallelisms' between the writings of Marlowe and Shakespeare. Marlovians make much of these textual parallels. A well-known example occurs in *Romeo and Juliet*, where Romeo's famous lines about Juliet on the balcony ('But soft, what light through yonder window breaks? / It is the East, and Juliet is the sun', 2.1.44–5) seem to echo the words of Barabas in *The Jew of Malta* about his daughter Abigail, also on a balcony ('But stay, what star shines yonder in the East? / The lodestar of my life, if Abigail', 2.1.41–2).

Particular interest is focused on *As You Like It* (*c.* 1599), because it contains numerous glancing allusions to Marlowe, including an acknowledged quotation, in which the late poet is directly addressed: 'Dead shepherd, now I find thy saw of might: / "Whoever loved that loved not at first sight"?' (3.5.81–2). This quotation from *Hero and Leander* can doubtless be related to the recent publication of the poem by Edward Blount (1598). Recurrent references to Ovid in the play would also be topical in relation to Marlowe, whose translation of Ovid's erotic *Elegies* was among the 'unseemly' works banned by Archbishop Whitgift's book-burning edict of 1 June 1599. But the lines which command the attention of Marlovians are those spoken by Touchstone:

When a man's verses cannot be understood, nor a man's good wit seconded with the forward child, understanding, it strikes a man more dead than a great reckoning in a little room. (3.3.9–12)[19]

Since the recovery of the inquest narrative that last phrase has been interpreted as an allusion to the death of Marlowe, who was struck dead in a little room in Deptford in a quarrel over the 'reckoning'. There may also be an echoing of a line from *The Jew of Malta*, 'infinite riches in a little room'. Marlovians profess puzzlement at this. How – they ask – could Shakespeare have known about the detail of the 'reckoning', which is not mentioned by any contemporary commentator? This is typically disingenuous. That we don't know how he knew does not mean that he couldn't have known. The question is framed in order to elicit a desired answer, which is that (like the Machevil prologue) the lines are a veiled communiqué from the true author of the play.

The idea that Shakespeare's plays contain clues as to their true authorship – anagrams, acrostics, ciphers – is a commonplace of anti-Stratfordian theory, but the echoes of Marlowe are perfectly explicable as the influence of one writer on another. One can trace the trajectory of this influence. In his earlier histories and tragedies – the *Henry VI* plays, *Titus Andronicus, Richard III, Richard II* – Shakespeare is consciously writing in a Marlovian idiom, but by the later 1590s the echoes are more ironic. In *Henry IV Part 2* Falstaff's swaggering sidekick Pistol is full of faulty scraps of Marlowe – his 'hollow pampered jades' (2.4.161) garbles a line from *Tamburlaine*, 'Holla, ye pampered jades of Asia.' In *The Merry Wives of Windsor*, Hugh Evans soothes his 'melancholies' by crooning a couple of stanzas from Marlowe's famous lyric, 'Come Live With Me', complete with comic Welsh pronunciations ('And we will make our peds of roses', etc.). In *Hamlet* the speech of the First Player (2.2.471–521) – that epitome of outdated theatrical histrionics – is a parodic version of lines from Marlowe and Nashe's *Dido Queen of Carthage*. The nature of these later references suggests the audience's familiarity with the Marlowe canon: their very casualness is a kind of tribute. Yet there is also a note of desertion – the poet who had so inspired Shakespeare in his early years is now made light of. These comic characters quote him as if they were whistling an old tune.

There is the hint of a human story here – two great writers, the sparks of admiration and rivalry – but any tendency to see these writers as real breathing people is drowned out by the vociferous anti-Shakespearian agenda of codes and conspiracies.

Calvin Hoffman, who died in 1987, continues to dominate the world of Marlovian authorship studies. There have been various further explorations and refinements of his theory, but no great changes or new directions. The late Dorothy Wraight mined the Sonnets for refractions of Marlowe's post-mortem biography (*The Story that the Sonnets Tell*, 1994). David More has proposed that the corpse used in the body-switch was that of the anti-episcopal agitator John Penry, who had been hanged on 29 May at St Thomas a Watering, not far from Deptford (less arbitrary than Hoffman's sailor but harder to square with the procedures of the inquest, given the obvious physical evidence of execution).[20] Peter Farey, one of

the more industrious and level-headed of current Marlovians, has sought
to prove that on 30 May 1593 the royal court was at Nonsuch Palace
rather than Greenwich, that the Deptford killing did not therefore fall
infra virgam ('within the verge', defined as a twelve-mile radius around the
body of the Queen), and that the involvement of the Royal Coroner in
the case was a suspicious intervention rather than a routine requirement.[21]
The late Louis Ule, one of the more fantastical, claimed that after 1593
Marlowe lived in the Countess of Pembroke's household under the name
'Hugh Sanford'.[22] In a wide field of improbable theories this is surely a
champion. The real Sanford edited the 1593 edition of Sidney's *Arcadia*,
had a reputation as a grammarian pedant and an expert on heraldry, and
wrote some theological tracts which suggest Puritan leanings. He has no
connection with or similarity to Marlowe, and has anyway a perfectly
legitimate biography of his own. It is hard to see how Marlowe might have
'taken' his name after 1593. Was Sanford locked up like Mrs Rochester in
an attic at Wilton House? Did no one notice?

Hoffman's influence also persists in the form of the Hoffman Prize,
endowed by a bequest in his will and administered by King's School,
Canterbury. An annual prize is awarded for a 'distinguished publication
on Christopher Marlowe', but the true grail is the 'principal prize', which
consists of one half of the capital of the trust fund, an unspecified but very
sizeable amount. This, it is stipulated, will be awarded to anyone who 'has
furnished irrefutable and incontrovertible proof and evidence required to
satisfy the world of Shakespearian scholarship that all the plays and poems
now commonly attributed to William Shakespeare were in fact written by
Christopher Marlowe'.[23] This pot of gold has not yet been claimed, and it
is a fairly safe bet it never will be.

CHAPTER 4

The life and theatrical interests of Edward de Vere, seventeenth Earl of Oxford

Alan H. Nelson

For sixty-three years following the 1857 publication of Delia Bacon's *The Philosophy of the Plays of Shakspeare Unfolded*, conspiracy theorists unwilling to concede that William Shakespeare wrote his own poems and plays tended to accept Delia's namesake Sir Francis Bacon as the true author. This all changed in 1920, with the publication of J. T. Looney's *'Shakespeare' Identified in Edward de Vere the Seventeenth Earl of Oxford*. Looney drew up a list of propositions declaring what Shakespeare must have been like given the particular characteristics of his surviving poems and plays. Thus, for example, because the plays often portray aristocrats, the author himself must have been an aristocrat. Predictably (judging from his title), Looney discounted the authorship of the historical William Shakespeare and promoted the authorship of the hyper-aristocratic seventeenth Earl of Oxford, Edward de Vere.

Looney's primary source of information on Oxford was Sidney Lee's entry in the respected *Dictionary of National Biography*.[1] In 1928 B. M. Ward followed up with *The Seventeenth Earl of Oxford, 1550–1604, From Contemporary Documents*. True to his title, Ward significantly increased the number of historical documents from which Oxford's life can be reconstructed; but his Victorian sensibilities balked at Oxford's apparent homosexuality. Two years later (1930), Percy Allen published, as the first of many titles, *The Case for Edward de Vere 17th Earl of Oxford as 'Shakespeare'*. Allen eventually embarrassed the cause by consulting spiritual mediums.[2] In 1952 Dorothy and Charlton Ogburn published *This Star of England: 'William Shakespeare,' Man of the Renaissance*. The elder Ogburns represent an odd tradition in which Americans, having cast off English monarchy, grow besotted with English aristocracy; the Ogburns also promote the 'Prince Tudor theory' (discussed below) which undermines the scholarly integrity of the entire Oxfordian enterprise. A generation later, in 1984, their son Charlton Ogburn (the younger) published *The Mysterious William Shakespeare: The Myth and the Reality*. This Ogburn was more a publicist than a scholar, but what a publicist! He is more responsible than any individual since Looney for the current vitality of the 'authorship debate'. In 2003 Alan H. Nelson (author of this present essay) published *Monstrous Adversary: The Life of Edward de Vere, 17th Earl of Oxford*. Having inspected and transcribed the reports which so scandalized B. M. Ward, along with other 'new' documents, Nelson remains the rare sceptic among Oxford's biographers. In 2005 Mark Anderson published his complexly titled *'Shakespeare' by Another Name: The Life of Edward de Vere, Earl of Oxford, The Man Who Was Shakespeare*. For Anderson, scarcely an incident in Oxford's life remains unconnected to the Shakespeare canon; and scarcely a detail of the Shakespeare canon remains unconnected to Oxford's life.

My list of post-Looney biographers barely scratches the surface of the Oxfordian movement. By 1992 some 4,000 'authorship' books and articles clogged the shelves of public, private and institutional libraries.[3] The rate of publication has only increased in subsequent years, promoted by the internet, the worldwide web, and the ease of publishing – including newsletters and self-publishing – in the wake of the computer revolution.

To understand what the fuss is all about, we must first look into the life of our subject.[4] For the sake of convenience we may divide Oxford's life into three periods: minority; young adulthood; and maturity. Born 12 June 1550 in remote but picturesque Castle Hedingham, Essex, Edward de Vere was baptized a few days later, as evidenced by the gift of a gilt-silver cup from the young King Edward (recorded on 17 June 1550). Edward de Vere was the sole son of John de Vere, sixteenth Earl of Oxford, by his second (or possibly third) wife, Margery née Golding. Upon John's death on 3 August 1562 the twelve-year-old Edward became a royal ward. He was put under the care of William Cecil, master of the wards. Cecil kept a grand house on the Strand, between London and Westminster. Here Edward had access to Cecil's library, and may have been tutored by his uncle Arthur Golding, the translator of Ovid, and by the notably learned Sir Thomas Smith. As one of many grandees accompanying the Queen's royal visits, Edward picked up unearned MA degrees at both Cambridge (1564) and Oxford (1566). On 23 July 1567 he killed an undercook in Cecil's household, escaping a charge of capital murder on the plea that the undercook committed suicide by deliberately running himself upon the young earl's rapier. Edward – or Oxford as we shall call him henceforth – attained his majority on 12 June 1571.

On 3 December 1571 Oxford married Anne Cecil, his guardian's daughter. In March 1572 he fell under suspicion of trying to facilitate the escape of the Catholic Duke of Norfolk from the Tower of London. A year later Gilbert Talbot wrote to his father, the Earl of Shrewsbury:

[The Earl of Oxford] is lately grown into great credit; for the Queen's Majesty delighteth more in his personage and his dancing and valiantness than any other. I think [the Earl of] Sussex doth back him all that he can; if it were not for his fickle head, he would pass any of them shortly.[5]

Future events show that Oxford's 'fickle head' got the best of him.

In July 1574 Oxford fled to the Low Countries, where he tried unsuccessfully to make contact with Catholic refugees. An old friend, Thomas Bedingfield, was sent over to retrieve him. Back in England, Oxford finally paid enough attention to Anne to get her pregnant. Rather than await the birth of his first child, however, Oxford went abroad again, this time with permission. He travelled to Venice, which over the course of some eleven months became both his principal residence and a springboard for touristic visits around northern Italy. At his return to London in April 1576 Oxford deliberately bypassed Gravesend, where Anne had gone to meet him. His father-in-law Cecil – now Lord Burghley – complained that Oxford had been 'enticed by certain lewd persons to be a stranger to his wife'. Refusing a reconciliation, Oxford denied paternity of his baby daughter Elizabeth and took up residence in London with Orazio Coquo, a choirboy he had brought back from Venice.

Apart from paying the occasional marital debt which eventually led to five pregnancies, Oxford had very little to do with his wife or his three surviving daughters, Elizabeth, Bridget and Susan Vere. Rather, Anne and her three girls lived in the household of their doting grandfather, Lord Burghley, while Oxford, a classic dead-beat father, financed a self-indulgent lifestyle by selling off virtually all his inherited properties.

Beginning in 1577 Oxford joined forces with Henry Howard, younger brother of the late Duke of Norfolk, and with Charles Arundel, scion of a family still faithful to the Old Religion. The threesome secretly considered how England might be restored to Catholicism. A quarrel with Sir Philip Sidney at Greenwich in 1579 seemed headed for a duel until the Queen told Sidney, who was Oxford's superior in everything but rank, to know his place. In late 1580 Oxford turned on his Catholic friends, who soon languished in prison or under house arrest. In March 1581 Anne Vavasour, a royal maid of honour, scandalized the court by giving birth to Oxford's illegitimate son, Edward Vere. While Oxford returned to his wife following a stint in the Tower, the Vavasour clan was less willing to be reconciled, for Anne's uncle, Sir Thomas Knyvet, challenged Oxford to a duel. Single combat and lethal gang warfare threatened the Queen's peace until May 1583, when Elizabeth finally called a halt to Oxford's private adventures. Then, beginning in 1586, in exchange for his good behaviour, Oxford accepted an annuity of £1,000 carefully disbursed in quarterly increments.

In August 1585 Oxford sailed with John Norris to the Netherlands, where he remained less than two months before returning to England, impelled by a private 'humour' grounded in an unwillingness to co-operate with the Earl of Leicester. The Armada events of 1588 saw a repeat performance, as Oxford refused Leicester's direct order to assume the governorship of the important port of Harwich. Leicester wrote to Walsingham even before the action was concluded: 'I am glad I am rid of my Lord Oxford.'

Anne died of a fever in 1588. Some four years later Oxford took as his second wife Elizabeth, daughter and heiress of Thomas Trentham of Rocester Priory, Staffordshire. She soon gave birth to a son, Henry, who would eventually succeed as eighteenth earl. Meanwhile, the seventeenth Earl and his Countess removed to Hackney, whence his final letters are addressed. Most of these letters concern Oxford's project to repair his fortunes by gaining control over tin mining in Devon and Cornwall. Having become a virtual recluse, Oxford survived the devastating plague of 1603 only to die in April 1604, scarcely a year into the reign of James I.

Arguments for Oxford's authorship of the Shakespeare canon begin with the fact that he is the acknowledged author of sixteen poems and the probable author of four more.[6] His poems mostly derive from the early years of his adulthood. Thus in 1573 a poem in English and a literary essay in Latin appeared in a publication dedicated to himself, his old friend Thomas Bedingfield's translation of Jerome Cardan entitled *Cardanos Comforte*. Eight more poems followed in print, beginning in 1575, while still more poems survive in manuscript, the latest estimated date of composition being 1592. Oxford's poems, while not bad for a courtier, are an embarrassment to his proponents, who like to excuse their crude rhymes and old-fashioned metrics as Oxford's 'juvenilia' – even though they were all composed well past his twenty-first birthday.

Two contemporary imprints commend Oxford as a writer of comedies (but not tragedies). The first is *The Arte of English Poetry* (1589), technically anonymous but generally attributed to George Puttenham:

... for Tragedie, the Lord of Buckhurst, & Maister Edward Ferrys for such doings as I haue sene of theirs do deserue the hyest price: Th'Earle of Oxford and Maister Edwardes of her Maiesies Chappell for Comedy and Enterlude...

The second imprint is Francis Meres's *Palladis Tamia* (1598), which draws on the first:

... so the best for Comedy amongst vs bee, Edward Earle of Oxforde, Doctor Gager of Oxforde, Maister Rowley once a rare Scholler of learned Pembrooke Hall in Cambridge, Maister Edwardes one of her Maiesties Chappell, eloquent and wittie Iohn Lilly, Lodge, Gascoyne, Greene, Shakespeare, Thomas Nash, Thomas Heywood, Anthony Mundye our best plotter, Chapman, Porter, Wilson, Hathway, and Henry Chettle.

Meres includes both Oxford and Shakespeare in his list, being obviously of the opinion that these were two different men, each an author in his own right. Confirmation that Oxford was not Shakespeare occurs in John Bodenham's *Bel-vedere or the Garden of the Muses* (1600). In a list of some forty English poets, Bodenham puts Oxford – where he belongs – among earls and knights, and he puts Shakespeare – where he belongs – among commoners.

As no play-text survives from Oxford's pen, it is not possible to compare his comedies to those of the Shakespeare canon. Chronology, however, presents a fatal stumbling-block to the Oxfordian hypothesis. Shakespeare's *Tempest*, for example, was written in or about 1611, well within Shakespeare's lifetime, but seven years after Oxford's death. Evidence for a late date of composition is rich and complex. *The Tempest* is clearly based on reports of a shipwreck which occurred off the island of Bermuda in late 1609. The earliest documented performance of the play was at court during the winter of 1611–12. The play's free-form metrics are entirely consistent with a late date of composition, while its elaborate stage-directions are consistent with indoor performance at the Blackfriars Theatre, which opened in 1609. *The Tempest* is obviously of the same approximate date as *The Winter's Tale*, which is first mentioned in the very same record of a performance at court during the winter of 1611–12. From a document dated 1623 we learn that *The Winter's Tale* was licensed by Sir George Buc.[7] As Buc entered the office of Master of the Revels in 1610, he must have issued the licence in 1610 at the earliest. Simon Forman attended a performance of *The Winter's Tale* on 15 May 1611.[8] Similarly (to take an earlier play), *King Lear* followed the non-Shakespearian *King Leir* published in 1605, was performed at court on 26 December 1607 and was first published in 1608.

So how could *The Tempest* have been written by Oxford? Looney dealt with this obstacle by the simple expedient of ejecting the play from the Shakespeare canon. *The Tempest*, he declared, is not only not by Shakespeare, but is thoroughly un-Shakespearian.[9] Looney's followers, unwilling to follow their leader to such an absurd conclusion, generally take one of three 'outs': (1) they invent an Oxford-friendly chronology by pushing every play and every poem back before April 1604, the month of Oxford's death; (2) they fantasize that Oxford left drafts which were released after his death, perhaps touched up by a reviser; or (3) they take a page from the Marlovian playbook and imagine that Oxford faked his death and continued to write from some place of hiding.

Equally fatal to the Oxfordian cause is the fact that Oxford was a patron of his own theatrical company. In 1580 he acquired the Earl of Warwick's players. For the next twenty-two years, with no known break, this company went under the title of Oxford's Men. The earlier years of the company are richly documented from records of provincial performances, while its later years are best known from the sub-titles of two anonymous plays, *The Weakest Goeth to the Wall*, whose text survives in print (1600), and the lost 'True Historye of George Scanderbarge', entered into the Stationers' Register on 3 July 1601 'as yt was lately playd by the right honourable the Earle of Oxenford his servantes'. In 1602 Oxford involved both the Queen and the Privy Council in transferring patronage of his company to the Earl of Worcester (see below). Oxford's household employees over the years included the playwrights John Lyly and Anthony Munday. If Oxford himself wrote plays for the professional, as distinct from the private, stage – and there is no evidence that he did – it is impossible to imagine that he would have given his plays to the Lord Chamberlain's Men, a rival company.

More persuasive to many of Oxford's partisans are perceived parallels between aspects or events of Oxford's private life and the characters or plot details of the Shakespeare canon, particularly *Hamlet*. Oxford's father died in 1562; his mother then re-married. Oxford became a ward of William Cecil, by all accounts a kind of Polonius. Cecil had a daughter, Anne, whom Oxford wooed. She had a brother (actually several brothers). Oxford was temporarily captured by pirates on his way (back) to England. And so forth, and so forth.

Parallels between Oxford's life and aspects of the Shakespeare canon are both superficial, however, and inexact. It is true that Oxford's father died before his allotted time of three score years and ten, but he was not murdered, and certainly was not poisoned by having a fatal dram poured into the porches of his ear. Edward de Vere was a child of twelve at the time of his father's death, far younger than Hamlet at the time of King Hamlet's murder. Far from re-marrying within a month, Edward's mother remained a widow for more than the conventional year of mourning. Her second husband was not her first husband's brother, but a respectable knight who remained on friendly terms with young Edward. Far from rejecting Burghley's daughter and consigning her to a nunnery, Oxford married the girl, who didn't commit suicide but lived sixteen more years until she died a natural death. Neither of Anne's brothers was particularly fond of Oxford, who made their sister's life a misery, but neither challenged him to a duel or killed him with an empoisoned rapier.

As for parallels with other plays, Oxford remained on reasonably good terms with his three surviving daughters, none of whom was a Goneril or a Regan; nor was any a Cordelia. Nor was Anne Cecil a Helena as in *All's Well that Ends Well*: she did not follow her husband abroad in disguise, but remained in England, pregnant, giving birth to a daughter (not a son) long before Oxford's return.

The typical Oxfordian litany inevitably recalls the pedantic and tiresome comparativist Fluellen in *Henry V* (4.7):

> . . . I tell you, captain, if you look in the maps of the 'orld, I warrant you sall find, in the comparisons between Macedon and Monmouth, that the situations, look you, is both alike. There is a river in Macedon; and there is also moreover a river at Monmouth: . . . 'tis all one, 'tis alike as my fingers is to my fingers, and there is salmons in both. If you mark Alexander's life well, Harry of Monmouth's life is come after it indifferent well; for there is figures in all things. Alexander, God knows, and you know, in his rages, and his furies, and his wraths, and his cholers, and his moods, and his displeasures, and his indignations, and also being a little intoxicate in his prains, did, in his ales and his angers, look you, kill his best friend, Cleitus.

Academic Shakespearians are like the spoil-sport Gower: 'Our king is not like him in that: he never killed any of his friends.' (Oxford did however kill a poor undercook.)

As for the conspiracy theory – called the 'Prince Tudor theory' – which makes Oxford the son of Princess Elizabeth and the father-by-incest of the Earl of Southampton, and which forms the main plot of Roland Emmerich's film *Anonymous*, this is invented out of thin air and invokes an English court quite unknown to history.[10] To accept the theory we must deny the known facts of Oxford's life, including the dates of his birth and baptism. If Oxford was not born on 12 June 1550, then he had no right to celebrate his majority on 12 June 1571, and no right to the inherited properties which he liquidated to support his extravagant lifestyle. If Oxford was not the biological son of Margery Golding he was not the biological nephew of the poet Arthur Golding. If Oxford was not the son of John de Vere, sixteenth Earl of Oxford, then he had no link through the marriage of his aunt Frances Vere to the famed poet Henry Howard,

Earl of Surrey. To make him the son of Thomas Seymour and Princess Elizabeth is, in short, to strip him of any familial predisposition to be a poet.

But why would anyone even think that the 'true Shakespeare' should have been the illegitimate son of Princess (later Queen) Elizabeth and consequently the unacknowledged King Edward VII? A crucial element of the self-styled 'authorship debate' is Looney's post-Romantic (and anti-classical) proposition that all literary composition is quintessentially auto-biographical. An author must write what he (or she) knows; and all that an author knows is the experience of his (or her) own life. A glover's son from Stratford could not possibly know or even imagine what it is to be a king because he is not a king. Perhaps an earl could imagine what it is to be a king, even though no adult male had sat on England's throne since the death of Henry VIII in 1547. So it helps that Edward de Vere was an earl. But what if he was actually a king? This, surely, and this alone, would make it possible for the author to create convincing dramatic characters out of historical kings!

An even more serious fault than the film's descent into historical absur-dity is its unwillingness to face up to Oxford's fondness for young boys. In the life of the real Oxford this inclination is enshrined in his relationship to Orazio Coquo, and in the witticism attributed to him by his Catholic friends: 'When women are unsweet, young boys are in season' (reminiscent of the saying attributed to Christopher Marlowe, that 'All who love not boys and tobacco are fools'). The film is as squeamish as B. M. Ward on the subject of homosexuality. If it had followed its own plot to its logical con-clusion, then Oxford would have conducted a homosexual affair with the Earl of Southampton, Oxford's own biological son by an incestuous union with his own mother. As the present writer wrote in a different context,[11] these implied relationships do not prove that Oxford was William Shake-speare, but they do prove that he was John Milton, for how but by personal experience could Milton have conceived the variously incestuous trio in *Paradise Lost*, Satan, Sin and Death? By depriving the Oxford biography of homoeroticism, both the 'Prince Tudor' theory and the film sever an essential link to the Sonnets, of which some of the first 126 (out of 154) are clearly written to a young man, putatively the Earl of Southampton.

Turning back from pornographic fantasy to documented historical fact, I conclude by examining a letter addressed by the Privy Council to the Lord Mayor of London on 31 March 1602, about one year prior to the death of Queen Elizabeth on 24 March 1603 and two years prior to Oxford's death on 24 June 1604. The reader is invited to detect any remote hint in the letter that 'our verey good L[ord] the Earle of Oxford' was a playwright, or a poet, or a courtier obsessed with protecting his literary legacy, or that the Queen was his biological mother and ex-lover.[12]

A lettre to the L[ord] Maior for the Bores head to be licensed for the plaiers.

After our verey hartie Commendacions to your L[ordship]. We receaued your letter, signifieinge some amendment of the abuses or disorders by the immoderate exercise of Stage plays in and about the Citie, by meanes of our late order renued for the restraint of them, and with all [=withall] shewinge a speciall inconvenience yet remayneinge, by reason that the seruants of our verey good L[ord] the Earle of Oxford, and of me the Earle of Worcester, beinge ioyned by agreement together in on[e] Companie (to whom, vpon noteice of her Maiesties pleasure at the suit of the Earle of Oxford, tolleracion hath ben thought meete to be graunted, notwithstandinge the restraint of our said former Orders), doe not tye them selfs to one certaine place and howse, but do change their place at there owne disposition, which is as disorderly and offensiue as the former offence of many howses. And as the other Companies that are allowed, namely of me the L[ord] Admirall and the L[ord] Chamberlaine, be appointed there certaine howses, and one and noe more to each Companie. Soe we doe straightly require that this third Companie be likewise to one place, And because we are informed the house called the Bores head is the place they haue especially vsed and doe best like of, we doe pray and require yow that the said howse, namely the Bores head, may be assigned onto them, and that they be verrey straightlie Charged to vse and exercise there plaies in noe other but that howse, as they will looke to haue that tolleracion continued and avoid farther displeasure. And soe we bid your L[ordshi]p. hartely farewell, from the Court at Ritchemond the last of March, 1602.

Your lordshippes verey lovinge friends,

T Buchkhust	Notingham
E. Worcester	W. Knowlis
Iohn Stannop:	Ro: Cecyll
Io: fortescu	I: Herbert

The eight signatories are all members of the Privy Council. That Oxford was not a member of the Council is evident both from the absence of his name in the list of signatories, and from reference to him in the body of the letter in the third person (as compared to first person for Edward Somerset, fourth Earl of Worcester). The Oxford-Worcester company is a third London company, clearly distinct from both the Lord Admiral's (Nottingham's) company and from the Lord Chamberlain's company (Shakespeare's). It is impossible indeed to imagine that Oxford could or would have been allowed to stick his nose into the affairs of the company patronized by the Lord Chamberlain (George Carey, second Baron Hunsdon). Oxford's men, moreover, played (past, present and future) at the Boar's Head (within the City of London), whereas the Lord Chamberlain's men played at the Globe (across the Thames on Bankside).

Oxford's involvement in the petition was twofold: he had already petitioned Queen Elizabeth for toleration of his own playing company to make a third to the two 'approved' companies, and he had come to an understanding with Worcester that their two companies might proceed as one single company to be called Lord Worcester's men. Neither aspect of Oxford's involvement is compatible with the assumption that he had supplied play-texts to the Lord Chamberlain's men. This letter to the Lord Mayor, moreover, and not *The Tempest*, is Oxford's farewell to the theatre.

CHAPTER 5

The unusual suspects

Matt Kubus

In April of 1995 the popular science magazine, *Scientific American* famously published an article by art historian Lillian Schwartz entitled 'The Art Historian's Computer'. The article advances Schwartz's findings after electronically juxtaposing and superimposing the faces on famous portraits so as to forensically uncover hidden secrets of the past. Comparing da Vinci's *Mona Lisa* with his self-portrait, for instance, and revealing striking similarities between the two legendary countenances, Schwartz boldly claimed that the former must have been completed with the latter in mind since it so clearly is 'infused . . . with his own features'.[1] Among other assertions, Schwartz also adds to the conversation that concerns this collection of essays, a contribution that in itself situates the Shakespeare authorship discussion within the spectrum of the greatest of history's artistic mysteries. Comparing Droeshout's engraving of Shakespeare on the title page of the First Folio with a number of portraits of Shakespeare's contemporaries, Schwartz concluded that the iconic image of the man from Stratford is actually an engraving based on George Gower's 'Armada' portrait of Queen Elizabeth I: 'A detailed comparison on the computer', Schwartz remarks, 'revealed that most of the lines in the Droeshout engraving and the queen's portrait by George Gower are the same. The eyes, noses and curvature of the faces match perfectly. But there is an odd shift in some features.'[2] To reconcile this 'odd shift', Schwartz proposes two solutions. First, '[i]n having to *invent* a face for Shakespeare, Droeshout must have based his engraving on a *cartoon* of the queen's face', and secondly, because '[e]tching metal is hard laborious work, . . . Droeshout came back to the engraving sometime later . . . perhaps [after] having finished the left side of the face, and inadvertently (or deliberately) shifted the cartoon' (italics mine). And finally, while she does not implicitly argue that the plays of Shakespeare were written by the Virgin Queen, she states that 'lively debates continue as to who wrote Shakespeare's works' in spite of, or perhaps partly because of her artistic comparison.

In gathering material for this chapter, I encountered article after article, book after book, some less and some more convincing, some less and some more self-assured, some through similar and some through quite different methods; but each staking claim to the same discovery: the real author of the plays and poems attributed to William Shakespeare. And as I continued to collect what seemed to be endless amounts of data, it became evident that what is more interesting than the conclusions of these arguments is the way in which each proposition is fashioned. Intellectually, what is most concerning about Schwartz's contention, for example, is less her conclusion and more her methodology. It is standard scientific method to start with a hypothesis, to analyse the data, and to make a logical con-clusion based upon that information. Schwartz, however, begins with the major assumption that Shakespeare's face needed to be *invented* in the first instance. This is a tactic used by so many of the supporters of candidates of Shakespeare authorship – a line of reasoning with an unsubstantiated premise that influences how the argument will be constructed. It is the approach that begins *in medias res* without ensuring that the premise is corroborated by data. It is therefore the goal of this chapter to exploit methodology and use it as a way in – a means to synthesize the myriad of other, lesser candidates of the authorship discussion.

This chapter deals with plurality – the proliferation of candidates for Shakespeare authorship that, according to Paul Edmondson and Stanley Wells, 'should be enough in itself to topple the whole house of cards. Every additional name added to the list only serves to demonstrate the absurdity of the entire enterprise. All of these nominations are equally invalid; none has a greater claim than any of the others.'[3] Mathematically, each time an additional candidate is suggested, the probability decreases that any given name is the true author. In economic terms, we can apply the law of diminishing returns; or, the law that states that as a single factor of production is increased (as each name is put forth), the marginal output of production decreases (the overall reliability of the case decreases). Any way we look at it, the outcome is the same.

By the end of the chapter, we should be able to see that there is a formula emerging into which one can place nearly any name of any person living in Shakespeare's day and the same conclusion will be realized: that they are both a viable candidate and an unviable candidate in the sense that anyone can be one. You will see that anti-Stratfordians have created an unsubstantiated-premise-based machine, a self-sustainable mechanism that churns out candidates for authorship. At the same time, this chapter deals with a very specialized group of people – a literary coterie made up of only the well-educated, well-travelled and those of the highest status. James Shapiro's prophecy in *Contested Will: Who Wrote Shakespeare?* that making a complete list of candidates would be futile because it would soon be outdated proved to be true, as since work began on this chapter, three more candidates for authorship have been proposed, bringing the total number (as far as we know) to eighty – a rather startling figure. In seeking to understand the extent of each theory's influence and how the myriad of anti-Stratfordians organize themselves, we should want to look at the theoretical framework of each case. What *kind* of an argument is being made? Each section, then, will analyse the longevity of the case being made, and finally, will make clear just how each argument does not stand up to historical fact and/or rationality.

READING BIOGRAPHICALLY: THE CASES FOR WILLIAM STANLEY, SIXTH EARL OF DERBY (1561–1642) AND ROGER MANNERS, FIFTH EARL OF RUTLAND (1576–1612)

Edward de Vere, seventeenth Earl of Oxford, discussed in a previous chapter of this volume, is the most famous example of a proposed candidate whose case heavily relies on the idea that in order to create the wealth of thoughts, characters and settings found in Shakespeare's plays and poems, the real author required sufficient enough exposure to life on the Continent, at University and in Court. This methodology – what I call reading biographically – is not without its reputable supporters. The great American essayist, Ralph Waldo Emerson, for instance, notoriously described his contempt for the idea that someone like the man from Stratford was able to write the plays attributed to his name for the reason that he was in want of sufficient cultural exposure. 'Shakespeare, Homer, Dante, Chaucer', he begins, 'saw the splendor of meaning that plays over the visible world; knew that a tree had another use than for apples, and corn another than for meal, and the ball of the earth, than for tillage and roads: that these things bore a second and finer harvest to the mind, being emblems of its thoughts, and conveying in all their natural history a certain mute commentary on human life. He converted the elements which waited on his command, into entertainments. He was master of the revels to mankind.' Yet, Emerson's Shakespeare – the far-removed artist-creator – cannot be the man from Stratford, for Emerson goes on to say that

[t]he Egyptian verdict of the Shakespeare Societies comes to mind; that he was a jovial actor and manager. I can not marry this fact to his verse. Other admirable

men have led lives in some sort of keeping with their thought; but this man, in wide contrast. Had he been less, had he reached only the common measure of great authors, of Bacon, Milton, Tasso, Cervantes, we might leave the fact in the twilight of human fate: but that this man of men, he who gave to the science of mind a new and larger subject than had ever existed, and planted the standard of humanity some furlongs forward into Chaos, – that he should not be wise for himself; – it must even go into the world's history that the best poet led an obscure and profane life, using his genius for the public amusement.[4]

This marriage between verse and experience that Emerson eloquently describes is what is at the heart of reading works of literature biographically, and the methodology, it seems, is contagious – for the cases for Robert Cecil, first Earl of Salisbury, Robert Devereux, second Earl of Essex and Charles Blount, eighth Baron Mountjoy and Earl of Devonshire, among others, all pivot around this notion. Two particularly representative cases are described below.

During the two-year period of 1891–2, three articles by James Greenstreet appeared in *The Genealogist*, the collective thesis of which would lay the foundation for the case of William Stanley, sixth Earl of Derby's authorship of the plays. The original Derbyite, Greenstreet, in an article entitled 'A Hitherto Unknown Noble Writer of Elizabethan Comedies', revealed to the world two previously unknown excerpts from domestic state papers written in 1599 that declare that the Earl of Derby is 'busied only in penning comedies for the common players'.[5] Greenstreet then asks, 'How comes it that this mention in a printed State Paper of a nobleman writing Comedies, at the very time the (so-called) Shakespearian Plays were appearing has been so long overlooked?' He then asked his readers to take that morsel of previously unknown documentary evidence and jump to the conclusion that these comedies must have been those written by a professional dramatist, like the one who penned the theatrical masterpieces of *Hamlet*, *A Midsummer Night's Dream* and *King Lear*. It is unnecessary and misleading to the logical mind to describe the gaping maw – the deep, yawning chasm – between Greenstreet's discovery and his conclusion.[6]

Notwithstanding the absurdity to this logic, though, the Derbyite's claim has been more sustainable than most of the other seventy-nine candidates for the reason that there exists that shred of documentary evidence – even though it is highly speculative. That evidence, paired with the way in which his life is read against the plays in the Shakespeare canon, makes a stronger case than most competing theories. Indeed, William Stanley is an ideal candidate for disciples of Emerson's verse/life methodology. He was born into a noble family and at the age of eleven matriculated at Oxford. After becoming a member of Gray's Inn, where he would study for six years, Derby journeyed to the continent where it is said he travelled under a licence for three years throughout much of France, as well as for an additional two, unlicensed, in Italy and Spain – just the sort of experience Derbyites require in a dramatist of Shakespearian calibre. Furthermore, Derbyites stress the importance of Stanley's strong ties to the theatre community in London that he made upon his return to England. It is well known, for instance, that Derby patronized his own acting troupe, Derby's Men, for whom it is entirely possible he had written plays, though none are extant. His experience in the theatre would have put him in close contact with canonical dramatists like John Marston and Thomas Middleton. Further to his own personal involvement in the theatre, Derby received a number of poem dedications from some of the most popular poets of the day, none greater than John Donne, with whom Derby seems to have travelled throughout Spain and Italy.[7] Yet, in spite of this abundance of circumstantial evidence, the Derbyite theory seems to have proven unsustainable, fizzling out around 1919, less than thirty years after the publication of Greenstreet's articles, predominantly due to the lack of a corpus of writing to which Shakespeare's plays could be compared.

Roger Manners became fifth Earl of Rutland when he was still a boy of eleven years of age – just before he was created a ward of Lord Burghley, and consequently cementing ties between the Manners and Cecil families. Manners furthered his courtly connections by establishing contact with Robert Devereux, second Earl of Essex while he was matriculated at Corpus Christi College, Cambridge. After leaving Cambridge, Rutland ventured on a journey to the continent where in 1596 he would matriculate at Padua University. One can undoubtedly begin to see why in 1912 Celestin Demblon of the University of Brussels published his *Lord Rutland est Shakespeare*. Yet again, the link between life and works laid the foundation upon which Rutlandites would erect an argument, though it would prove to be not much more than a meagre dwelling of insufficient substantiation. Nevertheless, in the minds of the supporters of the case for Rutland, a courtier with strong connections to the earls of Southampton and Essex as well as to the Cecil family, who travelled extensively on the Continent, and who had a university education is an ideal candidate to have written the plays attributed to Shakespeare.

What, then, is the problem with reading biographically? It is best evidenced by the notion that even the most sophisticated of readers and thinkers – the Ralph Waldo Emersons of the past and present – rely so heavily on the critical assumption that there is an inherent connection between the author and the content of his works. There is no more credence in saying that the author of Shakespeare's plays must have visited Vienna, Venice and Athens in order to paint such an illustrious picture of them than there is in saying Dante must have visited the depths of the Inferno, Homer had to have encountered a one-eyed giant, or Milton only could have written *Paradise Lost* because of his conversations with a talking snake. It is historically and literarily irresponsible to assume that fictions always have and always will be based on actual events. And perhaps it is for this reason that this type of rationale began to fall out of fashion in the decades following, and a new method of decoding the Shakespeare authorship mystery gained momentum.

THE CRYPTOGRAM AND THE ANAGRAM: SIR HENRY NEVILLE (1561/2–1615) AND WILLIAM HASTINGS

To understand the Shakespearian cryptographer's method, we need to take as a premise that hidden within the confines of the Shakespeare canon there is a code to be broken – for without this assumption the cryptographic enterprise is foolhardy. This is where Brenda James and William D. Rubinstein began in their endeavour to crack the code of Shakespeare authorship – or in their phrase, 'unmask the real Shakespeare'. In her 2008 monograph, *Henry Neville and the Shakespeare Code*, Brenda James reveals that while doing her postgraduate research, she decided to leave academia to pursue her long-time dream of cracking the Dedication code: that is, trying to find out definitively who was the Mr W. H. of the Sonnet Dedication. She began to develop a methodology by which she would be able to discover why 'the Dedication to the Sonnets is written in a form which invites mystification and stimulates attempts at solving its strange syntax' and to whom the Sonnets were dedicated.[8] First, James memorized the text on the dedication page,

TO.THE.ONLIE.BEGETTER.OF.
THESE.INSUING.SONNETS.
Mr.W.H. ALL.HAPPINESSE.
AND.THAT.ETERNITIE.
PROMISED.

BY.

OUR.EVER-LIVING.POET.
WISHETH.

THE.WELL-WISHING.
ADVENTURER.IN.
SETTING.
FORTH.

T.T.

so that it could repeatedly run through her mind whenever necessary.
'Eventually, then', James eagerly shares, 'I began to visualize how the code
might be solved. However, I realized that this initial visualization wouldn't
be nearly enough on its own. The subsequent sleuthing I had to carry
out led to unexpected areas of research. The solution to the Code was
so unexpected and innovatory that I could not ask outsiders for help, for
fear of having my discovery – and my work – taken over. Nevertheless,
this is how it all began, and but for that order of commitment, Sir Henry
Neville might never have been uncovered as the author of the Shakespeare
Works.'9 Noticing that there are 144 letters in the dedication, James placed
each into its own square in a 12 × 12 grid, as shown below:

	1	2	3	4	5	6	7	8	9	10	11	12
1	T	O	T	H	E	O	N	L	I	E	B	E
2	G	E	T	T	E	R	O	F	T	H	E	S
3	E	I	N	S	U	I	N	G	S	O	N	N
4	E	T	S	Mr	W	H	x	A	L	L	H	A
5	P	P	I	N	E	S	S	E	N	N	D	T
6	H	A	T	E	T	E	R	N	I	T	I	E
7	P	R	O	M	I	S	E	D	B	Y	O	U
8	R	E	V	E	R	L	I	V	I	N	G	P
9	O	E	T	W	I	S	H	E	T	H	T	H
10	E	W	E	L	L	W	I	S	H	I	N	G
11	A	D	V	E	N	T	U	R	E	R	I	N
12	S	E	T	T	I	N	G	F	O	R	T	H

The shaded boxes are meant to draw attention to the word 'twelve', the
number of boxes across and down the grid. James reasons that the compiler
of the code is telling her that she must be on the right track because the
word 'twelve' is written out in a block of letters, with 'TT' directly below
it. The letters 'TT' act, James would have us believe, as a reference to
Thomas Thorpe, the publisher and printer. This is where the code becomes
increasingly complex, and over the course of eighteen pages, James delves

deeper and deeper into the depths of code cracking until she is able to find the sequence in the grid that reveals the name Sir Henry Neville, which she extends beyond the mystery of the Sonnet Dedication to the authorship discussion as a whole.

It is difficult to relate James's argument without appearing derisive. The logical mind undoubtedly will find basic flaws in the approach, none more crucial than that there is no documentary evidence to suggest that any such a code exists. Moreover, James's argument is peppered with assumptions and littered with the qualifying terminology of 'probably', 'most likely' and 'it may be', which do a great disservice to the Neville theory of Shakespeare authorship. It was just three years prior to the publication of *Henry Neville and the Shakespeare Code* that Brenda James, along with William D. Rubinstein completed the book, *The Truth Will Out: Unmasking the Real Shakespeare* – a book with a very different type of methodology behind it. Looking closely at what is known about Neville's political and social involvements, James and Rubinstein set out to describe why his life matches up well with the man who wrote the Shakespeare canon. And though there was no more credibility behind these claims made in the latter of the two books, the cryptographic argument stood to discredit their previous work on the case for Neville.

An equally invalid, and altogether less satisfying cryptographic argument was put forward in 2007 by Robert Nield in his book, *Breaking the Shakespeare Codes: The Sensational Discovery of the Bard's True Identity*, wherein Nield brings William Hastings, secret son of Elizabeth I and Robert Dudley, to the fore of the authorship discussion. 'In my opinion', states Nield, 'the combination of thesis and evidence presented here is the most compelling, complete and logically satisfying of all the attempts that have been made to resolve the Authorship Controversy. It seems to me that this case answers all the major questions – and many more besides.'[10] According to Nield, the truth is found in a series of non-linear anagrammatic codes that were constructed by Hastings and a group of his contemporaries so as to keep secret his identity. 'The solutions – or "keys" – that link the clues to the answers consist of interlocking horizontal and vertical words, arranged in a two-dimensional array rather like *Scrabble*. But, because there is no general formula, each anagram must be solved individually by a process of informed trial and error.'[11] The non-linear anagram based on the first line of Jonson's commendatory verse in the First Folio, for instance, might look like this:

Clue: To draw no envy (Shakespeare) on thy name
Anagram:

```
          W    A    S
               T    H   Y
                    A
                    K
                    E             N
V   E   N   D   O   R    S        O
                    P    O    E   T
               H    E
                    A
                    R
          N    A    M    E
```

Answer: Shakespeare, thy vendor's name (he was not any poet)

Nield's phrase, 'no general formula', is the one that is most intellectually disconcerting because without standardization – without a homogeneous set of rules by which to abide – subjectivity impedes objective analysis, and we are then dealing in the realm of coincidence rather than design. And this is the inherent problem with using the cryptogram and the anagram as a means of unveiling Shakespeare authorship. In these sorts of endeavours, one must alter and contort Shakespeare's text until it lines up flush to a hypothesis. It is working on a micro-level, sometimes with units as small as the word, or even the individual letter – a process also used by advocates of one of the methodologies to which we now turn.

FROM INTERTEXTUALISTS TO THE UNUSUALLY EXTREME: MARY HERBERT (NÉE SIDNEY), COUNTESS OF PEMBROKE (1561–1621), SIR PHILIP SIDNEY (1554–86), MIGUEL DE CERVANTES (1547–1616), ST EDMUND CAMPION (1540–81)

Whereas cryptographers alter the text to find hidden clues, intertextualists examine micro and macro similarities between two bodies of work, trying to find enough of a resemblance to make an educated suggestion about the real author of Shakespeare's works. The most famous case that employs this method, in part, is Christopher Marlowe, to whom Charles Nicholl has devoted an entire chapter in this volume. Certainly, this is also the same type of work performed by the attribution scholar and the stylometricist – the work by someone like MacDonald P. Jackson in *Defining Shakespeare: 'Pericles' as Test Case*, wherein he demonstrates that the wide range of internal evidence in any given play can be put to good use in an effort to discover answers to issues of attribution, as well as the chronologies associated with them. But why, then, is there consensus among the scholarly community on the stylometric analysis on plays like *Pericles, Edward III* and *Arden of Faversham*, and not on the cases made by those advocating for their stylometric testing on the Shakespeare canon against any number of authors from Shakespeare's time? As we will soon see, the evidence purported by attribution scholars has a great deal more logical stability than do such theories for Christopher Marlowe or Mary Sidney.

The Sidney family maintains the distinction of having more authorship candidates than any other Elizabethan or Jacobean family – Philip and his younger sister, Mary, both of whom have been put forth, the latter seeming to have more advocates. Robin P. Williams, in her book, *Sweet Swan of Avon: Did a Woman Write Shakespeare?*, makes the intertextual case for Mary by alluding to a number of similarities between her writings and translations and the text of the plays and poems of Shakespeare. Compare Claudio's 'To sue to live, I find I seek to die, / And seeking death, find life' (*MM* 3.1.42–3) with the end of Sidney's translation of *A Discourse of Life and Death*, as an example:

Neither ought we to fly death, for it is childish to fear it; and in fleeing from it, we meet it . . . It is enough that we constantly and continually wait for her coming, that she may never find us unprovided. For as there is nothing more certain than death, so is there nothing more uncertain than the hour of death, known only to God, the only Author of life and death, to whom we all ought endeavor both to live and die.

> Die to live,
>
> Live to die.[12]

It is typical of an intertextualist to make this sort of connection between two texts, and to make the assumption that the same author must have written the two works, based solely on coincidental use of syntax and theme. And just when it would seem we have reached the end of the methodological rope, there emerges something even more unusual to grab a hold of.

The 2010 publication of Brean Hammond's edition of *Double Falsehood* for The Arden Shakespeare series received ample media attention for its scholarly dealing with the compelling textual questions and performance histories that surround the play, as well as for its inclusion, for the first time, in a major Shakespeare series. For the most part, this media attention was positive, and was used to stimulate debate around complex areas of Shakespeare studies like canonicity. What Brean Hammond and the General Editors of The Arden Shakespeare surely could not anticipate, however, was the way in which their publication of a play by Lewis Theobald would cause several bloggers, one of which is known only as Frank, to take exception with the notion that Shakespeare used *Don Quixote* as a source, and to jump to an astonishing conclusion:

What interested me about this theory is that Cardenio was a character in *Don Quixote*! Why would Shakespeare include a character from another author's work[?] The obvious answer is that Cardenio was not the creation of Cervantes but Shakespeare[']s. This raises another intruiguing [sic] possibility – that the works of Shakespeare are not the creation of one man but a group collaboration by various authors which may have included the real William Shakespeare and Cervantes. Walt Disney films are not made by the man Walt Disney but the production company known as Walt Disney Company and William Shakespeare could have just been a brand name in the same way as Disney. It may be that scholars who have championed one author or another as the real author of the works of Shakespeare may be barking up the wrong tree. William Shakespeare may have been all of them.[13]

To omit one theory on the basis that it is not published in book format is giving precedence where none is due. Furthermore, the democratization of the Shakespeare authorship discussion – that is, the putting of the discussion into the hands of the amateur – is a primary reason for its perpetuation. The blogs of the amateur are an ideal platform for those unusually extreme cases for Shakespeare authorship. A further example is Joanne Ambrose's website, *Shakespeare Unmasked*, which advocates for the case of St Edmund Campion, who died in 1581. Ambrose, who claims to be the first and only Campionist, makes the case for Campion assuming that the works of Shakespeare only could have come from someone with the beauty, wit and intellect, and the fiery energy that Edmund Campion was known to have had. She does not consider, however, that Campion's death in 1581 would have precluded him from writing any of the plays that contain reference to political or social events during the years after.

By way of concluding, I should like to return to Lillian Schwartz and rethink her theory in light of comments about the case made for Sir Francis Bacon by John Bull in an 1857 letter-to-the-editor of *The Illustrated London News*: 'I won't have Bacon', insists Bull. 'I will have my own cherished "Will." I . . . never thought that an Englishman . . . would try to prove that he was a swindler – a thief – a jackdaw – and died, in the odour of sanctity, the pilferer of Bacon. . . . First, a College of Monks wrote Shikspur; now it's the jurisprudist Bacon. Why not Sir Walter Raleigh? Why not Queen Elizabeth herself? But, as I began, we won't have "Bacon"!'[14] How did it come to be that the case for Elizabeth I has gone from an idea existing solely in the realm of hyperbole to a legitimate theory of authorship? And it is not just John Bull who sends up the far-fetched idea of Elizabeth I being the author of Shakespeare's plays. More recently, Woody Allen comically warned us in a 1975 piece, *But Soft. Real Soft*, that when one asks the average man or woman who wrote the plays of William Shakespeare you should not be surprised 'if you get answers like Sir Francis Bacon, Ben Jonson, Queen Elizabeth and possibly even the Homestead Act'.[15] Do we not see this as a severe problem, not just for the study of Shakespeare, but more importantly, for the very way that we conduct historical research? Indeed, George Elliott Sweet devoted an entire book to Elizabeth I's authorship wherein he defends his own arguments with rationales such as this: 'When would a busy queen have time to write plays? We might well ask: When would a busy actor, memorizing play after play, have time to write? It is a well-known maxim that you go to a busy person to get things done. The very fact that there are no plays with Elizabeth as authoress creates the suspicion that there must be hidden plays of hers.'[16] The standard of argument would seem to be at an all-time low, but it is my great fear that it may not be the bottom. This is no longer historical revisionism, which has the potential to be a healthy scholarly approach. This is negationism. This is pseudohistory.

Anti-Stratfordians have been their own worst enemies. The excess of theories gives ample testimony to the old adage that less is truly more. With the rise of literary detective fiction and the use of the cryptogram in the twentieth century, the candidates whose proponents rely on reading the plays biographically have fallen out of favour. It does seem, however, somewhat ironically, that these sorts of arguments are the ones that would be more advantageous for the anti-Stratfordians. Partisanship within the anti-Stratfordian cause will undoubtedly be its downfall. 'If twenty or forty million inhabitants of the earth were convinced that the moon was about to split in twain', George Elliott Sweet argues, 'there would be hearty laughter all day but at night most of our faces would be turned to the sky. Since twenty or forty million people think the disguise of Shakespeare is real and earnest, in these perilous times, we had best explore the implications as carefully as we know how.'[17] Perilous times, indeed.

PART II

Shakespeare as author

This second section reaffirms that William Shakespeare of Stratford-upon-Avon is the author, and in some cases co-author of the works attributed to him. We begin with Andrew Hadfield's reminder (Chapter 6) that the kinds of biographical evidence we might long for are often missing. It is perfectly normal to encounter gaps in the surviving records of people's lives during Shakespeare's period, and in fact we know more about him than about many of his contemporary writers. Absence of evidence is never the same as evidence of absence, but it affects the way we need to approach historiography and to understand authorial identities. This is followed by Stanley Wells setting forth an overview of allusions to Shakespeare up until 1642, a reminder of the diversity and complexity of evidence for Shakespeare's authorship which is denied by anti-Shakespearians seeking an alternative nominee (Chapter 7). John Jowett (Chapter 8) and MacDonald Jackson (Chapter 9) then demonstrate how Shakespeare studies have come increasingly to understand Shakespeare as a collaborative playwright, which surely puts paid to all anti-Shakespearian endeavour that offers only single authors as alternatives to Shakespeare. This severe gap between what is now an established orthodoxy for most Shakespeare scholars (that Shakespeare worked in collaboration with other writers) and the on-going, late nineteenth-century-style biographical theorizing of anti-Shakespearians, is perhaps the best illustration of how the professional Shakespeare scholar and the amateur enquirer work with totally different methodologies and expectations. Looking only at the printed textual evidence of the plays, James Mardock and Eric Rasmussen (Chapter 10) then ask: what do we learn from the texts of these works about the controlling mind behind them?

They demonstrate clearly that the plays' author is a professionally acute and deeply engaged man of the theatre, rather than a
non-professional aristocrat writing during his spare time. Two
essays then follow about Shakespeare's cultural and intellectual
formation. David Kathman (Chapter 11) explains how a sense
of Warwickshire is rooted in the works, and Carol Rutter
(Chapter 12) shows how they are demonstrably the product of
an Elizabethan grammar school education. No university experience was required. This section ends with Barbara Everett's
subtle unfolding of an imaginative and creative characteristic
that she discerns across the Shakespearian canon (Chapter 13).
The propensity for the author to 'tell lies' means that the
works evade and at the same time challenge any apparently
straightforward biographical readings by anti-Shakespearians,
and, indeed, by Shakespearians themselves.

CHAPTER 6

Theorizing Shakespeare's authorship

Andrew Hadfield

There are two types of problems in attributing works to authors, consistent over time, but especially acute in the late sixteenth and early seventeenth centuries. First, we do not often have much information about people, making it hard for us to reconstruct what they were like and so to decide whether they actually wrote what has been attributed to them. All too often decisions are made based on the assumption that a particular work could or could not have been written by someone because it bears no resemblance to the purported author of that work. Second, looking at the problem from the other way round, attributions are not always precise, safe or even made at all, so we often do not know whether we can assume that a work was really written by the author we think is responsible. And this is before we deal with more philosophical problems of authorship and the attribution of an author to such common sentences as 'I love you'; 'Hear your good father, lady'; or, 'I have forgotten my umbrella.' In theorizing Shakespeare's authorship we need to consider both sides of the question, before drawing to a conclusion. The evidence will demonstrate, I think, that what we do not know is often much more significant than what we do know and any case that we make about authorship has to consider ignorance as well as knowledge.

It is often argued that the gaps in our understanding of Shakespeare's life are particularly unusual. In an online blog discussion about the authorship question, William Rubinstein asked what looks like a series of pointed questions to his opponents:

No evidence exists as to how or why Shakespeare came to London, what his real religion was, how he became so erudite and learned although he had no formal education past the age of about 13, why he retired to a provincial town in his mid-40s, etc., etc., only stories and legends recorded long after his death. Not a single new important fact about Shakespeare's life has been discovered since the Mountjoy-Bellot lawsuit in 1910, and nothing whatever about his supposed career as a writer. Doesn't this strike you as peculiar?[1]

The answer should be no. We do not know why Christopher Marlowe, Thomas Nashe or John Fletcher came to London. We know virtually nothing about most writers' religious views, a list which would include the above, as well as Edmund Spenser (who is assumed to be a Protestant but who reared two Catholic sons); Sir Philip Sidney (who sided with Protestants but was connected to a number of Catholics, a common enough issue), Thomas Middleton (who was long thought to be a Calvinist, but whose religious allegiance is undoubtedly less clear);[2] Anthony Munday, who has been claimed as a Catholic pretending to be a Protestant and a Protestant pretending to be a Catholic;[3] or John Donne, like Ben Jonson, a man of conflicting allegiance whose religious beliefs look very odd indeed, belong to no recognized category of religious allegiance, and who has been claimed for a long deceased sect (one that may not have been especially obscure).[4] Furthermore, it is not true to say that Shakespeare had no formal education after the age of thirteen: we simply do not know where he went to school. Anyone reading the *Oxford Dictionary of National Biography* will find the words, 'There is no evidence regarding Dekker's education', and 'There is no evidence about Munday's education' in the entries for these two contemporary writers. Furthermore, there is no discussion of Henry Chettle's schooling; but then, we do not even know when he was born.[5] Life records are not as comprehensive as we would like them to be, to put it mildly.

It is also worth noting that we do not know why many writers took apparently momentous decisions, such as Spenser deciding to leave London for Ireland when he was about twenty-six, or Jonson changing his religious allegiance so often. Personal letters did not survive in an age when paper was scarce and expensive, and so was invariably re-used for a host of purposes. And, the appearance of very few new facts about Shakespeare, which is also true of most other writers, is a testimony to the energy and thoroughness of Victorian genealogists and archivists, not an anomaly that requires explanation. In short, what looks like a series of loaded questions that point to a strange series of lacunae, so odd that a disturbing conspiracy must be assumed to have taken place, is anything but challenging and simply describes a normal series of life records.

It is worth reminding ourselves that although English biography did exist in an earlier form than has often been recognized, biographers were not 'interested in minute and even apparently trivial information about remarkable persons' until the second half of the seventeenth century.[6] As is widely recognized, it is therefore no accident that 'Milton is the first English author for whom we have so much in the way of biography.'[7] The first biographer who appears to have taken a proper interest in the apparently inconsequential details of lives is John Aubrey (1626–97), whose *Brief Lives* remained in manuscript until 1813. Only after such a development could a biographer really hope to assemble the sort of material that we think of as essential to the construction of a life. Paradoxically, the serious work of biography, one of the key genres of writing that we depend on today, could only begin with a desire to document superfluous, ephemeral details, a sign that lives were being read in rather less solemn ways than when they were perceived in moral and theological terms. The history of biography and the history of gossip are intertwined.[8]

Even a superficial trawl through the *Oxford Dictionary of National Biography* will reveal how little we know about many important figures, making the gaps in the biographical records of Shakespeare seem typical rather than unusual and therefore in no need of explanation. Thomas Nashe (bap. 1567– d. *c.* 1601) was among the most significant literary figures of the 1590s, having forced the authorities to close the theatres and then censor the press within the space of two years, surely a unique achievement. Yet, no one saw fit to record the date, let alone the cause, of his death.[9] Gabriel Harvey (1552/3–1631), his bitter opponent, and a writer who did leave behind a large number of clues about his whereabouts and opinions, nevertheless disappeared into relative obscurity in Saffron Waldon for the last thirty years of his life.[10] The same might be said of John Lyly (1554–1606), a major court poet and dramatist. His *ODNB* biographer, G. K. Hunter, notes that 'The only expression of Lyly's literary talent in the last sixteen years of his life appears in the begging letters he wrote to Elizabeth and to the Cecils.' The case is no different if we turn to Thomas Lodge (1558–1625), another prominent literary figure, whose work had a major impact on the course of Elizabethan literature. His *ODNB* biographer, Alexandra Halasz, is also clear about the frustrating gaps in our knowledge: 'Although Lodge was occasionally recognized by his contemporaries, his name occurs less frequently than might be expected from the range of his work and the length of his life', adding further 'Some of the mentions, moreover, are not easily understandable in relation to what is taken to be Lodge's *œuvre*.'

If we turn to dramatists who largely relied on the stage for their income, the picture is, if anything, even worse. It is especially hard to determine the canon of Thomas Middleton (bap. 1580, d. 1627).[11] The important play, *The Family of Love* (pub. 1608) has been removed from the list of his known works, and, despite the interest in his life and work, many gaps remain in our knowledge of both.[12] The life records of John Webster (*c.* 1578/80– 1638?) are even more obscure.[13] Unless there is a reason to record lives because the narrative will tell the reader as much as a seriously learned book, or, details are preserved through the records of state or other official mechanisms, evidence invariably does not survive. What are left are scraps, fragments and clues in parish registers, court records and probate offices.[14]

It is hardly surprising, given the state of the evidence, that often a great deal is made of one or two facts, which, read in particular ways, determine how a whole personality – and more – might be seen in relationship to their work. Again, the case of Shakespeare indicates how problematic such interpretations invariably are. As there are virtually no literary remains left behind by Shakespeare outside his published works, and most of the surviving records deal with property and legal disputes, a revisionist impulse has attempted to correct the familiar picture of Shakespeare as a wild and untutored genius by representing him as a hard-headed provincial citizen with an eye for personal gain.[15] Moreover, a whole scholarly sub-industry hinges on what we might understand by the gift of the second-best bed to Anne Hathaway, whether the gesture signals the contempt of a husband trapped in a loveless marriage, or a sign of intimate affection because the second-best bed was the one the couple slept in.[16] If the former connection is made, the life and the works are then read as a symbiotic whole, with Shakespeare's plays and poems compensating for what he did not get at home and revealing his contempt for women.[17] The problem of life records goes beyond their paucity. Readers on both sides of the authorship divide assume that they know who Shakespeare was and judge the relationship between the life and the works accordingly.[18]

How can and how do we link works and lives in order to locate authors? Perhaps it is as well to acknowledge that all early modern authors have had attribution problems, which is hardly surprising in a time when many works, plays in particular, were not thought of as the exclusive property of their authors.[19] Again, a list of authors who have doubtfully attributed works includes most major writers and, therefore, duplicates those who have problematic life records: Chettle, Donne, Marlowe, Middleton, Munday, Nashe, Ralegh, Sidney and Spenser, to name only a few. There is now a great deal of work on authorship and attribution in the early modern period, notably by Jonathan Hope, MacDonald Jackson, Brian Merriman and Brian Vickers.[20] Even if one is sceptical about the benefits of stylometric analysis and the ability to separate writers based on a study of significant stylistic features, it is clear that certain distinctions can be made. In his work, Jonathan Hope distinguishes between the scenes written by John Fletcher and Shakespeare in *Henry VIII* through an analysis of their use of the auxiliary 'do'. Shakespeare's use of 'do' in sentences is unregulated and varies from scene to scene and play to play, whereas Fletcher exhibits a much more consistent use of the auxiliary throughout his work. In the two plays they wrote together, a clear distinction can be made between scenes which have a high incidence of unregulated usage, which can be attributed to Shakespeare, and ones that are more regulated, which can be assumed to have been written by Fletcher. The reason, according to Professor Hope, is that Fletcher was fifteen years younger than Shakespeare, from a higher class, and better educated, having gone to university.[21] There may not be an obvious and clearly detectable linguistic DNA that can be isolated, but there are features of writers' styles that do indeed matter.

Similarly, Brian Vickers's incisive study of *Titus Andronicus* was based on the analysis of rhetorical features, notably the vocative, as well as the use of alliteration and polysyllabic words. Vickers concluded that the highly educated George Peele used forms of direct address based on his reading of Latin literature significantly more often than Shakespeare, enabling the reader of the play to distinguish which writer wrote which scene. Following a number of earlier studies, Professor Vickers concluded that Peele wrote Act 1, Act 2.1 and Act 4.1.[22] Such studies are far more valuable than assertions either that Shakespeare simply wrote what was attributed to him, or that his style looks a bit like Marlowe's so the two must obviously have been the same writer (a judgment no one familiar with much Elizabethan drama could possible make).[23]

Such analysis can take us so far but cannot prove beyond any shadow of doubt that Shakespeare wrote every part of every work attributed to him and it is hardly surprising that there is room for argument about sections of works and that new evidence and ways of reading plays and poems emerges from time to time. It is now generally accepted that Thomas Middleton had a hand in *Macbeth*, as well as *Timon of Athens*, but exactly how much is open to some debate.[24] And, while we know that Thomas Nashe contributed to the first tetralogy, we are not yet sure what he wrote, or who else was in the writing team along with Shakespeare.

However we read it, the evidence for collaborative authorship serves to strengthen our understanding that Shakespeare wrote much that was attributed to him. We may find that some passages, even some widely beloved sections of plays or favourite lines, were not all his own work. But there is no question of duplicity or disguise, merely a better understanding of the writing conditions that existed in early modern England and the fact that authors as we understand them, exercising close control over everything they wrote, did not really exist. At the end of his lament for Sir Philip Sidney, *Astrophel*, published in 1595 some years after Sidney's death, Edmund Spenser announces that there will now follow a lament by the poet's sister, Mary Sidney, 'The Doleful Lay of Clorinda'. It is not clear whether this text was actually written by the Countess or whether Spenser was impersonating the poet's sister, or whether Spenser and the Countess co-operated to produce the poem.[25] There is a problem with these lines, which were printed as a separate poem in the 1596 edition but then incorporated into the other poem in 1611, and arguments can be made about their authorship. Moreover, there are other works that may not be wholly by him, or which are not quite what they seem to be: we cannot be sure whether the letters he wrote to Harvey, which were published in 1580, appear in their original form; it is quite likely that he had a hand in the notes to *The Shepheardes Calender* (1579); and we cannot be certain that he translated the pseudo-Platonic dialogue, *Axiochus*, attributed to him when published in 1592. But, as with Shakespeare, such uncertainty only makes us more secure in the knowledge that Edmund Spenser was an author who wrote a corpus of works which have been attributed to him, even if we are less certain of the range and extent of his contribution to literature than we can be about a Victorian man of letters, for example. Nevertheless, one suspects that if more were at stake with Spenser as a famous national poet, doubts about his status would exist, especially as he is often referred to as 'Edward Spenser'.[26]

In order for us to believe that there is a case to answer that Shakespeare from Stratford may not have been Shakespeare the author we would need evidence from the period that it was possible for writers to impersonate other people; that they had the motives to do so; and that they had the ability to carry this out. No one, I think, disputes that Shakespeare collaborated with other writers – indeed one of the theories of some of the prominent figures who have signed the 'Declaration of Reasonable Doubt' is that the plays were written by a group of writers.[27] This means that all of those who wrote with 'Shakespeare' must have known that he was a front and had the ability to keep silent. The list would include at a conservative estimate John Fletcher, Thomas Middleton, Thomas Nashe, George Peele, George Wilkins and some others. Writers such as Robert Greene, Ben Jonson, Thomas Kyd, John Lyly and Christopher Marlowe would surely also have known of the disguise. Already the list is growing larger than seems feasible and it is hard to believe that all remained silent. Then again, perhaps they did not and there are some clues that Shakespeare was not Shakespeare. William Rubinstein, this time in his book (co-authored with Brenda James) arguing that Sir Henry Neville (1564–1615) was the true author of the works, claims that there is indeed evidence that Jonson was a co-conspirator. In his poem prefacing the First Folio Jonson famously describes Shakespeare as the 'Sweet Swan of Avon'. James and Rubinstein comment 'native swans in Britain are mute, so this might well be a subtle hint that we are not speaking of a true writer here'.[28] One hopes that Neville was not too perturbed by this revelation and that few contemporary readers were alive to the true meaning of the text, as Jonson had clearly felt unable to keep the terrible secret to himself. Such explanations rely on the assumption that interested parties would have been attuned to these nuances at the time, while others missed them. Modern readers have been able to decode them through a proper understanding of Renaissance poetry, clearly a more advanced knowledge than many early modern readers possessed, although it is not entirely clear why the deception had to be broken in this dangerous manner.

Nevertheless, other writers were prepared to act in an underhand and devious manner and we should see whether they provide any useful evidence about the nature of authorship in the period. There is the notorious plagiarist, Anthony Nixon (fl.1592–1616), who has been attributed a particular style replete with Latinate phrases, 'Nixonese', always eager to pass work off as though it were his own.[29] This is not quite the same phenomenon and, in any case, Nixon's attempt to defraud his fellow writers was noted by sharp-eyed contemporaries such as Thomas Dekker, another writer who would surely have known about Shakespeare's true identity as he collaborated with him to write *Sir Thomas More*. More promising, perhaps, is the case of the astonishingly prolific Anthony Munday (1560–1633), playwright, pamphleteer, poet, translator and author of civic pageants. Munday is certainly a devious and slippery author, as his complicated religious position suggests. Furthermore, we cannot be certain of exactly what he wrote. The problem, however, is not that Munday pretended to write things that he did not write, but that he wrote things which were not attributed to him, or that were not what they seemed to be. He may have been the author of the anti-Martinist satire, *Almond for a Parrot* (1590), one of the tracts commissioned by the bishops to counter the aggressively Protestant satires written by the pseudonymous Martin Marprelate.[30] These tracts are further evidence that our conception of early modern authorship may be more limited – and limiting – than the fluid reality and attempts to attribute them securely are doomed to failure unless failsafe ways of isolating individual stylistic features do eventually emerge.

Such evidence does not help to sustain the notion that Shakespeare was used to conceal another writer. What it shows us is that in many cases attribution is a difficult and messy business and that writers were often responsible for more than we thought they had written, or that more works were written collaboratively than we had assumed. Works such as *Edward III*, once attributed to Shakespeare and then banished from the canon, are now thought to contain scenes that he wrote.[31] If a more secure case is made for *Arden of Faversham*, for example, and it can be shown that Shakespeare probably did write scene 8, it will not significantly change our understanding of the authorship question. It is likely that as time goes on more works that we once assumed to be written by Shakespeare will be shown to be collaborations and more complicated in genesis than has been hitherto assumed. After all, even though we do not know as much about how plays were written as we would like, we do know that they were often written at great speed; that scenes were assigned to different writers; and that parts were written for particular actors, which might suggest an element of co-operation between writer and actor.[32]

It is also true that early modern texts could hide secrets and were not always produced in good faith. Writers and publishers sometimes misled the public about the nature and status of the books that they produced, as many anti-Stratfordians allege. False colophons were common enough, especially with Italian material that might have attracted the hostile attention of the authorities. John Wolfe (1548?–1601), the publisher and close friend of Gabriel Harvey, who made his name as the principal importer of Machiavelli, Aretino and other scandalous Italian works, was often more than economical with the truth and advertised his wares as if they had been imported rather than his actual publications.[33] And, of course, there were plenty of other unscrupulous booksellers, like John Trundle (1577–1629), publisher of popular works, who published a pirated edition of *Hamlet* with Nicholas Ling and who was clearly not beyond several forms of sharp publishing practice. Certainly, the account he published in 1614, *True and Wonderfull A Discourse Relating to a Strange and Monstrous Serpent (or Dragon) lately discouered, and yet liuing, to the great annoyance and diuers slaughters both of men and cattell, by his strong and violent poyson, in Sussex two miles from Horsam, in a woode called S. Leonards Forrest*, complete with fire-breathing beast and his human and animal victims depicted on the cover, cannot quite be all that it seems.[34] The author 'A. R.' has not been traced, and neither have the three witnesses, John Steele, Christopher Holder and 'a widow woman dwelling near *Faygate*'.[35] Most significant of all are the ruses of William Cecil, Lord Burghley, who cleverly placed books in the public domain via nefarious and underhand means. In 1572 he commissioned a translation of George Buchanan's treatise detailing the crimes of Mary Stuart and her part in the murder of her husband, Lord Darnley, into fake Scots. This was published as *Ane Detectioun of the Doingis of Marie Quene of Scottis*, and made to look as if it were an independent publication which expressed the views of an informed public opinion, when it was nothing of the sort. It is a measure of Burghley's success that the picture of Mary as a politically incompetent Catholic Jezebel has influenced subsequent views of Mary up to the present.[36] Burghley was probably also behind the publication of John Stubbes's criticism of Elizabeth's plans to marry the Duc d'Alençon in 1579, *The Discouerie of a Gaping Gulf whereinto England is like to be swallovved by another French marriage*, a similar subterfuge designed to convince the queen that her loyal subjects simply could not tolerate her plans. This work, for which the author had his hand severed, was published along with Edmund Spenser's *Shepheardes Calender*, which asserts the independence of the queen and the fears of her subjects. Both were produced by the same printer, Hugh Singleton, suggesting that they were part of a plot against the match.

All this material is indeed fascinating and is an important element of the early modern publishing industry as writers, booksellers and publishers experimented with what they could do with the new medium of print and the new, expanding market for books. It is more than likely, especially given the relatively recent discovery of the extent of Lord Burghley's successful attempt to manipulate the public, that material is yet to come to light detailing the ways in which readers were hoodwinked. Nevertheless, nothing found here provides evidence that one writer was able to pretend to be another writer for a sustained period. It may be that the 'A. R.' who wrote the treatise about the dragon in Horsham was really John Trundle himself, just as the 'E. K.' who wrote the notes to *The Shepheardes Calender* may have been Spenser himself, perhaps giving us a clue and expecting readers to realize that he was 'Edmund of Kent', because he worked for the Bishop of Rochester.[37] But this is hardly the same thing at all. Trundle and Spenser, assuming they are attempting to deceive the public, are not borrowing or stealing another man's identity and passing it off as their own. They are either playing a smart literary game, or inventing a character to authenticate one particular text. Most likely, Spenser is doing the former, Trundle the latter.

We can look at early modern ideas of authorship in a variety of ways and from very different positions. Moreover, notions of an author's authority changed significantly during Shakespeare's lifetime. When he started writing, no one really placed much value on drama but by the time he died playwrights could publish their collected works. However we approach the question of authorship, whether from the establishment of the author's identity and persona; the words that they wrote; who they wrote with; or the personae and guises that they adopted, we can rarely be absolutely certain that we have always identified the extent of the work of one particular writer beyond a significant margin of error. But we can be certain, beyond any reasonable doubt, that early modern authors did not ever pretend to be other people.

CHAPTER 7

Allusions to Shakespeare to 1642

Stanley Wells

Anyone wishing to suggest alternative nominees for the authorship of Shakespeare's works needs to disprove everything that goes to show that they were written – sometimes in collaboration with other writers[1] – by the William Shakespeare who was baptized on 26 April 1564 in Stratford-upon-Avon and was buried there on 25 April, 1616. The purpose of this chapter is to demonstrate that there is an abundance of such evidence and to set out some of the more significant items.[2]

What is usually taken to be the first printed reference to Shakespeare comes in a book named *Greene's Groatsworth of Wit Bought with a Million of Repentance* of 1592, written ostensibly by the popular playwright, poet and prose writer Robert Greene, but possibly in part or in whole by Henry Chettle.[3] In it Greene on his deathbed portrays himself, or is portrayed by Chettle, as attacking an 'upstart Crow, beautified with our feathers, that with his Tiger's heart wrapped in a Player's hide, supposes he is as well able to bombast out a blank verse as the best of you: and beeing an absolute *Johannes fac-totum* is in his own conceit the only Shake-scene in a country.' There are two strong reasons to identify the object of attack with Shakespeare. One is that the words 'Tiger's heart wrapped in a Player's hide' parody a line from Shakespeare's play *Richard Duke of York* (*Henry VI Part Three*) in which the Duke of York inveighs against Queen Margaret in the words 'O tiger's heart wrapped in a woman's hide!' (1.4.138). Another reason is the apparent parody of the name Shakespeare in 'Shake-scene'. Moreover, soon after the book appeared Chettle published *Kind Heart's Dream* with a preface in which he offered an apology for not having (presumably in his capacity as publisher or printer) toned down the criticism made in the earlier book. He says that two men had been offended by the attack. He cares nothing for what one of them (usually supposed to be Christopher Marlowe) thinks, but regrets having offended the other, 'because myself have seen his demeanour no less civil than he excellent in the quality he professes. Besides, divers of worship have reported his uprightness of

73

dealing, which argues his honesty, and his facetious [skilful] grace in writing that approves [demonstrates] his art.'

The cryptic nature of the attack in the *Groatsworth of Wit* means that we cannot say definitively that it refers to Shakespeare. There are however numerous subsequent references in both printed and manuscript documents of the time, most of them written by highly reputable, university-educated men, to someone named Shakespeare, often giving his forename as William, and identifying him either as a writer in general or as the author of specific plays and poems from the Shakespeare canon. In what follows I aim to list all explicit references surviving up to the closing of the theatres in 1642. On top of this is the evidence provided by entries of books in the Stationers' Register and on the title pages of editions, which I provide at the end of this chapter. This is generally reliable, though there is reason to believe that as Shakespeare's reputation grew certain publishers used his name fraudulently.

The earliest direct reference to Shakespeare as a writer comes at the end of the dedication to his poem *Venus and Adonis*, published by his fellow Stratfordian Richard Field in 1593 and entered without author's name (as was common) on the Stationers' Register on 18 April of that year. In itself this belongs to the category of publication evidence; I mention it here because on 12 June 1593 – which must be no more than a matter of weeks after the poem appeared – an elderly gentleman named Richard Stonley listed his purchase of a copy of '*Venus and "Adhonay"* pr Shakspere' in a manuscript note which was mentioned by the great scholar Edmond Malone in a book of 1796. Malone says that he was told about it by his fellow scholar George Steevens, who had seen it in an 'ancient manuscript diary'. The note was believed to be lost until 1972 when it turned up in San Francisco and was bought by the Folger Shakespeare Library.[4]

The Rape of Lucrece was published by John Harrison and printed, again by the Stratfordian Richard Field, in 1594. As in *Venus and Adonis*, the dedication is signed 'William Shakespeare'. And Shakespeare is named as the author of a poem about Lucrece in the commendatory verses that introduce *Willobie his Avisa*, a poem by Henry Willobie, an Oxford graduate, published in 1594:

> Though Collatine have dearly bought
> To high renown a lasting life,
> And found, that most in vain have sought,
> To have a fair and constant wife,
>   Yet Tarquin plucked his glistering grape,
>   And Shakespeare paints poor Lucrece' rape.

We may pass quickly over a reference to 'W. S.' in the body of the book since although Shakespeare is probably the person referred to, only initials are given.

Lucrece and its author are praised in a terse note by the Cambridge-educated clergyman William Covell in his *Polimenteia, or The Means Lawful and Unlawful to Judge of the Fall of a Commonwealth* of 1595: 'All praiseworthy. Lucrecia Sweet Shakespeare. Eloquent Gaveston. Wanton Adonis. Watsons heyre.' (Gaveston is a leading character in Marlowe's play *Edward II* and also the central figure of Michael Drayton's popular poem *The Legend of Piers Gaveston*, which first appeared in 1593. Thomas Watson (*c.* 1556–92) was a successful and influential poet, friend of Marlowe.)

The first substantial documentation and discussion of Shakespeare as a writer comes in 1598 in the critically naive and derivative, but historically invaluable treatise *Palladis Tamia, or Wit's Treasury* described as 'A Comparative Discourse of our English Poets, with the Greek, Latin, and Italian Poets' by Francis Meres, at that time a thirty-three-year-old Cambridge-educated gentleman who was to be ordained in the following year and who became a schoolmaster. Meres writes of Shakespeare as both poet and dramatist, listing him among a number of writers, including Sidney, Spenser, Marlowe and Chapman, by whose work 'the English tongue' has been 'mightily enriched and gorgeously invested in rare ornaments and resplendent habiliments'. Referring to him specifically as a non-dramatic poet Meres declares that 'the sweet witty soul of Ovid lives in mellifluous and honey-tongued Shakespeare, witness his *Venus and Adonis*, his *Lucrece*, his sugared sonnets among his private friends, etc.' This is the first evidence we have of Shakespeare as a sonneteer. Meres goes on to discuss his stage works in a passage which is invaluable especially because it gives us a date by which the plays he lists must have been written. Meres writes that

As Plautus and Seneca are accounted the best for comedy and tragedy among the Latins, so Shakespeare among the English is the most excellent in both kinds for the stage; for comedy, witness his *Errors*, his *Love's Labour's Lost*, his *Love's Labour's Won*, his *Midsummer's* [sic] *Night's Dream*, and his *Merchant of Venice*; for tragedy his *Richard the Second, Richard the Third, Henry the Fourth, King John, Titus Andronicus* and his *Romeo and Juliet*. As Epius Stolo said that the Muses would speak with Plautus' tongue if they could speak Latin, so I say that the Muses would speak with Shakespeare's fine-filed phrase if they would speak English.

Meres continues by listing Shakespeare again among writers who, as Horace boasts of himself, '*Exegi monumentum aere perennius*' ('deserve monuments more lasting than bronze'), and also in lists of the best lyric poets, of 'the best for tragedy' and of 'the best for comedy'. Among a long list of other writers who receive Meres's commendation for comedy is 'Edward Earl of Oxford'. The fact that Oxford – often touted as the author of Shakespeare's works – is mentioned in the same list as Shakespeare shows clearly that Meres knew – like John Bodenham (see p. xxx) – they were two different people. Meres's final naming of Shakespeare comes in another long list, this time of 'the most passionate among us to bewail and bemoan the perplexities of love'.

Though there is something mechanical about Meres's mindless making of lists, he demonstrates familiarity at least with one of Falstaff's speeches in *Henry IV Part One* when, speaking of Michael Drayton, he alludes to 'these declining and corrupt times, when there is nothing but roguery in villainous man, and when cheating and craftiness is counted the cleanest wit and soundest wisdom'.[5]

Shakespeare was the subject of several complimentary poems addressed to him by contemporaries. The first of these was written by the Oxford-educated poet Richard Barnfield and printed in a collection called 'Poems in Diverse Humours' published, like Meres's book, in 1598. Headed 'A Remembrance of Some English Poets', it praises first Edmund Spenser, then Samuel Daniel, then Michael Drayton and finally Shakespeare,

> whose honey-flowing vein.
> Pleasing the world, thy praises doth obtain.
> Whose *Venus*, and whose *Lucrece* – sweet and chaste –
> Thy name in fame's immortal book have placed.
> Live ever you, at least in fame live ever;
> Well may thy body die, but fame dies never.

In the following year, 1599,[6] a poem addressed specifically to Shakespeare appeared in a collection by the Cambridge-educated poet and antiquary John Weever[7] (1576–1632) called *Epigrams in the Oldest Cut, and Newest Fashion* which also contains epigrams on the poets Samuel Daniel, Michael Drayton, Ben Jonson, Edmund Spenser, William Warner and Christopher Middleton. Headed 'Ad Gulielmum Shakespeare' it takes the form of a Shakespearian sonnet, opens with the words 'Honey-tongued Shakespeare!', and includes references to *Venus and Adonis*, *The Rape of Lucrece* and, somewhat cryptically, 'Romeo-Richard; more whose names I know not'. Shakespeare is named explicitly again in the penultimate line where, in a metaphor that interestingly foreshadows later criticism, characters he created are referred to as his 'children'. At around the same time the controversialist Gabriel Harvey, friend of Edmund Spenser and Fellow of Pembroke Hall, Cambridge, scribbled a long note about contemporary writers in his copy of an edition of Chaucer (now in the British Library) in the course of which he remarked that 'the younger sort take much delight in Shakespeare's *Venus and Adonis*, but his *Lucrece*, and his *Hamlet, Prince of Denmark* have it in them to please the wiser sort'.

A body of references to Shakespeare comparable in quantity and importance to those in *Palladis Tamia*, though entirely different in tone, comes in the series of three topically informative plays written anonymously and performed by students of St John's College, Cambridge between 1598 and 1602, known as the *Parnassus* plays. The authors were clearly aware of Shakespeare both as a poet and as a theatrical celebrity. In the second play, *The First Part of the Return from Parnassus*, a foolish fellow named Gullio (a gull was an affected and easily duped man about town, as in the title of Thomas Dekker's satire *The Gull's Hornbook* of 1609) adapts lines from *Venus and Adonis* in wooing his mistress, provoking the comment 'we shall have nothing but pure Shakespeare and shreds of poetry that he hath gathered at the theatres'. In his next speech he says his mistress is 'in comparison of thy bright hue a mere slut, Antony's Cleopatra a black-browed milkmaid, Helen a dowdy'. Here he alludes to Mercutio's 'Laura to his lady was a kitchen-wench . . . Dido a dowdy, Cleopatra a gypsy' with a glance at Juliet's 'black-browed night' (*Romeo and Juliet* 2.3.37–9, 3.2.20).[8] Ingenioso helpfully identifies the source of the allusion: 'Mark, *Romeo and Juliet!*' Gullio continues by quoting almost the whole of the second stanza of *Venus and Adonis*, which provokes Ingenioso to exclaim 'Sweet Mr Shakespeare!', and a few lines later, Gullio, after alluding explicitly to Chaucer, Gower, Spenser and 'Mr Shakespeare',[9] quotes the opening two lines of *Venus and Adonis* before exclaiming 'O sweet Master Shakespeare! I'll have his picture in my study at the court.' Later in the play Gullio asks Ingenioso 'Let me hear Mr Shakespeare's vein', upon which Ingenioso speaks lines written in the 'rhyme royal' form of *The Rape of Lucrece* which, judging by the ludicrous couplet, surely form the earliest parody of Shakespearian verse:

> Fair Venus, Queen of beauty and of love,
> Thy red doth stain the blushing of the morn,
> Thy snowy neck shameth the milk-white dove,
> Thy presence doth this naked world adorn.
> Gazing on thee all other nymphs I scorn.
>> Whene'er thou diest slow shine that Saturday
>> Beauty and grace must sleep with thee for aye.

Gullio responds with more adoration of Shakespeare: 'Let this duncified world esteem of Spenser and Chaucer, I'll worship sweet Mr Shakespeare, and to honour him will lay his *Venus and Adonis* under my pillow.'

The name 'William Shakespeare' occurs again in the third play of the series, in the context of a satirical allusion to Ben Jonson ('the wittiest fellow of a bricklayer in England'). In a later episode, Burbage and Kemp audition recent undergraduates who aspire to a career in the theatre. Kemp, a true professional, fears that as writers for the popular theatre they will be too keen to show off their classical education: they 'smell too much of that writer Ovid, and that writer Metamorphoses, and talk too much of "Proserpina" and "Jupiter"'. They are not a patch on Shakespeare and Jonson: 'Why, here's our fellow Shakespeare puts them all down, ay, and Ben Jonson too. O, that Ben Jonson is a pestilent fellow: he brought up Horace giving the poets a pill, but our fellow Shakespeare hath given him a purge that made him bewray [beshit] his credit.' 'It's a shrewd fellow indeed', responds Burbage. When the aspiring actors arrive, Burbage, remarking 'I like your face, and the proportion of your body for Richard III' – a dubious compliment – asks one of them, Philomusus, to act a little of it, in response to which Philomusus speaks the first two lines of Richard's opening soliloquy. This passage alludes obliquely to an episode known to later ages as the War of the Theatres centring on plays written from 1599 to 1602 by Jonson – *Every Man Out of his Humour* – John Marston – *Histriomastix, Jack Drum's Entertainment* and *What you Will* – and Dekker together with Marston – *Satiromastix* – in which they girded satirically at each other.

Shakespeare's name occurs in passing in a literary context in the epistle to a book of 1600, John Bodenham's verse anthology *Belvedere, or The Garden of the Muses*, along with references to fellow writers including John Marston, Christopher Marlowe and Ben Jonson. In 1602 comes the famous piece of gossip recorded by the Cambridge-educated future barrister John Manningham in his diaries suggesting that Shakespeare – like most of his fellow playwrights – may have been a womanizer:

Upon a time, when Burbage played Richard III, there was a citizen grew so far in liking with him that before she went from the play she appointed him to come that night unto her by the name of Richard the Third. Shakespeare, overhearing their conclusion, went before, was entertained, and at his game ere Burbage came. Then, message being brought that Richard the Third was at the door, Shakespeare caused return to be made that William the Conqueror was before Richard the Third.

Though Manningham does not explicitly identify Shakespeare as a writer, he clearly associates him with both his fellow-actor Burbage and his play *Richard III*.

In the following year the unidentified author of 'A Mournful Ditty, entitled Elizabeth's Love' called upon Shakespeare (unsuccessfully, as far as we know), along with other writers, to memorialize the newly dead Queen:

> You poets all, brave Shakespeare, Johnson [*sic*], Greene,
> Bestow your time to write for England's queen,

and in 1604 an epigram by John Cooke names Shakespeare again in caustically pointing out that by including Greene, who had died in 1592, the author had called on 'help of spirits in their sleeping graves'.

There is a cryptic allusion to Shakespeare in the context of an allusion to *Hamlet* in the epistle to Anthony Scoloker's *Diaphantus, or The Passions of Love* of 1604, with its reference to 'friendly Shakespeare's tragedies, where the comedian rides, when the tragedian stands on tip-toe: faith, it should please all, like Prince Hamlet; but in sadness, then it were to be feared he would run mad'. And in the following year the great historian William Camden, friend and teacher of Ben Jonson, includes Shakespeare in his *Remains of a greater Work, concerning Britain* among a long list of the 'most pregnant wits of these our times, whom succeeding ages may justly admire'. In 1607 Shakespeare achieves the dubious honour of a passing, self-abasing mention in the final lines of a long and boring poem by the young actor, later playwright, William Barksted, called *Myrrha, the Mother of Adonis; or Lust's Prodigies*:

> But stay, my muse, in thine own confines keep,
>   And wage not war with so dear loved a neighbour;
> But having sung thy day song, rest and sleep,
>   Preserve thy small fame and his greater favour;
> His song was worthy merit – Shakespeare, he
> Sung the fair blossom, thou the withered tree.
>   Laurel is due to him, his art and wit
>   Hath purchased it. Cypress thy brow will fit.

A second poem explicitly addressed to Shakespeare appeared in John Davies of Hereford's collection of epigrams *The Scourge of Folly*, entered in the Stationers' Register on 8 October 1610. Characteristically of epigrams in this period it is somewhat obscure in its allusiveness, but certainly names him as an actor, and in its title compares him to one of the greatest of Roman playwrights:

To our English Terence, Mr. Will. Shakespeare.
Some say (good Will) which I, in sport, do sing,
Hadst thou not played some kingly parts in sport,
Thou hadst been a companion for a king
And been a king among the meaner sort.
Some others rail; but, rail as they think fit,
Thou hast no railing, but a reigning wit;
And honesty thou sow'st which they do reap
So, to increase their stock which they do keep.

One of the greatest playwrights contemporary with Shakespeare, John Webster, paid tribute to him in the epistle to his tragedy *The White Devil*, in 1612. Responding to unnamed critics, Webster claims that he has always reacted to the writings of his contemporaries with generosity. In particular, he has admired 'that full and heightened style of Master Chapman, the laboured and understanding works of Master Jonson, the no less worthy composures [compositions] of the both worthily excellent Master Beaumont and Master Fletcher; and lastly (without wrong last to be named) the right happy and copious industry of Master Shakespeare, Master Dekker, and Master Heywood'. In 1614 Shakespeare is among many writers mentioned in *The Excellency of the English Tongue* by another antiquarian, Richard Carew (1550–1620), who was also a translator and wrote a *Survey of Cornwall* (1603).

A third poem explicitly addressed to 'To Master W. Shakespeare' was included in the Oxford-educated Thomas Freeman's collection of epigrams 'Run and a Great Cast', of 1614, and is written in Shakespearian sonnet form. It praises him both as a poet and as a playwright comparable to classical writers:

Who loves chaste life, there's *Lucrece* for a teacher:
Who list read lust there's *Venus and Adonis*,
True model of a most lascivious lecher.
Besides, in plays thy wit winds like Meander,
Whence needy new composers borrow more
Than Terence doth from Plautus or Menander.
But to praise thee aright I want thy store:
    Then let thine own works thine own worth upraise,
    And help t'adorn thee with deservèd bays.

Shakespeare is also the subject of a Latin epigram by the Cambridge-educated Thomas Porter included in a manuscript collection dated 1614 (but probably written earlier). He figures too in a long list of 'modern and present excellent poets which worthily flourish in their own works' named by Edmund Howes in his 1615 continuation of John Stow's *Annals of England*. Another relatively passing compliment comes in a manuscript poem ascribed to Francis Beaumont of around 1615, and addressed to Jonson. The author desires to 'keep these lines as clear / As Shakespeare's best are'. And in another manuscript, dating from around 1616, the historian and poet Edmund Bolton (*c*. 1575–*c*. 1633) explicitly names Shakespeare and Beaumont among writers from whose books 'we gather the most warrantable English'.

Among the allusions that I have cited so far, despite the mass of evidence that the works were written by a man named William Shakespeare, there is none that explicitly and incontrovertibly identifies him with Stratford-upon-Avon. Anti-Shakespearians often proclaim this fact in self-satisfied triumph, brandishing the phrase 'in his lifetime' like a mantra. But to refuse to credit the considerable amount of posthumously derived evidence linking the writer with the Stratford man is totally illogical. To put it at its most basic level, if we refused to accept posthumous evidence we should have to refuse the evidence that anyone has ever died. The death of 'William Shakespeare, gent.' recorded in the Stratford registers for 1616 is memorialized in the monument and epitaphs which clearly identify the Stratford man as a great writer and which, along with other evidence, are discussed by David Kathman elsewhere in this volume (Chapter 11). On a literary level, the death was mourned in an elegy first printed in a collection of John Donne's poems in 1633 but certainly written by 1623, if not earlier. The poem, generally attributed to a minor poet named William Basse (*c*. 1583–*c*. 1653), was extremely popular, circulating widely, with many minor variants, in manuscript. The editors of the Oxford Complete Works of Shakespeare, published in 1986, wrote: 'We have searched for manuscript copies in the Bodleian, British Library, Folger, Harvard, Huntington, Rosenbach and Yale collections; most of the manuscripts listed below were unknown to earlier investigators. No doubt a further search would uncover further copies.' They listed and collated twenty-seven manuscript and six seventeenth-century printed texts, with many minor variants.[10] Later, in an essay called 'Who Wrote William Basse's "Elegy on Shakespeare"?: Rediscovering a Poem Lost from the Donne Canon',[11] Brandon S. Centerwall revealed an additional six early manuscript copies along with an additional printed one. He proposed that both the poem and the memorial inscription in the church were composed by Donne. The poem clearly owes its popularity at least as much to the fact that it memorializes the 'rare tragedian' (the word could be used of either a writer or an actor) Shakespeare as to its poetic qualities.

The elegy's date of composition is uncertain. Its opening lines, recommending that Shakespeare should be buried alongside other great poets in Westminster Abbey, might suggest that it was written even before Shakespeare was buried.

> Renownèd Spenser, lie a thought more nigh
> To learnèd Chaucer; and rare Beaumont, lie
> A little nearer Spenser, to make room
> For Shakespeare in your threefold, fourfold tomb.
> To lodge all four in one bed make a shift
> Until Doomsday, for hardly will a fifth
> Betwixt this day and that by fate be slain
> For whom your curtains need be drawn again.

But the later reference to Shakespeare's 'carved' ['carven', 'sacred', 'sable', 'vncarved', 'curled' and 'incarved' in other versions] monument' seems rather to indicate that the memorial in Holy Trinity Church, Stratford-upon-Avon was already in place, and even that the author may have hoped his verses would have adorned it.

> But if precedency in death doth bar
> A fourth place in your sacred sepulchre,
> Under this carvèd marble of thine own,
> Sleep, rare tragedian Shakespeare, sleep alone.

The poem was certainly in circulation by 1623 – ten years before it appeared in print – since Jonson alludes to it, and dissociates himself from its recommendations, in his great elegy printed in the First Folio:

> My Shakespeare, rise. I will not lodge thee by
>   Chaucer or Spenser, or bid Beaumont lie
> A little further to make thee a room.
>   Thou art a monument without a tomb,
> And art alive still while thy book doth live
>   And we have wits to read and praise to give.

Centerwall suggests that the monument, created in London, was originally intended for the Abbey where it would have surmounted a tomb, whereas in Stratford it is placed in the wall not quite adjacent to the stone traditionally supposed to cover Shakespeare's burial place.[12] The poem's final lines read

> Thy unmolested peace, unsharèd cave,
> Possess as lord, not tenant, of thy grave,
> That unto us or others it may be
> Honour hereafter to be laid by thee.

Figure 7.1. A memorial bust to Shakespeare, designed by Gheerart Janssen and installed in Holy Trinity Church, Stratford-upon-Avon by 1623 (when it is mentioned by Leonard Digges in the First Folio). The inscriptions refer to Shakespeare as a writer, and the Latin can be translated: 'Earth covers, the nation mourns, and heaven holds / A Nestor in counsel, a Socrates in mind, a Virgil in art.' Photo and copyright John Cheal.

The poem, then, along with its survival in multiple versions, bears witness to Shakespeare's popularity as a great writer, worthy of comparison with England's finest. Moreover the headings of some versions make clear that this is the Shakespeare of Stratford-upon-Avon; one of them, indeed, reads 'On Willm Shakespear buried att Stratford vpon Avon, his Town of Nativity.'[13]

In 1618, Ben Jonson undertook a long walk from London to Scotland, where he visited the poet Sir William Drummond of Hawthornden, staying with him for a couple of bibulous and garrulous weeks. Drummond had already, sometime around 1614, spoken of Shakespeare as a writer about love, presumably referring to the Sonnets.[14] During Jonson's visit he and his host talked much about the contemporary literary scene. Drummond reported Jonson as saying that 'Shakespeare wanted art', and that 'Shakespeare in a play brought in a number of men saying that they had suffered shipwreck in Bohemia, where there is no sea near by some 100 miles.' But Jonson was to be far more generous in expression of admiration for his friend and rival when it came to the publication of the First Folio, in 1623, and the preliminaries to this volume alone, boldly entitled 'Mr. WILLIAM SHAKESPEARES COMEDIES, HISTORIES, & TRAGEDIES' bear extensive witness to the fact that William Shakespeare of Stratford-upon-Avon wrote Shakespeare.

Opposite the title-page engraving by Martin Droeshout is placed a short poem attributed to 'B. I.' – in context, clearly Ben Jonson – praising it as a likeness. The dedication of the volume to William, Earl of Pembroke and his brother, Philip, Earl of Montgomery signed by Shakespeare's fellow actors John Heminges and Henry Condell, declares their ambition to 'keep the memory of so worthy a friend and fellow alive as was our Shakespeare, by humble offer of his plays to your most noble patronage' and declares that they 'consecrate to your highnesses these remains of your servant Shakespeare'. Their epistle 'To the Great Variety of Readers' refers to their author as dead but does not name him. There follows Jonson's great tribute headed 'To the memory of my beloved, the author Master William Shakespeare, and what he hath left us.' The poem names Shakespeare five times and refers to him as 'Sweet Swan of Avon!' And as I have said, it alludes unmistakably to the poem ascribed to William Basse, with all its associations. There follows yet another poem addressed to Shakespeare and written in the sonnet form with which he is associated: the Cambridge-educated Hugh Holland's 'Upon the Lines and Life of the Famous Scenic Poet, Master William Shakespeare' which calls upon 'You Britons brave' to wring the hands that they had formerly clapped in applause, 'for done are Shakespeare's days'. After the volume's table of contents comes another poem, this one headed 'To the Memory of the deceased author Master William Shakespeare', by Leonard Digges, a poet and orator of University College, Oxford, which in its reference to 'thy Stratford monument' unequivocally links the author of *Romeo and Juliet*, *Julius Caesar* and other plays with the man of Stratford. (A considerably longer version of the same poem was printed after Digges's death in the 1640 volume of Shakespeare's *Poems* published by John Benson.) Digges (1588–1635) is a particularly interesting witness since his mother married as her second husband Thomas Russell who lived only a few miles from Stratford, at Alderminster, and whom Shakespeare named in 1616 as one of the overseers of his will. The poem that follows Digges's, headed 'To the Memory of Master. W. Shakespeare' also names Shakespeare as one who has gone 'From the world's stage to the grave's tiring-room'. Printed over the initials 'I. M.' it has usually been supposed to have been written by James Mabbe, a translator, of Magdalen College, Oxford. But the Milton scholar Gordon Campbell has suggested that it is the work of the elder John Milton who was a trustee of the Blackfriars playhouse where Shakespeare's company performed from 1609.[15]

In 1627 Michael Drayton published an elegy headed 'To my most dearly loved friend Henry Reynolds Esq., of Poets and Poesy' which includes the lines

> And be it said of thee,
> Shakespeare, thou hadst as smooth a comic vein
> Fitting the sock, and in thy natural brain
> As strong conception and as clear a rage
> As anyone that trafficked with the stage.

An anonymous tribute to Shakespeare appeared in verses printed in the Second Folio, of 1632, headed 'Upon the effigies of my worthy friend the author Master William Shakespeare, and his works', and a poem by Sir William Davenant first printed in 1638, headed 'In remembrance of Master William Shakespeare', again associates the poet with the River Avon:

> Beware, delighted poets, when you sing
> To welcome Nature in the early spring,
> Your num'rous feet not tread
> The banks of Avon, for each flower,
> As it ne'er knew a sun or shower,
> Hangs there the pensive head.

And a few years later the prolific dramatist Thomas Heywood, who in his *Apology for Actors* of 1612 had referred to Shakespeare without explicitly naming him as having been 'much offended' with William Jaggard for piratically publishing some of his poems in *The Passionate Pilgrim* of 1599, mentioned him again in his *The Hierarchy of the Blessed Angels* of 1635 as one whose given name was often 'curtailed' to 'Will':

> Mellifluous Shakespeare, whose enchanting quill
> Commanded mirth or passion, was but 'Will.'

Finally, to take the story up to the closing of the theatres in 1642, in 1640 appeared the volume of *Poems* ascribed to Shakespeare (but including some by other poets, and greatly altering some of Shakespeare's own) published by John Benson with a preface cribbed from one written by Thomas May),[16] alluding to the 'excellent and sweetly composed poems of Master William Shakespeare'.

PUBLICATION EVIDENCE

Many plays of the period appeared in print with no author's name. However, Shakespeare is named as the author, either as 'William Shakespeare' or 'W. Shakespeare' in the following publication of his works as well as in the First Folio of 1623:

Venus and Adonis (dedication 1593 and the fifteen reprints up to 1636)
Lucrece (dedication 1594 and the seven reprints up to 1632)
Henry VI Part Two (Q3 1619)
Richard II (Q2 1598, Q3 1598, Q4 1608, Q5 1615)
Richard III (Q2 1598, Q3 1602, Q4 1605, Q5 1612, Q6 1622)
Love's Labour's Lost (Q1 1598)
Henry IV Part One (Q2 1599, Q3 1604, Q4 1608, Q5 1613)
A Midsummer Night's Dream (Q1 1600, Q2 1619)
The Merchant of Venice (Q1 1600, Q2 1619)
Henry IV Part Two (Q1 1600)
Much Ado About Nothing (Q1 1600)
The Merry Wives of Windsor (Q1 1602, Q2 1619)
Hamlet (Q1 1603, Q2 1604)
King Lear (Q1 1608, Q2 1619)
Shakespeare's Sonnets (Q1 1609)
Pericles (Q1 1609, Q2 1609, Q3 1611, Q4 1619)
Troilus and Cressida (Q1 1609)

Shakespeare is also named as the author of one of the poems (now generally known as 'The Phoenix and Turtle') in *Love's Martyr*, by Robert Chester, published by Richard Field in 1601 and of *The Passionate Pilgrim* (1599), which includes versions of two of his sonnets and three extracts from *Love's Labour's Lost* as well other poems not known to be by him or now clearly ascribed to other writers. This is an unauthorized publication. Somewhat similarly, the title page of *The London Prodigal* of 1605 claims that it is 'by William Shakespeare' and *A Yorkshire Tragedy* appeared in 1608 with the title-page statement that it was 'written by W. Shakespeare'; neither ascription is accepted by modern scholars, though it is conceivable that Shakespeare had some as-yet-unidentified hand in the composition of these plays. *Sir John Oldcastle*, published anonymously in 1600, was ascribed to Shakespeare on its republication by Thomas Pavier in 1619 (falsely dated 1600) though it is clearly, and no doubt accurately, ascribed to Anthony Munday, Richard Hathaway, Michael Drayton and Richard Wilson in the Henslowe papers. The Stationers' Register names Shakespeare as the author in the entries for the quarto of *King Lear* published in 1607, *Shakespeare's Sonnets* published in 1609 and for the sixteen plays first printed in the Folio of 1623.

No one expressed doubt that William Shakespeare of Stratford-upon-Avon wrote the works attributed to him – give or take a few suggestions that some of the plays might have been written in collaboration with other professional writers, as was extremely common at the time – until the middle of the nineteenth century. It was a period of intellectual ferment in which many orthodoxies – social, religious and scientific – were being challenged. Gaps in the record began to make people uneasy. There are certainly gaps in the records of Shakespeare's life, but there is nothing unusual about them. We know more about him than about many of his contemporaries, such as John Lyly, Thomas Kyd, John Webster or John Ford. While aristocratic families had their muniment rooms in which personal papers were preserved, the lives of most middle and lower class people – even those who achieved fame in their time – were little memorialized, and then generally through court records of slight personal interest, such as those that tell us about Shakespeare's financial dealings and purchases of property. All this should give the doubters pause. And anyone wishing to question the evidence I have set out in this chapter needs to disprove all of it, not simply, as is often done, to express scepticism about individual items. The evidence that Shakespeare wrote Shakespeare is overwhelming, and to dispute it is to challenge the entire validity of historical research.

CHAPTER 8

Shakespeare as collaborator

John Jowett

> If he did collaborate, or used researchers, or perhaps had a wonderful
> editor, that is interesting and important to me.
>
> Mark Rylance[1]

This essay describes William Shakespeare as a dramatist who worked in
collaboration with other writers for the professional theatre. The evidence
for this account lies largely in the field of stylistic analysis – typically computational stylistics – whose methodology MacDonald P. Jackson describes
elsewhere in this volume (Chapter 9). Some of the conclusions reached by
attribution scholarship remain speculative, as will be indicated where this is
the case. This is a field of on-going investigation and evolving techniques.
But there is nothing speculative about the outlines. The core findings are
that Shakespeare collaborated with other dramatists on *Titus Andronicus*,
Henry VI Part Two, *Henry VI Part One*, *Edward III*, the revision of *Sir
Thomas More*, *Timon of Athens*, *Pericles*, *All Is True* (*Henry VIII*) and *The
Two Noble Kinsmen*.[2] Recent attribution studies have suspected his work
elsewhere too: in *Arden of Faversham*, and in the revisions added to *The
Spanish Tragedy*, as first printed in the edition of 1602, and perhaps *Mucedorus*, as first printed in the edition of 1610.[3] He is also likely to have collaborated in the lost tragicomedy *Cardenio*,[4] and his sole authorship of *Henry
VI Part Three* has fallen under suspicion. Furthermore, two of his plays,
Macbeth and *Measure for Measure*, were adapted after his death.[5] Shakespeare was a regular collaborator at the beginning and end of his career, and
an intermittent collaborator at other stages. The dramatists with whom he
almost certainly or probably worked who can be named include Christopher Marlowe, George Peele, Henry Chettle, Thomas Dekker, Thomas
Heywood, Thomas Middleton, George Wilkins and John Fletcher. If he
revised *The Spanish Tragedy*, he worked on a play that was also revised by
Ben Jonson. The two posthumous adaptations were undertaken by Middleton. This picture conflicts utterly with the anti-Shakespearians' usual

preferred candidates for the authorship of Shakespeare's plays, who are usually aristocrats such as the Earl of Oxford or Francis Bacon who had no day-to-day dealings with the theatre and its dramatists.

BEAUTIFIED WITH OUR FEATHERS

The earliest account of Shakespeare as a dramatist is found in the reputation-spinning pamphlet *Greene's Groatsworth of Wit* (1592). The extent to which Greene wrote this work is debatable, so I will refer to the author of the famous letter addressed to '*those Gentlemen his Quondam acquaintances, that spend their wits in making plays*' by the initials appended to the epistle, 'R. G.'[6] The gentleman-playmakers are warned against 'an upstart Crow, beautified with our feathers, that with his Tiger's heart wrapped in a Player's hide, supposes he is as well able to bombast out a blank verse as the best of you: and being an absolute *Johannes fac-totum*, is in his own conceit the only Shake-scene in a country'. The 'Shake-scene' is clearly Shakespeare by virtue of both the allusive play on his name and the paraphrase of 'his' line in *Henry VI Part Three* (1.4.137). Shakespeare is accused of being a Johannes Factotum, or Jack of all trades. The exact meaning of R. G.'s accusations has been debated, but it seems likeliest that he implies that Shakespeare is attacked as an actor who has become involved in writing plays.[7]

If, in contrast, Shakespeare were invoked only as an actor who delivered lines on stage with bombast, as anti-Shakespearians claim, there is no obvious sense in which he could be described as a Jack of all trades; the point is that the phrase accuses the actor of doing something else in addition to acting – namely, writing plays. And it would be puzzling for a reader to understand what deep offence Shakespeare in particular had caused if he were invoked purely and simply as a performer of the playmakers' texts. In any case, it was dramatists, not actors, who were remembered by lines that were metonymic for their style of writing: Christopher Marlowe the dramatist by 'Holla, ye pampered jades of Asia', elsewhere Thomas Kyd the dramatist by 'O eyes, no eyes, but fountains fraught with tears' – hence comparably here William Shakespeare the dramatist by 'O tiger's heart wrapped in a woman's hide'. The trajectory of the epistle is partly disrupted by R. G.'s address of his attack on the players including Shakespeare to an unnamed third dramatist 'no less deserving than the other two'. R. G.'s target is the abuse perpetrated by the wayward dramatists, each of whom is identified cryptically. The tragedian Marlowe lapsed into 'Diabolicall Atheisme', to his cost; the 'Sweet boy' Thomas Nashe, 'that lastly with mee together writ a Comedie', is advised against deviating into 'byting' satire and 'bitter words'; Peele deserves his misfortune 'sith thou dependest on so meane a stay' as the players, and so allowed himself to be maltreated by Shakespeare. Peele is not, like Marlowe and Nashe, a wrong-doer in his writing, but a victim. Shakespeare in effect usurps Peele's role in the triad of playwrights as writer of the third kind of drama, the history play. He is guilty of 'bombast', of encroachment on the territory of the dramatists and perhaps of plagiarism. This shift of address from perpetrator to victim, we are to understand, re-enacts the usurped authorship of the play or plays to which R. G. refers. Hence it is Shakespeare, with 'his' famous line from a history play, who complements the tragedian Marlowe and the comedian Nashe.

If plagiarism is one possible implication of R. G.'s words, yet it is not quite the right term if the line parodied is, after all, 'his', Shakespeare's. R. G.'s suggestion of stealing conflicts with the contrary suggestion that Shakespeare writes in a distinctive and memorable style. The exact implication of the charge against Shakespeare's writing techniques may well be left deliberately obscure. Perhaps the point is that Shakespeare has picked up the techniques of dramatic writing from the plays in which he and his company have performed, and that, not content with imitating, he now claims to outdo the established dramatists. Having accused Shakespeare of being 'an upstart Crow, beautified with our feathers', R. G. goes on to advise writers to stop delivering new plays to the actors: 'let those Apes imitate your past excellence, and never more acquaint them with your admired inventions'. Shakespeare might be accused of a non-consensual form of collaboration: in other words, of adapting the play-scripts that the theatre company had received from other dramatists in ways that lay beyond their control. The roles of 'poet' or 'playmaker' and 'player' were usually distinct, with the theatre 'poet' of the early 1590s often being a university-educated if impoverished gentleman – hence Greene customarily made sure that on the title pages or epistles of his printed works he was identified by his gentrifying title of Master of Arts.[8] The stereotypically uneducated actor would not be expected to have the training in classical literature and rhetoric that would seem to be needed for the task of writing plays. In a sense, the complaint in *Greene's Groatsworth of Wit* is the same as that of the anti-Shakespearians of later centuries: that Shakespeare, a mere provincial actor, had no right to act as a playmaker. But R. G.'s protest would be meaningless without the premise that he indeed had been transgressing in this way.

There would have been little to prevent such behaviour. The playwrights would have had no rights over their scripts once they had sold them on to the players, and one of R. G.'s concerns is surely that, if the acting company could generate scripts in-house, the income stream as well as the professional standing of the dramatists would be endangered. More specifically, *Greene's Groatsworth of Wit* accuses Shakespeare of abusing professional demarcations between actor and dramatist, and undermining the protocols for collaboration. He is 'beautified with our feathers', and yet, as it were in annoying contradiction, beautified with well-recognized feathers of his own.

EARLY COLLABORATIONS

The play R. G. misquotes, *Henry VI Part Three*, is now suspected of itself containing traces of a hand other than Shakespeare's, and is therefore one possible instance of Shakespeare, in R. G.'s real or supposed view, mis-appropriating the work of others. But no one has argued in any detail that *Henry VI Part Three* is in its greater substance anything other than a Shakespeare play. It is the other members of the trilogy that lack credibility in this respect. *Henry VI Part Two* was, according to Hugh Craig's compelling study, written by Shakespeare along with another dramatist, identified as Marlowe, who supplied the scenes showing Cade's rebellion.[9] *Henry VI Part One* is probably a prequel, that is to say, a play that, although it depicted earlier events than the other parts, was actually written after them. Shakespeare's hand in this play has emerged in a number of recent studies as comprising no more than the 'rose-plucking' scene (2.4) and most of Act 4. No doubt there is more to be written about the evolution of the *Henry VI* trilogy in terms of both author attribution and theatre history. But this less-than-straightforward sequence of events supplies one context in which R. G.'s accusations against Shakespeare can be understood.

There are, however, other plays that R. G. might potentially have had in mind. One of the earliest surviving dramas containing Shakespeare's hand may well be the anonymous *Arden of Faversham*, written at some point between 1587 and its publication in 1592. Though it has yet to be included in any Shakespeare edition, its part-authorship by Shakespeare has been convincingly demonstrated by MacDonald P. Jackson, who identifies scene 8, the 'quarrel scene', as Shakespeare's, and by Arthur F. Kinney, who identifies other probable Shakespeare scenes in the same area of the play.[10] The exact attribution by scene is less clear from Kinney's study; it may well be that one dramatist added to another dramatist's work. What remains quite clear is the presence of Shakespeare, alongside one or more other unknown dramatists.

Furthermore, it happens that the year in which *Greene's Groatsworth of Wit* appeared is also the likeliest year for the first performance of a play in which Shakespeare's work is conjoined with that of another dramatist, *Titus Andronicus*. Peele wrote the first act and 2.1; he may also have provided drafts of 2.2 and 4.1 that were later revised by Shakespeare. It is probably Peele whom R. G. most directly warns against Shake-scene: 'I would swear by sweet St. George, thou art unworthy better hap, since thou dependest on so mean a stay.' 'St. George' glances both at Peele's forename and the patriotic tenor of much of his writing. *Titus* is one play in which the practice of collaboration between Shakespeare and Peele is established, and the potential for real or perceived malpractice therefore exists.

Shakespeare seems to have been involved in an uncharacteristically large number of plays around 1592, at a time when the theatre companies were undergoing major upheavals. The greater extent of his collaborative writing can be read in this light: at most points during his career he wrote no more than a couple of plays per year. After 1592 – which was the year before literary success with *Venus and Adonis* – Shakespeare committed himself to single authorship, with some exceptions. *Edward III*, which was probably written around 1595, may be another play where Shakespeare's input may have followed after the other dramatists had completed theirs, for the editor Giorgio Melchiori emphasizes how Shakespeare added complexity by writing against the grain of the plan devised by the original plotter.[11]

Traces can therefore be seen of a pattern that would be consistent with a strong reading of R. G.'s accusation: that Shakespeare not only imitated other dramatists, but completed or re-completed scripts they had prepared. He added scenes presenting some striking confrontations that were of his own invention, of the kind typified in Margaret's tormenting of Richard Duke of York; others too involve key female roles (Mistress Arden, the Countess of Salisbury). Shakespeare's hand has additionally been posited to be present in the passages added to Kyd's *Spanish Tragedy* and, more speculatively, the 'new additions' advertised and first printed in the 1610 edition of the anonymous *Mucedorus*. These are activities entirely consonant with his position as a member of the theatre company who also wrote dialogue for performance, whether that dialogue constitutes entire plays or passages designed to augment existing scripts.

'Sir Thomas More'

The summary description of Shakespeare's additions given above applies in various ways also to his part in the manuscript play *Sir Thomas More*, which was revised probably in 1603–4. The main passage he contributed in scene 6 shows More pacifying supporters of an insurrection against foreigners in London by appealing, in long set speeches, to the citizens' sense of loyalty to authority and their humanitarian fellow-feeling for the strangers. This is a key document for our understanding of Shakespeare as a collaborator. The first version of the play, known as the Original Text, is in the hand of the dramatist Anthony Munday. The manuscript in this state was sent to the Master of the Revels, Edmund Tilney, whose duties included licensing plays for performance. Tilney marked various passages for deletion, mainly those that staged an insurrection of London citizens, and wrote in to the margin of the first page his demand that the insurrection should be left out. To this script has been added a series of additions designed to replace or expand upon passages in the Original Text, including parts of the insurrection episode. These Additional Passages are written in the hands of an unknown copyist probably working for the theatre, known simply as Hand C, and of four dramatists identified as Chettle, Heywood, Shakespeare and Dekker.[12]

From the point of view of Shakespeare study, the most consequential finding is that the hand otherwise known simply as 'Hand D' is Shakespeare. The evidence is complex, but finally compelling. The most numerous and most expert studies of the handwriting find strong links between Hand D and the few samples of Shakespeare's writing in legal documents. No remotely comparable affinity has been discovered between Hand D and any other hand. The stylistic evidence is equally strong. Investigations have established a compelling case based on establishing unique associations between Hand D and Shakespeare, including both transparent and probably irrefutable statistical analysis and unique individual parallels. There are also traits of spelling shared by Hand C and Shakespeare, such as 'scilens' for *silence*, that point in the same direction. Thanks to advances in methodology, in particular the use of computational analysis, and the recent availability of searchable texts of virtually all early-modern books, the claim that Hand D is Shakespeare can now be advanced with far greater confidence than has been possible hitherto.

There are inescapable consequences for the anti-Shakespearian case. *Sir Thomas More* establishes a clear documentary connection between William Shakespeare of Stratford and the author of Shakespeare's plays. The handwriting cannot be associated with any other dramatist, nor with any of the more prestigious figures that have been put forward as alternatives to Shakespeare. Moreover, the Stratford signatory writes dramatic verse in *Sir Thomas More* that displays a range of stylistic features that connect him with the author of the more familiar canonical plays and with no other writer. To this may be added less quantifiable aspects of writing such as the intellectual and emotional temper of the writing, and the techniques of dramatization, all of which are fully Shakespearian.

Shakespeare is seen working as a member of a team of professional dramatists. Hand C's task in piecing together the revisions was complicated, and the Hand D passage needed particular attention. Paradoxically, however, the lack of fine-tuning in some of the staging details reflects not so much Shakespeare's remoteness from the project as his pragmatic willingness to allow someone else with responsibility for the revision as a whole to make the final adjustments. He is certainly not as attuned to the revision as was Hand C, but he was attuned to theatre practice. Speech-prefixes for 'other' (or more briefly 'oth' or 'o') recognize the symbiosis between dramatist and theatre annotator. So too does the extra space Shakespeare left around a stage direction when he was uncertain as to whether More needed to enter. Both features signify incompletion; both invite supplementation; both are based on a collaborative understanding of playmaking.

It should not be forgotten, however, that Shakespeare's contribution to *Sir Thomas More* consisted of a small proportion of the play as a whole, and indeed only a fraction of the revisions. His contribution seems not to have been confined to the Hand D passage. One and perhaps two short soliloquies spoken by More seem also to derive from this writer.[13] If one or both of the speeches as copied by the scribe-annotator Hand C is based on a draft by Shakespeare, his role in the revision looks entirely different. These short soliloquies at the beginning of scene 8 and scene 9 show that their writer was fully aware of the scenes that come before and after, and indeed that their author was engaged in an attempt to draw together the scattered episodes that constitute the middle part of the play in order to create a more coherent drama. But even the Hand D passage taken in isolation is not a work of the periphery. Shakespeare, working evidently at the same time that Heywood revised the previous scene, supplies the most crucial episode in the insurrection sequence that takes up the first two-fifths of the play, and shows an imaginative engagement matched by none of the other contributors.

The manuscript confirms the picture that has been seen already of Shakespeare as a dramatist who was a man of the theatre. He worked alongside playwrights who are now considered of less note, contributing to a collaborative revision overseen by a theatre functionary. Unless the identification of Hand D as Shakespeare can be disproved, which at the current point in time looks highly unlikely, this play manuscript demonstrates that William Shakespeare of Stratford was a professional dramatist who was willing and able to work alongside fellow professionals.

NEW GENRES: 'TIMON OF ATHENS', 'PERICLES'

Timon of Athens, written a few years after the revision of *Sir Thomas More* in about 1606, might be described as a tragic response to city comedy. The spirit of writing is at times close to *King Lear*, but *Timon* is if anything an even more extreme play; it has virtually no space for women, and no recourse to reconciliation. Instead, it suffuses its bleak vision of aggressively economistic man with a harsh strain of satirical comedy. And for this Shakespeare turned to the foremost proponent of that sharp, new style of writing, Thomas Middleton.

Middleton contributed the first banquet scene (2.1), the mid-play scenes in which Timon's servants are rejected by his friends when they petition him for loans, Alcibiades's plea to the Senate for mercy on behalf of one of his soldiers, and various episodes within individual scenes, particularly those dealing with Timon's steward Flavius. The creditor scenes are set pieces of city comedy, if with a keenly serious edge.

Middleton is evidently seeing a work initiated by Shakespeare to completion (or near completion). For instance, the first banquet scene can be read as a pre-response to the long Shakespearian scene later in the play where Timon discovers gold buried in the earth: Timon, in his gift-giving, is an artificial, regendered reconfiguration of mother earth. The senate scene has some basis in Plutarch; it was Shakespeare, not Middleton, who read Plutarch, so Middleton is probably following a plan devised by Shakespeare. And a few scenes have short passages at the beginning or end that were evidently added by Middleton; again, the implication is that he is the finisher, not the starter. This is a significant conclusion. In most other plays, either Shakespeare seems to come to the project belatedly, or there is no clear sequence to the dramatists' labours. *Timon* not only shows Shakespeare collaborating; it extends the range of situations in which he did so.[14]

Pericles, written in the same period (*c.* 1607) conforms instead to the model supplied by *Titus Andronicus*. Another writer, in this case George Wilkins, supplied the opening scenes; Shakespeare then took over and completed the play. Both plays (like *Timon*) represent extremes of generic experimentation: *Titus* indulges in the bloodiest kind of revenge tragedy, *Pericles* engages whole-heartedly with the popular genre of romance, complete with the sensational theme of incest. As in other collaborative plays, many readers identify a transformation in the poetic depth and emotional temperature where Shakespeare takes over. But the telling point is that he saw no need to reject and replace Wilkins's more humdrum style of writing. His mentality in this respect remains that of the paid professional dramatist, someone not averse to joining with a co-writer, and a far less experienced and inferior one at that. Shakespeare's participation in the revision of *Sir Thomas More* alongside Chettle, Dekker and Heywood is less surprising if one takes *Pericles* into account.

HANDING OVER: THE FLETCHER COLLABORATIONS

John Fletcher and Francis Beaumont's *Philaster* (1609) shows that Fletcher was an accomplished dramatist before his collaborations with Shakespeare, and indeed *Philaster* may have given Shakespeare some hints for the development of his later style as next seen in *Cymbeline*.[15] Perhaps Shakespeare was again in some way beautifying his own writing with feathers from another bird – or at least using the distinctive timbre of another dramatist's writing to develop his own – though, as elsewhere, there can be no doubting the stronger dramatic energy and greater stylistic complexity flowing from Shakespeare's pen. The Shakespeare–Fletcher partnership led to the joint authorship of two extant works, the play identified as *Henry VIII* in the First Folio but otherwise known as *All Is True*, and *The Two Noble Kinsmen*. *All Is True* is hard to separate into clearly defined authorial stints; *The Two Noble Kinsmen*, in contrast, shows Fletcher and Shakespeare collaborating in the middle part of the play, with Fletcher predominating, and Shakespeare writing the long and monumentally ceremonial opening scene and most of Act 5. A growing body of scholarship argues that the lost *Cardenio*, which the mid-seventeenth-century publisher Humphrey Moseley attributed to 'Mr Fletcher & Shakespeare', belongs to the same group.[16]

The dramatist who collaborated with Fletcher was alive and well as late as 1613, when *All Is True* was first performed. The development of Shakespeare's metrical style, seen most obviously in the increased usage of flow-overs and feminine endings, can be associated with plays written in the post-1609 period; the traits were shared with Fletcher and are found in the collaborative plays. Yet Shakespeare and Fletcher can usually be differentiated. The Shakespearian portions of both plays are written in a style elsewhere found exclusively in a book whose credentials as a testament to the activity of William Shakespeare as a dramatic author could scarcely be higher. This is the 1623 Folio of Comedies, Histories, and Tragedies based on texts supplied by the King's Men and prefaced by an epistle by two of the company's leading actors.

PARTS AND WHOLES

The importance of the Folio as evidence for Shakespeare's authorship of the plays it contains is established elsewhere in this book. There is, however, a complication that will be evident from the ground covered in the present essay. The Folio presents all the plays as if they were in Shakespeare's sole hand. He is a dramatist untainted by any suspicion of collegiality with other dramatists. Given this view, the anti-Shakespearian project of denying that Shakespeare was the author of these plays, for all its implausibility in other respects, would have at least this in its favour: that the detached and abstracted dramatist presented in the Folio would need only his name changing to sustain the case for the plays in that book being the work of another man or woman. But this is not the case. The grand simplicity to the Folio's claim is misleading. The title page of the 1634 quarto of *The Two Noble Kinsmen* advertises that it was 'Written by the memorable Worthies of their time; Mr *John Fletcher*, and Mr *William Shakspere. Gent.*' The book was issued by Moseley, the same publisher who recorded Fletcher and Shakespeare as authors of *Cardenio*. What Moseley tells us, but the 1623 Folio denies, is that Shakespeare on occasion wrote plays in collaboration with other dramatists. This necessary counter-Folio account of Shakespeare places the author of the plays within the regular practices of playmaking up to 1613.

It might, however, be asked whether our recognition that the canon we call 'Shakespeare' is not entirely written by Shakespeare is in any way con-nected with the view that Shakespeare did not write those plays at all. The short answer is an emphatic 'no'. Indeed, the question would scarcely be worth addressing were it not implied in some anti-Shakespearian perspec-tives. Hence William Leahy, referring to the claims of anti-Shakespearian studies to be treated seriously, writes: 'Equally significant, however, is the fact that many of the plays are now considered to have been produced in collaboration, as was normal among playwrights at the time, and are none the worse for it. To my mind, this development within the field of Shakespeare criticism has been one effect of the Authorship Question and the research carried out in its name.'[17] The exact implication of these words is unclear. They are presumably not intended to make the reasonable claim that attribution studies have effectively responded to and dismantled anti-Shakespearian arguments, but rather, and absurdly, that the weight of the anti-Shakespearian 'research' advanced under the appropriative ban-ner of the 'Authorship Question' has forced Shakespeare 'criticism' into a compromising admission that Shakespeare is not entirely Shakespeare.

The admixture of a second ingredient is, of course, categorically distinct from the substitution of one sole ingredient with another. As applied to attribution studies, this principle emerges in the following form: the evidence of dramatists other than Shakespeare within the Shakespeare canon is also, by the same token, evidence that the residual body of writing (maybe ninety per cent of the canon) is by Shakespeare. Each of the writers involved has a distinct and demonstrable stylistic profile. The sophisticated analysis that allows, say, Peele to be identified as author of parts of *Titus Andronicus* has the incidental but important effect of establishing a more accurate and nuanced account of Shakespeare's own style, and of affirming his presence in the larger part of the play.

This principle applies most critically to Marlowe, the one alternative candidate for the authorship of Shakespeare's plays who, though dead for most of Shakespeare's writing career, is known for his ability to compose brilliantly effective dramatic verse and to construct stageable plays. The fact that Marlowe qualifies in these respects certainly singles him out from other claimants, but it demonstrates nothing beyond that. The success of attribution study in differentiating between Shakespeare and Marlowe is based on the establishment of two distinct stylistic identities. This is nowhere more clearly the case than in the plays that Craig has argued to contain the work of both dramatists, the first and second parts of *Henry VI*. The point at which Marlowe has indeed been identified in the Shakespeare canon is also, definitively, the point at which Shakespeare and Marlowe can be seen to be different, even though they are writing the same plays at about the same point in time.

This is entirely consistent with the findings in relation to *Sir Thomas More*. When palaeographers point out that Hand D has rare and highly individual characteristics in common with the Shakespeare signatures, it follows that Hand D cannot be Marlowe. But we can go further, as Marlowe's hand survives as witness to a will. Hand D's writing is certainly not Marlowe's writing. In the first instance at least, the case based on palaeography is separate from the case based on a variety of stylistic evidence. But the two forms of investigation say the same thing: Shakespeare is different from Marlowe. In contrast, the biographical Shakespeare and the stylistic Shakespeare – the Shakespeare who signed wills and the Shakespeare who wrote plays – are one and the same person. Marlowe is a different man.

Shakespeare worked in the popular theatre until about 1613, the date on which it is recorded that his and Fletcher's *All Is True* was first performed, and over twenty years after Marlowe's death. Some of the key stages in the development of Shakespeare's dramatic writing are associated with him working in conjunction with other dramatists: his establishment as a well-recognized dramatist excelling in history plays infused with moments of high rhetorical tragedy, his first uneven experiments with the tragicomic mode and his perfection of that mode in the late plays. Careful scrutiny of the Shakespeare collaborations shows him both writing a draft for someone else to complete (as is clearly seen only in *Timon of Athens*) and (as is more common with Shakespeare) completing a play begun by another dramatist. Elsewhere, he interacts closely with fellow-dramatists in such as way as to suggest unsequenced co-writing. He also revises plays that have been previously completed by others. Thus our survey of a broad range of collaboratively written plays reveals a dramatist closely involved in active and various interactions with other dramatists. In some of the early plays and in the revised plays, Shakespeare was evidently participating as a member of the theatre company, in that he was making improvements to the work of the paid professional dramatists. Here, most clearly, we see a writer embedded in the process of putting plays on stage, writing at a point in between the initial scripting and the appearance of the play on stage. That picture of a dramatist embedded in the process of playmaking is, however, one that emerges at no matter where we look at collaboration in Shakespeare's work.

CHAPTER 9

Authorship and the evidence of stylometrics

MacDonald P. Jackson

Shakespeare is widely held to be the greatest writer in English. There must therefore be such a thing as literary value upon which agreement can be reached, and the best of those works attributed to Shakespeare must possess qualities that distinguish them from the works of other dramatists and poets. This is demonstrably the case. Most of Shakespeare's plays are mainly in verse, and his poetic style differs from that of each of the several playwrights who at times collaborated with him. It tends also to be more complex, concentrated and expressive – to carry a heavier freight of meaning. The poetry enriches the dramatized events in subtle ways. Shakespeare's dramatic verse is unmatched by that of his professional contemporaries. Its remoteness from the amateur compositions of noblemen proposed as 'the real Shakespeare' is even greater. This essay aims briefly to indicate the literary critical grounds for such a claim and, more especially, to describe certain kinds of quantitative tests that differentiate Shakespeare's writing from writing by his co-authors and those 'Shakespeare claimants' who have left poems or plays for comparison. The terms 'stylometrics' or 'computational stylistics' refer to this numerical measurement of style.

Scores of candidates have been put forward as sole or partial authors of Shakespeare's œuvre. Many of these have left no poetry or drama under their own names, so that it is impossible to investigate whether creative writing acknowledged to be theirs is stylistically compatible with the writings of the Shakespeare canon. The Claremont Shakespeare Clinic has, however, devised a series of tests that in combination differentiate every extant work of the core Shakespeare canon from a very large number of other early modern poetic and dramatic works, including those by the fifteen full claimants and twenty-two partial claimants for whom relevant material was available.[1] 'Full' claimants are alleged to be the true authors behind the Shakespearian *nom-de-plume*. 'Partial' claimants are held to have composed portions of the canonical works and include several men accepted by orthodox scholars as collaborators with Shakespeare.

But before describing the Claremont research, it seems worth making a few remarks about the literary compositions of the three candidates who have received most support from anti-Shakespearians: Francis Bacon, Christopher Marlowe and Edward de Vere, seventeenth Earl of Oxford. Bacon was, in the nineteenth and early twentieth centuries, the leading contender, a status now held by the Earl of Oxford. Marlowe's candidacy was vigorously promoted by Calvin Hoffman in *The Man Who Was Shakespeare* (1955)[2] and is still urged in books and articles and on websites.

Bacon, lord chancellor, politician and philosopher, was one of the great English thinkers of his time, who, in fine discursive prose, addressed a vast variety of topics. His *Works*, as edited by James Spedding and others, fill fourteen weighty volumes.[3] But the genius they display is for cogitation and exposition. They are the products of reason, not of the imagination that created *Venus and Adonis*, *A Midsummer Night's Dream* and *King Lear*. Bacon's *Essays* have the expanded title *Counsels Civil and Moral*, an apt description of their unShakespearian nature. As poet, Bacon did indeed compose a verse adaptation of a Greek epigram, and metrical versions of seven Psalms.[4] He can handle rhyme and metre. But his vein is moralistic, tending towards generalized statement. The poem from the Greek begins:

> The world's a bubble, and the life of man
> less than a span;
> In his conception wretched, from the womb
> so to the tomb:
> Curst from the cradle, and brought up to years
> with cares and fears.

It goes on to find court, country and city wanting and pronounces unsatisfactory both married and single life, having and not having children, staying at home and travelling abroad, wartime and peacetime, concluding that it is better never to have been born or 'being born to die'. One need only read Hamlet's 'To be, or not to be' soliloquy (3.1.58–92) or Shakespeare's Sonnet 66, where the theme is somewhat similar, to observe a far more lively play of figurative language. The imagery of 'Whether 'tis nobler in the mind to suffer / The slings and arrows of outrageous fortune, / Or to take arms against a sea of troubles, / And, by opposing, end them' or of 'The undiscovered country from whose bourn / No traveller returns' or of 'And thus the native hue of resolution / Is sicklied o'er with the pale cast of thought' is utterly foreign to Bacon's habits of mind. Even Bacon's opening metaphor, 'The world's a *bubble*', is trite compared to, say, Shakespeare's vivid verbal snapshot in Jacques's Seven Ages speech of the soldier, 'bearded like the *pard*' and 'Seeking the *bubble* reputation / Even in the cannon's mouth' (*As You Like It* 2.7.149–53). Shakespeare's language is always richly particular. Bacon is not averse to using illustrative analogies in his prose works, but the areas of experience on which his and Shakespeare's imagery draw form sharply dissimilar patterns, Bacon especially favouring domestic life, Shakespeare nature. Caroline Spurgeon demonstrated this over three-quarters of a century ago.[5]

Bacon's voluminous output included a handful of speeches for devices or masques presented at Gray's Inn and before the Queen during the period 1592–5, but these are long prose orations, lacking any trace of the dramatic and more akin to his essays than to anything spoken on the public stage.[6]

Sixteen poems by Edward de Vere, born in 1550, survive to form the uncontested canon, and others are doubtfully ascribed.[7] The earliest datable work belongs to 1572, and another eight had certainly been written by 1575. They are not negligible, but to compare them with Shakespeare's narrative poems or sonnets is to measure intergalactic distances. De Vere's models are of the mid-sixteenth century and earlier, with heavy use of alliteration and the rhetorical figure *amplicatio*, which 'generates content by multiplying examples to illustrate a given theme',[8] and a liking for metrical forms with long lines of twelve or fourteen syllables and six or seven stresses, such as fourteeners and 'Poulter's measure'. No Shakespeare poem is written in these metres, though he employs a fragmented version of the fourteen-syllable, seven-stress line for comic effect within the 'Pyramus and Thisbe' burlesque in *A Midsummer Night's Dream* (5.1). De Vere's is typical mid-Tudor verse, in what C. S. Lewis characterized as the 'drab' style:[9]

> My life through ling'ring long is lodged in lair of loathsome ways,
> My death delayed to keep from life the harm of hapless days;
> My sprites, my heart, my wit and force in deep distress are drowned;
> The only loss of my good name is of these griefs the ground.

The poetic imagination at work here is of a different order from that which created Shakespeare's Sonnet 29 ('When in disgrace with fortune and men's eyes') and Hamlet's dying request to Horatio:

> O God, Horatio, what a wounded name,
> Things standing thus unknown, shall I leave behind me!
> If thou didst ever hold me in thy heart,
> Absent thee from felicity a while,
> And in this harsh world draw thy breath in pain
> To tell my story.   (5.2.296–301)

Some of De Vere's later poems – such as the question-and-answer dialogue between the poet and Desire – have a certain lyric grace, but they remain formulaic. In 1589 George Puttenham praised 'Th'Earl of Oxford and Master *Edwards* of her Majesty's Chapel for Comedy and Interlude',[10] which probably implies De Vere's authorship or part-authorship of court masques or entertainments, but they are no longer extant.

Marlowe has the advantage over Bacon, De Vere and a whole bevy of nobles of having been the brilliant poet of *Hero and Leander* and a splendid public-theatre playwright, whose *Tamburlaine* galvanized early modern English drama. But he has the disadvantage of having been killed in a brawl in 1593 before all but a handful of Shakespeare's plays were in existence – or at least so the coroner's report on an inquest attended by sixteen local jurors asserted. At the time of his death Marlowe's dramatic output rivalled the young Shakespeare's in quality. But Marlowe had shown no talent for the kind of comedy evinced in Shakespeare's already staged *The Two Gentlemen of Verona* (1590–1) and *The Taming of the Shrew* (1590–1), and his dramatic verse is clearly distinguishable from Shakespeare's by stylometric tests, as we shall see. Moreover, the dominant sources of his poetic images – classical texts, the firmament and its celestial bodies – contrast markedly with Shakespeare's.[11] Typical of Marlowe at his best is Faustus's enraptured response to the beauty of Helen, whom he judges 'fairer than the evening air, / Clad in the beauty of a thousand stars'.[12] Typical of Shakespeare is the contrite Posthumus's outpouring of emotion as the wife he had rashly spurned '*throws her arms about his neck*': 'Hang there like fruit, my soul, / Till the tree die' (*Cymbeline* 5.6.263–4). The point is not, of course, that Marlowe invents no images of nature or that Shakespeare invents none of the heavens, but that their overall patterns of usage are dissimilar.

Advocates of Marlowe's authorship of the Shakespeare canon surmount the most massive obstacle by theorizing that his death was faked. De Vere's supporters are also confronted with chronological difficulties. He died 24 June 1604, when a dozen Shakespeare plays were, orthodox scholars agree, yet to be written. Oxfordians must therefore challenge the conventional dating of these plays to the period 1604/5–1613/14 and claim that, having all been written by June 1604, they were posthumously released year by year till near the end of front-man Shakespeare's life. Stylistic evidence helps render such an explanation incredible.

The approximate order in which Shakespeare's plays were written and their dates of first performance (spanning the period 1590–1614) have now been securely established, only small modifications having been made to the determinations of E. K. Chambers over eighty years ago.[13] A skeleton chronology can be provided by such matters as entry of plays in the Stationers' Register and/or their appearance in print; the date when known sources became available; records of performance or other references to particular plays; and allusions within plays to identifiable historical events and circumstances. It then becomes obvious that Shakespeare's dramatic verse developed in comprehensible ways as his career progressed. End-stopped iambic pentameter conforming rigidly to the paradigm (ti-túm ti-túm ti-túm ti-túm ti-túm) gradually acquired greater freedom, variety and flow. Increasingly the sense ran straight on from one line to the next, without pause; greater use was made of extra unstressed syllables, particularly those forming a 'double ending' (also known as a 'feminine ending') to a line (ti-túm-ti); pentameters shared by two or more speakers became more common; the position and weight of pauses *within* lines evolved. These and other metrical features can be counted and indices computed that place plays in an order closely corresponding with the order that can be deduced from 'external' evidence.[14]

Nobody imagines that a play in which twenty-five per cent of the blank verse lines have double endings *must* be later than a play in which the percentage is twenty. Artistic change is not so mechanical. But the trends in the several metrical variations that make for greater freedom from the norm are unmistakable and strongly correlated with one another. Some of these had not been analysed in Chambers's day. Moreover, different and independent kinds of data, also unknown to Chambers, support the chronology fleshed out by metrical statistics. Plays of about the same date are apt to share a higher proportion of rare words than those written many years apart. From about 1600 onwards Shakespeare, like other dramatists, adopted more third-person verbs ending in '-s' rather than '-th' and a more colloquial orthography that included a wider range of contractions. Progressively, he employed larger numbers of short speeches. Even from common words that in Shakespeare's usage became more frequent (such as 'most') or less frequent (such as 'unto'), mathematical analysis can calculate an 'omnibus predictor' that orders plays in a chronology correlating remarkably well with that ascertained by other means. While elements of Shakespeare's style remained constant, aspects of it – including his way with imagery and his handling of language itself – steadily evolved throughout his career.[15]

Oxfordian attempts to concoct a chronology whereby De Vere could have written all Shakespeare's plays by 1604 confound this natural progression.[16] The beginnings of the Shakespearian output are moved back a decade or more to 1580 at the latest. Plays with large proportions of double endings and run-on lines are thus assigned dates at which they would be utterly anomalous on the Elizabethan stage and when De Vere's own poems were absolutely devoid of double endings. In his last plays, from *Antony and Cleopatra* (1606) onwards, Shakespeare often ended a line with a word that began a phrase completed in the next line: Alexas 'went to Jewry on / Affairs of Antony' (4.6.11–12); 'with / His bounty' (4.6.20–1). Oxfordian chronologies place Shakespearian plays making liberal use of these extreme forms of enjambement, known as 'weak' and 'light' endings, ten or more years before Shakespeare introduced this metrical innovation to dramatic blank verse.

Playwrights responded in their individual ways to what might be termed a changing rhythmical climate. In the 1580s the position in the pentameter line at which pauses most frequently fell was after the fourth syllable. It was not until 1597 that the verse of any surviving play, whoever the author, contained more pauses after the sixth syllable than after the fourth. Yet in the latest Oxfordian chronology, by W. Ron Hess, *All's Well That Ends Well, Measure for Measure, King Lear, Hamlet, Antony and Cleopatra* and *Coriolanus*, in all of which this development has occurred, are given dates within the period 1591–6. Likewise, plays reflecting the general shift in drama towards the replacement of 'hath' and 'doth' by 'has' and 'does' and recourse to various colloquial contractions are dated by Oxfordians long before this advance took place. The knotty, elliptical, condensed poetic style of *Cymbeline, The Winter's Tale* and *The Tempest* that was innovative in 1609–11 would have been unthinkable in the Elizabethan years 1598–9, to which Oxfordians assign these plays. Moreover, Shakespeare's final plays reflect, both in structure and content, the acquisition by the King's Men in August 1608 of the indoor Blackfriars Theatre.[17] The challenges posed by playing in this new venue, so ably met by Shakespeare with his inside knowledge, could not possibly have been anticipated by De Vere. Older Oxfordian chronologies, which had all Shakespeare's plays completed by 1590, were even more wildly incompatible with the whole development of early modern dramatic verse.

But there are even more solid barriers to supposing that the last twelve Shakespeare plays could all have been written by 1604. For at least seven, topical allusions, the dates at which sources became available and connections with non-Shakespearian plays of known dates provide good grounds for believing in composition after De Vere's death.[18] Oxfordians are forced to dismiss every single item of this evidence as illusory or posit late interpolations into the texts first published in the First Folio of 1623. But the dependence of Shakespeare's last unaided play *The Tempest* on reports of events surrounding the shipwreck of the 'Sea Venture' off Bermuda during a voyage to Virginia, and William Strachey's 'A True Reportory' in particular, is manifest to any unbiased judge.[19] Moreover, four of the dozen plays were undoubtedly works of co-authorship – *Timon of Athens* with Thomas Middleton, *Pericles* with George Wilkins and *All Is True* (*Henry VIII*) and *The Two Noble Kinsmen* with John Fletcher. Middleton had no association with the King's Men – to whom alleged front-man Shakespeare is held by Oxfordians to have released De Vere's scripts – before 1605; Wilkins's short stint of playwriting was restricted to 1606–7; and Fletcher first emerged as a playwright in 1606. Documentary evidence proves that *All Is True*, on which Fletcher and Shakespeare collaborated, was first performed in 1613. The two playwrights clearly planned their collaborative plays as joint enterprises.

The Oxfordian ploy of pushing the Shakespearian œuvre back in time is in any case self-defeating. It makes Shakespeare's earliest works contemporary with De Vere's surviving poems, so that the glaring disparity between the literary talents on display cannot be explained away as due to De Vere's progressive acquisition of greater literary skills. The stylometric research of the Claremont Shakespeare Clinic, led by Ward E. Y. Elliott and Robert J. Valenza, furnishes some confirmation that objectively measurable characteristics demarcate all writing attributed by mainstream scholarship to Shakespeare from the writings of his contemporaries, including all testable anti-Shakespearian claimants. Elliott and Valenza's project began as an attempt to use computerized stylistic tests to cast light on 'The Authorship Problem', as popularly understood, but was soon extended to furnish answers to questions about First Folio plays suspected to be not wholly of Shakespeare's authorship and non-Folio plays haunting the fringes of the canon.

Over more than two decades the Claremont group has devised a variety of tests for Shakespearian authorship. There have been many interim reports and articles in academic journals. So far the fullest published account of their work is in a 2004 issue of the *Tennessee Law Review* devoted to a symposium on 'Who Wrote Shakespeare?'[20] The team worked with electronic texts modernized according to principles governing the highly respected *Riverside Shakespeare*. In brief, their approach was to determine the rates of use of various features in the twenty-nine Shakespeare plays generally accepted as of his sole authorship; to compare the inter-play range of these rates with the rates for a large and diverse sample of plays by Shakespeare's near-contemporaries; and to establish 'profiles' of usage that included nearly all the Shakespearian plays but excluded many of the non-Shakespearian.

Some tests thus derived were straightforward and simple – the rate of occurrence of 'ne'er', for instance. The Shakespeare range for this locution per 20,000 words was reckoned at 1–10. All twenty-nine core Shakespeare plays had rates falling within this range, whereas thirty-one of fifty-one securely ascribed non-Shakespeare plays and fourteen of twenty-eight plays of questioned authorship and classed as 'apocrypha' did not. The co-authored *Henry VI Part One* and *Timon of Athens* also yielded rates outside the Shakespearian range or profile, as did George Wilkins's *Pericles* acts one and two (treated separately from Shakespeare's acts three and five) and Peele's portion of *Titus Andronicus*. Other tests were 'hi-tech', utilizing statistical computations that were sometimes quite elaborate. An example is the 'Thisted-Efron New Words Test', devised by the professional statisticians, Ronald Thisted and Bradley Efron to estimate how many words within a Shakespeare play or block of text of a specified size might be expected to appear only in that play or block among all those by Shakespeare. Claremont testing based on the Thisted-Efron formula subtracts actual rates of occurrence from expected rates. The resultant range for the twenty-nine core Shakespeare plays was −14 to +5. Scores for thirty-three of the fifty-one undoubtedly non-Shakespeare plays yielded figures outside this range ('rejections'), as did eight of the twenty-eight 'apocryphal' plays. On this test, *Henry VI Part One*, *Henry V*, *Henry VIII* and *Timon of Athens* were also anomalous. *Henry V* had been excluded from the Shakespearian core because of its scenes in French, and the results for the other three plays were consistent with their co-authored nature.

Eventually three rounds of tests were run, totalling forty-eight tests in all. No core Shakespeare play accumulated more than two rejections. Rejections were possible for core plays because actual ranges for all twenty-nine were trimmed to exclude clear 'outliers' and so create a Shakespearian 'profile'. But no core play produced the outlier, thus failing to fit the restricted profile, more than twice. For the fifty-one non-Shakespeare plays the average (mean) number of rejections was seventeen, the lowest was ten, and the highest twenty-nine. For the apocrypha the average number of rejections was fifteen, the lowest seven and the highest twenty-two. Marlowe's seven plays, with between ten and twenty-six rejections, belonged clearly within the non-Shakespearian category. So did plays by Greene, Kyd, Lyly and Peele that some Baconians or Oxfordians have implausibly attributed to their claimant, in order to lend him some credibility as a playwright.

Refinements to the Claremont Clinic's methods included formulating separate profiles for pre-1600 and post-1600 Shakespeare when a definite distinction emerged; dividing core canon dramatic verse into blocks of 3,000, 1,500 and even 750 words; and establishing profiles for

Shakespeare's undisputed *poetic* corpus: *Venus and Adonis, The Rape of Lucrece* and the Sonnets. Fourteen 3,000-word blocks from all Shakespeare's poems were used for comparison with eighty-seven 3,000-word blocks of verse by some thirty-five other poets. Fourteen tests proved efficacious when applied to 3,000 word blocks from poems. Only two blocks out of the fourteen taken from Shakespeare's poems yielded so much as a single rejection. All but three of the eighty-seven blocks by other poets yielded more rejections, with Bacon's yielding seven, De Vere's six, and two blocks from Marlowe's *Hero and Leander* three and four.

In establishing profiles for Shakespeare's poems, Elliott and Valenza also took account of tests on eighty-two 3,000-word blocks of verse from a sample of fourteen plays covering the full generic and chronological range. And for particular metrical features they took the added precaution of employing 1,500-word verse blocks to compare with De Vere's iambic pentameter verse, which constituted a little less than half of his 3,042-word corpus. For De Vere they were able to apply a further test, using hand-counts – the rate of use of relative clauses – for which De Vere's figure fell outside the range for Shakespeare's poems. Elliott and Valenza discuss in detail the limitations of each of the tests flunked by De Vere. Despite any individual imperfections, in bulk they decisively distinguish De Vere's poetry from Shakespeare's – and from Bacon's and Marlowe's.

An especially potent test was a mathematically sophisticated one derived from signal testing and called 'modal distance', which, put simply, measures the extent to which authors use, or avoid using, certain words together.[21] Elliott and Valenza's analysis relied on fifty-two of the fairly common, but not most common, words of Shakespeare's poetry and, while unreliable across genres, proved highly effective on poem–poem comparisons. An early report of modal analysis of 500-word blocks, ninety by Shakespeare and 1,303 by twenty-six contemporary poets, demonstrated 'high internal consistency among Shakespeare's poems, and notably sharp discrimination between Shakespeare's poems and the poems of others'.[22] Marlowe, and especially De Vere and Bacon, emerged as among the most remote from Shakespeare. In their 2004 article Elliott and Valenza cited a Shakespearian modal range for 3,000-word blocks of 281–1,149 and a score of 2,892 for De Vere, almost eight standard deviations removed from Shakespeare's mean and six beyond his maximum.[23] 'By this test, the two authors were on different planets.'[24] Stylometrics thus objectively confirm what must be obvious to any reader sensitive to poetic style and value.

The Claremont methodology and battery of tests are not immune from some criticism.[25] But the Clinic's findings, with regard to matters unrelated to the so-called 'authorship problem' of anti-Shakespearianism, are almost entirely in accord with orthodox scholarly opinion: that *Henry VI Part One*, *Titus Andronicus*, *Timon of Athens*, *Pericles*, *All Is True* and *The Two Noble Kinsmen* were co-authored, not by Shakespeare alone; that doubts whether *The True Tragedy of Richard Duke of York* (*Henry VI Part Three*) is solely Shakespeare's are also justified; that attempts to ascribe *A Funeral Elegy* and *Edmond Ironside* to Shakespeare were misguided; and that Shakespeare *may* have contributed to the anonymous *Edward III* and *Arden of Faversham*.[26] Elliott and Valenza are wrong, in my view, in thinking that the three pages penned by 'Hand D' of the manuscript play *Sir Thomas More* are not Shakespeare's, though right in finding that it yields fewer rejections as a post-1600 than as a pre-1600 composition. They also strike me as wrong in rejecting from the canon the 329-line poem *A Lover's Complaint*, published as Shakespeare's in the Quarto of *Shakespeare's Sonnets* (1609). But scholars remain divided on these last two problems and the unique textual origins of editions of Hand D could have been responsible for its failure on at least one Claremont test.

To explain the disparity between Shakespeare and De Vere, some Oxfordians have claimed that several of De Vere's poems are really songs, perhaps from his lost dramatic works, but none is known to have been set to music and none bears the least resemblance to such Shakespearian songs as 'Who is Silvia?' in *The Two Gentlemen of Verona* (4.2.38–52), 'O mistress mine' in *Twelfth Night* (2.3.39–51) or 'Full fathom five' in *The Tempest* (1.2.399–407). Another desperate Oxfordian resort is to downgrade De Vere's extant poems as juvenilia, some composed when he was as young as fifteen. Since De Vere was born in 1550, this tactic has the damaging effect of opening up a huge gap in the surviving record of De Vere's artistic productivity: a handful of youthful poems in a prosaic mid-Tudor style is followed by two decades of silence before the dazzling narrative poet of *Venus and Adonis* (1593) and playwright of *The Two Gentlemen of Verona* and *The Taming of the Shrew* (both 1590–1) bursts onto the scene, when De Vere is in his forties, and creates the whole Shakespearian œuvre within a dozen or so years. Postulating lost and unattributed works that might bridge the chasm merely compounds the improbabilities.

An alternative kind of computational stylistics, undertaken by a team led by Hugh Craig and Arthur Kinney, addresses only problems recognized by orthodox Shakespeare scholars, but does have implications for anti-Shakespearian theories and especially for that identifying Marlowe as 'the man who was Shakespeare'. The team's methods are explained and results displayed in *Shakespeare, Computers, and the Mystery of Authorship*.[27] Craig and Kinney employed an electronic database of some 109 early modern play-texts of single, undisputed, non-Shakespearian authorship and of twenty-seven core plays accepted as by Shakespeare alone.[28] All were standardized in modern spelling. It has long been recognized that various aspects of a writer's style may be reflected in his or her rates of use of high-frequency words, such as 'the', 'of', 'by' and 'that'. These 'function words' form the framework around which sentences – with their nouns, verbs, adjectives and adverbs – are constructed. They form one of two sorts of data that Craig and Kinney investigated. The other consisted of lexical words – such as 'gentle', 'answer', 'brave' and 'hopes' – that are used much more, or much less, often by one particular dramatist than by others. Their methods of attribution were validated on plays and sections of plays whose authors are known: before they applied them to doubtful texts, Craig and Kinney regularly assessed the degree to which their statistical computations correctly credited texts to the playwrights agreed to have written them.

The tests seldom yield perfect separation between authors, but they classify texts of known authorship correctly in the vast majority of cases. The evidence is particularly compelling when, as is usually the case, the two independent modes of testing – through function words and through lexical words – clearly point to the same conclusions. Like Elliott and Valenza, Craig and Kinney confirm current orthodox views about Shakespeare's collaborations and anonymous plays that have been attributed to him. They disagree with Elliott and Valenza's Claremont Clinic only in endorsing Shakespeare's authorship of Hand D's pages and, much more cautiously, *A Lover's Complaint*.[29] They are less doubtful than the Clinic about *Arden of Faversham* and *Edward III*. Their research has both general and specific relevance to anti-Shakespearian claims. They demonstrate that 2,000-word segments of the whole Shakespeare core canon have certain kinds of consistency that enable almost all to be differentiated from almost all 2,000 segments by other playwrights, including playwrights whom some Baconians and Oxfordians have wished to enlist under Bacon's or Oxford's banner. More particularly, they firmly distinguish between Shakespeare and Marlowe, while suggesting that Marlowe – who was Shakespeare's exact contemporary – may have contributed to the *Henry VI* plays, whose solely Shakespearian authorship has long been doubted. Stylistically, Shakespeare and Marlowe are again shown to be different men.

The critical and computational analysis of style gives no support whatsoever to the notion that anybody but William Shakespeare of Stratford was the author, or in some cases co-author, of the works printed in modern editions under his name.

CHAPTER 10

What does textual evidence reveal about the author?

James Mardock and Eric Rasmussen

A careful consideration of Shakespeare's dramatic texts reveals that their author was a professional man of the theatre who always wrote with a nuanced understanding of the specific requirements and limitations of his acting company. Many readers of Shakespeare may never have noticed that his plays are exquisitely structured to enable the practice of doubling – having individual actors portray more than one character. By this means, Shakespeare could write plays with as many as seventy speaking parts for a company that generally had no more than a dozen or so actors.

In order to facilitate this doubling of roles, Shakespeare constructed his plays with a meticulous oscillation of parts. In *Hamlet*, for instance, the thirty-one speaking roles could be performed by eleven actors (eight men and three boys), because characters such as Laertes and Guildenstern or the Ghost and Claudius never appear onstage together. Thus, one actor could begin the play as Laertes (who figures in 1.2 and 1.3) and then change costume to re-enter as Guildenstern in Acts 2 and 3 (in which Laertes does not appear). Guildenstern's role continues through the first three scenes of Act 4, after which Laertes returns at line 109.1 of 4.5 (the first hundred lines of dialogue would presumably have provided time for a costume change). Similarly, a single actor could play both the Ghost of Hamlet's father and Claudius: the Ghost appears in 1.1; Claudius in 1.2; the Ghost in 1.4; Claudius in 2.2–3.3. The Ghost reappears at line 93.1 in 3.4, then exits at 127.1; during the subsequent seventy lines of dialogue between Hamlet and Gertrude, the actor could change his costume in preparation for his entrance as Claudius at the opening of 4.1.

This example from *Hamlet* illustrates the care that Shakespeare took in balancing sets of characters and building in the time necessary for costume changes. Consider the 'closet scene' in the Q2 and F versions of the play, where the Ghost/Claudius doubling possibility may account for the decidedly drawn-out leave that Hamlet takes before lugging the guts of Polonius into the neighbouring room. After the Ghost's exit, Hamlet bids his mother 'good night' fully four times, with at least that many separate admonitions to repent. To be sure, each iteration adds much excellent verse but little new information, with the result that the end of the scene feels extravagantly padded. If we imagine that one reason for the drawing out is to give the actor of the Ghost time to shift from his presumably quite complicated armour costume into the similarly complicated finery of the King of Denmark, then the length of the scene has technical as well as thematic justification.

The need for the Ghost/Claudius costume change may also help explain the curiously domestic stage direction in the First Quarto of *Hamlet* (1603) which specifies that the Ghost enters '*in his night gowne*'. In the longer Q2 and F texts of the play, seventy lines separate the Ghost's exit from Claudius's entrance. In the Q1 text, this interval is reduced to twenty-one lines. Since the shorter scene fails to give the actor sufficient time to change from armour to royal regalia, the Ghost's costume is simplified: the actor dons a nightgown over his kingly robes before entering in 3.4, and removes it before resuming the role of Claudius in 4.1.

The stratagems required to balance characters and create time for costume changes in a play with a large number of doubled roles could be extraordinarily complex. Indeed, the editors of the Arden Shakespeare edition of *King Henry VI Part Three*, John Cox and Eric Rasmussen, were long puzzled by that play's elaborate design. In the end, they determined that its sixty-seven roles could be played by twenty-one actors, because individual actors could play as many as ten roles – not merely the two that the term 'doubling' implies. For example, one actor could play Norfolk, John Mortimer, Soldier, Dead Father, Bourbon, Second Watchman, Stanley, Lieutenant, Alderman and the Mayor of Coventry!

Every one of Shakespeare's plays is structured to facilitate doubling.[1] Clearly, only a professional man of the theatre who recognized the limitations imposed by the available resources of his company (e.g., a certain number of adult and boy actors) would have understood the necessity of a doubling structure. A dilettante writer of plays might have included King Lear's Fool in the opening court scene of that tragedy, not realizing that the Fool had to be absent because the actor was needed to double as Cordelia; so too, a writer outside of the theatrical orbit might have included Paris at Capulet's ball in *Romeo and Juliet*, not realizing that the actor was needed to double as Mercutio. But Shakespeare deployed his characters with full knowledge of the exigencies associated with his company of players.

Moreover, only someone with an intimate knowledge of such details as the amount of time required for a costume change could have devised the structures of the plays with such aplomb. Rasmussen has pointed out elsewhere that in the extant playbook of *Sir Thomas More*, Shakespeare rescued a script with doubling problems by contributing a speech of twenty-one lines – which was transcribed onto a slip of paper and pasted into the manuscript – in order to provide time for the actor playing the Second Officer in scene 7 to transform himself into More's servant Randall in scene 8 (a doubling first identified by Scott McMillin).[2] Such a costume change would have had to be fairly rapid, but we must not underestimate the dexterity of actors. Although David Bradley claimed that 'even in late Morality Plays an actor very rarely if ever changes identity in under twenty-seven lines of dialogue', David Bevington located thirty-eight instances in Tudor popular drama of changes covered by twenty-five lines or fewer.[3] Given the doubling possibilities in the revised version of *Sir Thomas More*, a company of eighteen actors (thirteen men and five boys) could perform the play's fifty-four roles.

It is worth noting that Shakespeare's handwriting in the manuscript additions he supplied while serving as a play-doctor to *Sir Thomas More* provides solid links between this man of the theatre and the printed texts of his plays. For instance, one idiosyncrasy of Shakespeare's hand is that he closed up his manuscript 'u' at the top. As a result, it could easily be mistaken for an 'a' – and there are many *a/u* misprints in play texts set from Shakespeare's manuscripts, such as Q2 *Hamlet* where the Queen is called 'Gertrad', 'sallied' is printed for 'sullied' and 'deule' (Shakespeare's characteristic spelling of 'devil') is misprinted as 'deale'.

Shakespeare knew not only how long his fellow players would take to change from a particular costume to another, but also how long it would take to execute a technical effect, given the (often creaking) technology of the working theatre. In the scene of Posthumus's dream vision in *Cymbeline* (5.5.186.1–2), we find the extraordinary stage direction '*Jupiter descends in thunder and lightning, sitting upon an eagle. He throws a thunderbolt.*' Since Shakespeare knew that the eagle's subsequent retraction from the stage would not be instantaneous, he wrote a covering speech for Sicilius – a nine-line, present-tense description that invites the audience to see this special effect in poetic terms:

> his ascension is
> More sweet then our blest fields. His royal bird
> Preens the immortal wing and claws his beak
> As when his God is pleased.   (5.5.210–13)

Similarly, Jupiter's necessarily laborious exit through a trap door is transfigured by Sicilius's speech into a moment of wonder: 'the marble pavement closes, he is entered / His radiant roof' (5.5.214–15).

Other textual traces reveal Shakespeare's intimate working relationship with his acting company. It appears that in the late 1590s, there were two boy actors in the Lord Chamberlain's Men who performed the female roles in Shakespeare's love comedies. Although we don't know their names, we can deduce that one was tall and fair, and the other short and dark, since Shakespeare during this period wrote parts for several pairs of female friends (Helena and Hermia in *A Midsummer Night's Dream*, Rosalind and Celia in *As You Like It* and Beatrice and Hero in *Much Ado About Nothing*) and, in each instance, one is tall and fair and the other short and dark.

Certain aspects of Shakespeare's early printed texts reveal the author's revising mind at work, and these too can give us clues to his familiarity not only with theatrical practice generally, but with the particular resources of the Lord Chamberlain's Men. Take, for example, Leonato's wife, Innogen, the famous 'ghost character' (appearing in stage directions but speaking no lines) in *Much Ado About Nothing*. The opening stage directions in both the 1600 quarto and 1623 folio versions of the play call for the entrance of '*Leonato Gouernour of Messina, Innogen his wife, Hero his daughter, and Beatrice his Neece*', and the opening stage direction of Act 2 again mentions her presence. Yet Innogen is never addressed and never speaks, and she disappears even from the stage directions after the beginning of Act 2. Her excision from the play is evidently the result of Shakespeare's second thoughts, and critics usually explain her status as a textual ghost in terms of literary craft: Shakespeare cut the mother figure who appeared in the play's source material in order to enhance Hero's dependency on Beatrice, and also to make her slander by her fiancé and abandonment to death by her own father more logical. An Innogen fully aware of her daughter's predicament but remaining silent would be difficult to stomach; as E. K. Chambers put it, '[a] lady, whose daughter is successively betrothed, defamed, repudiated before the altar, taken for dead, and restored to life, ought not to be a mute. It is not motherly.'[4]

We would suggest that the excision of Innogen happened for more mundane and practical reasons: that is, Shakespeare as he wrote the play continued to plan for Innogen until it became clear that his company could not provide an actor to play her. Innogen is included in the text of *Much Ado* only until the play requires Ursula and Margaret (both introduced in 2.1), two female parts for boy actors who could obviously not double with Hero and Beatrice, since all four appear together. Other plays written around the period of *Much Ado*'s composition require two, or at most four, female characters to share the stage at one time, because of the scarcity of qualified boys in the company – *As You Like It*, for example, could handle a Rosalind, a Celia, a Phoebe and an Audrey, but no more. Shakespeare continued planning for Innogen only until he reached the shallow end of his casting pool, a clear indication that he wrote with a specific company in mind.

We can take this point further by noting that Shakespeare often seems to have had specific *members* of his company in mind. In a scene in the first quarto of *Much Ado About Nothing*, the speech-prefixes use the names of the comic actors Will Kemp and Richard Cowley, for whom Shakespeare apparently wrote the parts of Dogberry and Verges. Kemp's name also appears in the 1599 quarto of *Romeo and Juliet*, where Peter's entrance is indicated by the direction, '*Enter Will Kemp*'. Similarly, the name of the actor John Sinklo appears in several printed plays, including *Henry VI Part Three*, *Henry IV Part Two* and *The Taming of the Shrew*.

An authorship conspiracy theorist might object that anyone with enough interest in London's theatre business to try to pass off his work as Shakespeare's would have been sufficiently familiar with a celebrity player like Kemp (or even, less likely, a Sinklo or a Cowley) to substitute the player's name for the character's when writing a scene. After all, even the authors of *The Second Part of the Return From Parnassus* (*c.* 1602), an academic satire penned by the students of St John's College, Cambridge, knew enough about the Lord Chamberlain's Men to include two of them, Will Kemp and Richard Burbage, as characters *in propria persona*. However, other clues from Shakespeare's plays indicate not merely that they were composed by someone familiar with the names of the primary members of the company he wrote for, but that their author was a player himself, and a fellow of that company.

For example, the best dating evidence for the plays and poems suggests that there was an increase in Shakespeare's output during periods when the playhouses were closed due to the plague. This is exactly what we would expect if the author were a player: he would have more time on his hands when there were no performances. The particularly violent plague visitation of 1592–4, during which the playhouses were closed for twenty-three months, saw the composition of seven Shakespeare plays – *Henry VI Part One*, *Richard III*, *The Comedy of Errors*, *Love's Labour's Lost*, *Romeo and Juliet*, *A Midsummer Night's Dream* and likely *Richard II* – as well as the erotic epyllions *Venus and Adonis* and *The Rape of Lucrece*, the printing of which Shakespeare seems to have carefully supervised. During the lengthy playhouse closures of 1603–4, Shakespeare produced *Measure for Measure*, *All's Well that Ends Well*, *Othello*, *Timon of Athens*, the first draft of *King Lear* and possibly *A Lover's Complaint*. By contrast, during the relatively plague-free years of 1600–2, he seems to have written only three plays, *Hamlet*, *Twelfth Night* and perhaps *Troilus and Cressida*.

This pattern of increased writing activity during times when theatres were closed suggests that Shakespeare's plays were authored by a man whose primary income came from his role as a sharer in a company, receiving a portion of what we would today call box office receipts. When the theatres were closed, the player-sharer had to live by his writing alone. In contrast, no pattern of heightened productivity during playhouse closures appears in the career of the jobbing playwright and pamphleteer Thomas Dekker, who wrote plays for more than one company and never acted or held a share in one. The same is true of Thomas Middleton, whose income was substantially augmented by repeated and reliable commissions by the city to write civic pageants like the annual Lord Mayor's Show.

A player-sharer who also wrote was an uncommon thing, but one of Shakespeare's colleagues in the King's Men shared that status, and his literary output increased when he was not able to act and his regular income was in jeopardy. Robert Armin, the principal comic actor in Shakespeare's company after the departure of Will Kemp in 1600, created the roles of Touchstone, Feste, Lavatch and other 'allowed fools' like King Lear's – musically talented professionals in motley as opposed to the bumbling, malaprop-prone 'naturals' originated by Kemp. But Armin, though nowhere near as prolific as Shakespeare, was a published poet and playwright as well, writing a collection of anecdotes about fools, *Fool upon Fool, or, Six Sorts of Sots* in 1604 during one extended closure of the theatres, and issuing an expanded version, *A Nest of Ninnies*, in 1608, at the outset of the longest closure to occur during James I's reign. That period also saw the publication of Armin's romance *The Italian Tailor and His Boy*, his comedy *The Two Maids of Mortlake* (both 1609) and a collection of humorous dialogues called *Quips upon Questions* (1608). Armin's example lends support to the traditional picture of the author of Shakespeare's plays as a theatre man.

Armin and his predecessor, Will Kemp, are relevant to our discussion for another reason as well. The comedies written before Kemp's departure feature clowns like Dogberry and Bottom, who dominate the scenes in which they appear and whose plots are only loosely integrated into the main plots, allowing a talented improviser like Kemp to ad lib his own jokes. Thus, when multiple texts of 'Kemp plays' survive, one finds additional lines in the comic scenes that have the look of actorly interpolations. It has been suggested that Hamlet's complaints about clowns' antics, written shortly after Kemp's departure, can be read as Shakespeare's own opinions of his company's former clown:

let those that play your clowns speak no more than is set down for them; for there be of them that will themselves laugh to set on some quantity of barren spectators to laugh too, though in the meantime some necessary question of the play be then to be considered. That's villainous and shows a most pitiful ambition in the fool that uses it. (3.2.38–45)

This sounds like the complaint of a playwright who knew Kemp's habits and had grown tired of writing around his improvisational skills. By comparison, comedies written to feature Armin play to the new clown's talent for singing, and his roles are more tightly woven into the plays' fabric, making improvisation less possible or desirable.

An alternate candidate for Shakespearian authorship would be less likely to have backstage familiarity with a player's habits and talents, though such knowledge would not be impossible to acquire. And such a candidate would have no reason to comment at length on the state of the London theatre business in 1601, as the author of *Hamlet* does. When Rosencrantz and Guildenstern introduce the players that they have 'coted . . . on the way' to Elsinore (2.2.319), there follows a lengthy conversation between them and the prince regarding the playing company's identity and circumstances. The players have fallen on hard times; like a permanent London company during a plague closure, they have been forced to travel, but only because of what Rosencrantz calls 'the late innovation' (2.2.334): 'there is, sir, an eyrie of children, little eyases, that cry out on the top of question, and are most tyrannically clapped for't. These are now the fashion' (2.2.340–2).

This exchange is a direct allusion to London's theatres at the time of the play's writing. The 'tragedians of the city' are a thinly veiled London playing company; no 'city' is elsewhere mentioned in the environs of Elsinore, and companies did not have permanent homes elsewhere in Europe. Even in London, permanent playhouses attached to playing companies were something of an innovation; before 1576 a travelling company would have been the rule, not the exception. Hamlet's players are an adult company – their 'young lady and mistress' (2.2.428) being a boy in drag whose voice Hamlet hopes is not yet broken – forced onto the road by the fickle tastes of playhouse audiences. The 'little eyases' whose ascendance Rosencrantz laments are boy companies like the Children of Paul's and the Children of the Chapel, both of which had been licensed in 1600 to play in public theatres, taking revenue from adult companies like Shakespeare's Lord Chamberlain's Men.

This *Hamlet* passage constitutes Shakespeare's oblique incursion into the so-called 'War of the Theatres', a vitriolic public exchange started by John Marston, who satirized Ben Jonson in *Histriomastix* (1599) and *Jack Drum's Entertainment* (1600), two plays performed by the newly fashionable Children of Paul's. Jonson responded with *Every Man Out of His Humour* (1600), a Lord Chamberlain's Men play that satirized Marston's prolix style. As Rosencrantz says, there had been, at the time of *Hamlet's* writing, 'much to-do on both sides. . . . the poet and player went to cuffs in the question' (2.2.353, 356–7). The War of the Theatres, however, was a short-lived phenomenon that played itself out by 1602, and the *Hamlet* exchange, bewildering to today's audiences without extensive footnotes, is invariably shortened or cut from modern performances; indeed, the reference only appears in one of the original printed texts of *Hamlet*, the Folio of 1623, which is generally thought to reflect the script of a version of the play performed while the 'War of the Theatres' was still current. In the quarto version printed in 1604, when the controversy had played itself out (the Second Quarto, or Q2), the exchange takes only ten lines, not the Folio's thirty-six, and Rosencrantz's reference to the boys' companies is completely absent. The second quarto is thought to have been printed from an early authorial draft, so this discrepancy between the texts means either that the stale allusion to the competing playing companies was removed when Q2 was printed or, more likely, that its appearance in the Folio text represents the temporary insertion of material topical at the time of that version's performance. In either case, while it is not impossible that the Earl of Oxford, or another amateur candidate for Shakespearian authorship, might have noticed and alluded to the 'War', a playwright without a personal stake in the business of London playhouses would have no reason to include such a specific, instantly dated passage in *Hamlet*.

Perhaps the best evidence from the plays that Shakespeare wrote for a working theatre whose practices he knew intimately – in a way that an amateur would not – comes from his use of actors' parts. Tiffany Stern's excellent work on early modern rehearsal practices has led to a deeper understanding of the ways that players learned and prepared their roles, an understanding that culminates in a book she wrote with Simon Palfrey, *Shakespeare in Parts* (2007). Like all early modern players, members of the Lord Chamberlain's and King's Men received only a scroll containing their characters' speeches, each preceded by two or three words as cues. They did not receive the full script from which modern actors work. These actors' 'parts' would be memorized in private, and the full play – an invaluable document with only one reference copy in use in a playhouse – would only reassemble in performance.

'[T]he part', Palfrey and Stern write, 'was the first (and perhaps only) unit of text designed by Shakespeare to be examined, thought about, learned, and "interpreted".'[5] Moreover, they argue, Shakespeare experimented with the limited and subjective understanding of a play that the practice of learning parts produced. According to their analysis, Shakespeare consistently manipulated the players by including 'repeated' or 'premature' cues within long speeches. An actor hearing his cue-phrase spoken not at the end, but in the middle of a preceding speech, would interrupt the other actor, provoking a 'battle for the cue-space' in which each player struggled to maintain control of the play text as he understood it. Without a thorough understanding of the details of playhouse practice, no dramatist could have produced the part-based characterization effects apparent in these plays.

That Shakespeare conceived of his texts as parts is clear from the evidence we have of revised versions of texts. As James J. Marino's recent work has ably demonstrated, when multiple versions of a play exist, changed speeches are most often cut or expanded in the middle, leaving cue-lines intact and thus requiring a change to one scroll only.[6] A change to a character's name might involve similarly limited revision. In the shorter first quarto of *Hamlet*, for reasons much discussed but still unknown, the character of Polonius is called 'Corambis'.[7] Effecting the change to 'Polonius' required only a minimal amount of scribal work: throughout the play, only the king refers to the counsellor by name; all of the other characters refer to him as 'old man' or 'father'. The change of a name in a *Hamlet* script already rendered into parts and distributed to actors would entail revision only to Claudius's part, saving the company valuable time and paper.[8] The additional fact that only Claudius speaks Gertrude's name in any version of the text bears out Marino's argument: Shakespeare seems to have reserved the right to rename the Queen as well.

The plays' characters themselves explicitly demonstrate their author's knowledge of the practices that Palfrey and Stern have described. Viola's protest in *Twelfth Night, or What You Will* that she cannot answer Olivia's demands alludes to the player's method of 'conning' his role: 'I can say little more than I have studied, and that question's out of my part' (1.5.171–2). And most famously, in the rude mechanicals' parody of playhouse practice in *A Midsummer Night's Dream*, Flute fails to understand the convention of waiting for his cues, and drives through all of his speeches in the order they appear on his scroll; he 'speak[s] all [his] part at once, cues and all' (3.1.93–5). Authors of closet drama do not allude to the backstage craft of the public playhouse in this way, and neither would an amateur, aristocratic playwright hiding his authorship behind the false front of an illiterate player, as Oxford is imagined by his supporters to have done. The plays of Shakespeare were indisputably created by a working theatre professional.

CHAPTER 11

Shakespeare and Warwickshire

David Kathman

Ever since some people began openly to question William Shakespeare's authorship in the mid-nineteenth century, attacks on Stratford-upon-Avon have been a common anti-Shakespearian theme. For example, Ignatius Donnelly wrote in his 1888 pro-Baconian book *The Great Cryptogram* that 'the lives of the people [of Stratford] were coarse, barren, and filthy', and that 'the people of Stratford were densely ignorant'.[1] J. Thomas Looney similarly wrote in his Oxfordian tome *'Shakespeare' Identified* (1920) that 'dirt and ignorance . . . were outstanding features of the social life of Stratford in those days and had stamped themselves very definitely upon the family life under which William Shakspere was reared'.[2] More recent anti-Shakespearians are usually not quite so blunt, but they typically present a bleak picture of sixteenth-century Stratford, and lament an alleged lack of correspondence between 'the mundane, wholly uninspiring record of the Stratford man's life' (as the Oxfordian Charlton Ogburn Jr. put it) and the great works of Shakespeare.[3]

As with so much else that anti-Shakespearians write, such claims are based on distortions and ignorance of historical context. It's true that a time-travelling visitor from the twenty-first century would probably not find sixteenth-century Stratford to be very clean or progressive, but in the context of English society at that time, it was a prosperous market town with a fairly educated populace. Despite the picture painted by anti-Shakespearians, books were relatively common in Stratford, and middle-class people such as Shakespeare were typically literate in both English and Latin. William Shakespeare's friends in and around Stratford were a rather cultured bunch with numerous literary ties, not the ignorant dolts one might expect from reading anti-Shakespearians. Shakespeare's works are peppered with signs that the author came from the area around Stratford, which was famous from the 1620s onward as the home of the poet and playwright William Shakespeare.

SIXTEENTH-CENTURY STRATFORD-UPON-AVON

Stratford-upon-Avon already had a long history by the time William
Shakespeare was baptized there on 26 April 1564. There were settlements
in the area at least from Roman times, and Stratford was a manor of the
Bishop of Worcester from the seventh century AD, but the town itself
properly dates from 1196, when the bishop granted it borough status. In the
following centuries, Stratford thrived as a market town and produced some
notable citizens, including John Stratford, who in the fourteenth century
became Archbishop of Canterbury and chancellor of England. John's
brother Robert and nephew Ralph also became bishops (of Chichester and
London respectively), and Robert Stratford succeeded John as chancellor
under Edward III. The wealthy Guild of the Holy Cross was a very important force in medieval Stratford, building the guildhall and guild chapel
that still exist today, and founding and maintaining a school in the town by
the late thirteenth century. This school was one of the first in England to be
founded by a religious guild, and an endowment in 1482 by Thomas Joliffe,
a wealthy local priest, made it free to the children of Stratford townsmen.[4]

The two decades before Shakespeare's birth had seen major changes in
Stratford, part of the disruption wrought by the English Reformation. In
1547 the Guild of the Holy Cross was dissolved along with similar religious
guilds across England, and two years later the Bishop of Worcester was
forced to give up his ownership of the manor and borough of Stratford. In
1553, nine days before his death, King Edward VI granted Stratford a charter
of incorporation, under which the town has operated ever since (with
some modification). The charter provided for a government of fourteen
aldermen, led by a bailiff, and gave a royal imprimatur to the Stratford
school, now called the King Edward VI School. The new Corporation of
Stratford inherited most of the property that had belonged to the Guild of
the Holy Cross, and many of its responsibilities.

Stratford grew rapidly starting in the mid-sixteenth century, as England's
population increased following a long fallow period and many people
migrated to towns and cities from the countryside. William Shakespeare's
father John was part of this migration, arriving in Stratford-upon-Avon
by 1552, when he was fined for having an unauthorized dunghill in
Henley Street. Anti-Shakespearians have sometimes used this fine to
disparage John Shakespeare and depict the town as a filthy place, but
several prominent citizens were fined for the same offence at the same
time, including Adrian Quiney and Richard Symons, deputy steward of
the manor.[5] In the following decade, John Shakespeare became one of

the more prominent members of the governing class in Stratford, being named chamberlain in 1561, alderman in 1565 and bailiff in 1568, when William was four years old. In 1572, when he was deputy to bailiff Adrian Quiney, the two men were sent to London on borough business.

Accompanying this growth was a general improvement in education and literacy, so that William Shakespeare's generation was much more literate than his father's.[6] John Shakespeare's prominent position in Stratford would have entitled his children to free admittance at the King Edward VI School, which was an excellent one, to judge by the evidence. The schoolmasters in the 1560s and 1570s were experienced Oxford graduates, including John Brownswerd, whose published Latin verses were later praised by Francis Meres in *Palladis Tamia* (1598) on the same page as William Shakespeare. Brownswerd was brought to Stratford by his former teacher John Bretchgirdle, the vicar who had presumably baptized Shakespeare. When Bretchgirdle died in 1565, his will listed twenty-five books by name, including two bequeathed to Brownswerd, one 'to the comon vse of the scolars of the free scole of stretford vpon Avon', and eight others to the sons of Stratford alderman William Smith.[7] Such bequests illustrate that Stratford-upon-Avon was very far from being the allegedly bookless neighbourhood often depicted by anti-Shakespearians. When John Marshall, curate of the chapel at Bishopton (in the north-east quarter of Stratford) died in 1607, his will bequeathed several specific books, and an inventory of his goods lists 171 books, mostly Latin and Greek but also including some in Hebrew and English.[8] No specific surviving books can be traced to William Shakespeare, but his friend Richard Quiney and son-in-law John Hall are both known to have had studies of books, the latter's presumably inherited from Shakespeare when the bulk of his estate passed to his daughter, Susanna, Hall's wife. A memorandum from a 1596 lawsuit over the sale of some disputed property in Stratford notes that the property included 'one boke' bought by 'Mr. Shaxpere', who must have been either William or his father John.[9]

The second half of the sixteenth century was also a period when travelling players became increasingly popular across England, and Stratford was a regular stopping place for such players. The very first record of travelling actors in Stratford is from 1568–9, the year when John Shakespeare was bailiff, and it is not too hard to imagine four-year-old William sitting on his father's lap and watching the performances that the players were required to give before the town authorities. Other playing companies to visit Stratford included James Burbage and Leicester's Men in 1573 and 1577, and seventeen-year-old Edward Alleyn and Worcester's

Men in 1583–4, when William Shakespeare was a newly married father. The peak year for travelling players in Stratford was 1587, when five companies visited the town, including the Queen's Men with their famous clown, Richard Tarlton. One of the leading Queen's Men, William Knell, was killed by his fellow actor John Towne at Thame, Oxfordshire, in June 1587, and some Shakespeare biographers have speculated that young Will might have joined the short-handed company when they visited Stratford soon after.[10] Whether or not such speculation has any validity, William Shakespeare was regularly exposed to top-flight professional players when he was growing up in Stratford.

SHAKESPEARE'S WARWICKSHIRE FRIENDS

In addition to denigrating Stratford-upon-Avon, anti-Shakespearians typically attack William Shakespeare himself, often depicting him as a barely literate 'grain merchant' with no known intellectual interests. As with so many anti-Shakespearian claims, such character assassination has very little to do with historical reality. By the normal standards of literary historians, there is plenty of evidence for Shakespeare's friendship with such literary figures as Ben Jonson, but anti-Shakespearians refuse to accept this evidence, insisting that it refers to the author 'Shakespeare' and not to William Shakespeare of Stratford. However, even if we restrict ourselves to Shakespeare's known friends from Stratford and the surrounding area, we find them to be primarily cultured, educated men with connections to the nobility and court, in sharp contrast to the picture painted by anti-Shakespearians.

First, consider Richard Quiney, author of the only surviving letter to William Shakespeare. Quiney was eleven years older than Shakespeare but very similar in social status, according to all the evidence we have.[11] The fathers of the two men were friends and neighbours for nearly fifty years; as Edgar Fripp puts it in his biography of Richard Quiney, John Shakespeare and Adrian Quiney 'had much in common, and they climbed together, Quyny leading, the ladder of municipal promotion, from Taster to Constable, and thence to Principal Burgess, Chamberlain, Alderman, Bailiff and Capital or Head Alderman'.[12] As we saw earlier, the two men travelled to London on Stratford business in early 1572, when Adrian Quiney was bailiff and John Shakespeare was high alderman. Adrian Quiney was a mercer (a dealer in fine fabrics) and John Shakespeare was a glover, though they both had additional sources of income. Richard Quiney was also a mercer by trade, and though he was fairly well off, he did not own land, as Shakespeare did. Quiney's famous letter to Shakespeare is addressed 'to my loving good friend and countryman, Master William Shakespeare'. Quiney's son Thomas eventually married Shakespeare's daughter Judith, and they named their first son, born in 1617, 'Shakespeare'. The Quineys and the Shakespeares were close, in both friendship and social status, over a span of three generations.

The correspondence of Richard Quiney was preserved in the town archives by a fluke when Quiney died in office as bailiff, and it provides an interesting snapshot of the life of one of Shakespeare's closest Stratford friends. This correspondence contains Quiney's famous letter to Shakespeare, in which he mentions that he is going to Court on business and may not be back that night. It also includes: a letter in Latin from Quiney's eleven-year-old son Richard, in which the younger Quiney adapts a quotation from Cicero's 'Epistolae ad Familiares';[13] several letters from fellow townsman Abraham Sturley to Quiney, some entirely or partially in Latin, in which Sturley quotes Erasmus's *Adagia* and Terence's *Eunuchus* and alludes to Quiney's study of books;[14] a letter in which Quiney's wife advises him to read Tully's *Epistles*;[15] a letter from a representative of Sir Fulke Greville (father of the courtier and poet), sending Greville's 'love' and inviting Quiney and his friends to spend Christmas with Greville at Beauchamp's Court;[16] a letter from Quiney to an unidentified Privy Councillor;[17] and lots of other interesting material. It is only by the purest luck that this cache of letters managed to survive to the present day, but it presents a picture of a man who, despite having no documented education (just like his 'loving friend' William Shakespeare), seems to have been very well-read and to have been perfectly capable of interacting easily with the rich and powerful.

Next, consider Thomas Greene. He was also one of William Shakespeare's closest friends in Stratford, to judge by the surviving evidence.[18] He was living in Shakespeare's house, New Place, in 1609 and probably for some time before, and in his diary he refers affectionately to 'my cosen Shakespeare' numerous times around 1614.[19] Three of his children were born in Stratford, and he named two of them 'William' and 'Anne', most likely after Shakespeare and his wife. In 1595 Thomas Greene entered the Middle Temple (one of the four Inns of Court, the equivalent of law schools), with his sureties being John Marston junior and senior, the future playwright and his father. In 1601 he accompanied Richard Quiney to London on Stratford business; they tried unsuccessfully to see the Attorney General, Sir Edward Coke, but Coke was preoccupied because the Essex rebellion had just happened. Greene was a close friend of the poet

Michael Drayton, a native of Warwickshire, and in 1603 he wrote a sonnet which appeared in Drayton's *The Barons' Wars*. In the same year he wrote a poem in honour of King James called *A Poets Vision and a Princes Glorie*, which was published by William Leake, who also held the rights to Shakespeare's *Venus and Adonis*. Drayton, in turn, later wrote an elegy for Sir Henry Rainsford, Greene's good friend and fellow Middle Templar whom he often mentions affectionately in the same diary where he mentions Shakespeare. Some of Greene's papers managed to survive at Stratford, and they include Latin verses and some English jottings about the nature of love.

Greene's literary endeavours (at least those that were published) were confined to the period 1602–03, when he was in London finishing up his formal studies at the Middle Temple. He was probably in the audience when Shakespeare's *Twelfth Night* was performed there on 2 February 1602. He was called to the Bar of the Middle Temple in October 1602 and in August 1603 he was appointed Steward of Stratford. He held this position for the next fourteen years, during which time he negotiated a new town charter, bought a lease of tithes (as Shakespeare had done in 1605) and was heavily involved in the enclosure controversy of 1614–19, during which he wrote the diary in which he mentions Shakespeare. In 1617 he resigned his post and sold his house for £240 and his tithes for £400. He became a Reader at the Middle Temple in 1621, Master of the Bench in 1623 and Treasurer in 1629. He died in Bristol in 1640. Here we have a close friend of William Shakespeare's who also happened to be a published poet, a friend of Michael Drayton and John Marston and an accomplished lawyer.

The final Shakespeare friend to consider is Thomas Russell.[20] He was one of two overseers of Shakespeare's will, an honour which implies a close friendship. Russell was born in 1570, six years after Shakespeare, to Sir Thomas Russell, a former Member of Parliament. The boy was brought up by his mother and her second husband, Sir Henry Berkeley, in very comfortable circumstances. He was educated at Queen's College, Oxford, and in 1590 he married Katherine Bampfield. After Katherine's death, Russell moved to Alderminster, about four miles south of Stratford, and sued a Stratford butcher, William Parry, for debt in 1596. In 1599 he began wooing Anne Digges, the widowed mother of Leonard Digges (author of a eulogy to Shakespeare published in the First Folio of 1623) and Dudley Digges (future knight and Member of Parliament). Anne Digges had a London house in Philips Lane, Aldermanbury, just around the corner from John Heminges and Henry Condell, and she also had an estate in Rushock, Worcestershire, a few miles from Heminges's birthplace of Droitwich. Russell and Anne Digges could not get married right away because of the onerous conditions of her husband's will, but in 1600 she and her children moved in anyway, to Russell's estate in Alderminster. In 1601 Russell tried to buy Clopton House, one of the largest houses in the Stratford area, four years after Shakespeare had bought New Place (the second largest house in Stratford), but in the end William Clopton refused to complete the sale. In 1603, Russell finally married Anne Digges officially, and they divided their time between Alderminster and Rushock until his death in 1634.

Russell had plenty of friends and relatives in high places. The half-brother with whom he was raised, Sir Maurice Berkeley, became a prominent Member of Parliament, as did Russell's stepson Sir Dudley Digges. One of his stepfather's good friends and neighbours was Sir John Harington, the courtier, godson of Queen Elizabeth and author of *The Metamorphosis of Ajax*. Another family friend was Tobie Matthew senior, Dean of Christchurch at Oxford and Archbishop of York. Thomas Russell was at Oxford with Matthew's son, Tobie Matthew junior, and the two men maintained a friendship for many years after. Tobie junior was one of Francis Bacon's closest friends (Bacon called him 'my alter ego' and asked for his advice in writing his *Essays*); he was also a friend of John Donne and a retainer of the Earl of Essex. Still another of Thomas Russell's friends was Endymion Porter, a courtier, patron of poets and favourite of Kings James and Charles I; the two men's families were close for years, and there survives a letter from Russell to Porter in which he offers to take in Porter's wife and children during a plague outbreak, promising to give them 'fatherlike care'. Russell himself was invited to be knighted at the coronation of King Charles I, but he refused the honour, preferring to pay a fine of £15 instead.

Quiney, Greene and Russell were just three of William Shakespeare's friends in Stratford, but they were representative of the type of people he associated with outside of London. The Combe family, with whom Shakespeare was friendly for many years, had lots of connections with the Inns of Court and other power centres in London, and Dr John Hall, Shakespeare's son-in-law and friend, was another well-educated man with lots of connections. These do not seem like the type of people with whom an ignorant, uncultured man would associate; they were conversant in Latin, at ease with both literary types and courtiers. Could it be that William Shakespeare too was a cultured man at ease with literary types and courtiers?

WARWICKSHIRE IN THE PLAYS

Many anti-Shakespearians, in addition to attacking the character of William Shakespeare and his hometown, claim that an alleged lack of correspondence between Shakespeare's life and the plays disqualifies him as the author. They question how somebody from a small town like Stratford could have written plays about kings and courtiers, many set in faraway lands such as Italy and having an allegedly aristocratic point of view. They go on to suggest that their favoured candidate (such as the Earl of Oxford, Francis Bacon or Christopher Marlowe) is a better biographical fit as the author. Such claims require a wholesale dismissal of all the documentary evidence showing that William Shakespeare of Stratford wrote the plays, but even apart from that, they are based on fundamental misunderstandings about how literary history is done, and ignore evidence suggesting that the plays were written by someone from Warwickshire.

Underlying these anti-Shakespearian arguments is the seductive but mistaken assumption that there is a straightforward, transparent relationship between an author's biography and his works. Most literary works, including those of Shakespeare, are undoubtedly influenced to some degree by their authors' life experiences, but that doesn't mean that it's possible to tell just from reading a literary work what the writer was like, or to treat such works as biographical puzzles to be solved. T. S. Eliot wrote that he was used to 'having my personal biography reconstructed from passages which I got out of books, or which I invented out of nothing because they sounded well; and to having my biography invariably ignored in what I *did* write from personal experience'.[21] If this was true of a well-documented twentieth-century figure such as Eliot, it is much more true of someone like Shakespeare, writing four hundred years ago in a society that was very different from ours in many ways.

Certainly, many people have perceived elements of William Shakespeare's biography in the Shakespeare plays and poems. For example, Constance's grief at Arthur's supposed death in Act 3, scene 4 of *King John* has often been seen as Shakespeare's reaction to the death of his son Hamnet in 1596; many people have seen Shakespeare's supposedly unhappy marriage to Anne Hathaway reflected in the contentious marriages found in many of the plays; and countless commentators have tried to identify a fair youth and a dark lady in the Sonnets, which are commonly assumed to reflect Shakespeare's personal experiences. Anti-Shakespearians typically disparage such biographical links to William Shakespeare of Stratford, claiming that their candidate's life 'fits' the plays much better, but this way of looking at things is fundamentally flawed. For the reasons noted above, biographical parallels are inherently suspect in the absence of independent evidence of the type that doesn't exist for Shakespeare's time (e.g. relevant letters or diaries). They can't bear the weight placed on them by many commentators, both traditional and anti-Shakespearian, and they certainly can't override external documentary evidence; all they can do is add speculative flavour to the picture that the documentary evidence presents.

While there is good reason to be sceptical of the rather heavy-handed, overly literal biographical parallels beloved by anti-Shakespearians, there are plenty of subtler signs in Shakespeare's plays and poems suggesting that the author was intimately familiar with Warwickshire. For one thing, those works are peppered with dialect words from Warwickshire and the West Midlands. These include 'unwappered' for unfatigued or fresh (*The Two Noble Kinsmen* 5.6.10); 'ballow' for cudgel (Folio *King Lear* TLN 2693); 'batlet' for a paddle used to beat laundry (*As You Like It* 2.4.46); 'gallow' for terrify (*The Tragedy of King Lear* 3.2.44); 'honey-stalks' for clover (*Titus Andronicus* 4.4.91); 'mobbled' for muffled (*Hamlet* 2.2.504); 'pash' for smash (*Troilus and Cressida* 2.3.201); 'potch' for poke or thrust (*Coriolanus* 1.11.15); and 'tarre' for provoke (*King John* 4.1.116; *Troilus and Cressida* 1.3.384; *Hamlet* 2.2.354).[22] The presence of such words doesn't prove anything, but it's entirely consistent with the authorship of Stratford native William Shakespeare.

In addition, the plays include numerous offhand references to people and places from the area around Stratford. For example, in Act 5, scene 3 of *Henry the Fourth Part Two*, Silence calls Falstaff 'Goodman Puff of Barson' (line 90), alluding either to Barston, a village fifteen miles northeast of Stratford, or to Barcheston (pronounced Barston), twelve miles southeast of Stratford. The induction to *The Taming of the Shrew* has several such allusions. Christopher Sly calls himself 'old Sly's son of Burton Heath' (Ind 2.17), referring to Barton-on-the-Heath, a village sixteen miles south of Stratford where Shakespeare's aunt Joan Lambert lived, and a few lines later refers to 'Marian Hacket, the fat alewife of Wincot' (line 20). Wincot is a village four miles from Stratford where a real Hacket family was living in 1591, though the name also suggests Wilmcote, the hometown of Shakespeare's mother Mary Arden. Christopher Sly also mentions 'Stephen Sly', the name of a real servant of William Combe of Welcombe (near Stratford) in 1615, though the surname was common enough for this to be a coincidence.[23] As with the dialect words, such references are not proof of anything, but they do suggest an author who was at home in the area around Stratford.

SHAKESPEARE AND STRATFORD AFTER 1616

William Shakespeare died in 1616 and was buried in Holy Trinity Church in Stratford-upon-Avon. While Stratford did not become a real tourist mecca until the late eighteenth century, it quickly became well known as the birthplace of the famous poet and playwright, William Shakespeare, contrary to the implications of many anti-Shakespearians. A wealth of evidence from the decades after Shakespeare's death illustrates Stratford's fame.

The first important piece of evidence (also discussed by Stanley Wells in Chapter 7 above) is William Basse's famous elegy, in which he calls Shakespeare 'famous tragedian' and suggests that he should be buried with Spenser, Chaucer and Beaumont (who had died just two months before Shakespeare). This poem was written no later than 1623, when Ben Jonson responded to it in the First Folio, but was not printed until 1633, when it appeared in the first edition of John Donne's *Poems* before being omitted from subsequent editions. The poem was printed five more times in the seventeenth century and survives in at least thirty-four manuscript copies, making it extremely popular by the standards of the day. It clearly refers specifically to William Shakespeare of Stratford. Seven of the manuscript copies, including one in Basse's autograph, specify that the Shakespeare in the poem died in April 1616, as does the version printed in the 1640 edition of Shakespeare's poems, attributed to Basse, and one manuscript copy specifies that he was 'bury'd att Stratford vpon Avon, his Town of Nativity'.[24] The popularity of this poem puts the lie to the frequent anti-Shakespearian claim that Shakespeare's death went entirely unnoticed and unremarked.

The monument to Shakespeare in Holy Trinity Church in Stratford is another illustration of his posthumous local fame as a writer. It was presumably in place by 1623, when Leonard Digges referred to it in the First Folio as 'thy Stratford moniment'. The monument depicts Shakespeare writing on a cushion, with a Latin inscription that compares him to Nestor, Socrates and Virgil, and an English inscription that refers to 'all that he hath writt' and his 'living art'. Anti-Shakespearians try to discredit this clear evidence by pointing to an engraving in William Dugdale's *Antiquities of Warwick-shire* (1656) which depicts the monument with a much thinner figure and no pen; the suggestion is that Dugdale depicted the 'original' monument, which supposedly depicted Shakespeare as a grain merchant and was later replaced or altered by conspirators. This wildly implausible conspiracy theory ignores the fact that Dugdale explicitly identified the monument as being for 'our late famous Poet Will. Shakespeare' and transcribed the verses from the monument and gravestone. Also, Dugdale's engravings were demonstrably inaccurate in many other cases, as M. H. Spielmann showed in 1924, and Dugdale's original 1634 sketch of the Shakespeare monument is significantly closer to the monument we see today, proving that Wenceslaus Hollar introduced errors into his engravings.[25]

Dugdale is just one of many seventeenth-century writers who independently noted Stratford's fame as the birthplace of Shakespeare. Soon after the publication of the First Folio, a contemporary hand transcribed the poems from the Shakespeare monument and gravestone into a copy of the First Folio (now in the Folger Shakespeare Library), along with another poem not recorded elsewhere.[26] Richard Hunt (*c.* 1596–1661), vicar of Itchington, Warwickshire, annotated his copy of Camden's *Britannia* by adding 'et Gulielmo Shakespeare Roscio plané nostro' ('and to William Shakespeare, truly our Roscius') to Camden's sentence on famous residents of Stratford-upon-Avon, indicating Shakespeare's local fame as a man of the theatre.[27] In 1630 an anecdote in *A Banquet of Jeasts or Change of Cheare* mentions Stratford-upon-Avon as 'a Towne most remarkable for the birth of famous William Shakespeare', and in his 1631 book *Ancient Funerall Monuments*, John Weever, who in 1598 had written a sonnet to Shakespeare and probably knew him personally, printed the poems from the monument and gravestone in his section on Stratford-upon-Avon, adding 'Willm Shakespeare the famous poet' in a marginal note. In September 1634 a Lieutenant Hammond, from a military company of Norwich travelling through Stratford, wrote in his private diary that the church contained 'A neat monument of that famous English Poet, Mr. William Shakespeare; who was borne heere.'

Anti-Shakespearians tend either to ignore such references, or to assert that all these people must have been mistaken, fooled by a virtually omnipotent conspiracy. Charlton Ogburn Jr. in *The Mysterious William Shakespeare* is typically mendacious on this point;[28] he only mentions Lieutenant Hammond, who visited in 1634, out of these witnesses, and scornfully suggests that the only people who connected Stratford with Shakespeare in the seventeenth century were those who stumbled upon the monument while travelling through the town, being presumably too simple to know otherwise. Such a suggestion requires a gross distortion of the evidence, and reflects a dismissively condescending view of seventeenth-century English society that is all too common among anti-Shakespearians.

In general, anti-Shakespearians' depictions of sixteenth-century Stratford-upon-Avon and Warwickshire are rooted in distortions, driven

by an irrational hatred of William Shakespeare of Stratford and all he represents. Those who would deny Shakespeare's authorship and disparage his
hometown must turn a blind eye to a mountain of evidence showing that
Stratford's leading residents, including Shakespeare's closest friends there,
were educated and cultured by just about any standard.

CHAPTER 12

Shakespeare and school

Carol Chillington Rutter

Know ye that we, induced by the singular love and affection which we greatly bear the young subjects of our Kingdom in our said country of Warwick, do not lay it a little to heart, that from their cradles they may be imbued with polite literature, which before our times was neglected, [so that] when they become of more riper years, they may go on to be more learned, and increase in number to be useful members of the English Church of Christ, . . . [we] create erect found ordain make and establish to endure for ever a Free Grammar School in the said town . . . And that the said school . . . shall for ever be called and named . . . 'The Kyng's newe Scole of Stratford upon Avon'.[1]

OF APES AND ART

How did he do it? A working-class lad from a modest provincial market town (population 1,500) two days' ride (or ten days' walk) from London and from the public, purpose-built playhouses that only in his adolescence were being built in the metropolis (the Theatre, 1576; the Rose, 1587), establishing a brand new cultural industry, the one that would occupy his adult life: how did the boy from Stratford-upon-Avon become the playwright who wrote *King Lear*? *Hamlet*? *Twelfth Night*? *Measure for Measure*? *Troilus and Cressida*? *The Winter's Tale*? The eight plays of the double history tetralogy, *Richard II* to *Richard III* by way of the three parts of *Henry VI*, the two parts of *Henry IV* and the life of the 'mirror of all Christian kings', *Henry V*?

'How did he do it?' was a question that occupied, probably, William Shakespeare's playwriting contemporaries.[2] In late 1592, when he had only *The Two Gentlemen of Verona*, *Titus Andronicus*, *The Taming of the Shrew* and the *Henry VI*s as Shakespeare's theatrical output to date to go on, the rival playwright, Robert Greene (who was then on his deathbed and perhaps as sick at heart as he was in body) complained bitterly that Shakespeare 'did it' monkey-fashion, the way 'Apes imitate'. Greene didn't consider the

Shakespeare who'd so recently appeared on the London scene a writer. He
was a player (cf. John Jowett's and Eric Rasmussen and James Mardock's
chapters in this volume. And that made him a 'puppet'. An 'antick').
Turning to scribbling, he was a thieving jackdaw who stole the playwriterly
work of university-trained men like Christopher Marlowe, George Peele,
Thomas Nashe – and Greene himself; a self-styled 'absolute *Johannes fac
totum*' who, 'in his own conceit', imagined himself 'the only Shake-scene
in a country'. But in reality, he was just 'an upstart Crow beautified with
our' – that is, the university men's –'feathers'.[3]

Twenty years later, in about 1615, when everything Shakespeare would
write was written, and when he had the playwright's life's work to go
on, work that showed Shakespeare simply outstripping every pattern or
precedent or possible rival for imitation, Francis Beaumont didn't see him
as apish, but as artless. He 'did it', his writing, 'cleere' 'from all Learning',
without any 'scholarship'. He 'did it' led only 'by the dim light of Nature'.[4]

Ben Jonson (to whom those lines of Beaumont's were directed) could
have told Beaumont otherwise. For twenty years, Jonson's career ran a
parallel course to Shakespeare's, sometimes working in the same company;
sometimes, in competition. Shakespeare played in at least one of Jonson's
comedies. Jonson wrote eulogistic lines to the First Folio, 1623. Jonson
knew Shakespeare very well, and knew that while 'Nature' certainly had 'a
part' in Shakespeare, 'Nature' wasn't 'all'. There was also 'His Art'. 'Nature'
provided 'the Poets matter', wrote Jonson, but it was his 'Art' that gave the
'matter' its 'fashion'. Art was the *fashioner*. Writing was hard work. It was
labour. 'A good Poet's made', wrote Jonson, 'as well as born', and any he
'Who casts to write a living line, must sweat'.[5]

So where did Shakespeare learn his 'art'? How was the poet 'made'? Over
what did he 'sweat'? If he'd been asked those questions, Jonson would
doubtless have pointed to the Royal Charter, quoted above. It established
from 1553 a 'free grammar school' in Stratford-upon-Avon, and with it, what
by then had settled into the *de facto* national curriculum, a programme of
humanist education derived over the past fifty years from the pan-European
teachings of Battista Guarino and Desiderius Erasmus.[6] That curriculum
taught Latin grammar, literature – the 'polite literature' alluded to in the
Royal Charter – and rhetorical exercises; the object of this education being,
as Peter Mack has written, to 'inculcate virtue', to produce pupils who were
'wise, pious, and eloquent';[7] that is, 'useful members of the English Church
of Christ'. (Or, as the statutes for Chester grammar school, executed in
1558, the first year of Elizabeth's reign, put it, to 'instruct' youth 'to live
well' and to 'furnish their minds with knowledge and cunning'.)[8]

For humanists like Erasmus, Thomas More, John Colet and Roger Ascham (all of them educational innovators), the connection between rhetoric and ethics was clear, as also between the art of persuasion and the promotion of individual and public morality.[9] In 'the grammar' boys were not just taught to read classical texts and to compose their own writing out of their reading. That reading, that composition in turn taught them ways of ethical thinking and of expressing their thinking. The curriculum established the relationship between literary culture and Elizabethan discourse. The texts taught and the skills learned to study those texts installed habits of mind that produced ways of thinking, talking, writing, arguing, feeling, remembering; habits of reflection, but also of activity. Ultimately, the study of *bonae literae* aimed not only at individual wisdom and virtue but at a social programme of reform: the eradication of 'greed and indolence, the taproots of injustice and social disorder'.[10]

The 'Kyng's newe Scole' was not exceptional. It was part of the Tudors' post-Reformation expansion and reformation of the education system: a project so comprehensive that by 1660 only in two counties of England would a boy have lived further than twelve miles from a free grammar school.[11] Ben Jonson was a grammar school boy. So, I believe, was William Shakespeare. And if the educational system that produced England's greatest theologians, ambassadors, lawyers, physicians, moral philosophers and political thinkers also produced its best playwrights, Erasmus, for one, wouldn't have been surprised. As we will see, play was foundational to the curriculum he formulated. But first, boys – and it was *only* boys in the early modern grammar schools – had to acquire a second language, and they started by learning its grammar.

'IN THE GRAMMAR'

For Erasmus in *De ratione studii* (*On the Method of Study*, 1512) it was evident that 'grammar . . . claims primacy of place' on the school syllabus and that 'at the outset boys must be instructed in two – Greek, of course, and Latin'.[12] Why? 'Because almost everything worth learning is set forth in these two languages.' As things developed in England, however, Erasmus's hopes for Greek teaching at school level couldn't be met, certainly not outside London. Before about 1600, the provinces simply could not be supplied with enough teachers. Latin, then, was the core curriculum: the key qualification, the language of instruction, the default setting for the transmission of human knowledge giving access to the early modern internet that connected men of learning across Europe, no matter what their native mother tongue, in a shared patriarchal discourse.[13]

A boy arrived 'in the grammar' aged about seven, having spent the previous year or two in a 'petty school' learning the basics of reading and writing English, probably from a 'dame', probably in mixed classes (or 'forms') with girls: his *ABC*, 'Our Father', and numbers off a hornbook; the *Catechism*; prayers and psalms from the *Primer*. Entering the 'lower school', his first 'sweat' was, armed with 'Lily's Grammar' and under the eye of the school 'Usher', to learn the eight parts of speech and the 'accidence', that is, the declension and conjugation of Latin nouns and verbs. He worked by memorization, repetition and continuous drilling, first on elementary sentences that demonstrated points of grammar, then on longer phrases (an anthology of which were helpfully collected into a little school text, *Sententiae Pueriles*):

> Amicis opitulare. (Help your friends.)
> Cognosce teipsum. (Know yourself.)
> Arcanum cela. (Keep a secret.)
> Mendacem memorem esse oportet. (A liar needs to have a good memory.)

The other beginner's textbook he would have had to hand was the collection known as *Cato's Distichs* (or more simply, *Cato*), which organized moral sentences into couplets laid out as binaries: 'Be gentle to all men; but be familiar only with the good'; 'Be neat and cleanly in your apparel; but not brave and sumptuous' (cf. *Hamlet* 1.3.70–2). He read simple texts – Aesop's *Fables* in Latin; Cicero's easiest letters; extracts of Ovid and Terence – and he began composition: writing short themes of his own devising; for example, composing a story that linked a narrative to a moral sentence, culled perhaps from Erasmus's *Adagia*. He worked long hours: from six or seven in the morning to five or six at night (with perhaps a two-hour mid-day break), six days a week, most weeks of the year, with short vacations and occasional one-day holidays. Sweat indeed.

Proceeding to the upper forms, now aged about eleven and under the supervision of the school 'Master', boys perfected their grammar with exercises in double translation: from Latin into English then back into Latin, the object being to match the pupil's efforts against the model author's, and to impress the original on his memory so that the precedent served as the internalized pattern for imitation. In this pedagogic model, memorization was the method and imitation (not invention) was the first object: students were apprentices learning their craft the way a goldsmith's or dyer's apprentices learned theirs, by copying the master craftsman. Plagiarism – the word derives from the Latin, *plagiarius*, '*one who abducts the child or slave of another, a kidnapper*' (OED: *plagiary*, sb.); we use it today for someone who steals someone else's writing – was foreign to early modern poetic theory and practice. Instead, as Robert Miola writes, what was stressed was 'the importance of *imitatio*, the creative imitation of others'. Poets 'demonstrated originality not by inventing new stories but by adapting extant, particularly classical, ones. The genius lay not in the invention but in the transformation.'[14]

More difficult assignments followed that *did* move students beyond imitation to invention, like composing letters and orations in the style of the great master of Latinity, Cicero. As prep and crib, boys had to hand a letter writing manual that helped them to recognize the genre of each letter (a begging letter, a letter of introduction, of apology, of advice, persuasion) and to analyse its structure before writing their own letter, following the textual model and employing appropriate topics to achieve their effect. Always, it was tacitly understood, writers needed to consider their audience, needed to anticipate their writing's reception. Always, the pupil kept the master text in front of him because he was interested not just in its content, its subject 'matter', but in its form, its 'art'.

Further on, the principles of rhetoric were introduced from Lily's *Brevissima institutio* and Erasmus's *De copia* (another core handbook), teaching the student to recognize the rhetorical tropes and figures (among them, metaphor, allegory, irony, hyperbole, synecdoche, metonymy; anaphora, ploce, anadiplosis, ellipsis, apostrophe), to see them as elements of a writer's style, to discriminate their appropriate use in their own writing and to understand them not as 'dry formulae' or mere ornamentation but 'pockets of energy', channels for re-enacting feeling.[15] As G. K. Hunter reminds us, 'rhetoric' for the Elizabethans was not flattery, insincerity or bombast; it was 'a science (or art or *techne*) of persuasion, an art, that is of public activity'; 'a science of *doing* rather than knowing'.[16] And in the grammar, it was taught as a science. The elements of rhetorical construction were laid out in the writing models given in Aphthonius's *Progymnasmata* (the third essential handbook in the upper forms), students being assigned composition exercises to imitate and practise them (fable, narrative, chreia, proverb, commonplace, encomium, vituperation). From these, boys learned how to structure, build and amplify an argument directed at a specific purpose. The art of persuasion was aimed at making your point. So, for example, as Aphthonius defined it, a 'commonplace' was an oration arguing the good or bad qualities in something. It worked by amplification (intensifying the goodness of the good man or the badness of the bad) to excite either pity or rage in the audience. It was structured thus: preface (telling the seriousness of the crime or the need for mercy); argument from contraries, exposition of the case, comparison, argument from a moral maxim, digression, moving or removing pity, arguments from the lawful, the just, the useful and the possible and a conclusion.

In all of this reading and composition, boys were learning by imitating the best authors in all kinds of writing: history and biography; poetry, comedy and tragedy; moral essays and orations; the epic. Their reading list included what today would constitute the curriculum of a university classics degree: the plays of Terence; Virgil's *Eclogues* and *Aeneid* (and sometimes the *Georgics* as well); Ovid's *Fasti*, sometimes *de Tristibus* and/or *Epistolae Heroidum* and certainly *Metamorphoses* (which in some schools boys in the upper forms memorized, word for word, at the rate of a book a year); Cicero's *Epistles*, *De officiis*, *De amicitia* and *De senectute*, Caesar or Sallust, Horace.[17] But they weren't just reading and writing Latin; they were turning writing into speaking, learning to pronounce 'naturally and sweetly without vaine affection' (as one pedagogue put it), for speaking Latin was as important to the Elizabethan syllabus as Latin literacy. By the end of his schooling a boy would have delivered several declamations and might have performed parts of a number of Latin plays: every Thursday at Shrewsbury – Philip Sidney's grammar school – the boys in the top class were required to 'declaim and play one act of a comedy' before breaking up for the afternoon, which, Katherine Duncan-Jones suggests, probably explains 'Sidney's ready familiarity with the plays of Terence'.[18] Every boy would certainly have had experience composing and delivering *ethopoeia* (literally, 'character making' or 'impersonation': a 'speech for a character').

This exercise required him to use texts already to hand to 'speak in character', evoking according to set rhetorical conventions (repetition, variation, figuration) the feelings of a specific character in a specific situation, usually states of high emotion, anxiety or agitation, which encouraged students to examine the psychological as well as the technical aspects of rhetorical techniques. In short, by 'becoming other', *ethopoeia* schooled them in emotional literacy.[19] For what is striking about this exercise, given the grammar school's near-exclusive maleness, is that it routinely found its material in texts that focused on women's feelings: Niobe mourning her children; Juno railing against the surviving Trojans' escape; 'infelix Dido', betrayed, furnishing her own funeral pyre; abandoned Ariadne, watching from the cliffs of Naxos Theseus's sails disappearing; Hecuba clamouring over her husband's slaughter, her daughter's sacrifice, her last boy-child's murder. All of these were stories boys would have encountered in Ovid, in Virgil, in Aphthonius. The immediate point of *ethopoeia* was to find 'the best words to suit the meaning and . . . feelings of sorrow and anger appropriate to the majesty of the character he impersonated'.[20] But the larger educative point of the exercise was that by 'becoming' women, by role-playing feelings that as adult men they would be expected to contain or repress, boys learned to express themselves: to weep, and to make others weep. And the aim was perfect impersonation. So, as the educational theorist, John Brinsley, wrote in his *Ludus Literarius*, almost as if describing a kind of early modern method acting, students must 'pronounce every matter according to the nature of it . . . as if they themselves were the persons which did speak . . . & . . . imagine themselves to have occasion to utter the very same thing'. Memorization was a key skill. Boys who memorized their authors word for word, 'without book', wrote Brinsley, made 'the very phrase and matter of their Author' 'their own to use perpetually'. A boy literally incorporated those texts into the fabric of his being, into his muscle-memory, by 'imprinting the originals in his hart'.[21]

In sum, then, the grammar school, as Peter Mack writes, 'cultivated particular skills in a range of different ways but it also emphasized a range of skills'; and it 'inculcated knowledge as well as skills. The poems and histories pupils read, the maxims and stories they learned and reproduced, provided a shared stock of principles' that added up to a 'shared heritage of cultural knowledge'.[22] Most significantly, grammar school training, writes Robert Miola, 'fostered certain habits of reading, thinking, and writing' that would have spilled over into students' writing in English. They 'acquired extraordinary sensitivity to language, especially its sound'. Reading aloud and reciting verse *viva voce* were practices that not only encouraged the performative but helped students develop 'acute inner ears that could appreciate sonic effects which are lost on moderns'. Such 'aural sensitivity led to delight in wordplay of all kinds, repartee, *double entendre*, puns, and quibbles', wordplay that 'exploited the energies of language and intellect'.[23] The grammar school boy, we should remember, would always in some sense have been working in two languages, and hearing the Latin legacy, its DNA, left in his English. So when Ben Jonson wrote that 'Art' gave 'the Poets matter' its 'fashion', he would certainly have had in mind the Latin root of 'fashion', *facere*, to make, and the way that verb would play in the line against 'poet', the Greek for 'maker'.

Learning by rote (word for word, 'without book'), developing prodigious memories, students could, for the rest of their lives, dip into the archive of the personal memory bank they'd stocked as children for quotation, allusion, analogy, example – and not just of the classics but of the Bible, the Psalms and the Book of Common Prayer. But the student wouldn't have had to depend wholly on memory, for he'd been taught another organized system for reading and remembering his authors – and retrieving what he'd read: he could turn to his commonplace book. Essentially a personal dictionary of quotation, it was compiled from sentences, words and phrases that the boy collected and copied into his book, filed page by page under subject headings ('Friendship'; 'Justice'; 'Constancy') that made the entries accessible for using as 'matter' when it came time to write a letter, say, or a theme. The process of building a commonplace book taught the student to read actively, analogically as well as logically, and opportunistically: looking not just at a writer's argument and where he could find parallels and cross-glosses but how he could raid it for his own future invention. The collective habits of the commonplace book sponsored a kind of self-reflectiveness (what *I* find interesting; what catches *my* eye), while the need of the student always to be on the look-out, as a reader, for material for themes, for declamations, for *ethopoeia*, prompted an outwardness registered in annotation, marginalia. (Erasmus advised students, when they found something they wanted to remember, to mark the text with a finger post.) Finally, the habits of reading inculcated 'in the grammar' forged in the early modern mind connections between rhetoric and ethics, between the art of persuasion and the promotion of individual and public morality, ideas about right and wrong. And one thing more. The cultivation of play in the grammar school – that place that Erasmus wanted to be 'playful', and Ascham (and Brinsley following him) called the *'ludus literarius'* – installed habits of 'becoming other', of imagining other minds and voices: excellent preparation for a playwright.

But was this education sufficient to equip Shakespeare to write Shakespeare? Certainly, it was enough to equip any school leaver to read any 'modern' English writing: Chaucer, Gower, Holinshed, Hall, Elyot, Nashe, Greene, North's Plutarch, Florio's Montaigne, Hoby's Castiglione, and to know how to turn such source material to his own uses. Certainly, too, it was sufficient to equip Jonson to write Jonson: young Ben had only three or four years at Westminster School before being removed to learn his step-father's trade of bricklaying.[24] And it was enough to equip Richard Field, another Stratfordian, Shakespeare's near contemporary and doubtless his school fellow, to secure, aged seventeen, an apprenticeship with the distinguished Huguenot printer Thomas Vautrollier in 1579, to take over the business eight years later and thereafter to rise rapidly to 'become one of the most versatile and up-market printers of his age', handling works in French, Italian, Spanish and Welsh, with occasional passages in Greek and

Latin. As far as literary equipment goes, it was T. W. Baldwin's exhaustive research back in 1944 in the two thick volumes of *Small Latine & Lesse Greek* that comprehensively demolished the notion that Shakespeare would have needed a university education to write Shakespeare by tracking back to the grammar school almost every quotation, allusion and reference that appears in the plays. The majority of them derive, Baldwin found, 'from the standard books and curriculum of the Elizabethan grammar school'.[25]

WILL-INGLY TO SCHOOL?

But Baldwin's statement begs a question: did Will Shakespeare actually attend the local grammar school? Was he remembering himself the 'whining schoolboy with his satchel / And shining morning face, creeping like snail / Unwillingly to school' in Jacques's lines (*As You Like It* 2.7.145–7)? Or not?

We have no direct evidence. Class lists for the 1570s – if they were ever kept – don't exist. In fact none survive before the nineteenth century. But certainly attendance at the free grammar school would have been an expectation and indeed a civic right for the only son of so prominent a local as John Shakespeare, a man who had held civic office since 1556: elected alderman in 1565, bailiff – that is, mayor – in 1568 and head alderman in 1571, the year young Will would have started school.

Beyond domestic circumstance, we have the evidence of the plays. The numbers of scenes and scenarios they contain of schooling (and side-swipes *at* schooling) smack of first-hand knowledge of the classroom. In 4.1 of *The Merry Wives of Windsor* there's the Latin lesson. Parson Evans (a send-up of the Welshman, Thomas Jenkins, master of the King's new school, 1575–9?) puts young William (a glance at the playwright himself, in the Elizabethan equivalent of short trousers?) through his paces. Evans poses William questions on the accidence straight out of Lily, the schoolmaster's Welsh tongue making glorious nonsense of the Latin pronunciation ('*hing, hang, hog*'); the lad's imperfect memory making a pig's ear of double translation ('*lapis*' = '*stone*' = '*lapis*', not 'pebble'), both of them showing, perhaps, what teaching and learning was really like 'in the grammar' as against Erasmus's ideal. In *Love's Labour's Lost* there's the delicious satire on pedantry (that surely looks sideways at the young noblemen's dedication to their monastic 'Academy' of learning) presented in the absurd Holofernes, he who educates 'youth at the charge-house on the top of the mountain', constantly smells 'false Latin', fastidiously corrects punctuation ('You find not the apostrophus and so miss the accent') and talks habitually in elementary 'construings': '*caelo*, the sky, the welkin, the heaven . . . *terra*, the soil, the land, the earth'. In 3.1 of *The Taming of the Shrew*, Lucentio-as-Cambio, the fake schoolmaster, tutors Bianca across Ovid, using the opening letter in the school text, *Heroides*, that has Penelope writing to Ulysses about trouble in Ithaca. Cambio, practising a formal construing, phrase by phrase ('*Hic ibat . . . Simois . . . Sigeia tellus*'), uses the exercise to cover seduction, his translation not of the text but of his desire ('as I told you before . . . I am . . . disguised to get your love', 3.1.31–3). Bianca, 'no breeching scholar in the schools' (3.1.18), knows enough of her accidence to answer in imperatives: '*regia*, presume not; "*celsa senis*", despair not'. (Others in Shakespeare's plays will remember *Heroides*: Cleopatra taunting Antony ('What says the married woman?', 1.3.20) recalls Dido in the seventh letter; and Lorenzo star-gazing with Jessica in *The Merchant of Venice*, thinking on 'Dido with a willow in her hand' (5.1.10) is actually remembering Ariadne in *Heroides* x.)

There are many more such rememberings. Little Lucius in *Titus Andronicus* '*flies*' into 4.1, '*with Bookes under his Arme*' (as the Folio stage-direction has it): anachronistically, bound Elizabethan schoolbooks. One of them, his mutilated aunt Lavinia paws through. It's Ovid's *Metamorphoses*. She searches it to find her own story in its precedent: the rape and mutilation of Philomela in Book vi. Ovid, it turns out, served her rapists as 'precedent'. Chiron and Demetrius know the story. As they say, they've both been 'in the grammar' (4.2.23). But Ovid also serves the 'hard-handed men' who 'work for bread' upon Athenian stalls in *A Midsummer Night's Dream* (5.1.72 and 3.2.10) who put on a play based on Pyramus and Thisbe (Book ix). And Ovid serves Prospero. 'Ye elves of hills, brooks, standing lakes and groves' (*The Tempest* 5.1.33) is straight out of Book vii.

All over Shakespeare characters remember their school friends, their school days, their school exercises: Hamlet, Rosencrantz, Guildenstern and Hecuba; Brutus and Cassius; Helena and Hermia. (And some, like the ignorant goon, Jack Cade, in *Henry VI Part Two*, would make learning a capital offence: 'Thou hast most traitorously corrupted the youth of the realm in erecting a grammar school; . . . thou hast men about thee that usually talk of a noun and a verb', 4.7.10–11, 16–17.) The great general Mark Antony may be one of the 'triple pillar[s] of the world' (*Antony and Cleopatra* 1.1.12), but he keeps among his globe-trotting retinue his schoolmaster. It's his schoolmaster he sends, in defeat, to broker a deal with Octavius. In *The Two Gentlemen of Verona*, in a complicated scene of disguise and double bluff, Julia-as-Sebastian talks about 'Pentecost . . . pageants' when 'he' 'play[ed] the woman's part': ''twas Aridane, passioning / For Theseus's perjury . . . / Which I so lively acted . . . / That my poor mistress . . . / Wept bitterly' (5.1.155–68). S/he, of course, is remembering '*ethopoeia*', perhaps the very 'speech for a character' the boy Shakespeare might have composed from *Heroides* x and performed 'in the grammar'.

All over Shakespeare, too, characters use school as a point of metaphoric reference: Gremio, in *The Taming of the Shrew*, comes from Petruccio and Kate's wedding 'As willingly as ere I came from school' (3.3.23). The rebel army, at the end of *Henry IV Part Two*, de-mobs 'Like youthful steers unyoked . . . or, like a school broke up' (4.1.328–9). The Fool in *The Tragedy of King Lear* wishes the king would 'keep a schoolmaster that can teach thy fool to lie' (1.4.160–1); his daughters consider that 'The injuries' that 'wilful men . . . themselves procure / Must be their schoolmasters' (2.2.474–5).

It might be argued that Shakespeare acquired such familiarity with school through reading. There was plenty else he got from books, not from experience: travel in Italy; the geography and customs of Venice; Mediterranean shipwrecks; Cleopatra's spectacular arrival at Cydnus; fratricide; witchcraft; men turned into asses. But what he couldn't have got simply from reading about school would have been the habits of mind, the habits of thinking and talking and expressing installed, inculcated via the curriculum over many years *at* school, habits like Polonius's 'distich thinking': 'Give every man thy ear but few thy voice. / Take each man's censure, but reserve thy judgement' (*Hamlet* 1.3.68–9). We hear grammar school habits in the rhetorical organization of Hamlet's 'To be, or not to be', the proposition of that initial binary argued out in subsequent lines: 'Whether . . . ', 'Or . . . ', 'And . . . ' (*Hamlet* 3.1.58, 61, 62). And in Ophelia's lines on 'a noble mind . . . o'erthrown': 'The courtier's, soldier's, scholar's eye, tongue, sword . . . ' (*Hamlet* 3.1.153, 154). This learned rhetoric is what structures Richard III's opening soliloquy, and a thousand other speeches in Shakespeare ('Now is the winter of our discontent / Made glorious summer by this sun of York; . . . Now . . . Our . . . Our . . . Our . . . And now . . . But I . . . I . . . I . . . why, I . . . And therefore . . . ' (*Richard III* 1.1.1–2, 6, 7, 8, 10, 14, 16, 18, 24, 28). The legacy of the grammar school is heard in the letters that fly across the plays ('They met me in the day of success . . . ', *Macbeth* 1.5.1.); in the themes composed ('I dreamt there was an emperor Antony', *Antony and Cleopatra* 5.2.75); the fables told ('There was a time when all the body's members, / Rebelled against the body . . . ', *Coriolanus* 1.1.94–5); the orations delivered ('Friends, Romans, countrymen . . . bury . . . not praise . . . ', *Julius Caesar* 3.2.74, 75), proofs offered ('The speciality of rule hath been neglected . . . O, when degree is shaked . . . Take but degree away . . . ', *Troilus and Cressida* 1.3.77, 101, 109; 'These are the forgeries of

jealousy... thy brawls... Therefore the winds... The ox... The plough-
man... the green corn... We are their parents and originals' (*A Midsummer Night's Dream* 2.1.81, 87, 93, 94, 117). Young Will's Latin lesson in
Windsor returns, transformed, in an argument upon which a man's life
depends, an argument organized around modal verbs. Will the deputy who
has power to execute a man show 'mercy'? 'I will not do't'; 'But can you if
you would?'; 'Look what I will not, that I cannot do'; 'But might you do't,
and do the world no wrong...?' (*Measure for Measure* 2.2.52–4). And it
returns every time someone 'construes': 'There's no art to find the mind's
construction in the face' (*Macbeth* 1.4.11–12). Or someone makes a breath-
taking pun or awful Dogberryism ('If he do bleed... gild... guilt', *Macbeth* 2.2.54–5); 'comparisons are odorous', *Much Ado About Nothing* 3.5.15).
The extravagant invention of Thersites's invective ('How the devil Luxury
with his fat rump and potato finger tickles these together!', *Troilus and Cressida* 5.2.55–6), of Hal and Falstaff's traded insults ('bed-presser... horse-
breaker... hill of flesh'; 'starveling... elf-skin... bull's pizzle', *Henry IV
Part One* 2.5.246–7, 248–9); of Dromio of Syracuse's horrified description
('she's the kitchen wench and all grease... if she lives till doomsday she'll
burn a week longer than the whole world', *The Comedy of Errors* 3.2.96–
7, 100–1) and of Romeo's enthralled observation ('O, she doth teach the
torches to burn bright... she hangs upon the cheek of night / As a rich
jewel in an Ethiope's ear', *Romeo and Juliet* 1.5.43, 44–5) all might trace
back to the schematic collecting of the commonplace book and to the
playfulness Erasmus endorsed in the development of the imagination in
writing. On every page, in every speech, every line Shakespeare wrote we
see the mental imprint of the grammar school. The wonder is, he makes
the 'sweat' appear so effortless. But Jonson was right: the poet playwright
who was Shakespeare was, if 'natural', also 'made'. And his making was in
'The Kyng's newe Scole of Stratford upon Avon'.

CHAPTER 13

Shakespeare tells lies

Barbara Everett

The obvious place to look for information about a writer is in contextual sources. Hence the relevance of historical and biographical study of litera-ture. But there are distinctions to be made. Poets of the Romantic period seem far nearer to us, and more is in fact known about them: as a result, they appear much more symbiotic on the world about them. Elizabethan writers derive much less, or less clearly, from their time and place. Such knowledge as can be gained may prove a matter of generalization, gossip and myth. Because of the lapse of four centuries, even what is recovered and regarded as circumstantial data may well conflict with deep-rooted snobbish or romantic or simply wilful presuppositions in the enquirer.

Being foxed can lead a researcher to search the work itself for answers it was never intended to give. Some editors and critics suppose that they can find in the Sonnets of Shakespeare a fair young man, and then settle to dispute which Earl he might turn out to be. This kind of interpretation will be wrong from the start, a fact not encouraging to historical scholars. Literature is, as Aristotle once came near to arguing, metaphorical. But there are closer studies of poets' work that look for information. Scholars who hope to find evidence there, in questions – for instance – of collaboration and attribution, will test Shakespeare's literary and verbal style for what it tells of identity. Such analyses are often interesting, but dogged by a problem that I have never seen properly articulated. Most good actors are brilliant mimics, of their colleagues, their friends and any passing public figures. This seems certain to be true of Burbage and likely to be true of Shakespeare. The gift of imitation was equally likely to have pervaded the poet's verbal style, its gigantic richness, inventiveness and variety gratefully or amusedly absorbing anything of character that offered itself.

I suspect that examinations of verbal style can't give back very securely much information about the writer's authenticity. But there are other kinds of questioning of the text which may render up a sense of Shakespeare, and moreover of Shakespeare within a given social world. I have just touched

briefly on the probability of Shakespeare's verbal mimicry. It is manifest
that as a writer he did what Hamlet urges on the actors, and held 'the
mirror up to nature' (*Hamlet* 3.2.23–4), learning from all he saw and heard,
watched, and read: but this art of mimicry never ended in an approach
to the modern newspaper or cinematic image. The master of styles was
also and simultaneously the great inventor of dramatic characters, who are
true but not factual, dreamed into existence but never overstepping what
Hamlet calls 'the modesty of nature' (*Hamlet* 3.2.9): or, as the Epilogue of
Henry IV Part Two tells us, of Falstaff, 'Oldcastle died a martyr, and this
is not the man.' Shakespeare was perhaps the first and greatest of English
artists who worked throughout his career to fuse the inner man with the
outside world, the dreamed and the lived; who in *Henry VI* invented
the history play, from that wealth of source-materials at the time held to
be factually true, but who then steadily developed his medium towards the
very different and fictive truth of the *Henry IV* plays, of *Julius Caesar* and
of *Hamlet*. The last remains a great and in fact a 'true' play even for those
who cannot believe in the vital ghost with which it opens.

   With a metaphor that includes both sexual infidelity and his profession
in the theatre, the poet speaks in Sonnet 110 of looking 'on truth / Askance
and strangely'. Similarly in Sonnet 53, since he reads love and imagination
as functions of each other he sees 'you' (at once both beloved and reader)
as attended by 'millions of strange shadows'. The reiteration of 'strange'
is notable. The strangeness lies perhaps in the struggle to hold together
ideals of love and creative thought with the life of public debauchery (110)
and with a context of illusions and fictions (53); the word 'shadows' in 53
implies at once empty images, darkness thrown by sunlight, and actors, an
involvement of love and art with darkness – even (as in 100) with simple
lies. All these implications suggest the great achievement of Shakespeare's
work, and tell something about the world of its immediate beginnings. If
Shakespeare made truth out of what might have been left mere lies, then
the process was begun in Stratford-upon-Avon. It remains probable that the
greatest moment in England's literary culture coincided with the emergence
through the Protestant revolution of what would several centuries later
come to be known as cultural Philistinism: the hostility on theological
and ecclesiastical grounds, mainly Calvinistic and Puritan, to the life of
intellect and the practice of the arts. Even if we had no more evidence than
the whitewashing over of the Doom pictures in Stratford-upon-Avon's
Guild Chapel, we could surely assume that this small and provincial if
successful country town would have provided a scene that a brilliantly
imaginative literary artist would need to fight his way out of. It may even

be that the Philistinism of Stratford explains the most lasting mystery in Shakespeare's biography. He seems to have begun his career peculiarly late by the standards of his contemporaries, being unlikely to have joined a theatrical company before the late 1580s (in 1589 he was twenty-five, and rising thirty when he began to be known and celebrated in London). What happened during the 'Lost Years'? It may well be that the aspiring poet and dramatist was held in Stratford by a loyal if reluctant bond with family, friends and neighbours who believed that his plain and sensible duty lay in carrying on his father's business and caring for his wife and children, rather than in making off to probable failure in distant London, working within a milieu as corrupt as it was profitless – a world of shoddy illusions, fictions, lies. If Shakespeare took to London with him this whole conflict of impulses and ideals, they are directly reflected in that numerically first of the Sonnets which sets the good Tudor yeoman and tradesman value of 'increase' against the apparent folly of a 'Thou', 'contracted to thine own bright eyes . . . / Making a famine where abundance lies'. Just conceivably, there is word play in this 'lies', a blow struck against the mere country town: as there was, many years later, when Claudius spoke (in *Hamlet* 3.3.61) of Heaven itself as unimaginable by him except as corrupt, 'there the action lies / In his true nature'. In the sonnet, the younger poet addresses himself, aware that his future will have to lie through lies.

I have been thinking in very general terms of the way in which a great Elizabethan artist might be characterized, quite exceptionally, by this creative conflict of values – a conflict that might even help to identify the universally admired writer with 'the man from Stratford'. I want to pause for a moment to consider a specific example of Shakespeare's life of lies. If asked what the name 'Shakespeare' meant to them, a startling number of the more sophisticated among contemporary readers would quote Ariel's song from what may be the poet's last completed play, *The Tempest*, 'Full fathom five thy father lies' (1.2.396).[1] Up until some fifty or seventy years ago, the more popular choice might have been Hamlet's 'To be, or not to be; that is the question' (3.1.58). This is a highly interesting choice in itself, because the whole soliloquy is certainly not what many editors and readers (even the best) suppose it to be, a meditation on suicide. *Hamlet*, alongside *Troilus and Cressida* and *Measure for Measure*, presents the writer at his most self-aware and meta-theatrical. Through Hamlet there speak the dramatist, the actor, the reader or theatregoer and the mere human being who are all caught by the play into the question of who or what the true being is, agent or patient, tradesman or poet, prince or player.

But Ariel's song too, that has so magical an effect on so many modern readers and playgoers (its resonance beginning with Eliot's *The Waste Land*, 'A Game of Chess', lines 123–4, 'I remember / Those are pearls that were his eyes') comes to us comparably spacious and complex. It should perhaps be quoted here in full:

> ARIEL
> Full fathom five thy father lies.
> Of his bones are coral made;
> Those are pearls that were his eyes;
> Nothing of him that doth fade,
> But doth suffer a sea-change
> Into something rich and strange.
> Sea-nymphs hourly ring his knell:
> Hark! now I hear them, ding dong bell.
> [*Spirits dispersedly echo the burden 'ding dong bell'*]
> (*The Tempest* 1.2.396–402.1)

It is unsurprising that the modernist, and now postmodernist consciousnesses are haunted by the late, highly sophisticated and courtly Shakespeare of the romances, and especially by the lucidities of this song, that seems simple, and is not.

One of its simplicities needs stating at once. The song or poem tells a lie, and is, in fact, a lie throughout. Ariel sings to Prince Ferdinand on Prospero's instruction, and both royal magician and spirit-servant well know that Ferdinand's father, the enemy King Alonso, does not lie drowned under thirty feet of sea water. Less than two hundred lines earlier, and in the same scene, Ariel assures Prospero that the voyagers in the ship he has been ordered to wreck are now ashore 'safe / . . . Not a hair perished'. Just over two hundred lines later, in the next scene and act, Alonso is discovered among his courtiers, some of them discussing their survival.

The lie that is Ariel's marvellous song goes undiscussed, or even unmentioned, by most critics and commentators. Of all *The Tempest* editions I know, only David Lindley's New Cambridge version notes that 'The song is literally untrue but represents the situation as Ferdinand believes it to be': which is appropriate, given that an orphaned princeling, now presuming himself King of Naples, will feel free to love and woo his future Queen, Miranda – thus fulfilling Prospero's (often unnoted) purpose in the play, which is primarily to bring about a good future life for his child ('I have done nothing but in care of thee – / Of thee my dear one, thee my daughter', 1.2.16–17). Although it is often supposed that the fantastic and romantic mode of these late romances forbids much psychological observation in them, they in fact include quite remarkable penetration of human mind and character, detailed and factual.

And yet it is hard to feel that Prospero is initiating his future son-in-law's love with a deception. *The Tempest* does sometimes care very much for literal truth; Prospero insists that his servants speak the truth to him. More largely, there is an odd authority in the way the invisible Ariel's flat denials to the vicious court servants in 3.2 ('Thou liest', line 39) come out of the air like that voice of Nature itself which in the next scene (3.3) Alonso hears as a condemnation: 'Methought the billows spoke and told me of it; / The winds did sing it to me' (lines 96–7). This is even a play in which one bad man may correct a worse in the cause of factual truth; thus, when Antonio in 2.1 hopes to persuade Sebastian that a second usurpation and in fact murder would be feasible because Tunis, where they have just left Ferdinand's sister Claribel, is unreachable, is 'ten leagues beyond man's life', a startled Sebastian defines the distance crisply as 'some space', adding: 'What stuff is this? What say you?' (lines 243 and 251).

There are plenty of such moments in *The Tempest* that articulate a respect for factual truth. And some of them are acted out by (for instance) a magician's invisible spirit-servant, a role originally written for that 'shadow', a boy-player on the stage of a theatre now centuries gone to dust. That theatre-construct and text to be read which we call *The Tempest* calmly juggles many different kinds of truth and untruth, whereby a certain kind of lie may manage to be more far-ranging, high-flying and deep-sounding than one of the kinds of truth, the merely literal. All the romances practise, impassively, this kind of lying: the sea-coast of Bohemia, '*Exit, pursued by a bear*' (*The Winter's Tale* 3.357). If 'Full fathom five' leaves so many experts untroubled by its lie-telling (apart from the fact that, as all opera-goers know, music may justify some weird utterances), this may be partly because the song is truth-telling as well. Alonso actually has been drowned. My *actually* here is of course a weasel-word, such as major poetry can sometimes drive an analyst to. Prospero's expository narrative in 1.2 takes him plunging back into memory and the whole 'dark backward and abysm of time' (line 50), and while he revives his unhappy past for Miranda, we may glimpse – as it were out of the corner of imagination's eye – other bodies than his falling through deep waters to rest on the sea-bed.

The extraordinary shocks and reversals of the first two scenes of *The Tempest* should wake up any auditor, even if they put Miranda to sleep. A violent wreck and apparent drowning of most of the play's characters is followed by Prospero's 'No harm done' (1.2.15), an assurance supported by his long, passive narrative of exposition, an autobiography that transforms into romantic and classical epic. The contrasts here are aesthetic, even Symbolist. Or, to use a term less anachronistic to Shakespeare, they are tragicomic: a form which the poet had more or less invented for himself by the time of *Measure for Measure*, though he may well have known (I think myself that he did) the inventions in the form by the Italian courtly writer, Giovanni Battista Guarini. In tragicomedy, Englished by Shakespeare's younger contemporary John Fletcher, characters are presented with a seriousness earned both by their status and by their passions, brought close to death, but allowed to evade it and revive. This trickery Shakespeare magics into true art by a lifelong devotion to metaphor, to fictions, to myths and dreams – in a word, to lies. Alonso, the bad King, is both wrecked and revived both metaphorically and morally. He dies out of a life of brutal power-seeking (the weight of his silence among his courtiers through the curious long 2.1 is memorable) and is revived by remorse and by grateful joy for the survival and marriage of his loved son, Ferdinand.

Late in the poet's work as it comes, Ariel's song of drowning and surviving may derive from much earlier, from a magnificent dream in *Richard III*. *The Tempest* carries behind it, like a long slipstream, a history or memory of a great classical theme or topos of human and political and cultural shipwreck. It first seems to enter Shakespeare with Clarence's dream in the early history (1.4.9–63): he imagines that he dies by drowning, falling from the high ship in which he travelled and drifting down to a sea-bed strewn with human bones and treasure from wrecks. The account moves on – 'O then began the tempest to my soul!' (line 44) – into an afterlife judgment on his ambition and worldly crimes. The condemning 'shadow like an angel, with bright hair / Dabbled in blood' (lines 53–4), hints at some early foreshadowing of Ariel; and just as striking are the 'heaps of pearl, / Inestimable stones, unvalued jewels' (lines 26–7) that reflect from the eye-holes of skulls on the sea-bed; these too, surely, survived in the poet's memory over long years to 'reflect' again in the coral and pearls of Ariel's song.

In Clarence's dream, the jewels are decorations of a topos, rhetorical ornaments illustrating a classical, even Senecan meditation on those stages of public life we call history. Ariel's jewels are like them, up to a point: tokens of courtly wealth and power shaken off by the usurpers in their fall through the water. But in their new form they have become musical, unhistorical and unpolitical. The translation of bones into coral and eyes into pearls – at once beautiful and blank – may begin from a point of moral wit, but the inexplicitness reached here, the deep-sea images and sounds ('Ding-dong bell') move the whole well beyond history into the personal and what we have to call the aesthetic. As with most music, the song gets its meaning from the attention of its auditors, 'lie' transforming into play and magic, and leaving behind its base in the story of the play. It is this Symbolistic or postmodernist element of illogic or self-denial that probably makes modern readers so revere the poem, while Ben Jonson – a major poet who loved and appreciated his contemporary and rival – clearly regretted Shakespeare's irrational flights into these late, lying romances.

Jonson had, as ever, good sense on his side. A critic goes wrong in trying to make Ariel's song, or *The Tempest* or anything in the romances, mysterious or even mystical. The playwright plainly did not want Prospero to be mistakeable for God, even if he has both drowned and salvaged Alonso – and does in fact at 5.1 claim to have raised the dead 'by my so potent art' (line 50). Salvaging is not saving. The divine connotations of resurrection are set aside, deflected throughout the play by such strategies as music and magic, functions of 'potent art' that enclose reader and auditor unquestioning in its autonomy, entangling in itself what must be at least in some sense untrue, the King of Naples drowned and caught in a net. The truth of the play is in turn rendered into coral, pearls and bell-notes, things inhuman or immaterial enough to last even after the powers of the magician prove disposable, a book drowned and a lie 'melted into air, into thin air'.

To look back from *The Tempest* over Shakespeare's preceding career is to observe a long course of often superb comedies from what was probably the first, *The Two Gentlemen of Verona*, through work at once entertaining and by category also 'mature', 'dark' and 'romantic'. The comedies frustrate criticism by the doubleness in the poet that I have been hoping to describe: a profound committed seriousness *and* a throwaway coolness reflected in sceptical titles like *Much Ado About Nothing* and *As You Like It*, and in the business-likeness of the singing Clown who closes *Twelfth Night, or What You Will* – 'our play is done, / And we'll strive to please you every day'. Not only the elusiveness but the strength of the comedies lies in this shared balance of art, however various the plays themselves. Both the wild romance of *The Two Gentlemen of Verona* and the farce of *The Comedy of Errors* enfold passages of sane and tender feeling; savagely intellectual experiments like *Troilus and Cressida* and *Measure for Measure* are both funny and touching, and remain (however seriously taken) entertainments.

It seems clear that Shakespeare loved, rather than merely endured, many of the maddening shifts of Tudor entertainment writing (the going 'here and there' by which Sonnet 110 manages to hint at once at emotional treachery, the enforced touring of the Elizabethan actor and playwright, and even a kind of cultural promiscuity, prostitution — sale of the self to bad books). Given a silly plot in *The Two Gentlemen of Verona*, Shakespeare adds a dog; given identical twins in *The Comedy of Errors*, he doubles them and then throws in a magician – and when he reaches *Twelfth Night, or What You Will*, as a climax makes the twins this time impossible, identical male-female siblings. The most splendid of the early comedies, *A Midsummer Night's Dream*, makes heroic Greek aristocrats audience to stage-struck Tudor workmen, and sends the Queen of the Fairies mad with passion for Bottom's body and his ass's head. But, as Theseus says, 'the best in this kind are but shadows' (5.1.210), the last word folding together 'players', 'fairies', dreams and images and nonentities, as well as darkness thrown by the moon, the planet of love. But Hippolyta calls the love that blinds the young at its best a transfiguration of the mind that goes beyond mere fantasy towards 'something of great constancy; / But howsoever, strange and admirable' (5.1.26–7). Where the poet has his characters reflect on what others may call lies in love and art, the word *strange* re-echoes, right up to the romances. When at the beginning of *Cymbeline* a visiting Gentleman laughs a little at the unbelievable pre-history of the play's plot, he is answered stiffly by a resident courtier, 'Howsoe'er 'tis strange . . . / Yet it is true, Sir' (1.1.66 and 68); and Hippolyta's idea of transfiguration suggests the 'sea-change' of Ariel's Song, which also invokes the 'rich and strange'.

Attention paid to words like 'strange' must remain somewhat abstract and theoretical. Something more solidly real is joined to a sense of Shakespeare's double vision of his art if we note that all the greatest characters of the first half of Shakespeare's career are liars: Richard of York an ironist, Bottom a born actor, Shylock a lethal joker, Falstaff a king of fantasy. At once liars and heroes, they are all, like their plays, strange but true. The two *Henry IV* plays that Falstaff straddles are at once the best of the histories, and the least constricted by the factual. Consonantly, the late last of the histories, known to us as *Henry VIII*, seems to have been called in its own time *All Is True*: a fine title for the most romantic of all history plays, the most sweetly mythical.

It is in no way surprising to find this balance in Shakespeare's comedies and histories – fact and fiction, lies and truth and almost, one might add, Stratford and London, in conflict but also completing each other. I want to close this essay by touching on four tragedies. *Hamlet, King Lear* and *Macbeth* I will contribute only a brief note on, for lack of space; *Othello* demands slightly more. First, *Hamlet*. The admirable edition by Harold

Jenkins quotes with some approval in its Introduction Harry Levin's assertion that *Hamlet* is 'the most problematic play ever written by Shakespeare
or any other playwright'.[2] One of the major problems (Jenkins, like many
other editors, agrees) is the Ghost of Hamlet's father, whose terrifying
appearance forms the climax of the superb first scene; but who is not universally observed, and who disappears half way through the play. As Dover
Wilson pointed out some seventy years ago, to this variability in human
terms must be added the fact that the Ghost may not work at all escha-
tologically (the fires he inhabits must be either Hellish or Purgatorial; the
first would forbid the phantom freedom of movement, the second imply
Roman Catholic affiliation in himself and presumably in his kingdom,
since the denial of purgatory was a turning-point of the Reformation; but
the Denmark of Shakespeare's time was Protestant, and Hamlet himself
attends the University of Wittenberg, Luther's own city). None of these
complexities makes for actual impossibility, but it is understandable that
Hamlet wonders if the Ghost could be an evil spirit, just as some modern
productions make him something like an emanation from Hamlet's own
troubled mind.

This last is a half-sympathetic assumption. I want to propose myself that
the Ghost of Hamlet's royal father is – like much else in the play – less of a
problem than a lie: a lie meaning in this context a conventional or fictional
vehicle standing in for the many things which actual human beings may
experience without being able to categorize or analyse them rationally.
The Ghost is, in *Hamlet*, what falling in love is for the comedies, or the
Crown is for the histories. Like the drowned and undrowned Alonso, the
Ghost must be allowed not to work theologically or politically because he
works so well poetically and theatrically. Beyond a mere theatrical device,
he works so well in terms of human experience as to approximate in the
tragedy to what Henrik Ibsen would much later have a character call the
'life-lie' – not an evil spirit, not even a bad man, but a step forward into
the abysm. The tragedy's opening vista of history, of the whole civilized
past, stretches beyond the old King's victories and defeats to encompass
the murder of Caesar by a friend, and the betrayal of Christ at cock-crow
by a disciple, all of what Prospero calls the 'abysm of time' (*The Tempest*
1.1.50). The very uncertainty about the Ghost when he comes only secures
the sense in reader or auditor that the spectre is true *only* in the response of
love, duty, misery and implication that he calls forth from his only son. In
his 1.5 encounter with the Prince, the Ghost at once becomes recognizable
as the shadow of those demands which the whole great patriarchal past of
civilized Europe makes on its children – that they should not merely or

only have to revenge the past, to carry its burden, but also become it: 'This is I, / Hamlet the Dane' (5.1.254–5) Hamlet echoes his royal father in the graveyard.

King Lear leaves behind it the modernity of *Hamlet* to evoke an archaic past set in a Britain before modern and Christian Europe. But there are shared life-lies. The old dead and failed Danish King longed for a son who would turn an experienced defeat (at the hand of his brother) into victory. Lear, threatened by age and death, needs love publicly articulated as glory, given political resonance and meaning – all of what Sonnet 124 calls 'state'. Lear is surely, no more than Hamlet Senior, an evil spirit, a villain, not even any kind of bad man; his hunger for state is hardly unnatural or infrequent in more commonplace human experience. But as in Hamlet's first scene, high up on the cold midnight battlements, the Ghost walks out of the dark past to hunt down his son, so in the first scene of *King Lear* the life-lie is generated.

The opening court scene of *King Lear* is a beginning which academic critics seem unanimously to have regarded as a mere technical shift, a convention that must be accepted and rapidly forgotten. But Lear's love-test is surely much more than this, a true life-lie. The tragedy's first words show the King 'affecting' this person or that. The word meant at the time 'liking', 'being fond of'. But its use here remains a curious hint of violent and even amatory passion, plus some faint colouring of the modern sense of lying. Lear is a man who, because of his royal power and his old age, cannot either control or make real truth out of his dreams and desires. Full of approval for what seems to him his own rationality ('we shall express our darker purpose', 1.1.35) he sets about bringing into harmony the private and public kingdoms of love – uniting what Sonnet 124 names 'my dear love' with the 'child of state'. By the love-test, his three daughters shall each inherit that share of the kingdom equivalent to their feeling.

But the whole plan is a lie, rife with fallacy. Whatever he took from a source, the very brilliant dramatist that Shakespeare had become, full at once of imagination and plain good sense, could have so deployed his difficult means as to make the test seem reasonable. What happens here makes it plain that princesses and daughters are not mere actors ('shadows' to be auditioned or directed; a kingdom is not its map; love is not political rhetoric). Moreover, the life-lie enlarges in practice. The King must already have divided his kingdom, or he could not hand it out in chunks as he goes along, proclaiming the justice of the process; and there is a strong probability in his helpless rage that he was guided by 'affection' for Cordelia, his 'last and least', to apportion to her that biggest share. This her furious taciturnity prevents. In the wholly undiplomatic chaos that succeeds, it becomes strikingly clear that the old King's powers are hopelessly limited, and he will pull his Court down around himself to disguise that fact. Like Old Hamlet before him, Lear cannot do what he needs to do – and this is what the formal court scene makes surprisingly clear: he cannot do what any good theatre artist does, bring lies to a good end. It in fact takes all the rest of the play to clear the air of this mastering life-lie, that love is what power makes it. When, at the play's end (*The Tragedy of King Lear* 5.3.232 onwards) Lear sees that his now provably loving Cordelia is dead, and himself not blameless for her fate, the understanding kills him. But, far from the illusion of life so many good recent critics and editors still make of it, his last 'Look on her. Look, her lips. / Look there, look there' (5.3.286–7) suggests that in dying he moves at least into the domain of truth. The play is done, the lie is over.

To these great tragedies, *Macbeth* may be so read as to add a kind of luminous footnote, which is all I want to make of it here. The poet and dramatist has given all his life to working with what artless enemies call 'lies'. That opposition he has accepted, and built the lying into his work: which reads more and more deeply into human hungers and dreams, passions and fictions. The entertainment lie becomes the life-lie, the walk into the abysm with eyes closed or blinded. At the beginning of *Macbeth*, witches who may or may not be what we call 'real', factual and proven, invoke into the moral atmosphere of the world it presents a 'fog and filthy air' (1.1.11); they order into existence the simplest of human lies – 'Fair is foul and foul is fair' (1.1.10, a lie that, it needs to be noted, speaks for the aesthetic before it reaches the moral). Rooted as he is in a royalist and warrior-led culture, Macbeth is led to believe that he loves his King; and loving him, wishes to be him; and wishing to be him, must take on royalty by destroying him, as Tarquin rapes Lucrece. All the extreme and glittering ambiguity of the play's language, its wickedly beautiful ironies and cliff-edge doubling of phrases, are bred by that first lying game of 'fair' and 'foul'.

I have taken *Othello* out of what may well be its chronological place in the sequence of major tragedies, which is after *Hamlet*, because it illuminates the issue of lying and truth with an articulacy all its own, and needs therefore to be a little more spaciously thought about. Some of the remarkable things that take place in the tragedy's last scene are not always found as interesting by critics as they are. The dying Desdemona tries to protect her husband from culpability by saying that nobody is to blame, or alternatively that she has smothered herself. But the Moor, jealous even of her claim to heroic goodness here, silences her with 'She's like a liar gone to burning hell. /

'Twas I that killed her' (5.2.138–9). This is of course less criminal than the
murder of an innocent wife, but in other ways is surely Othello's low-water
mark. His snarl is *low*, because shockingly vulgar, raw in the sense that it
relies on social tones and formulae while refusing to honour the inner spirit
of a wife, a woman and a fellow human being. Any justification in terms
of Jacobean misogyny is made doubtful by the truths Posthumus reaches
before the end of *Cymbeline*: 'If each of you should take this course, how
many / Must murder wives much better than themselves / For wrying but
a little!' (5.1.3–5), and 'Is't enough I am sorry? / . . . For Innogen's dear life
take mine; and though / 'Tis not so dear, yet 'tis a life' (5.4.105 and 116–117).
Adulterous or chaste, Innogen is a better human being than himself.

Othello's brutality to the dead Desdemona is 'low', or as Elizabethans
might have said, ignoble, lacking in honour, not because he is mistaken,
as he may or may not be, in calling her a liar: but because he is wrong
in thinking that truth consists in stating facts correctly. Desdemona is
true because true to Othello; Othello is low because not true to her. His
dramatic successor the jealous Posthumus was, as his name suggests, twice-
born, born after death (like the revived Alonso) in coming to understand
that truth does not consist in word or report or any such social mechanism,
but in fidelity to the self and to others – in the course of the play, the
Princess Innogen changes her name (along with her clothes) to that of the
unsexed Fidele, the faithful one. Tragically once-born, the almost pedantic
Othello, for all his passionate love more soldier than artist, cannot change
like Posthumus but only suffer his own full mistaken human fate locked
in the life-lie of romantic love and military honour, whose glory he briefly
retrieves in his last minutes, 'Soft you, a word or two before you go' (*Othello*
5.2.347).

To name Othello's sense of love and honour a 'life-lie' may disturb
some lovers of the play and of the character. This touches on a violent
debate that animated criticism of the play during the second half of the
twentieth century. Eighty years ago, T. S. Eliot dropped the comment that
the magnificent last speech of Othello's spoke for a Senecal arrogance, a lack
of true self-knowledge.[3] This cool appraisal, far from A. C. Bradley's respect
for the Moor as 'noble' (in his *Shakespearean Tragedy* of 1904) triggered two
brilliant studies of the play by F. R. Leavis and William Empson, each as
different from the other in tone and substance as both were from Bradley,
but both with at least some reservations in its response to the Moor.[4] Helen
Gardner took up arms against what she reads as their partisanship for Iago
(and Empson does indeed speak of Iago's 'claim to honesty') in her essay,
'The Noble Moor'. Her reaction to Empsom's word on Iago is 'I cannot

resist adapting from Johnsonian expressions and saying this is "sad stuff"; the man is a liar and there's an end on't'.[5]

This is important because not precisely true: and the whole issue explains the dissension between such able critics over the modern period; sometimes called a tragedy without a meaning, *Othello* is now mostly – understandably but very regrettably – simplified into the political: this is a tragedy of racism. Gardner's 'the man is a liar' allows us to back-track and make a new beginning. She is mistaken: because at critical moments, the play simply doesn't allow us to know whether a character is lying or telling the truth (and one of its sources, *Much Ado About Nothing*, is so different in this way as to imply purpose in the later work). As with all the other major tragedies the fault-line begins in the play's first scene. Iago tells his cat's paw the gentlemanly Roderigo how his own important friends and backers have begged the Moor, General Othello, to promote Iago (on the grounds of length of service) instead of Cassio (who is, says Iago, merely a well-born and graceful type). But, the narrative continues, Othello refused the request, and Iago hates him as a result: secretly (he says) in general, though voicing his attitude publicly to Roderigo here: 'I follow him to serve my turn upon him' (1.1.42).

Did any of this ever, in fact, happen? The play doesn't say. Later in *Othello*, at 3.3, Iago leads the Moor to a climax of jealousy by telling him of a bed-sharing with Cassio and of the man's sexual dreams of Desdemona, part-enacted on Iago's disgusted body (3.3.418–30). Did any of this in fact ever happen? The play doesn't say. These areas of silence in the work seem to me of peculiar importance, though never discussed. 'The Noble Moor' attaches the issue of lying to Iago alone, and sees the character as special in his dishonesty: but this moral contraction is false to the work. The fact is that areas of silence can affect Othello too. At 1.3.170 the Duke says diplomatically of the Moor's recounting of the wooing of Desdemona, given here in public to the Senators, 'I think this tale would win my daughter, too'; and there is something in that word 'tale' (fiction? dream? lie?), and in the whole fabulous autobiography itself, beginning 'her father lov'd me' (1.3.127–68), that leaves a reader or auditor just a little thoughtful. Did any of this ever happen? The play doesn't say. Much in the tragedy turns, or is made to turn, on the handkerchief, woven by holy worms, and with 'magic in the web of it' (3.4.69), but did any of that ever happen, either? Even that last memory of what passed 'in Aleppo once' (5.2.361) is perhaps too good to be entirely true. It might be safe to assume that most of the important characters of Othello lie a little from time to time, or invent romantic myths, or metaphors, or ironies.

But (to return to Desdemona's dying) there are perhaps lies of love, and
lies of hatred – the first involving a truth not of words, but of fidelity to
the self. The marvellous, gruelling first scene of the tragedy creates a world
of urban gossip, metropolitan myths and lethal chattering crowds, where
truth inheres not in babble but in the lonely individual's capacity for trust,
for fidelity. Roderigo is caught in mid-phrase and as it were overheard (as
in a crowd) with his 'Tush, never tell me . . .' (1.1.1), complaining that he
has been drained of money by the man who (he assumed) would use it to
woo Desdemona for him: yet she has, with Iago's connivance perhaps, just
eloped with Othello – 'I take it much unkindly / That thou, Iago, who hast
had my purse / As if the strings were thine, shouldst know of this' (1.1.1–3).
In the tragedy's opening lines, the sense of obscure overhearing, as from a
window over a dark city street, is very perfectly achieved – this is the superla-
tively gifted actor-dramatist I began by supposing: these opening exchanges
are thoroughly opaque, if vaguely and oddly sexual ('who hast had my
purse'). But the lines contain dangerous suppositions. To allow another
person freedom with one's money is effectively to buy that person, even if
the giver intends to profit from the transaction. It is to own and thus direct
the other's right not merely to act, but to think, to 'know of this'. We are in
a world of what the film-maker Mike Leigh has called *Secrets and Lies* – but
the secrets are not beautiful and the lies do not (as in a poem) chart truth.

Roderigo's ugly and messy triangle of propositions about love and money,
self-interest and trust, business and friendship, buying and thinking seems
to have a source, originating (or at least appearing) in a purer form in *The
Merchant of Venice*, where Shylock, tormented by what the Christians have
done to his child and his possessions, two things he himself fuses ('I would
my daughter were dead at my foot, and the jewels in her ear . . .' (3.1.81–2))
determines that Antonio owes him his life-blood; Antonio for his part
believes that he owes all he can give to his friend Bassanio. In Shakespeare's
savage comedy, money, power and love are symbiotic, and this dark vision or
life-lie descends into *Othello* in a street-wise and muddied form, spreading
trouble from the first words: Iago's way of reassuring Roderigo that he is
true to him is to tell the subliminally jealous man that if he, Roderigo is
not manifestly loved then at least his rival is loathed: 'I hate the Moor'
(1.3.278). Tossing hatred between them as in a vicious game, Iago moves
the ball along to Desdemona's father Brabantio, whose peasant 'how got
she out?' (1.1.171), and comparison of his house to some grange (or rustic
farmhouse) as if Desdemona were a fugitive cow or pig, sets circles widening
outwards through the senatorial to the commercial and political: who owns
Desdemona? Who owns Othello?

Desdemona, a good and wise woman though capable of many mistakes, knows the true answer: 'Nobody, I myself' (5.2.133). But, in loving Desdemona, Othello has fallen for Venice too. His outsider status, something in him that is provincial in all his grandeur (he might almost be said to have come from Stratford), fails to understand the underworld of Venice, a noise of vicious gossip threaded through with the malign: 'I take it much unkindly' (1.1.1); 'I follow him to serve my turn upon him' (1.1.42); 'with as little a web as this . . .' (2.1.171). This sinister undertow is a kind of original sin that takes mercenary form in the grandest and richest of capital cities, and there is, strictly speaking, nothing at all Othello can do about it until he has learned its power, even in himself – and by that time, Desdemona is dead. There is perhaps a common-sensical voice, especially in a female reader, that can't be silenced (like Emilia) in the perception that the General might have followed *Much Ado About Nothing*'s Benedick and adjusted the rules of male friendship in a military milieu. He should have told Iago that he couldn't discuss his wife's morals with his sergeant-major, and walked away. But tragedies are neither sermons nor guides to conduct.

Othello may or may not be 'noble', or his heroism may lie in living out the discovery of what it is to possess and to lose nobility: he is merely human. He at first doesn't know, but the play brings him to know, what close neighbours his dreams and desires are to malevolent illusions, all the life-lies of existence. Great general as he is, and lover of Desdemona, he is hopelessly at a loss. But he is a soldier, a child of state even (to quote and adapt a later phrase from this same Sonnet 110) a 'fool of time'. Emilia herself calls him 'gull', 'dolt' and 'ignorant' (5.2.170–1), and the last insult is perhaps the truest: Othello has to have lived and experienced to find out what is, and is not, 'heavenly true' (5.2.144).

Whatever Shakespeare's own factual life was like, and biography is not going to tell us, he must at moments have felt gratitude for a fate unlike his characters'. He had only to write, absorbing in with his materials even the most sceptical or hostile elements in the world around him. Those who saw poetry and drama as a lie, an enemy of what Sonnet 1 calls 'increase', 'abundance', are themselves drawn into a fuller understanding of the great life-lies. For this, Shakespeare must often have been grateful to his own beginnings in provincial small-town Stratford, which taught him to distrust mere art, but to trust true creativity. Those who fail to be able, for snobbish or other 'ignorant' reasons, to locate the genius of the work in Shakespeare of Stratford, have failed to do what the editors of the First Folio in their prefatory epistle demanded: which is, that we should 'Read him.'

PART III

A cultural phenomenon: Did Shakespeare write Shakespeare?

This third and final section considers the dynamic afterlife of the authorship discussion, since it originated more than a century and a half ago with the writings of Delia Bacon. Kathleen E. McLuskie (Chapter 14) discusses how and why anti-Shakespearian stories are told, their political, cultural and psychological dynamics. The kinds of evidence that the doubters summon into play need always to be carefully contextualized. Andrew Murphy (Chapter 15) gives a fascinating account of Delia Bacon's influence (almost half a century after her death) on Hester Dowden (daughter of the famous Shakespeare scholar Edward Dowden). Murphy provides one illuminating example of how and why anti-Shakespearianism can take a powerful hold on an intelligent person's intellect. Paul Franssen then identifies narrative tropes in fictional accounts of the authorship discussion, and shows how they have a propensity to re-invent as well as repeat themselves (Chapter 16). Stuart Hampton-Reeves (Chapter 17) presents a critical investigation into the anti-Shakespearians' online 'Declaration of Reasonable Doubt', its methodology and adherents. Douglas Lanier (Chapter 18) discusses the narrative, cultural and historical energies of Roland Emmerich's 2011 film *Anonymous* and lays out how it works towards (and in hindsight missed) its anti-Shakespearian goal. Although the film was a box office disaster it remains a fascinating document in the on-going history of anti-Shakespearianism. This final part of our book concludes with Paul Edmondson's consideration (Chapter 19) of the different kinds of antagonism which clash at the heart of the Shakespeare authorship discussion and its infiltration into at least two universities. His account is illustrated by close reference to The Shakespeare Birthplace Trust's Shakespeare Authorship Campaign.

CHAPTER 14

'This palpable device': Authorship and conspiracy in Shakespeare's life

Kathleen E. McLuskie

> We humans tend to marry, date, befriend and talk with people who
> already agree with us, and hence are less likely to say, 'Wait a minute –
> that's just not true.'[1]

Delia Bacon, we are told, went mad. John Thomas Looney's name can be
mispronounced to chime with an insult to mad people. Mockery of mental
illness is an unusual accompaniment to serious intellectual discussion. Its
persistent background in the authorship debate,[2] together with the anger
and name-calling that also accompany it, suggests that more than the facts
of the case are at issue.[3] The emotion that often accompanies discussion
of Shakespeare's life seems to involve more than the pathology of individual adherents to one side or another. It seems rather to travel along the
boundary between the life and the plays, between the recurring stories that
make emotional sense of the world and the systems of codified knowledge
that carry the authority of truth. The tension between knowledge and
emotion that this debate reveals can be explained in social and historical
terms.[4] However, its recurrence across two centuries suggests that psychology may also provide an explanatory model, not only for the authorship
debate but for the many occasions when the evidence for a case does not
meet the emotional demands that it makes on its proponents. Emotional
reaction to public issues is often dismissed as 'conspiracy theory', especially
by those who do not share it, but an attempt to understand the structure
of conspiracy as a narrative and as a set of emotions might illuminate the
psychological work that it performs.

Familiar stories, including those used in the plays of Shakespeare, are
often heard as part of the primary experiences of growing up: the development of affect within the fundamental relations of love and desire and
the process of understanding the difference between oneself and other
people. Adult knowledge of a complex world involves the often painful
business of rejecting those stories, putting away childish things, dismissing

the 'woman's story at a winter's fire' (*Macbeth* 3.6.64) of a world in which the wicked tyrant will be slain, the ghost will tell the truth and the lovers will live happily ever after. But the stories never go away. In moments of emotional pressure they seem to return. When a child dies, the codified knowledge of science may be angrily rejected;[5] when a public figure is killed, the sentence on the murderer must be equal to the public pain he has caused; when frightening economic change collides with people's lives, a sufficiently authoritative figure must be held responsible. 'The King, the King's to blame.'

The classical myths, including those of Oedipus and Medea, have long since been associated with the explanations of psychic states, and their recurring repetition in literature and popular culture increases their explanatory potency.[6] Shakespeare's stories also provide a rich store of emotionally satisfying ways of explaining the world. The psychology of his characters and their eloquent articulation of their emotional states play an important role in sustaining the continuing attention to his work. In what follows, I will suggest that it also structures the emotional satisfaction that we demand from the story of the life.

POLITICS AND LIES

In the middle of *Richard III*, as the action speeds towards Richard's triumph, there occurs a curious still moment. A Scrivener enters and shows the audience the fair copy of 'the indictment of the good Lord Hastings' that he had prepared so 'That it may be today read o'er in Paul's'. He then explains the puzzling time sequence between the order to write out the indictment and the charges levied against its subject:

> And mark how well the sequel hangs together:
> Eleven hours I have spent to write it over,
> For yesternight by Catesby was it sent me;
> The precedent was full as long a-doing;
> And yet, within these five hours, Hastings lived,
> Untainted, unexamined, free, at liberty.
>
> (3.6.4–9)

The fact that due process had not been observed in Hastings's execution is no surprise to the audience. We have already witnessed the extraordinary scene where Buckingham and Richard had frightened the Lord Mayor into thinking he was surrounded by enemies, Hastings's head had been carried in by Lovel and Ratcliffe, Richard and Buckingham had acted out their regret with crocodile tears of disappointment at Hastings's perfidy and the Lord Mayor had agreed that Hastings must have 'daubed his vice with show of virtue'. The layers of half-truth and falsehood, of counterfeit, persuasion and frightened acquiescence, are piled against the implacable reality of a severed head on the stage. The scene can be played as wit or tragedy, horror or comic grotesque. It shows us Richard and Buckingham at their most inventive: playing their multiple roles to the full, in complete control of the situation, managing and manipulating the politics and the personal relationships to keep the game in play.

The Scrivener's speech is different: as the keeper of the record, he is as clear about the difference between truth and falsehood as he is about the link between silence and fear:

> Who is so gross
> That cannot see this palpable device?
> Yet who so bold but says he sees it not?
> Bad is the world, and all will come to naught,
> When such ill dealing must be seen in thought.
> (3.6.10–14)

But the Scrivener never reappears. The rhyming moral of his conclusion has ethical force but no dramatic power. Richard is not finally overcome by civil servants or the anxious citizens whose passive resistance is 'like dumb statuas or breathing stones' (3.7.25) but by force of arms and the flight of his closest friends.

This sequence of scenes from *Richard III* presents a remarkable dramatization of a particular narrative of political power. It sets the charismatic, unscrupulous leader of men and events against the timid acquiescence of legal functionaries, local dignitaries and the common people. This model of politics has been reinforced again and again in twentieth-century adaptations of the play. It has become so recognizable that it only takes a change of settings and style to establish corroborative analogies between Richard and mythologized tyrants from Hitler to Saddam Hussein.[7] These productions work, because of the neat, recognizable familiarity of the Shakespeare analogy, but they also provide the theatrical pleasure of placing the audience in the know. They reinforce a widely held view that all tyrants behave in the same devious and violent way, regardless of their politics, and allow their audience to see the truth from the perspective of the powerless ones. The audience may be engaged by Richard's machinations but they also share the Scrivener's understanding of 'this palpable device'.

In this version of history and politics the alert audience can make the connection between the intention and the act: they see the whole picture, they watch from the secure ethical position that can distinguish between truth and falsehood, playing and deceit. Consequently, history makes sense: there are winners and losers, tyrants and victims, and their motivation is complex and contradictory enough to be interesting and even controversial. The controversy is possible because the audience knows and sees the truth, not only about this particular narrative but about the implied (though historically debatable) continuities of politics and power.

Many in the audience for the multiple versions of *Richard III* know, of course, that Shakespeare is not writing history: that other versions of the story have been told. They may even speculate that the author had an ulterior motive in offering this particular version of the triumph of the Tudor ascendancy, or that the director had a special reason to highlight the topical analogy. But even that speculation follows the same narrative model: the truth can be found by setting one story against another, by being alert to every 'palpable device' that the powerful might use against the unwary.

This satisfying model of politics as the complex interplay of competing interests is the antithesis of the dispersed and formalized power structures of contemporary democracies. Their adversarial party structures and celebrity political leaders allow occasional narratives of competing interests to structure journalists' narratives of public events. However, for the most part, the business-as-usual process of liberal democratic government is subject to scrutiny through formal procedures: periodic examples of malfeasance are dealt with by investigation through routine regulatory scrutiny of parliamentary committees and the Public Accounts Committee; more significant crises are followed by the painstaking analysis of evidence and deposition in lengthy public enquiries. These enquiries often deal with events that are disastrous for those affected by them: the Bloody Sunday enquiry or the report on the invasion of Iraq come to mind. Yet their process is too long, too painstaking, too complex and ultimately too distant to effect the satisfying closure of single combat, the villains vanquished, some pardoned and some punished, within a clear moral framework and a sense of satisfying inevitability.

Some twentieth-century productions of *Richard III* have used their modern setting to suggest 'that war had given way to bureaucracy', a state of affairs that one historian of the play's productions described as 'no great stretch of imagination' for post Second World War England'.[8] That view of contemporary due process, however, already suggests a scepticism about the effectiveness of democratically established protocols, seeing in them a mere obfuscation of the real machinations by which authority is sustained.

This consensus about the real story of politics allows the play's council meetings in Act 3, that eliminate Hastings from the courtly circle, to be played as civil servants round a conference table.[9] Those civic settings create a recognizable image of modern practice but often embody a knowing irony about the actual political relations that they are assumed to disguise.

Those images from *Richard III* are seldom directly referred to in modern discussions of political conspiracy, but the contrast that Shakespeare creates between the dangerously unpredictable leader and the ineffectual structures of civic power remains an important cultural image of the political process. As the comedian Bill Hicks fantasized,

> whoever's elected president . . . when you win, you go into this smoky room with the twelve industrialist, capitalist, scumfunks that got you in there . . . and this little screen comes down . . . and it's a shot of the Kennedy assassination.[10]

Hicks, like many satirical comedians, is playing the part of the Scrivener: the honest broker who can reveal the truth. He gathers around him sympathizers who will understand the truth even as they recognize that they are powerless to intervene in the story. They are 'but mutes or audience to this act': their role, if they are witnessing a tragedy, is, like Hamlet's final audience, to 'tremble and look pale'. If they are witnessing a satiric performance, whether given by Hicks or Thersites, it is to offer the knowing laugh. The connection between the play world of a Shakespeare performance or a stand-up's rant and the contradictory tangles of the life world exists only in the plausibility and effectiveness of the stories that they tell. Neither of them can offer a complete or even complex account of the truth about particular events, as most of their audience are aware. This lack of effective connection between play worlds and real-life agency is a political and an aesthetic problem, both of them tied up with the psychological satisfactions of pleasure and fear.

Shakespeare's own characters often explicitly reflect on that relationship. They discuss the gap between the strange and the true (*Cymbeline* 1.1), debating the power of imagination to embody forth the forms of things unknown but also its dangerous tendency to suppose a bush a bear (*A Midsummer Night's Dream* 5.1.1–23).[11] This intellectually pleasurable blurring of the truth of the onstage and off-stage worlds, the artistic exploration of the overlap between the imagination and the mirror up to nature, occasionally allows Shakespeare's characters, especially those in distress, to claim a more telling analogy between familiar narratives and their own situation. Hamlet is convinced that the truth of his father's murder can be revealed in the fiction of the murder of Gonzalo, and Lysander comforts Hermia with the tragic parallels to their story of thwarted love (*A Midsummer Night's Dream* 1.1). The comforting synergies between a particular intractable situation and analogous narratives allow the possibility of resolution in which the emotional and ethical can be resolved in satisfactory ways.

A similar confusion between narrative resolution and a literal understanding of complex historical events is evident throughout David Aaronovitch's powerful account of the recurring conspiracy theories of the modern era. These often widely believed, if counter-intuitive, stories attempt to explain the disastrous events of war, economic collapse, terrorist violence and random celebrity murders through narratives of good and evil. The recurrence of the anti-semitic myth of the Protocols of the Elders of Zion, or the knowing accounts of government collusion in disasters from the invasion of Pearl Harbour to the 9/11 attack on the twin towers in New York, take the same form of alleged secret plots, of a complicated denial of existing explanations and a knowing rejection of public knowledge as gullible or naive.

By their nature, the events these conspiracies refer to have either no explanation or one too complex to afford the expected allocation of punishment and expiation. Their occurrence in a world of modern communications also allows them to be explained in stories. Accounts from investigative journalism are followed by books and movies, whose narrative structure follows the familiar genres of the thriller as well as the tragedy. Distaste for the cold war triumphalism of the 1969 moon landings fuelled the narrative of a massive hoax, planned by NASA and the US government. But the story was also told in the 1978 movie, *Capricorn One*. The assassination of John F. Kennedy was the subject of enquiry and counter-enquiry but the voluminous evidence, analysed by the Warren Commission and the alternative committees that also investigated it, could be more effectively represented as the personal crusade of an eloquent single figure, dramatized in the 1991 Oliver Stone film, *JFK*. The film was subtitled 'The Story that Won't Go Away' in recognition of its potential for endless retelling that met commercial objectives, to be sure, but also played to audiences' pleasure in the narrative.

In every case, an undoubtedly significant event was turned into a narrative in which uncertainties in the sequence of events ('how well the sequel hangs together') are turned into the 'palpable device' of motivated action, a true story revealed by a heroic and indomitable 'ordinary man'. These powerless Scrivener figures become the heroes whose enemy, in order to be worthy of them, needs to be 'the perfect model of malice, a kind of amoral superman: sinister, ubiquitous, powerful, cruel, sensual, luxury loving'.[12] Because these stories are always in the past, the tragic outcome is unchangeable: the man of integrity remains unheard, the forces of evil are undefeated and nothing is but what it seems.

The connection between this model of the enemy and Shakespeare's Richard III is indirect and unexplicit. Nevertheless, the model of a powerless populace and an evil adversary has become generalized not only in recurring productions of Shakespeare's play but in its indiscriminate application in conspiracy theories to Trotskyites and Jews, bankers and mafia bosses. Shakespeare's stories often hover behind the modern conspiracies: the TV journalist Ed Murrrow quoted *Julius Caesar* in his account of the McCarthy hearings[13] and Shakespearian as well as eighteenth-century republican rhetoric shaped the final courtroom revelations in Oliver Stone's *JFK*.

The counter-traffic from political conspiracy to Shakespeare productions is even clearer. It has become common to end *Macbeth* with the victor's return to the witches or to undermine the heroism of Richmond's victory as the commonplace mid-twentieth-century view of the tragic cycle of history which flattens out the more complex connection between past narratives and contemporary truth.[14] The plays' narratives may not end this way: their explicit direction often denies the implication that all history and all politics is an unending conflict of evil with evil that pushes the knowing but powerless little people aside. Contemporary commonplaces about politics, informed, it must be said, by some actual examples of corruption and malfeasance, have however joined the circulating stories. If the stories are to offer a plausible sense that Shakespeare is our contemporary, the mirror that they hold up to nature must reflect a pleasurable image of the corrupted currents of this world.

As the social analyst Margaret Somers has suggested,

Narratives . . . not only convey information but serve epistemological purposes. They do so by establishing veracity through the integrity of their storied form . . . in the first instance the success or failure of truth-claims embedded in narratives depends less on empirical verification and more on the logic and rhetorical persuasiveness of the narrative. In this way the narrative . . . takes on the mantle of epistemology and endows the information it conveys with the stature of knowledge, fact and truth.[15]

The stories are not completely impermeable: the psychology of pleasure and fear is not the only determinant of adult human responses, and complex, democratic societies have a plurality of possible sources of information and authority. However invoking alternative knowledge in the middle of a performance only spoils the story. When the Duke himself intervenes in the play of Pyramus and Thisbe with suggestions for a more effective way to represent Wall, Pyramus fearlessly insists

> No, in truth, sir, he should not. 'Deceiving me'
> is Thisbe's cue. She is to enter now, and I am to
> spy her through the wall. You shall see, it will
> fall pat as I told you. Yonder she comes.
> (*A Midsummer Night's Dream* 5.1.182–6)

In order to fall pat, to make the sequence hang together, the story must be told in one way and not another. The way the story is told will not determine the audience's reaction to real-life parallels, but it may complicate the pleasures they provide.

TELLING THE SHAKESPEARE STORY

Shakespeare's dramatization of the complex and contested connection between narrative and truth has signally complicated the narrative and truth of his own lifestory. The connection between the plays of Shakespeare and a life that will be worthy of them lies across the boundary between truth and imagination. It also lies across the methodologies of history and literary appreciation. As records and documents are more systematically catalogued and their provenance more clearly established in modern library practice, the opportunity to cross the boundary bearing new evidence diminishes. Even scholarly re-examination of the old evidence tends to outline 'the more likely but distinctly less-exciting scenario'[16] that the author of Shakespeare's plays was a theatrical player, born and educated in a Midlands town with no unequivocally recorded connection to either the subversive or the high-born metaphorical players on the imagined stages of popular history.

That contrast between a likely story and an exciting one disappoints the growing passion for history in battle re-enactments and genealogical searches.[17] It also runs counter to the modern democratic prejudice against a settled consensus, especially one that is upheld by established institutions. The sense that the truth is always trammelled by the vested interests is not restricted to readings of *Richard III*. In the twenty-first century, the authority of academic research in particular is often seen as a combination of dry pedantry and special pleading. For those who have a special interest in challenging the likely story, as Samuel Schoenbaum and James Shapiro have shown, the conclusions of scholarly controversy can sometimes represent sinister collusion in an exclusive club. The stories of Shakespeare's life and the stories of secret knowledge and power-broking that link the plays and the world are never far behind.[18]

In the parallel world of conspiratorial analogies new stories may be imagined in which the teller, like Shakespeare's Scrivener, is cast as the one who reveals 'the palpable device' of received ideas. Alternative accounts of Shakespeare's life reveal not only the old conspiracy to disguise the true author of the plays, they also develop new stories of a modern plot to disguise the truth of their findings. For example, one such would-be truth teller, Charlton Ogburn, described resistance to his authorship theory as 'an intellectual Watergate'.[19] His charge was able to build on the familiarity of the Watergate affair, as told in popular film, to cast himself as the fearless journalists, Woodward and Bernstein, and the academic researchers as the bungling hirelings in the pay of the most powerful politician in the Western world.[20] In the conflict between imagined and hidden stories, the truth of Shakespeare's life and inspiration had become less a matter of established record than a contest over casting in a latter day psychomachia between adversaries whose effectiveness could be established by the style of their performance.[21]

The need for a constant recasting that will make the story new and exciting has had a permanent effect on the base-line story of the man from Stratford who made his fortune in London writing plays for both court and people. That story has been retold countless times and it appears in every genre and medium from children's comics to high-budget feature films. Its default narrative maps easily onto a familiar narrative structure in which outstanding achievement is the result of individual aspiration, initiative and creativity.[22] However, its familiarity and repetition, together with scepticism about the optimistic model of social development that it proposes, have given it the status of a folk myth, 'a woman's story at a winter's fire', and reduced its power as a narrative that will account for the position of Shakespeare in contemporary culture.

The raw records of Shakespeare's life and even the more extended documents that hint at relationships and a shared professional life, somehow fail to tell the story that will meet the psychological needs of later readers. Halliwell-Phillipps's regret that none of the documents discovered in his own time 'discloses those finer traits of thought and action we are sure must have pervaded the author of *Lear* and *Hamlet* in his communication with the more cultivated of his contemporaries'[23] evokes a wistful suggestion of the conversation that he himself might have had with Shakespeare. Even the scrupulous Edmond Malone, scourge of the fantasist and forger, allowed himself to imagine

That these letters, [in a recently announced find] if indeed they exist, and are dated 1606, or about that time, will turn out to be letters of thanks to the Treasurer, for some bounty transmitted through his hands by King James, in return for the tragedy of Macbeth.[24]

Both these writers, like many since, placed Shakespeare in an Elizabethan world framed by its writers and its monarchs. The modern archival work that suggests that King James VI and I himself had no personal connection to the playing company that used his name[25] or that Shakespeare's close companions included a head-dress maker and a violent pimp[26] come not only from different scholarly methodologies: they come from different kinds of story, from different worlds and different genres. They create different pleasurable locations for their readers and a different relationship to the authority of their narrators.

Those relationships and the subtlety with which they are framed are critical to how a story is to be believed. Stephen Greenblatt, for example, in *Will in the World*, gently distances its narrator from the 'dogged archival labour' of the 'eager scholars' who have provided him and other biographers with the information that shapes their stories. Acknowledging the 'huge gaps in knowledge that make any biographical study of Shakespeare an exercise in speculation', he moves elegantly from the telling anecdote to the imagined experience, weaving connections from the known story to the less well known but not implausible world. Evidence that the Earl of Worcester's Men and the Queen's Men were paid for performances in Stratford in the year that Shakespeare was five years old transmutes into an 'unspeakably thrilling' event in the imagination of the boy himself. Accounts of schooling in Stratford turn Jacques's 'whining school-boy . . . creeping like snail / Unwillingly to school' into the image of a boy running home during the lunch-break while the curriculum that apparently involved 'compiling lists of Latin synonyms' becomes the key to the repeated adjectives describing lust in Shakespeare's Sonnet 129. Elegant analogy replaces scholarly exegesis, the tentative subjunctive mood replaces the authoritative indicative one. As Touchstone found in his challenge to the lying courtier, 'Your "if" is the only peacemaker; much virtue in "if"' (*As You Like It* 5.4.100–1).

The overall effect is to create a Shakespeare who seems much more recognizable than before: he lives 'with bread like you; feel[s] want / Taste[s] grief, need[s] friends' (*Richard II* 3.2.171–2). He provides the reader with opportunities for empathy and reinforces the relationship between the reader and the universal genius of the twenty-first-century imagination.

The narrative strategy connects the narrative and themes of the plays directly to familiar images from the time without going through the elusive connections between events and their archival record. Shakespeare, it is alleged, could only reveal himself in his plays because his life took place in dangerous times, under the shadow of the traitors' heads on London Bridge, on the edges of such exciting events as the execution of the Catholic martyr, Campion, or Lopez, the Jewish physician to the Queen. The poverty-stricken death of his rival poet, Greene, made him wary of the temptations of bohemian profligacy, the mysterious murder of Marlowe warned him off political intrigue, but the fascination of courtly power drew him into a dangerous relationship with Southampton and royal patronage ensured his playing company's continued social and financial success.

The story teeters on the bridge between history and imagination. It is informed by recent social history that engages with the imagined mentalities of the period's disenfranchised groups[27] and the period detail offered has all the vividness of the continuity effects of heritage cinema, an authenticating background to the current Shakespeare myth with no jarring insistence on counter-intuitive fact. The narrative style is that of the 'time-traveller' genre: the narrator/hero from the present, like Virginia Woolf's Orlando, or, more recently, Woody Allen's Gill Pender,[28] wanders through a past landscape encountering its iconic figures whose presence authenticates its reality.[29]

The shift in genre and style is important. When a nineteenth-century writer asserts that Shakespeare attended the Earl of Leicester's Kenilworth festivities 'as a capable and gratified spectator in the suite of his high-minded kinsman, the head of the Arden family',[30] the form of the assertion as well as the snobbery of the attempted connection between the poet and socially elevated companions invites scepticism.[31] On the other hand, when Queen Elizabeth herself joins the delighted audience for the production of *Romeo and Juliet* in the finale of *Shakespeare in Love*, knowing that the Queen never attended the public theatre has no impact on the pleasure of the story. In the world of biographical entertainment, the truest poetry is the most feigning. The pleasures of the story always trump the facts of the case.

THE LIMITS OF THE STORY

These fluid connections between poetic truth and fantasized knowledge create a troublesome basis for distinguishing between the playful and the instrumental deployment of the counter-factual *jeu d'esprit*. The myth that writing was a dangerous business in Renaissance London or that it depended on courtly patronage, can inform an elegant narrative extrapolation from complex individual cases to analogous examples from Shakespeare's plays. It can also be generalized into the founding assumption of those who retell fabulous tales of the secret aristocratic author of Shakespeare's plays. The imagined story of the heroic independent individual who alone knows the truth can be used to create a labyrinthine narrative in which a quite different author has both to conceal his work and to foist responsibility on to the man from Stratford.

The narrator hero of these alternative stories is less the engaged time-traveller and more the authoritative omniscient narrator of the thriller. Their settings present an insistence on courtly power represented by the familiar signifiers of historical romance: tramping soldiers, clanging prison gates and torches flaming in the night. Perhaps paradoxically, their claims to offer a truth stranger than fiction are often located in mysterious 'archives', represented by shots of a disembodied quill pen writing black letters on parchment[32] that require special skills and secret knowledge to decipher them.[33] The necessary first premise of these stories is a necessary connection between systematic mendacity and absolute power. Individual examples of courtly plotting from the history of the Elizabethan court can then be generalized into manifestations of a totalitarian state machine controlling a chain reaction that links even the most random events. As Aaronovitch describes, this process of moving from one agreed view to another is fundamental to the non-sequiturs of contemporary conspiracy:

And if you thought that JFK had been killed by 'them', then why not his brother, gunned down in California in 1968? Or Martin Luther King, shot dead in Memphis in the same year? Or go back to 1965 and the New York slaying of black leader Malcolm X?[34]

These assertions of the virtue of 'If' create a closed circuit of false connections that depend on the fallacy of the primary assumption. Intervening to say 'wait a minute; that's just not true' disrupts the sequence, challenges the narrator's control, spoils the pleasure of the story and violates the social and psychic pleasures of sharing a world view.

Recognizing the false logic and exposing it, of course, offers a different pleasure. It is illustrated in Touchstone's account of

a certain knight that swore 'by his honour' they were good pancakes, and swore 'by his honour' the mustard was naught. Now I'll stand to it the pancakes were naught and the mustard was good, and yet was not the knight forsworn. (*As You Like It* 1.2.60–4)

The knight's honour does not exist, so the quality of either pancakes or mustard is beside the point. The pleasure that Touchstone offers is similar to the Scrivener's: the audience are allowed to be the knowing, clever people, superior, for now, to the absent and unfortunate knight. In the terms of the authorship debate if Shakespeare's writing was not a coded allegory of courtly intrigue or a sycophantic bid for patronage, then the story of fantasy and intrigue collapses. But the collapse also creates the psychic dissonance between the satisfaction of one story and the disruption of another.

When the works and life of Shakespeare are placed in the wider context of early modern society it becomes clear how similarly limited the 'if' connections are. William Ingram's comprehensive analysis of the entire archive that surrounds cherry-picked references to theatre demonstrates that the authorities in Shakespeare's England had more pressing tasks in hand than the regulation of theatre, and Richard Dutton has shown that cases of censorship against dramatists are more often the result of localized and personal offences than the systematic and sinister operations of an absolutist state.[35] These books and others like them return their readers to a quotidian world where the development of theatre and its relations to the court was a matter of negotiation based on a shared understanding of the necessary rituals and compromises of social existence. None of these accounts of early modern politics and culture denies the imaginative power of Shakespeare's plays. However, their work demonstrates the critical difference between a fictional world where all the characters are, often ingeniously, linked into the story and the historical life-world where, much more often, 'There is a sense of vacancy and effort, of a tragedy that has no crisis, of characters that meet but do not clash.'[36]

These forms of social history are directed towards larger historical patterns of continuity and change rather than the satisfactions of empathy with individuals.[37] The limits that they set on the story of Shakespeare's life not only circumscribe its plausibility, they also restrict the pleasures of an imagined relationship between the reader and the past.

The popular history of the twenty-first century, by contrast, depends on placing the reader or viewer at the centre of the story. Its multifarious manifestations in 'vintage fashions, historical painting, what if? novels, found magazines and items, outbound tourism and historical holidays'[38] offer their participants 'unique freedom to roam the centuries – to explore the intricacies of our ancestors' minds and habits'.[39] The search for 'Our ancestors' is an individual quest: it offers the appeal of a direct and recognizable connection to the past, most readily met by genealogical searches that literally reveal 'our ancestors' in the records now available online. This approach to the past is supported by the movement for freedom of information, the sense that it is possible to get behind the official reports to the 'original documents' (like the Scrivener's deposition) that will contain the truth.[40]

This new sense of a democratic right to access the raw data, combined with a belief that it will provide an indisputable truth, has had an interesting effect on the story of Shakespeare's life. In 2008, the actor Mark Rylance instituted 'The Shakespearean Authorship Trust', inviting a range of Shakespeare authorities, including academics, to sign up to a 'statement of reasonable doubt' about the connection between Shakespeare from Stratford and the authorship of Shakespeare's plays.[41] By using the term 'reasonable doubt', Rylance echoes the legal concept that protects litigants against wrongful conviction and places the truth about particular cases in the hands of citizens' rather than experts' judgments. The air of forensic objectivity implied in the phrase, however, neglects the important accompanying legal procedures of admissible evidence and the authority of a presiding judge. It presents doubt as the legitimating source of scepticism without establishing the terms or the nature of evidence through which that doubt might be resolved. It began, once again, the search for the key document that would resolve once and for all the questions addressed by each and every individual who might remain unconvinced. Sadly, the campaign to establish the principle of 'reasonable doubt' can no more resolve the story of Shakespeare's imagined life than earlier efforts to speak with the dead, or open the grave or read between the lines of the plays for coded messages. For all its secular, forensic language, the search for authoritative evidence that will resolve all doubts, end the story, declare the triumph of truth has closer analogies with desire for a more satisfying alternative reality than with logical reasoning. The pathos and comedy of that search are the stuff of stories, not history.

Shakespeare, once again, has provided the most telling example. Indulging his fantasy of power over Olivia's household, and encouraged by the isolated fact that 'the Lady of the Strachey married the yeoman of the wardrobe', Malvolio finds that the letter he discovers has all the marks of authenticity:

By my life, this is my lady's hand. These be her
very c's, her u's, and her t's, and thus makes she her
great P's. It is in contempt of question her hand.
(*Twelfth Night* 2.5.37–8, 85–7)

Different productions of *Twelfth Night* will treat Malvolio's fantastic find
with different degrees of sympathy or mockery. The way that they do so will
differently inflect the comedy or unease of the second half of the play where
he is punished for his presumption and the finale where he vows revenge.
Shakespeare's treatment of this story allows its audiences and adapters to
reflect on the relationship between truth and desire. Malvolio is clearly
comically mistaken but Mavolio's misprision can be treated as a harmless
consoling fantasy or as an act of insubordination that presents a dangerous
threat to the happiness of Illyria.

We might ask similar questions of the varied ways that the story of
Shakespeare's life is told in our own time. Doing so will open further
questions about genres and taste, about the borders between fantasy and
knowledge, and about writing history that reveals the complexity of the
past rather than endlessly arguing over the story that won't go away.

CHAPTER 15

Amateurs and professionals: Regendering Bacon

Andrew Murphy

Foiled Traill's plan of naming a Committee on Degrees for Women out of the supporters of that scheme, + helped to get the other side well represented. It will come to nothing.

Edward Dowden[1]

. . . they are, of course, and must needs be, the strong-holds of the past – those ancient and venerable seats of learning. . . . [Their principle] is, of course, instinctively conservative. Their business is to know nothing of the new. The new intellectual movement must fight its battles through without, and come off conqueror there, or ever those old Gothic doors will creak on their reluctant hinges to give it ever so pinched an entrance.

Delia Bacon[2]

Please don't become a Baconian. I am pestered, in the obsolete sense, by the number of them, + some are so nice + amiable you can't well tell them that they are natural philosophers in Touchstone's sense of the words.

Edward Dowden[3]

In 1855, John Kells Ingram, Fellow of Trinity College Dublin, extended his Chair of Oratory at the college to include a remit in English Literature. In London at the time Delia Bacon was living in Spring Street, Paddington, at the home of a greengrocer, Mr Walker.[4] Over the next several years, Ingram lectured on various literary topics, including the plays of Shakespeare, before being succeeded in the Trinity Chair by Edward Dowden, who would publish, in 1875, the highly acclaimed *Shakspere: A Critical Study of His Mind and Art* – one of the standard Victorian works on the poet's career and writings. Eighteen years prior to the appearance of Dowden's book Delia Bacon had, of course, as Samuel Schoenbaum nicely puts it, unleashed 'a streak of crazed lightning' across the literary sky by publishing a study claiming that Shakespeare had not actually written the plays attributed to him.⁵ Bacon gained – and continues, of course, if indirectly, to gain – many followers. Dowden, in his time, was briskly dismissive of them; in a letter to a fellow professor, W. F. P. Stockley, he writes: 'As to the Baconians – nothing disturbs their assurance, and the assurance goes with amazing ignorance.'⁶

Ingram and Dowden, on the one hand, and Delia Bacon, on the other, lived, we might say, in parallel worlds. This is true in the rather obvious sense that they had wholly different views about the authorship question. Ingram and Dowden both believed firmly that 'the man from Stratford' had written the plays which appeared under his name. Indeed, for Dowden, the Stratford connection was a fundamental part of the playwright's constitution. In *Mind and Art*, he offered a tripartite model of Shakespeare's psychological make-up, proposing that the playwright was prone to excesses both of passion (like Romeo) and of brooding thought (like Hamlet), but that these tendencies were balanced by the commercialist instinct of the Stratford speculator who invested heavily in land and property in his home town. For Dowden, this triangulated system functioned generally in a state of delicate equilibrium.⁷ Bacon, by contrast, could see *only* the commercialist Stratfordian in the historical William Shakespeare and, for her, the sheer fact of his being a speculator served as evidence, in itself, that he could never have written the plays. This, indeed, is a common theme within the multiple varieties of anti-Shakespearianism. As James Shapiro has noted, for those who deny Shakespeare's authorship of the plays there is an irreconcilable tension 'between Shakespeare the poet and Shakespeare the businessman; between the London playwright and the Stratford haggler; between Shakespeare as Prospero and Shakespeare as Shylock' and so the inevitable conclusion arises 'that we were dealing not with one man, but two'.⁸ As Bacon herself observed to Thomas Carlyle: 'you do not know what is really in the plays if you believe that that booby wrote them' (in response, Carlyle is said to have shrieked, loudly).⁹

Bacon stands, then, on the opposite side of the authorial divide from Ingram and Dowden. But there are other ways too in which she can be said to have lived in a different world from that occupied by the two Irishmen. Gary Taylor, in *Reinventing Shakespeare*, has noted that the anti-Stratfordian movement 'arose at the moment when Shakespeare was institutionalised and expropriated by the new civil servants of literature'.¹⁰ The 'civil servants' Taylor has in mind here are that group of professional, university-based literary commentators who emerged over the course of the nineteenth century and who came, in time, to dominate literary analysis. The professionalization of English as a discipline across the nineteenth century is all of a piece with a more general trend towards professionalism throughout the period. As Josephine Guy has noted, during the course of the century 'knowledge increasingly passed into the hands of the universities and learned societies (and their equally learned journals)'.[11] This was not just a process of the concentration of knowledge, of course: it was also a matter, effectively, of creating communities of insiders and – just as significantly – of outsiders. As Harold Perkin has observed: 'professional society is based on human capital created by education and enhanced by strategies of closure, that is, the exclusion of the unqualified'.[12] From this perspective, we can say that Ingram and Dowden were clearly insiders – academics with the full authority and resources of their college behind them; Bacon, by contrast, was an outsider, with no institutional affiliation or support. Thus, for example, where Ingram and Dowden pursued their work with the financial backing of their university employer, Bacon's extended stay in England – where substantial parts of *The Philosophy of the Plays of Shakspere Unfolded* were written – was funded by the New York lawyer and banker, Charles Butler. This was, effectively, a patronage relationship: already a rather old-fashioned form of support for literary or scholarly work by the beginning of the nineteenth century.[13] Butler eventually lost interest in Bacon and her project and he refused to continue supporting her, leaving her effectively destitute and on the brink, on at least one occasion, of starvation.[14]

There is one further – and rather obvious – point to be made here. Bacon was an outsider because she had no formal institutional training or affiliation. But there was, in fact, never any possibility of her accessing such training or securing such an affiliation – for the starkly simple reason that she was a woman. Bacon lived in an era before women were permitted to enter most universities in the US and the UK – indeed, relative to men, the amount even of general schooling they received was often quite limited. The contrast between her life and that of her brother, Leonard (her parents' eldest son), is very striking in this regard. Leonard attended Yale, going on to Andover Theological Seminary and becoming a Congregationalist minister and a figure of real standing in the New Haven community. His sister, by contrast, received a grand total of one year's formal schooling, at an institution run by Catherine and Mary Beecher. Leonard wrote home from Yale to his younger brother David, making reference to reading both Shakespeare and Bacon; his sister had to find her own way to these authors – and make her own sense of them when she read them. (There is also, we might note in passing here, a rather savage irony in the fact that, among Leonard's sponsors during his time at Yale and Andover were the Connecticut Female Society and the Female Society of New Haven.)

Delia Bacon was, then, an autodidact; she had no choice but to be. And she was, in fact, in some respects, quite a successful one: her command of history, in particular, earned her large audiences and much praise during stints spent giving public lectures in New York City and elsewhere. Nina Baym has characterized her as 'an aspiring, displaced intellectual', engaged in a 'lifelong work of inventing and reinventing herself as a female intellectual celebrity'.[15] Baym further helpfully notes that Bacon refused 'to stay in even the best place her local culture could provide for an intellectual woman'.[16] This is a key driver, I would suggest, in her anti-Stratfordian work. In proposing that anti-Stratfordianism is a product of the emergence of a professionalized literary commentariat, Gary Taylor has observed that, in the anti-Stratfordian project, the enthusiast, 'armed only with the truth, struggles against the massed repressive powers of a corrupt establishment'.[17] In Bacon's case that establishment was, specifically, male – and it was an establishment that actively refused her entry. This fact colours, I believe – and, indeed, to some extent, serves to motivate – her reading of Shakespeare, Bacon and early modern culture and politics.

Entering Delia Bacon's reading of Shakespeare is like passing through the looking-glass, intellectually. Nothing, she proposes, in the world of early modern England is quite as it seems; much of what we have always thought we knew is in need of being inverted. Shakespeare did not write the plays, and we must read the texts carefully to establish the new co-ordinates by which the cultural and intellectual world of early modern England will be made to yield up new sense. In looking at Delia Bacon's work, what I would like to propose is a reading of Bacon that might be thought of as, in effect, offering a 'Baconization' of *The Philosophy of the Plays of Shakspere Unfolded*. Just as Bacon reads Shakespeare in reverse, so we too, I would suggest, might read Bacon in her turn in reverse. And just as she finds in the plays a hidden intellectual narrative of the culture of Shakespeare's time, I would argue that we can also find a submerged narrative of the culture of Delia Bacon's time in her interpretation of the plays.

If we ask, to begin with, why it is that, in Delia Bacon's view, Francis Bacon and his collaborators ever felt it necessary in the first place to hide their cultural and political messages in the plays of Shakespeare, we find that the answer lies primarily in their monarch: Elizabeth I. In Delia Bacon's view, Elizabeth, though superficially benign and encouraging of the new intellectual movements in her realm, was, in fact, strongly opposed to them, since their new philosophies had the capacity to call in doubt the very principles of absolutist monarchy. Beneath the surface, Bacon proposes, the reality of Elizabethan power was that 'its iron was on every neck, its fetter was on every step, and all the new forces, and world-grasping aims and aspirations which that age was generating were held down and cramped, and tortured in its chains, dashing their eagle wings in vain against its iron limits' (p. 21). In Bacon's view, we might say, the Faerie Queene turns out, in fact, ultimately to be Duessa in disguise. The consequence of this repression is that Francis Bacon and the group of intellectuals around him were forced to advance their philosophies indirectly and covertly: specifically, through the medium of fiction, in the form of a set of stage plays. As a further precaution, the Bacon cadre could not be seen to have any direct connection with the texts – hence the need for the 'booby' Shakespeare to serve as a 'front' for the group. As she explains, the Baconians were 'men so far in advance of their time, that they were compelled to have recourse to literature for the purpose of instituting a gradual encroachment on popular opinions, a gradual encroachment on the prejudices, the ignorance, the stupidity of the oppressed and suffering masses of the human kind'. Furthermore, according to Bacon, 'they were compelled to play this great game in secret, in their own time, referring themselves to posthumous effects for the explanation of their designs; postponing their honour to ages able to discover their worth' (p. 16).

What Bacon presents us with here is, essentially, a gendered narrative. An aggressive female regime leads to intellectual repression, with the greatest (male) minds of the time driven to covert strategies in order to achieve their cultural and political programme. They work in the knowledge that they will be unappreciated in their own time, but hope that future ages will be 'able to discover their worth'. Suppose we follow Bacon's own analytical strategy and reverse the terms of the discussion here? What if we swap female for male, male for female? If we do this, we discover a narrative suggesting that an aggressive *male* regime leads to intellectual repression, with women forced to work outside the normal channels, knowing that they are likely to be unappreciated, but hoping that future ages will discover the value of their work. I am not pushing Bacon's own analytical strategy here so far as to suggest that this message is consciously and deliberately encoded by her in the text, but I am suggesting that, given how heavily marked the text is by a narrative that relies on gender, it may well be that Bacon is unconsciously threading an inverted version of the details of her own situation through her text. In essence, I would argue, the negative image that lies behind the positive of Bacon's *Philosophy* presents a narrative of her own time and her own situation. In the shadows of Francis Bacon, in other words, we can trace the outlines of the image of Delia Bacon.

Bacon argues of the anti-Elizabethan cadre that 'they were determined to make their influence felt in that age, in spite of the want of encouragement which the conditions of that time offered to such an enterprise' (p. 25). Formidable obstacles, however, lay in their path. It was not just a matter of their political position relative to the state. There was also no institution where they might immediately find a congenial home. Writing specifically of Walter Ralegh, she observes: 'No chair at Oxford or Cambridge is waiting for him.' This is the case, in Bacon's view, essentially because the early modern universities were hide-bound and unwilling to embrace change: 'they are, of course, and must needs be, the strong-holds of the past – those ancient and venerable seats of learning' (p. 22). The failure of the universities to provide a home for Ralegh and his like means, as Bacon sees it, that they were compelled to create their own intellectual space elsewhere:

he must needs institute a chair of his own, and pay for leave to occupy it. If there was no university with its appliances within his reach, he must make a university of his own . . . His library, or his drawing-room, or his 'banquet,' will be Oxford enough for him. He will begin it as the old monks began theirs, with their readings. (p. 40)

In the absence of access to the academy, Ralegh, Bacon and their collaborators 'could get no recognition of [their] right to teach and rule'. What then was left to the movement? Nothing, Bacon tells us, 'but *paper* to print itself on, nothing but a *pen* to hew its way with' (p. 23).

It is not a great leap here again, I would suggest, to think that, even as Bacon is writing about Ralegh and his milieu, she is also effectively writing about herself and her own situation. Unlike her brother, she could not attend Yale and so had to make her own 'university' as best she could, founding it precisely in her own reading. One might even push further and say that, in a way, she did try to 'institute a chair of [her] own', when she offered lectures in New York and elsewhere. And, as in her vision of Ralegh and his collaborators, in the final years of her life, all that was left to Bacon was paper and 'a *pen* to hew [her] way', as she dedicated herself, obsessively, to the business of writing and seeing to print her *Philosophy*.

In summarizing the position of the Renaissance men clustered around Francis Bacon, Delia Bacon sets them in the context of a state identified as 'Elizabethan' and gendered female:

The Elizabethan England rejected the Elizabethan Man. She would have none of his meddling with her affairs . . . She buried him alive in the heart of his time. She took the seals of office, she took the sword from his hands and put a pen in it. She would have him a Man of Letters. And a Man of Letters he became. A Man of Runes. He invented new letters in his need, letters that would go farther than the sword, that carried more execution in them than the great seal. (p. 31)

Again, the potential here in reversing the terms of the argument should be obvious: regender the passage and it could very easily be autobiographical – indeed, it could be a passage from a Victorian anticipation of *A Room of One's Own*. Bacon herself was deprived of cultural power, authority and position and sought to become a woman of letters – this being the only way she felt she could manifest her undoubted talent (she was the author of some short stories and of a play before she started work on the *Philosophy*). But what is also interesting in this passage is the claim to power that it makes. The Elizabethan Man is not just a Man of Letters, but, more specifically, *A Man of Runes* – someone who decodes secret meanings, who uncovers what is hidden in texts. This, to Bacon, ultimately offers greater power than that wielded by the repressive state: the 'new letters' that he invents carry 'more execution . . . than the great seal'. Delia Bacon too, of course, was a reader of runes, a discoverer of hidden meanings. In taking on the foremost figure in the Western literary canon, she was, in a way, challenging historical orthodoxy, an orthodoxy rooted in male hegemony.

Delia Bacon failed, of course, in real terms. Her theory, taken wholly on its own terms, is built on sand. The *Philosophy* is, as many commentators have observed, largely unreadable and it offers no worthwhile evidence in support of her claims. It is, precisely, we might say, the work of an amateur, of someone who is not engaged – indeed, *refuses* to engage – in the kind of scholarship based on external evidence that began to emerge in the humanities over the course of the nineteenth century: a methodology of real force and value that laid the foundations for modern scholarship. Excluded from being a professional, Bacon embraced amateurism in a way that is utterly fatal to her project. She is ultimately, we might say – intellectually as well as logistically – a victim of her own status outside the academy, outside the world of male power.

Had she been born in another age, Delia Bacon would undoubtedly have been a scholar, in the modern sense of the term – and an accomplished one at that. But the doors of the academy were closed to her and, indeed, at many institutions in the US and the UK, they remained closed for several decades beyond her death in 1859. Just under a decade after Delia

Bacon died, Professor Dowden became the father of a daughter, Hester. In 1882, when she was thirteen, he passed a fretful night: 'Painful dream woke me – Essie suddenly sinking under ice – instant disappearance – her voice faintly heard.'[18] In the following year, Dowden intervened to resist his fellow Trinity academic, Anthony Traill's plans aimed at paving the way for admitting women to the college. 'It will', Dowden wrote of Traill's initiative in his diary, 'come to nothing.' He was right: it would be January 1904 before Trinity admitted its first woman student. Hester Dowden was, by then, thirty-five years old; Delia Bacon had been dead for almost half a century.

Dowden dreams of Hester drowning, dreams of her voice fading as she disappears beneath the icy waters, of her dying, we might say, into inarticulacy. In the very next year, he blocks moves to allow women to study at Trinity. The narrative of this father and daughter is not, however, quite as straightforward as this stark juxtaposition might suggest. In the same year that he dreamt of her drowning, Dowden took his daughter to see Edwin Booth perform Shakespeare in Dublin and he also encouraged her in her reading, which included studying the work of Goethe and Blake.[19] But, of course, cultural encouragement is not the same as cultural empowerment and Hester Dowden's life was marked – like Delia Bacon's – by a high degree of intellectual frustration. Barred from entering Trinity, she moved instead to London, in 1891, to study music. On the eve of her debut as a concert pianist at the Crystal Palace Hester received word that her mother had died and she returned immediately to Dublin. Back at home, she was required to take her mother's place, running the house for her father, who entertained guests on a regular basis. In 1895 Edward Dowden married again but Hester detested her stepmother. Within a matter of months she married a Dublin physician, but increasingly, over the years, she found herself out of sympathy with him and, in 1916, they divorced.

By the time Hester separated from her husband, she had come to feel that she possessed psychic powers. She left Ireland in 1921 and in the following year she set herself up in London as a professional medium. She saw two or three clients a day, five days a week. This, presumably, helped to supplement the relatively modest alimony payment she received from her husband. What is striking about her work as a medium, however, is the extent to which it was marked by literary connections. She claimed that Oscar Wilde had come to her in a series of sessions and had dictated a new play in three acts, via the Ouija-board. Interestingly – given her own position – Wilde is, in Hester Dowden's version of him, peculiarly dismissive of Trinity College: 'These Dublin students could see such a short distance. I was a giant among pigmies.'[20] Asked by Dowden why he had chosen her as his medium, her Wilde replied: 'I had often fancied conveying my thoughts from this place of darkness to someone who had a fitting understanding of a mind such as mine is – fantastical and pained by a desire to express beauty in words.'[21]

In addition to her Wilde sessions, Dowden also connected with Francis Bacon, who confirmed – as her client on this occasion, Alfred Dodd, had hoped he would – that Bacon had written the plays ascribed to Shakespeare. Subsequently a further client, Percy Allen, approached Dowden, hoping to speak with Edward de Vere, the Earl of Oxford. This time, De Vere, Bacon and, eventually, Shakespeare all appeared; together they 'made up a wonderful trio of communicators who, between them, revealed, each in his own fashion, the *Shakespeare* mystery from beginning to end'.[22] What the trio revealed was that the plays were '*a group product*', written largely by Shakespeare and Oxford, but with Bacon serving essentially as overseer and advisor (Bacon nuanced the contradiction between the two sets of sessions by explaining that she had, effectively, been misled by a rogue spirit the first time round).[23] As proof of the trio's credentials, Dowden supplied Allen with three new 'Shakespearean' sonnets, specially composed for him. As James Shapiro has observed, they do not 'quite measure up to those collected in 1609', but they are certainly competent and, if considered outside their immediate context, reasonably well turned.[24]

What we witness here is, perhaps, something like a return of the repressed. Though she had a strong attachment to her father – her 'control', Johannes, bore such a close resemblance to him that she felt he 'might have been a twin brother' – her anti-Stratfordianism inevitably feels like a form of revolt against Edward Dowden's (masculine) authority.[25] Indeed, we might think of it as more than that: Hester Dowden knew her Shakespeare well – and knew her early modern English history well also; she was, truly, a professor's daughter. Her performances as Oxford, Bacon and Shakespeare (like her performance as Wilde) are – for the most part – reasonably convincing. Reading Percy Allen's account of the sessions it is hard not to feel that this is the daughter of an eminent Shakespearian who is turning her father's own expertise back against him. Perhaps we might think of this as a case of the most fanatical infidels being those who were once, themselves, true believers.

Hester Dowden presents us with a case of someone who, like Delia Bacon, clearly had a great deal of talent. That talent was frustrated both by a lack of opportunity and by opportunity dashed by domestic circumstances. Her mediumship provided her with an income, in a time when women's opportunities for work – and independent work at that – were few and far between. But it also provided her with something more than this: a chance to exercise her frustrated creative powers – not just in evoking imaginary worlds populated by the souls of the dead, but also by imagining 'new' works by some of the writers she connected with. The tragedy, of course, is that this work is – in a multiple sense – no more than a 'ventriloquization' of dead male writers. It is ultimately an exercise in mimicry and does not allow her to develop her own voice, to nurture her own, undoubted, talent.

Dowden's Wilde commented to her in one session: 'Belief is the refuge of those who are too dull to imagine.'[26] Both Hester Dowden and Delia Bacon imagined; they imagined fantastical worlds in which Shakespeare did not write the plays attributed to him; they imagined elaborate stories of collaborations and conspiracies, secrets and cryptic clues to be decoded. Unfortunately, for Bacon, certainly, and perhaps for Dowden too, this fabrication of the imagination became a form of belief. Delia Bacon really did think that Shakespeare had not written the plays. More to the point, perhaps, the tragedy is that, in their belief, they attracted – and continue to attract – believers. As Gary Taylor has noted: 'The theory that Shakespeare did not write Shakespeare's plays continues to appeal to amateurs, precisely because it has been utterly rejected by professionals.'[27] Forced into amateurism by a professionalized world that refused to admit her, Bacon used the tools of amateurism to create a narrative that inverted the truths of the professional world. The narrative is repeated and further elaborated by Dowden in her own time, as she, too, is excluded from the professional intellectual world and forced to inhabit a parallel realm in which her claim to psychic power grants her a status that she cannot otherwise achieve. These fantastical narratives then draw in those who – by virtue not so much of exclusion, but simply of not being scholars – feel a kinship with the non-professional, the outsider. And so the myth takes hold. And so it continues to fascinate.

Of the 'Elizabethan Man', Delia Bacon writes, in the *Philosophy*:

Banished from the state in that isle to which he was banished, he found not the base-born Caliban only, to instruct, and train, and subdue to his ends, but an Ariel, an imprisoned Ariel, waiting to be released, able to conduct his masques, able to put his girdles round the earth, and to 'perform and point' to his Tempest. (p. 31)

Bacon's recourse to *The Tempest* is interesting – and, perhaps, predictable. Configured as Calibans by their own society, Bacon and Dowden sought

to be Prosperos – readers of runes, communicators with spirits, expert
manipulators of arcane knowledge. The trouble is that, on their island, the
vision they evoked was fashioned of baseless fabric. Gifted, intelligent and
talented women, they were marginalized by their society and responded
by seeking to interrogate the standing of one of the central male cultural
icons of that society. Theirs was, we might say, an instinct that anticipated
the work of the first generation of feminist Shakespeare scholars.[28] The
pity of it is that they spent their potent, revolutionary energy chasing a
biographical chimera, rather than, as their scholarly successors would do,
analysing the plays themselves. Shakespeare's plays, that is.

CHAPTER 16

Fictional treatments of Shakespeare's authorship

Paul Franssen

Ever since Alexandre Duval wrote his short comedy *Shakespeare amoureux* in 1804, the popular imagination has been fed with fictions showing Shakespeare composing his works, inspired by his life. Such biofictions have been a fertile field for imaginative writers in all genres, including television and film. More recently, however, analogous fantasies have sprung up around the authorship controversy, denying or casting doubt on Shakespeare's authorship. Such fictions come in two kinds, which might be dubbed the emancipatory and the anti-Shakespearian ones.

The emancipatory fictions claim the authorship of Shakespeare's works for a character representing a special interest group. Typically, they give an underprivileged group a boost by crediting one of them with the authorship of Shakespeare's works. Some causes, obviously, such as various religious denominations, do not need to challenge Shakespeare's authorship to begin with, as they can simply claim him as one of their own: Shakespeare has been represented as Protestant, Catholic, agnostic and even Jewish. The cause of gay emancipation, too, was strengthened by fictions of a gay or bisexual Shakespeare extrapolated from the Sonnets. But in view of the historical record, it is difficult to claim that Shakespeare was, say, a woman or black; and this is where the notion of a conspiracy to hide the real authorship of the plays offers a way out. In Arliss Ryan's novel *The Secret Confessions of Anne Shakespeare*, for instance, Anne writes some of her husband's work, but modestly remains in the background.[1] Farrukh Dhondy's novel *Black Swan* combines an emancipatory approach with a Marlovian conspiracy theory.[2] Shakespeare's works are co-authored by Christopher Marlowe and a fugitive black slave from the Caribbean, who is also Marlowe's gay lover. Like Oscar Wilde's 'The Portrait of Mr. W. H.',[3] Dhondy's novel is cast in the form of a modern-frame story, showing how modern characters develop tentative theories around issues such as the identity of the addressees of the Sonnets or the authorship question. In true postmodern fashion, Dhondy first propounds the alternative authorship theory, then suggests it may be a form of self-projection by its originator, a former Caribbean politician with dubious credentials. This format allows for deliberate vagueness, so that awkward questions about the workings of the conspiracy can be avoided. Emancipatory fictions do not usually lay a strong claim to telling the truth about the authorship, nor do they usually paint a negative picture of Shakespeare: rather, in an exercise of self-conscious make-believe, they attempt to borrow some of his glory for an underprivileged group.

More or less the opposite is true for anti-Shakespearian fictions. There, Shakespeare's authorship is contested by a host of contemporaries, comprising rival playwrights like Christopher Marlowe, but mainly aristocrats and courtiers such as Sir Francis Bacon and the Earl of Oxford. It is aristocratic privilege that needs to be screened from public view, by a front man posing to the public as the author. Besides, fictions in this category typically evince dislike, even downright hatred, of 'the Man from Stratford', through his characterization and the invective heaped on him by other characters. One of the key arguments of anti-Shakespearianism has always been Shakespeare's presumed lack of education. In fiction this is stressed by portraying him as an ignorant country bumpkin whose talents are palpably inadequate to writing the masterpieces published under his name. The strategy of not just doubting Shakespeare's credentials, but heaping invective on him goes back to Delia Bacon calling him a 'stupid, illiterate, third-rate play-actor'.[4] Another common argument against Shakespeare's authorship is the many variant spellings of his name. Accordingly, anti-Shakespearian fictions often render his surname in an unusual spelling, the more ungainly the better, as if anagrammatizing his name – as the name of God in Marlowe's *Faustus* – can actually hurt the man himself. Usually the character of Shakespeare (or Shakspur, or Shaxper) stands in marked contrast to the intelligence and nobility of the preferred candidate.

Fictional representations of Shakespeare as ill-mannered seem to begin with Mark Twain's 1876 comic playlet *1601*, in which not just Shaxpur, but the entire court, including Elizabeth herself, discuss taboo subjects like farting and sex.[5] James Hirsh has argued that Twain's 'iconoclastic' attitude to Shakespeare here is of a piece with the Baconianism of his later pamphlet *Is Shakespeare Dead* (1909), in mixing admiration for Shakespeare with Bloomian anxiety of influence.[6]

A typical early anti-Shakespearian fiction is George Moore's comedy, *The Making of an Immortal*.[7] Bacon, who has used 'Shakspere' as his pen-name, is taken by surprise by the Essex rebellion: the Queen is clamouring for the author of that seditious piece, *Richard II*, believing him to be Essex or one of Essex's followers. Fortunately, a player is found who can act as a front for Bacon. He is so stupid that he may just convince the Queen that his plays are politically naive rather than seditious. He also happens to be called Shakespeare: the difference in spelling with Bacon's nom de plume is insignificant as the pronunciation is the same. The only thing that interests Shakespeare is his real estate, and he is at first reluctant to join the conspiracy. The plot succeeds: the Queen is fooled, and orders Shakespeare to write something about Falstaff in love. Shakespeare is completely at a loss, but when Elizabeth is gone, Bacon and Jonson promise to help him. Jonson concludes the play by saying, 'I think to-day we have assisted at the making of an immortal' (p. 59). The debunking of Shakespeare has always been one of the hallmarks of Baconianism, and Moore does this quite effectively. Cleverly deploying Shakespeare's well-documented business sense as an argument against his authorship, as if a shopkeeper could not be a literary genius, Moore stands in a long tradition of anti-Shakespearian snobbery.

A similar argument, transposed into a melodramatic key, is put forward by William R. Leigh's play *Clipt Wings*.[8] The plot is largely a fictionalization of the Baconian secrets unlocked by Orville Ward Owen with his 'cipher wheel', a mechanical device on which pages from the works of Bacon, Shakespeare and others were pasted, and then spun to reveal hidden messages, including the revelation that Robert Cecil and Francis Bacon had been Queen Elizabeth's sons.[9] Leigh's play traces Cecil's villainous machinations against his noble half-brother Bacon. Cecil raises the Queen's suspicions of Bacon; he, deprived of political influence, pours all his frustrations into his plays, which he does not openly acknowledge. Cecil in turn uses these plays, *Hamlet* in particular, to feed the Queen's paranoia. To satisfy Cecil, Elizabeth agrees to put a price on the head of the plays' author. Bacon consults Jonson and Marlowe about finding a 'screen' who can claim ignorance of political intentions, and so deflect attention from himself. They discuss the profile of a possible candidate:

BACON: We need a knave worthless enough to desire to live in idleness, reckless enough to be willing to undertake the role, and ignorant and grotesque enough to convince everybody at a glance that he is a dummy.

JONSON: Yet, withal, something of an actor, capable of keeping up the show.

MARLOWE: If he have some vice, like drink, 'twill be helpful. . . . The testimony of a drunken man is worthless. (p. 92)

A suitable man is soon found: the small-time actor Shaxper. He is an 'oaf', 'boorish', 'lazy', 'ignorant' and illiterate. They change his name to

Shakespeare, to make it sound better as a nom de plume. He will receive an allowance, and be taught basic writing skills, so that his authorship is not too implausible. After these decisions have been taken in his absence, Shaxper is invited in, and proves to be all the conspirators could ask for: stupid, greedy, fond of rum, and a morally weak person who has left his family penniless. He is repeatedly compared to a swine. Cecil seems, for the moment, to have been outmanoeuvred, but he plans his revenge, using Shaxper's weaknesses to his advantage. Many years later, just before murdering Elizabeth by poison and strangling, Cecil boasts to her of how he had stimulated 'the drunken pig Shaxper' to blackmail Bacon, until, in desperation, they had sent him to 'his native sty at Stratford' (p. 129). Finally, in 1616, Jonson and Drayton tell Bacon that they have silenced Shaxper forever: when the 'beast' was not amenable to reason, Jonson had put poison into his wine. Bacon is deeply grateful for their loyalty. That the poisoning of the beastly Shaxper by Bacon's henchmen resembles the Queen's death at the hands of the villainous Cecil is an irony that seems to have escaped Leigh; his Shaxper is so subhuman that killing him is an act of mercy.

A less lurid approach to Baconianism can be found in Colin Wilson's *The Philosopher's Stone*.[10] This novel deals with two scientists experimenting with expanded consciousness, which gives them immortality and a degree of clairvoyance. In their view, they are fulfilling mankind's full potential. They see the past as a benighted period, whereas the future is full of promise. The narrator has visions of Elizabethan London as a place of squalor and cruelty. He also comes to understand that Shakespeare's works had been written by Bacon, who had indulged in 'absurd pastiches of Elizabethan melodrama' (p. 159). Shakespeare had been a barely literate businessman, generally disliked in Stratford for suing his townsmen for minor debts and for supporting enclosures. He had married Anne when she was pregnant by Cecil, and had been set up in London as a reward. Not that it matters who wrote the plays: in a rare twist for a Baconian fantasy, Bacon is a 'second-rate mind', whether writing under his own name or as Shakespeare (p. 161). The other scientist has a vision of Shakespeare as a short, ill-mannered, aggressive and bibulous personality. In her introduction to the novel, Joyce Carol Oates remarks: 'Wilson's sweeping rejection of Shakespeare . . . is part of the recognition that belief in evolutionary humanism *as a progressive phenomenon* in history necessitates a systematic, remorseless examination and rejection of much of the past, not because it is the "past," but because its models of human behaviour are not really models any longer' (pp. 10–11). In this sense, the book is not so much anti-Shakespearian as anti-Renaissance.

As Baconianism faded away, Oxfordianism took its place. Rhoda Messner wrote a biographical novel about Oxford which mentions the Man from Stratford only once, in a list of Globe shareholders.[11] By pure coincidence, or so it seems – it is never explained – 'Shakespeare' is also Oxford's pen-name. His mistress affectionately calls him 'spear-shaker' (p. 193), and Oxford himself explains that his pseudonym 'described me precisely: invisible in the helmet of Pallas Athene, spearshaker and patron of the theatre' (p. 284). Oxford is forbidden to publish his works under his own name by both Elizabeth and James, partly because they lampoon Cecil Sr., partly because they are coded warnings to Elizabeth about treasonous plots.

Messner's polite reticence about 'the Man from Stratford' was not to last. Stephanie Caruana's unpublished play 'Edward Oxenford: Spear-shaker' follows Moore's model: Shacksper is hired as a facade for Oxford, who has (coincidentally) chosen the pen-name of 'Shake-speare' long before meeting him.[12] Caruana, too, postulates that the true author's identity had to be disguised for political reasons: if known to stem from the hand of a courtier, plays like *Richard II* and *Richard III* would be political dynamite, whereas the same plays written by a simpleton would be disregarded as innocuous fairy tales. Like Moore, Caruana represents the Man from Stratford as the most unlikely candidate for the authorship. Much of the play's humour derives from Shacksper's unfitness for anything in the least sophisticated. The plot is modelled on *The Taming of the Shrew*, with Shacksper cast as the Christopher Sly figure. The prologue shows how this drunken good-for-nothing is thrown out of his house by a shrewish Anne, and announces that he will go to London to complain to the Queen. On his arrival in London, he is treated as a gentleman, much to his surprise. He cannot read or write properly, and does not understand the theatrical sense of the verb 'to act'. His talents, he tells Oxford, lie in agriculture, butchery and brewing; none of the polite or warlike accomplishments that Oxford mentions. Called upon to defend his authorship in a law court, he admits to having had no more schooling than three years at Stratford Elementary School, and displays great naivety concerning the process of writing. The average play takes him about five days, he says, though *Hamlet* took somewhat longer. Other hilarious scenes include the request for a coat of arms, with an incredulous Herald having to be persuaded of Shacksper's worthiness to be made a gentleman, first by political pressure, then by a bribe. Throughout, Shacksper is a stooge, an ignorant and ignoble wretch. He dies of drinking too much, and his townsmen, surprised at the monument erected for him, remember him as a tight-fisted beer-brewer. Oxford, by contrast, is a tragic figure, who gives up his ambitions of achieving immortality through his poetry in the vain hope of seeing his son crowned king. His political struggle with the Cecils leads to the failure of his most cherished dreams.

The Oxfordian message was adapted to a juvenile audience by Lynne Kositsky in her time-travel fantasy *A Question of Will*.[13] Like Stratfordian equivalents, such as Susan Cooper's *King of Shadows*,[14] Kositsky's novel features a modern protagonist who travels to the past, works there in Shakespeare's company, and returns to the present after this formative experience. In this case, however, Shakespeare is far from a father figure to Perin, a Canadian schoolgirl on a summer course in London who is transported to 1599 by a time warp. She finds her way to the theatre, where she meets Shaksper, the Earl of Oxford and other historical characters. The plot focuses on the authorship of the plays. Sharing quarters with Shaksper, Perin is used to run messages to Oxford, which usually involves new manuscript plays and payments. She soon discovers that Shaksper is a front for Oxford, who writes plays for money, but cannot have them played or published under his own name. This is an open secret – so much so, that players of the rival theatre company try to rob Perin of Oxford's new manuscripts. Perin's disillusionment with Shaksper begins with his unimpressive performance as the Ghost in *Hamlet* (as an Oxfordian, Kositsky rejects the traditional chronology of the plays) and grows into a strong loathing as she gets to know him better. He drinks too much, lives in a 'pigsty' (p. 34), is miserly, anti-semitic and occasionally beats her. When she is forced to award a 'Bessie' to him for *Romeo and Juliet* – a variant on the Oscar awards introduced by Perin herself – she 'wanted to smash the statue to smithereens over his bald head. I wanted to flatten him like a fly on the wall' (p. 86). Shaksper keeps asking De Vere for more money. The economics of this are hazy – on the one hand, De Vere suggests that he writes for money, on the other, he has to pay Shaksper's company to produce his plays.

Although Oxford is rather arrogant, to Perin he is preferable to Shaksper, and she tries to persuade him to claim the plays for himself, but in vain. She then asks her friend John Pyke to ensure that the authorship secret will be revealed after Oxford's death, and when she returns to the present through another time warp, her copy of *Macbeth* has De Vere's name on it: through a well-known time-travel paradox, Perin has changed the past and therefore her own world.

In *Contested Will*, James Shapiro largely limits himself to Baconians and Oxfordians, claiming that support for other candidates works on the same principles (p. 3). Fictional works seem to bear him out. In Jaime Salom's *El otro William* (1994), a Derbyite play, Shakespeare is portrayed as an ignorant cheat, womanizer and schemer.[15] The title's other William is the penniless Stanley, the Earl of Derby, who needs to earn his money by writing and by a rich marriage, but cannot be known as an author. He chooses Shakespeare for his frontman, expecting that no one will believe that such an ignoramus has really written the works, but finds himself outwitted by the scoundrel. Rodney Bolt's Marlovian *History Play* works along similar lines.[16] Marlowe, entangled in a murky espionage plot, stages his own death in Deptford with the help of friends and flees to the Continent. He goes on writing plays, which are smuggled to England and produced and published under the name of Shakespere. Marlowe travels all over Europe, and is last seen stranded on Bermuda. While he soaks up the local colour and transmutes it into drama, humdrum Shakespere stays at home, reaping the fame due to Marlowe. Bolt's Shakespere, predictably, is untalented and ignorant, greedy and cocky. His own plays are invariably second-rate, like *The Taming of the Shrew* or *The London Prodigal*. He earns his fortune by sharp practice and by blackmailing Marlowe's sponsors. Fittingly, he dies from apoplexy, 'swine-drunk after a night spent swilling with his merchant cronies' (p. 310). Bolt paints a dismal portrait of a man with a mean, animalistic, second-rate mind, who through an accident of history reaps the fruits of another man's genius.

Still, Bolt's book also exemplifies a new direction in anti-Shakespearian fiction after the turn of the century, away from deadly seriousness to post-modern playfulness. For one thing, as emerges from Bolt's Afterword, this is not a serious intervention in the authorship controversy, but 'an exercise of purest (or most impure) conjecture' (p. 314). Bolt's intellectual game does have a serious point, however, namely that biographies, too, construct lives out of very few hard facts and a lot of speculation. Bolt, too, mixes established facts with guesswork – and, he admits, specious facts – 'to look a little more sharply at how we construct truth' (p. 314). Accordingly, this largely fictional book masquerades as a scholarly biography, ostensibly sifting evidence and weighing alternative theories, not to mention the apparatus of footnotes, appendices, bibliography and index. Only the attentive reader will notice the anagrams in the scholars' names mentioned in the notes: Norlet Boyd, Troy Blonde and Lord Yentob; or the first name in the sixteenth-century document reproduced in appendix 1: William Ireland (p. 316). Others may take Bolt's story at face value – as they do biographies.

Apart from Bolt, most anti-Shakespearian fictions discussed so far pretend to offer unmediated access to the truth about Shakespeare and the 'real' author, in clear-cut, stereotypical representations of the characters. Some, such as Leigh, Caruana and Kositsky, add author's notes or forewords to defend their view of the authorship issue and their characterization of Shakespeare as basically sound, in spite of some poetic licence. Over the last decade, however, a sense of indeterminacy, combined with the postulation of on-going conspiracies, seems to have taken over. In recent novels, the trend is for modern-frame stories, featuring present-day characters investigating past mysteries. These investigations suggest alternative authorship candidates, but closure is impossible due to on-going conspiracies. One advantage of this formula is that it does not require a fully developed explanation of the conspiracies, just some tantalizing clues of a hidden mystery.

Sarah Smith's *Chasing Shakespeares*, for instance, features Joe, a young American Shakespearian, who is converted to Oxfordianism once he delves into the evidence.[17] The religious metaphor is suggested by the parallel between Joe and his friend Mary Cat, who wants to become a nun, but is turned down because she had once promoted the use of condoms to fight AIDS. In religion as in literary studies, loyalty to one's personal conviction is paramount, it is suggested, although the nature of God's wishes is as elusive as the identity of the author of the works of Shakespeare. The novel casts doubt on the reliability of scholarship by evident signs of self-projection on the part of several characters: Joe, who is from a humble background, at first identifies with Shakespeare; his lover, Posy, hails from a rich family and accordingly champions Oxford. Other characters, too, have their correlatives in the Elizabethan age: the devious art trader Nicky Bogey, for instance, is the Cecil figure, the shrewd manipulator behind the scenes, who apparently spirits away Joe's one piece of genuine documentary evidence, a letter written by Shakespeare himself, and substitutes a fake. He has also painted a portrait of Cecil that can pass as an original, reminiscent of the forged portrait of Mr W. H. in Wilde's story (p. 289). In Smith's universe, all authority is to be distrusted, and hard facts do not exist: what counts is loyalty to one's personal convictions. For that, Joe gives up his job as a researcher, as a martyr to Oxfordianism. Because of the provisional nature of the theories bandied about, the historical figures of Oxford and particularly Shakespeare are constantly shifting, and never get fleshed out in Joe's imagination.

Shakespeare is similarly invisible in Norma Howe's juvenile novel *The Blue Avenger Cracks the Code*.[18] Blue, the teenage hero, becomes an Oxfordian thanks to his charismatic high school teacher, who dedicates a class to the Authorship question and gives him Charlton Ogburn's book to read. Blue, self-styled avenger of wrongs, makes it his mission to restore the injustice done to Oxford. Being obsessed with codes, he discovers an anagram in the Sonnets which points to Oxford's authorship. On a trip to Venice, he overhears a discussion of a notebook written by De Vere during his stay in Italy, which, Blue realizes, might contain evidence pertinent to the authorship of plays like *Romeo and Juliet*. However, before he can confirm his suspicions, the book is sold off, leaving Blue wondering whether the buyer was a genuine scholar or part of a conspiracy to cover up the truth and protect the Shakespeare industry. The suggestion is that Stratfordian conspiracies are as common now as in the past, but the ending remains open.

The most sophisticated of this genre of novels is Jennifer Lee Carrell's thriller *Interred with their Bones*.[19] This Shakespearian variant of Dan Brown's *The Da Vinci Code* (2003) traces the search of a female Shakespearian for the lost play *Cardenio*, as well as evidence pertaining to the authorship question. She is up against various interest groups, including Stratfordians and Oxfordians, some of whom are prepared to kill to protect their version of the truth. Although *Cardenio* is retrieved, the accompanying letter that might conclusively resolve the authorship question is lost when the Stratfordian villain snatches it away seconds before his death, taking the secret into his grave. Before that, there were hints that Shakespeare's works were produced by a conglomerate, consisting of Derby, Oxford, Lady Pembroke, Bacon and Shakespeare himself. What remains unclear is what precisely the nature of the co-operation was: were they sponsoring the plays together? Or also writing together?

However, the novel also contains five scenes set in Shakespeare's time, offering a direct representation of Shakespeare as an author, writing sonnets for the Dark Lady. He is obviously regarded as the author of *Cardenio* by his enemies, the Howards, and there is no sign of any co-authors. He is no simpleton: the Fair Friend remembers him as a 'man with mischief in his eyes – mischief, and cynical wit, and the quiet sorrow that fills the eyes of those who have seen that the world's brightest lights and deepest shadows are inextricably entwined' (p. 391). Shakespeare's ruling passion is his love for the Fair Friend. It is Shakespeare who asks the Dark Lady, his mistress, to seduce the Friend, to keep him from becoming a Jesuit, which he fears will be his death. When this fails due to the machinations of the Howard family, he takes his revenge on them by staging, and presumably writing, *Cardenio*, a damning allegory of their ambitions. Although Shakespeare is manipulative and vengeful, he is loyal to his friends and no fool. Thus Carrell leaves open the authorship issue, offering the reader conflicting clues.

Whether it springs from genuine belief or from the need for a good story, contemporary authorship fiction evokes a sense of mystery in the face of conspiracies past and present, which shroud the truth in an impenetrable smoke screen. We shall never know for certain who wrote what, the suggestion is, but someone is definitely trying to hoodwink us, even now. As a corollary of this new emphasis, Shakespeare is no longer represented as an ignoramus, but remains a mystery, too.

This also applies to Mark Rylance's unpublished comedy 'I am Shakespeare'.[20] Rylance, a prominent Shakespeare actor who has never made a secret of his anti-Shakespearian sympathies, wrote this play in the run-up to the internet campaign to gather signatures for a 'Declaration of reasonable doubt about the identity of William Shakespeare'. This campaign was designed to unite all anti-Shakespearians under one banner, but also sought to gain the middle ground: instead of confidently asserting that the conspiracy has been completely unravelled, it casts doubt on what we think we know; and in striving for reasonableness, it forgoes simple-minded caricatures of Shakespeare as a swinish idiot. As in a court of law, the suggestion is, every faction should get a fair hearing – but its weak sides will also be exposed. In this spirit, Rylance's play revolves around a modern character, Frank, who faces conflicting views of the authorship issue when some of the main candidates come to visit him from the past. A former Shakespearian disgraced for writing on the authorship question, Frank now runs an internet chat-show promoting the anti-Shakespearian cause. One day, Shakespeare himself turns up in Frank's studio, to defend his authorship. Shakespeare seems reasonable enough, and has plausible answers to all of Frank's questions. He stands up for the talents of the common man, and suggests that Frank is a snob in supporting an aristocrat. Just when Frank seems ready to convert to Stratfordianism, however, the other candidates start trickling into the studio; first Bacon, throwing out hints that he was the author; then a very aggressive Oxford, who claims that the works were his autobiography. Finally, Mary Sidney joins them, and widens the authorship issue by claiming that a group of aristocrats had published their works under a range of pseudonyms. Apart from herself, Oxford and Bacon, the group comprised Sir Philip Sidney and Marlowe; moreover, she, Oxford and Bacon were the illegitimate children of Queen Elizabeth. The works attributed to Shakespeare – and others – were written by all of them collectively.

Faced with these incompatible claims, the audience is asked to vote on whom they believe: they invariably favour Shakespeare. But Frank, reasonably enough, argues that the truth cannot be established by majority voting. When the historical characters disappear into thin air, Frank believes he has all their statements taped on video, but finds that the recording has failed. There is no final certainty, the play suggests, just lingering doubt, even when all the candidates' claims are given a fair hearing. In a deft stroke, Shakespeare himself approves of the debate: Frank is only asking obvious questions, he says, raised by the discrepancy between his life and his works.

Amy Freed's comedy *The Beard of Avon* is another playful production, which turns the authorship issue inside out.[21] Like a standard Oxfordian fiction, the play first presents Shaksper as an ignorant if amiable country bumpkin who follows some travelling players to London, where he is hired by Oxford to lend his name to his publications. Then the plot veers away from the usual Oxfordian fare, for Shaksper really does have a talent for writing, and is asked to improve Oxford's productions. Unaided, Oxford has so far written *Titus Andronicus*; he is aware that he lacks 'warmth' and 'humanity' (p. 27), a verdict borne out by the debaucheries he boasts of. Shaksper, who does have these qualities, helps his patron write sonnets on the basis of themes and odd lines supplied by Oxford. These are then published under Shaksper's name, but everyone at Court believes them to be Oxford's. Soon, other courtiers, too, including Elizabeth herself, are queuing up to have their works revised by Shaksper, produced on stage and published under his name. The quality of the works Shaksper is asked to revise becomes increasingly abysmal, and it is clear that all the brilliance in the resulting plays is due to him. For instance, Oxford's input on *Richard III* was: 'I see a . . . HUNCHBACK. YOU flesh it out' (p. 68). Gradually Shaksper, educating himself with books from Oxford's library, develops into a self-confident author who resents the exploitation of his work by the aristocracy and returns to Stratford in disgust. Promised a more respectful treatment by his desperate fellow players, he returns to London just in time to see Oxford on his deathbed. Oxford bequeaths him his manuscript plays: Shaksper was never good at plots, he says, but brilliant at poetry – so he can revise them. Shaksper's precise share in the plays remains vague, but it is clear that without his genius they would have been failures. Thus, Freed avoids the usual trap of confusing the advantages of birth with talent: given the chance to develop himself, Shaksper's genius quickly emerges, and puts his noble patrons in the shadow.

Freed's light-hearted take on the authorship issue contrasts with the doctrinaire and aggressive treatment of earlier anti-Shakespearian fictions. In giving Shakespeare talents that are then exploited by his vain betters, Freed comes close to parodying the anti-Shakespearian position. Such parodies were, of course, also written during the twentieth century: from the episodes ridiculing Baconianism in Vladimir Nabokov's *Bend Sinister*[22] and Harry Mulisch's *The Discovery of Heaven*,[23] to Luis Kutner's full-length play *The Trialle of William Shakespeare*, in which the Weird Sisters organize a public hearing on the authorship question to avenge themselves on Shakespeare for his negative portrayal of women.[24] In the comic novel *No Bed for Bacon*, Shakespeare's authorship is beyond doubt.[25] Yet Shakespeare and his wife cross Bacon's social ambitions by acquiring a bed the Queen has slept in, which Bacon had wanted for himself as a prestigious heirloom; and Shakespeare portrays him as Malvolio. Bacon swears to be revenged, 'something deep and literary to obscure Will's name to all posterity . . . But how?' (p. 250). There is no answer, but obviously the authorship controversy is glanced at here, and ridiculed. Most incisive is Anthony Burgess's sci-fi fantasy 'The Muse', in which a literary historian travels to the past, hoping to disprove Shakespeare's authorship.[26] What he finds is a hopeless hack, a ruthless plagiarist and a monster who makes a violent homosexual pass at him. His works were brought to him by mysterious Muses, who turn out to be time-travellers like the hero, who has himself taken a copy of the First Folio to the past. These texts Shakespeare patiently copies out, 'not blotting a line' (p. 160). In a familiar time-travel paradox, the authorship is elusive, lost in a cycle of infinite deferment. In view of Burgess's other works on Shakespeare, fictional and biographical, this can only be taken as a parody of the authorship controversy: the scholar who sets out to prove that Shakespeare did *not* write his works is punished by being imprisoned in the end.[27]

For most of the last century, anti-Shakespearian fiction has tended to represent Shakespeare as a fool or a cad. Rather than being grateful for his willingness to protect their candidate, Baconians and Oxfordians alike have ridiculed him, as a foil to their own candidate. In the twenty-first century, anti-Shakespearian stridency has given way to a sense of indeterminacy, in the face of missing historical evidence and enduring conspiracies. As a result, Shakespeare is no longer represented as an idiot but as an invisible man. On the positive side, there is a tendency to treat the authorship controversy with some humour, acknowledging how much we do not know.

CHAPTER 17

The 'Declaration of Reasonable Doubt'

Stuart Hampton-Reeves

The 'Declaration of Reasonable Doubt' is a petition whose signatories assert that there is reasonable doubt that William Shakespeare was the true author of the plays attributed to him. First launched in 2007 and principally authored by John M. Shahan, the Declaration has two principal aims: to petition for the authorship question to be treated as a serious academic topic and taught as such in schools and universities; and to present anti-Shakespearians as reasonable people. Since its launch, the Declaration has attracted over 2,000 signatories, among them university professors, Supreme Court judges and well-known actors. The Declaration is primarily an online document, although hard copies have been produced for highly publicized signing events in Los Angeles, Portland and, in the UK, Chichester. However, it is much more than just a document. The website, doubtaboutwill.org, is also a focus for anti-Shakespearian sentiment, and the organization behind both, the Shakespeare Authorship Coalition (SAC), has emerged as the organized voice of anti-Shakespearians, who may not agree on who did write the plays, but can agree on who didn't.

In his book *Contested Will*, James Shapiro praises the Declaration for its inspired title and 'skilfully drafted' text.[1] Shapiro does not critique the Declaration, and instead sets out his case for Shakespeare in the following chapter. The SAC's response, published on the Declaration website, thanks Shapiro for his generosity, and then attacks him for not engaging with the Declaration's arguments. This chapter will similarly disappoint SAC readers looking for a thorough, point-by-point rebuttal. My purpose here is to consider the Declaration and its aims, to evaluate its success and to look more closely at the people who have signed it, particularly academics.

As Shapiro notes, the Declaration of Reasonable Doubt draws its terminology (and some of its rhetoric) from legal trials, as if Shakespeare was in some way on trial (p. 218). In most Western legal systems, the concept of truth 'beyond a reasonable doubt' is used as a high standard of proof when securing convictions in a court of law. In television dramas and films,

201

the defence lawyer undermines the case for the prosecution with pointed rhetoric. Is this man capable of committing the crimes he is accused of? Are you sure – sure enough to send a man to the electric chair? In the more prosaic world of real court rooms, the question is not so much whether it is possible to doubt evidence brought before a jury, but whether that doubt is 'reasonable'. Doubt is always possible. Some philosophers doubt that we exist, and many philosophy students have been baffled by teachers pointing earnestly at a table and demanding they 'prove' it exists, or there is not an elephant in the room, or that you are not reading this at all, but dreaming that you are reading it. Few legal cases have been settled by recourse to radical existential doubt. The issue here is not whether there is any doubt about Shakespeare's authorship, but whether there is any *reasonable* doubt.

However, the Declaration is not just a declaration of doubt, it is also a declaration of faith, akin to the spiritual testament that Shakespeare's father kept to affirm his secret Catholicism. It encourages people who genuinely believe Shakespeare could not be the author of his plays by inducting them into a community which includes well-known and in some cases brilliant people. At the same time, it is a declaration of loss of faith – faith in Shakespeare. I've not encountered anyone in the anti-Shakespeare community who did not start out believing that Shakespeare was the true author of his plays. One does not need to propose an alternative author to sign the Declaration; one only has to be troubled by uncertainty. The narratives of the signatories who have defended their signing bring together the language of religious conversion and the language of loss of faith stories.

The Declaration normalizes and legitimizes the authorship question, allowing people to 'come out' with views that in the past (and in many situations in the present) would be regarded as fanciful, snobbish and of a kind with other famous conspiracy theories. In this respect, I believe the Declaration has been successful. It is no longer possible (if it ever really was) to dismiss anti-Shakespearians as ill-informed cranks. Many of us in the Shakespeare community are used to receiving emails and letters from anti-Shakespearians who are eccentric and in some cases fanatical, but this 'lunatic fringe' should not define a movement which includes some ordinary, reasonable people who have sincerely held views. The anti-Shakespearians I have corresponded with in the course of writing this chapter have been friendly, intelligent, witty and brave, since they know that what I have been writing is essentially a critique which is unlikely to put them in a good light.

I hope this chapter will serve as a corrective to these more outra-geous stereotypes of anti-Shakespearians, but at the same time I do not intend to provide any ammunition to the Declaration's other agenda, which is to confer academic legitimacy on the authorship question in the way in which they have framed it. It is perfectly possible (and if we're honest, probably normal) for reasonable people to hold unreasonable views.

The Declaration has an epigraph incongruously attributed to William Shakespeare: 'Time's glory is to calm contending kings, / To unmask falsehood and bring truth to light' (*The Rape of Lucrece* 939–40). The 'contending kings' in this case are, I take it, the different claimants to Shakespeare's crown. The Declaration's most striking contribution to the debate is its refusal to commit to any one alternative candidate, recognizing that establishing Shakespeare's illegitimacy is a crucial first step towards making a case for any new author. In this way, the Declaration is able to focus attention on demolishing Shakespeare's case, 'to unmask falsehood' even though it does nothing to 'bring the truth to light'.

BRINGING TRUTH TO LIGHT

In order to prove that they are actual individuals, those signing the petition have to enter the word 'doubt' into an anti-spam field before they hit 'submit'. Each signer has the opportunity to add a short comment which appears against their name on the website. They reveal that many of the signers are, indeed, eccentric in their outlook and already committed to the counter-knowledge that Shakespeare did not write his plays. These signers are not really doubters, they are quite certain that they know who did, and who did not, author the works. However, the list also includes many people who exhibit a genuine sense of doubt, and whose professional background indicates that they are, indeed, reasonable people.

They include Sabrina Feldman, a senior figure at NASA and the author of a book arguing that William Shakespeare was the author of the apocryphal plays with Thomas Sackville the author of the canonical plays. Feldman studied literature at university and although she asked me not to pass on further details about her educational background (unusually for contributors to the Declaration) I can at least confirm that it is first-rate. Feldman's doubts are, in my view, not reasoned but reasonable, in the sense that they are couched in a suitable level of scepticism and qualification. She told me, 'I signed the Declaration of Reasonable Doubt because I'm convinced that investigations of whether William Shakespeare actually wrote the Bard's works are useful and legitimate, whether or not the skeptics are right, and despite the difficulty in separating the wheat from the chaff among the authorship literature.'

The Declaration separates its reasonable people into three groups: 'notables', 'academics' and everyone else. I am going to focus on the academic group because it is through them that the Declaration hopes to achieve its main aim of making authorship doubt a legitimate area of study. The groups have separate lists on the website, and for the notables at least the Declaration authenticates the signature by insisting upon a hard copy of the signature. The notables and the academics are there to give weight to the Declaration and to make it easier for people to 'come out' with their own doubts. The academics are arguably the most important list here, since the Declaration's main aim is to make the subject a legitimate study in universities. Many in the anti-Shakespearian community are keen to assert their academic credentials and will often sign with their degree results to signal their intelligence, their reasonableness. For example, in the SAC's response to The Shakespeare Birthplace Trust's '60 minutes with Shakespeare' project, Michael York's preface is signed 'Michael York, MA (Oxon), OBE' and he is even listed in the contents as 'Michael York, MA, OBE.' A video posted on the Declaration's website is presented by 'Actor Keir Cutler, Ph.D'.

The academic list calls attention to how many of the Declaration's signatories (more than half) are not university educated – which is ironic given how Shakespeare's lack of a university education is so central to the doubters' case. Of the 415 names (at the time of writing) on the 'academics' list, many are not professional academics. Inclusion appears to depend on a self-declaration that the signer is either a current or former Faculty member. This is a very loose criterion for public identification as an academic and may include a range of roles beyond that of a traditional academic: very few of the ones I researched are published researchers or currently employed as an academic.

However, there are some heavy-weight names in the list and their willingness to risk professional scorn by association with a crank theory, demands attention. They include: Ekkehart R. A. Krippendorff, Professor Emeritus of Political Science, Free University of Berlin, who is the author of two monographs on Shakespeare; Dean Keith Simonton, a Psychology Professor at the University of California; Professor Charles David Duff, a theatre historian at Notre Dame and author of a well-received monograph on mid-twentieth-century theatre; Professor John David Griffin, from the Art Institute of Washington; Professor Cynthia Lee Katona, a Professor of Shakespeare at Ohlone College in California; Professor Patrick J. Buckridge, an

English professor at Griffiths University in Australia; and Professor Kristin Linklater, Professor of Theatre Arts at Columbia University and author of *Freeing Shakespeare's Voice*. These demand attention: not because they are numerous, but because they are serious and in some cases internationally well-known academics. Many of them have published detailed explanations of their anti-Shakespearian beliefs which are much more fully developed and thought-through than the usual discourse associated with such views.

At the same time, the combination of these professors from diverse disciplines creates a false impression of an international, cross-disciplinary acceptance of 'reasonable' doubt. In the next two sections, I will look more closely at some of the signatories from English literature and other disciplines, highlighting both the reasoned arguments put forward by some of them and evaluating their success at convincing colleagues in their own discipline of the appropriateness of their methodologies.

ENGLISH LITERATURE SIGNATORIES

A fifth of the 415 academic signatories are listed under English literature (eighty-one at the time of writing). Around half of them have PhDs or are at professorial level. Encouragingly, the number of recent signatories is small, suggesting that the Declaration has lost momentum among people with English literature degrees. There were only eighteen new signatories between 2010 and 2011, nine of whom signed in 2011. The majority (forty-eight) signed in 2007, six signed in 2008, nine in 2009. Approximately twenty-five of the signatories have or have had verifiable teaching positions as lecturers or Professors of English in a higher education institution. The HEIs are generally located in America, with a smattering in South America, some in Europe, one in Australia and just one in Britain. Virtually none of these English 'academics' have published significant (or insignificant) work on Shakespeare beyond the authorship question. However, two names stand out both for the quality of their Shakespeare scholarship and their contribution to the Declaration's agenda: Michael E. Egan and William Leahy.

Michael E. Egan has a prolific and varied career as a writer on topics ranging from Ibsen to Shakespeare. He is also the editor of *The Oxfordian* where he deserves credit (and much hostility from some Oxfordians) for insisting on a higher standard of academic rigour. Confusingly, he is also well-known for publishing a three-volume edition of the anonymous play *Woodstock* under the title, *The Tragedy of Richard II, Part One: A Newly Authenticated Play by William Shakespeare*.[2] In an email to me, Egan stressed that the words 'by William Shakespeare' in his book's title are important and deliberate. In an interview with the website *PlayShakespeare*, Egan explained that he is genuinely agnostic about Shakespeare's identity and is prepared to 'follow the evidence where it leads'.[3] He admits to changing his mind as new data emerges and fresh arguments are made, but he also explains why he signed the Declaration: 'I think there's a real question about the authorship of Shakespeare's plays – the disjunct between what we think we know about him and the mind and personality reflected in the Collected Works. Ascribing their astonishing range, wisdom and knowledge to genius is simply to invoke magic. One may be born with superior abilities but education must still be acquired.'

In correspondence with me, Egan further clarified that he regards himself as a Stratfordian until better evidence for another author comes along, but that he expects such evidence to be eventually produced. In order to clarify his thinking, Egan appropriates a watchmaker parable first developed in 1802 by the theologian William Paley as a 'thought experiment' to demonstrate the existence of a Creator (Paley's argument was famously dismissed by Darwin). In Egan's version, he finds a watch on a beach in the hands of a local native. The watch is clearly the result of an experienced craftsman, the native simply does not have the skills or experience to possibly be the creator of the watch. He reasons that there must therefore be a Swiss watch factory nearby. The watch is the Complete Works and the local native is, of course, William Shakespeare. When he devised his theory, Paley intended it to demonstrate that all created things must have a designer and this is essentially Egan's point as well. In effect, he is sceptical about the idea of 'genius' emerging without education as an explanation for the extraordinary achievement of the Complete Works.

A similar reasoning underpins the work of William Leahy, who is Head of the School of Arts at Brunel University, where he leads an MA on Shakespeare Authorship Studies and supervises doctoral students studying Shakespeare. William Leahy is the only academic signatory who has developed his career primarily as a Shakespeare scholar. He has published articles in *Shakespeare Jarbuch* and *Early Modern Literary Studies* on Shakespeare's history plays, and written a substantial history of Elizabeth Processions for Ashgate, as well as an edited collection on the authorship question.[4] In 2005, Leahy was asked to respond to Mark Rylance's views on the authorship question in *The New Statesman*. Leahy offered a conventional dismissal, but in researching the piece he was drawn to look at the issues more carefully and over time found himself less and less convinced by the 'orthodox' position. Following the launch of his MA, Leahy quickly became one of the figureheads of the UK anti-Shakespearian movement. He signed the Declaration publicly in 2007 and photographs of the signing are on the Declaration's website.

Leahy has brought together Shakespeare-deniers and postmodernists, and has even attracted the support of mainstream academics who admire his subversiveness even if they do not share his unorthodox views. Even so, Leahy is an unlikely ally of many of his co-signatories. As his published works, his courses and his interviews attest, his approach is grounded in continental philosophy rather than obscure cryptography. His works challenge the notion of Shakespeare 'the genius', Shakespeare 'the single author' even as he joins debating stands with Oxfordians and others who are more thoroughly invested in romantic fantasies of authorship than most modern Shakespearians.

Like Egan, Leahy's scepticism is rooted in the view that Shakespeare's education was not sufficient to explain the erudition of the works, although he accepts in an interview with the Oxfordian newsletter *Shakespeare Matters* (Summer 2006) that Shakespeare may have acquired the rest of his education informally. In his introduction to *Shakespeare and His Authors: Critical Perspectives on the Authorship Question*, Leahy brusquely argues that the education argument is not snobbery but 'sociology' (p. 1).

Egan and Leahy share a commitment to profiling as the best way to pick apart Shakespeare's authorship, but Leahy goes further than Egan in promoting this. Leahy seems to share with some Oxfordians a general distaste for Shakespeare. In his introduction to *Shakespeare and his Authors*, Leahy calls Shakespeare a 'money-lender', which is a curiously archaic and I assume pejorative term to describe a fairly normal practice which anyone with an interest-bearing savings account will also be guilty of. Does anyone today use 'money-lender' to describe creditors? The Shakespeare who emerges from Leahy's account reminds me very much of the character in Edward Bond's play *Bingo*. That play explored the disconnect between the portly capitalist Shakespeare and the author of *King Lear* and *Hamlet*. Leahy writes with disillusion, but endorses no other candidate.

OTHER DISCIPLINES

Leahy also notes that most 'Stratfordians' are English literature academics with no historical training, as if history would prove to be a more accepting discipline than English of the core anti-Shakespearian arguments. This is a line of argument echoed in the Declaration. Its caustic reviews of books and articles by James Shapiro, Stephen Greenblatt and Stanley Wells frequently

call into question their judgment and academic abilities (I don't doubt
that mine will also be examined at some point as well). However, these
rhetorical attempts to cast doubts on the academic validity of these and
many other scholars are challenged by the academic list itself. Few of those
disciplines which Leahy and the Declaration itself call upon are sufficiently
present to challenge the authority of English scholars.

There are far fewer historians prepared to publicly declare their reasonable doubt than almost any other discipline represented. Only sixteen
historians have so far signed the list, twelve of whom have PhDs or are at
professorial level. Among them is William Rubinstein, a professor of history
at the University of Aberystwyth who has made his own, well-publicized
intervention in the authorship debate in a book claiming Henry Neville
was the true author of the plays. However, some of these historians have
a weak claim to be regarded as such. The late Frank Ratliff held an MA
in History, but took his first degree in Journalism and spent his career as
a popular and much-loved English teacher. Professor Boria Sax specializes
in animal studies and, like Carl G. Estabrook, has a good reputation for
human rights advocacy.

One of the most distinguished historians on this list is Don Ostrowski,
a Russian historian who teaches at Harvard and is widely published.
Although Ostrowski has never, to my knowledge, written directly about
Shakespeare, he outlines a historical approach to literature in a paper titled
'Three Criteria of Historical Study' which gives some indications of the
structure of thought which has led him to signing the declaration.[5] At
the heart of Ostrowski's historical method is a radical scepticism and an
inherent distrust of documentary evidence. He begins the essay with a
quote from Buddha: 'Believe nothing just because you have been told it'
and moves on to discuss Einstein's challenge to conventional scientific wisdom. Ostrowski reacts against any predisposed views or conventions which
limit intellectual freedom and he challenges the conventional sanction in
historical method against making value judgments: 'Instead of castigating
ourselves for having them', he writes, 'we should learn to use them' (p. 2).
He continues, 'Value judgments are intuitive' and argues that intuitive
judgments have real value, even if they can sometimes be 'plain wacko'.
His paper is predicated on developing a historical methodology based on
intuition. He draws on Karl Popper's 'theory of refutation' (that the historian should try to refute hypotheses rather than confirm them) to argue
that historians should approach all written documents as potential forgeries
until they can be properly authenticated: 'It is not enough to assume they
are authentic merely because no one has questioned them or challenged

them' (p. 9). He continues, 'The only realistic approach to our source testimony then is one of distrust unless we have some specific reason for trusting it.' Most historians would agree that documentary evidence has to be understood in context and evaluating the reliability of any document is a basic skill for any historian. However, Ostrowski pushes academic scepticism to the extreme and creates a *reductio ad absurdum* argument. If all historical documents are presumed to be possible forgeries, how could they ever be validated, since most historical documents will be validated by other historical documents? Echoing Leahy, Ostrowski sees a political angle to the imposition of historical orthodoxy, speculating that students' 'resistance to learning the history taught in our secondary schools and colleges may be an existential resistance to being propagandized' (p. 16).

Ostrowski does not use the paper to justify his doubt in Shakespeare, although if he had done so the case would have made an excellent demonstration of his point. Having understood Ostrowski's position better, I can see why he was moved to sign the petition and endorse Mark Anderson's *'Shakespeare' by Another Name* (a book which develops the Oxford theory and includes a glowing tribute from Ostrowski on the cover).[6] Anyone following this method would indeed be inclined to doubt all documentary sources and to privilege intuitive judgments particularly when they challenge conventional histories. The paper is intelligently written and, indeed, reasonable; but as a historical methodology it is deeply flawed and has not won widespread acceptance, or for that matter attention, among historians. Ostrowski is a brilliant but iconoclastic historian, but hardly any other historian has followed his lead in challenging Shakespeare's authorship. Ostrowski's endorsement, made in December 2009, has only been followed by two further signatories with a history degree, neither of which are currently tenured academics. No historians have been moved to sign the list since the 2011 release of the film *Anonymous*.

Other disciplinary lists are similarly revealing. Despite Freud's very high-profile advocacy of the Oxford case, he was unable to convince his supporters at the time, and very few psychologists now will sign the Declaration, which lists only thirteen signatories, with only three new signatures since 2009. Leahy might be relieved to see more listed under 'social sciences' given that his own argument rests on a distinction between snobbery and sociology. However, of the twenty-four signatories, many are not sociologists but economists, political scientists, anthropologists and even theatre directors. The actual number of sociologists is twelve or less. Only eight names have been added to the list since 2009. Despite these low numbers, the Social Sciences section is strengthened by the signature of Geoffrey Hodgson, a

Research Professor in Business Studies at the University of Hertfordshire who holds a D.Litt. (a higher doctorate) from Oxford, edits a journal for Cambridge University Press and is the author of many highly respected works in his field. He is also a member of the De Vere Society and the Shakespeare Oxford Society. On his website (www.geoffrey-hodgson.info), Hodgson has posted an essay about his authorship convictions. Although he argues that 'no case has been proved' (echoing Egan's position) he clearly believes that Oxford has a stronger claim than 'Shaksper' and boasts that 'the lack of evidence on the Stratfordian side should put every serious thinker into a state of uncertainty and lead him or her to consider possible alternatives'.

Since the Declaration borrows 'reasonable doubt' as a standard of proof from criminal trials, it must be disappointing to the SAC that so few lawyers have been prepared to sign the document. By Spring 2012, only seventeen lawyers have signed, only three of them professors. More than half signed in the first two years of the petition; only four signatories have been added since 2010. It seems that very few in the legal profession are as convinced as the Declaration is that there is a case for applying notions of 'reasonable doubt' to Shakespeare's authorship. Fortunately for the Declaration, one of the seventeen is so distinguished as to make up for the lack of legal weight in the rest of the list. Justice John Paul Stevens is one of three Supreme Court judges to feel strongly enough about the authorship issue to publicly declare his support for the declaration. In 2012, Barack Obama nominated him for a Presidential Medal of Freedom, the US's highest honour, for a lifetime of achievements which included protecting civil rights. According to a number of reports, Justice Stevens is a committed Oxfordian (see the *Wall Street Journal*, 18 April 2009). Justice Stevens, who is now in his nineties, was drawn into the controversy in 1987 when he was one of three judges who presided over a mock-trial about the authorship question. Although the panel rejected the Oxfordian claim, Stevens thought Shakespeare's case marginal and in recent years has been more confident in putting out anti-Shakespearian points. Like Egan and Leahy, his starting point is Shakespeare's learning. Visiting Shakespeare's birthplace, Stevens was disappointed to find no books, no papers of any kind. The *Wall Street Journal* reports that he asked, 'Where are the books? You can't be a scholar of that depth and not have any books in your home . . . the evidence that he was not the author is beyond a reasonable doubt.' Stevens is more blunt than Leahy in advancing his own social views: 'a lot of people like to think it's Shakespeare because . . . they like to think that a commoner can be such a brilliant writer', he says. 'Even though there is no Santa Claus, it's still a wonderful myth.' Linking the idea that 'a commoner can be such a brilliant writer' to the myth of Santa Claus is not sociology.

Justice Stevens's distinguished career does not absolve him from obvious academic error. Once, learning that the Folger Shakespeare Library holds a Bible once owned by De Vere, Stevens decided to test a theory of his own: that Oxford was inspired by the bed-trick in Genesis 29:23 when writing *All's Well that Ends Well*. Stevens recounts this story in an interview with the *Wall Street Journal*. If that was the case, perhaps Oxford underlined the relevant passages in his copy of the Bible? Stevens asked to see the Bible but was disappointed to find no such markings: 'I really thought I might have stumbled onto something that would be a very strong coincidence . . . but it did not develop at all.' Any of the librarians at the Folger could have saved Stevens a wasted trip. As any good edition of the play should explain, the bed-trick derives from the play's source in the ninth story of Boccaccio's *The Decameron*. Stevens signed in July 2009; since then, only six more people with a legal education have joined him. Like Ostrowski, like Egan and Leahy, like Freud, Stevens's endorsement has not opened the door to widespread acceptance among his own profession.

LET'S BE REASONABLE

None of the people I've written about in this chapter could be called unreasonable people. Many are genuinely distinguished and have brilliant minds. Nevertheless, the numbers have to be seen in context. There are upwards of 100,000 academics in the UK alone, and the list has a global reach with many Americans in particular signing it. A large number of signatories are not professional academics but are listed because they have degrees, and the vast majority of those signing have no specialist knowledge of either the Renaissance or bibliographic studies. The number of academics with a firm grounding in the subject can be counted on one hand. The high-handedness with which some anti-Shakespearians attack Shakespeare studies is unwarranted, for few of these signatories are succeeding at even convincing their own colleagues. Reasonable people are still capable of holding unreasonable views.

This all assumes that being an academic, or having academic credentials, automatically confers authority. A frequent argument used by academics against anti-Shakespearians is that no one trained in academic methodology would ever seriously entertain the doubters' arguments. For example, Gordon McMullan, a Professor at King's College, London and himself a very eminent Shakespeare scholar, told *The Sunday Times*, 'Nobody with any professional training in the analysis of historical or literary evidence could think otherwise' (16 October 2011). Yet the Declaration provides nearly one hundred answers to this point. In this case, the folly is on both sides, since Shakespearians and anti-Shakespearians alike assume that all academics are reasonable people. This is a charming and generous view but as anyone who has ever spent any time in a university will know, the academic world has its fair share of eccentrics for whom specialism in one discipline hardly prepares them for the rigours of just about anything else. Indeed, some of the most notorious people in history have academic qualifications. In the UK, in just the last few years, there have been two notorious killers with PhDs (or studying for one). In Libya, Saif al-Islam Gaddafi holds a PhD from the London School of Economics (his late father, a notable anti-Shakespearian himself, is missing from the Declaration's list of notables). Robert Mugabe holds two Master's degrees and taught in colleges before entering politics. In fact, it is not hard to come up with a rogue's gallery of murderers, fraudsters and tyrants who have academic qualifications and even academic tenure. These are not reasonable people, but they would all qualify as 'academics' under the Declaration's criteria.

I am not for one moment suggesting that we should equate anti-Shakespearians with such appalling people, only that academics are as diverse as any other group of human beings, and as capable of eccentricity and folly as anyone. The object of creating a separate list of academic signatories is surely to normalize the anti-Shakespearian argument, to say to fellow doubters: 'look, even academics think the same as you'. Of all the academics I've looked at, only Ostrowski has developed a fully formulated methodology that defends the privileging of profile over documentary evidence. Hodgson, Leahy and Egan tend to fall into the same rhetorical traps as the Declaration itself does without recognizing the methodological differences between their approaches and standard historical methods.

What, then, has the Declaration achieved in its (to date) five years of existence? What is it capable of achieving? Like many anti-Shakespearian projects, the Declaration project thinks it needs publicity, hence the wave of books, websites and Hollywood films peddling the anti-Shakespearian position. The Declaration that Leahy publicly signed in 2007 has, next to his name, spaces reserved for The Shakespeare Birthplace Trust and the Shakespeare Institute, both of which are missing signatures (I could not find anyone at either institution that remembers being approached). The photograph seems to be a gauntlet thrown down at the 'orthodox'

Shakespearians, whom the Declaration seems to simultaneously deride for their small-mindedness and yet crave acceptance from.

The list has undoubtedly been successful in attracting some genuinely distinguished people. However, it has not been successful in attracting large numbers of them. Since its launch in 2007, the Declaration has struggled to maintain momentum. In the first seven months of its existence, the Declaration collected 1,161 signatures, and James Shapiro notes that by the spring of 2009, that figure had risen by 400.[7] In May 2012, at the time of writing, the figure advertised on the website is 2,379, just enough to squeeze into a single performance at Shakespeare's Globe. This indicates an increase of *c.* 900 signatures in the last three years, and it remains the case that fifty per cent of people signing the Declaration did so in the first year of its existence. I anticipated that the release of the film *Anonymous* would inevitably lead to a surge of interest in the Declaration, but this does not seem to have happened. In an email update to the SAC sent in April 2012, John Shahan noted that there had been an increase of eighty-five signatures in 2011 when compared to 2010 (260 in 2010, 345 in 2011), with the film itself probably responsible for attracting about one hundred people. To be fair to the Declaration, it did nothing to explicitly tie itself to the film, which is hardly mentioned on its website, but even so this is a low number given the wide publicity that the authorship question was given in the media in the film's wake.

These statistics put into perspective the initial disappointment I had when I saw some of the names on the list. In a way, the Declaration has performed an inadvertent service to the Shakespeare community by flushing out how few people around the world are prepared to sign such a document. Highlighting the number of academics as a strategy has back-fired for, far from isolating Shakespeare scholars as high priests of Stratfordian orthodoxy somehow divorced from academic logic and unable to accept a reasonable argument, the list reveals how few academics around the world have any truck with these arguments. Even those highly prominent academics who have signed the Declaration have failed to convince anyone in their profession to follow them. Again, momentum has slackened. Of these 415 'academics', 247 signed within the first two years. In 2011, only sixty names were added to the academics list. There have only been thirty-three new signatories since the release of the film *Anonymous* and by May 2012, the number of new names for 2012 stood at only fourteen. The 415 'academics', even if they are all bona fide higher education lecturers and professors, are dwarfed by the hundreds of thousands of academics across the world who have not, and will not, sign.

The 'notables' list is noticeably undistinguished in its recent signings. To date, no actor of the prominence of Michael York, Mark Rylance or Derek Jacobi has signed since 2007; with the exception of Justice Stevens and Justice O'Connor, who signed in 2009, no one of any real note has signed since.

That there are intelligent and highly qualified people in the world who sincerely believe that Shakespeare did not write his plays has been proved beyond all reasonable doubt – but we've known this since Mark Twain and Sigmund Freud endorsed the authorship sceptics. But even on this list, these reasonable people have to share internet space with people who use the Declaration to promote their own theories about 9/11, or argue (in one case) that Shakespeare was a woman. Reasonable people can hold unreasonable views. There does seem to be a common theme, or a common structure of thought, which binds together many of those on the list who have developed their views in public. However, this is a methodology which most academics will be deeply sceptical about, and until the Declaration is able to supplement its list of names with real, documentary evidence, the Declaration's second purpose, to legitimize the academic study of the authorship issue, will remain unfulfilled.

CHAPTER 18

'There won't be puppets, will there?': 'Heroic' authorship and the cultural politics of Anonymous

Douglas M. Lanier

At first glance, *Anonymous* (Sony Pictures, 2011) could not seem more different from other recent fictional treatments of Shakespeare's biography. Instead of imagining the circumstances of Shakespeare the man becoming 'Shakespeare' the author, the typical concern of such tales, it portrays Shakespeare as a reprehensibly opportunistic, illiterate buffoon and reassigns the role of author to the Earl of Oxford, the dashing nobleman and amateur playwright. Instead of focusing on backstage details of performance, it attends far more to the mechanics of how the plays got from Oxford's pen to the Rose. Though recent biographical fictions of Shakespeare have become more interested in political matters, *Anonymous* seems to stand out for its willingness to place courtly manoeuvering so squarely in the foreground. Even so, *Anonymous* is actually quite conventional in its conceptualization of authorship and shares with recent fictional treatments of Shakespeare a body of crucial assumptions. What makes the film distinctive, I will argue, is its conceptualization of Shakespearian spectatorship and of popular culture. There the cultural politics of the Oxfordian case it makes come most clearly into view.

The film's claim to historical authenticity is crucial to its case for Oxford as the true author of Shakespeare's plays, and so how it pursues that goal is worth examining. What becomes immediately apparent from the pile-up of factual errors is that the film's historicity is not a matter of fidelity to the verifiable historical record. It is worth observing, then, that the 'feeling' of historical accuracy often springs from details culled from other Shakespeare and Shakespeare-era films. The list of intercinematic references is long, particularly those that suggest we are getting an unromanticized vision of the Elizabethan past, a visual counterpart to the 'darker story of quills and swords, of power and betrayal' that the prologue promises. The muddy streets of London owe to *Shakespeare in Love* and especially to the sloppy battlefields of Agincourt in Branagh's *Henry V*, where mud serves as a signifier of the gritty political realities of early modern war;[1] the rainstorm in

215

the midst of the *Hamlet* performance owes to the rain-soaked performance of 2.1 in Olivier's *Henry V*, a reminder of the harsh realities of open-air performance; the sordid brothel scene involving Shakespeare owes to scenes with Burbage and Tilney in *Shakespeare in Love*; the darkly lit corridors of court power and myriad images of courtiers peering from behind screens or through leaded windows owe to *Elizabeth*; the erotic escapades of male-model handsome Oxford combined with spicy court intrigue owe to the hot-sex-and-politics formula of *The Tudors*; Oxford's ink-stained fingers, sign of the authentically early modern author, owe to Shakespeare in *Shakespeare in Love*. Even the film's structure – a cinematic tale framed by a theatrical prologue and epilogue – borrows from Olivier's *Henry V*, and the casting of Derek Jacobi as the Prologue draws on his towering theatrical reputation in the same way that Branagh did in his *Henry V*. These details (and others) aim to bring *Anonymous* in line with cinematic conventions for conveying historical authenticity, suggesting through cinematic pastiche that we are getting at unvarnished historical 'truth'.

The film's portrayal of authorship in this context is especially notable. In *Anonymous*'s vision of the plays, the public theatre milieu, so often the focus of Shakespeare authorship narratives, is quite literally an afterthought. Oxford's scripts are all single-authored without a thought to their staging outside of the court, and he has his go-between Jonson drop them off at the public theatre for production like an executive drops off his laundry to be dry-cleaned. His writing is unsullied by contact with other writer-collaborators, actors or the production process; his only link to the realities of staging is when we see him as a boy performing as Puck in a court per-formance of *A Midsummer Night's Dream*. When we first meet the mature Oxford, he is apparently attending the public theatre for the very first time, urged on by his companion Southampton who is enamoured of its superior production values. His only concern, a telling one, is that the experience not be vulgar – 'There won't be puppets, will there?' he worries. Only after seeing the crowd's response to a caricature of a foppish nobleman and the authorities' repressive response (they close the production) does Oxford consider having his work secretly produced for the public stage. Whereas recent scholarship has stressed the collaborative nature of Elizabethan stage production, the interplay between writers, actors, anticipated audiences, *Anonymous* prefers to conceive of Oxford working entirely in isolation, writing plays independently of any intention of their being performed, his shelves filling up with unproduced manuscripts.

In short, Oxford is presented as a private poet, not a public playwright, writing for the page not the stage. This may explain the gaffe of presenting

Oxford's *Romeo and Juliet* as the first play in iambic pentameter verse; the stress upon the novelty of verse marks Oxford's work as *poetry* rather than stage dialogue. By contrast, Shakespeare comes off as especially vulgar because he is a stage performer and, worse, one who panders to the public. We first see him as Carlo Buffone in *Every Man Out of His Humour*, hamming it up to get cheap laughs. Backstage, he exclaims 'Jesus, it's wonderful dialogue, absolutely wonderful!' when it's clear that the lines are wooden and the jokes stale, the first indication that Shakespeare has no literary taste. The scandal of Shakespeare laying claim to Oxford's verse, then, is that he is a common *actor*, concerned with mass entertainment rather than with court politics, the quality that gives Oxford's writing heft and force. In several ways, then, *Anonymous* presents Oxford the author as standing above the conditions of public stage production. It recoils at the idea that Shakespeare's works were conceived as popular entertainment, and so they are recast as covert court commentary.

This conception of authorship, the model of the lone, transcendent poet whose work stands apart from the vulgar marketplace and resists authoritarian powers-that-be, has deep roots in Romantic myths of literary genius, and it is the project of *Anonymous* to re-imagine Oxfordian authorship in those terms. In *Anonymous* the writing of Shakespeare's plays is emphatically *not* a matter of imitating or adapting prior models, a technique demonstrably at work in Shakespearian scripts. Rather, the author, a heroic figure near-tragic in his isolation, writes out of his personal experience; even when he is writing history plays or narrative poems, the tales he tells allegorize elements of his life. The biographical foundations upon which Oxford supposedly draws as an author – his training as a soldier and statesman, his classical education, his years on the continent – are sketched in, and the film focuses on how Oxford's vexed relationship with the venal Cecil family and failed romance with the young Queen Elizabeth shape his character and thus his writing. In his writing Oxford targets the oppressive upstart regime represented by the Cecils, the enemies of poetry and bearers of bourgeois morality, positioning himself as a rebel against what he calls the 'reptilian' court. To his wife Ann, Oxford speaks of the overwhelming vatic inspiration that drives his authorship, a channelling of others' voices that explains the negative capability of Shakespeare's characterizations:

The voices, Ann. The voices, I can't stop them. They come to me when I sleep, when I wake, when I sup. I walk down the hall, I hear the sweet longings of a maiden, the searching ambitions of a courtier, the foul designs of a murderer, the wretched pleas of his victim. Only when I put their words, their voices to parchment are they cast loose, freed. Only then is my mind quieted, at peace. I would go mad if I did not write down the voices.

Even Oxford's sexual exploits owe something to the Romantic notion that intense passion underlies genuine aesthetic vitality. And like the Byronic hero he resembles, Oxford pays a terrible price for devotion to his writing and political ideals, establishing the tragically idealistic, heroic nature of his artistic endeavour. (The stains on his fingers invite a double reading.) Elements of Shelley, Keats, Byron, Coleridge, Rimbaud – all feed into the film's portrayal of the author of Shakespeare's works as a Romantic poet *avant la lettre*.

Accordingly the performances of Shakespeare within the film are often shaped to accord with Romantic sensibilities, as if 'proving' the link between Oxford the author's Romantic biography and his work. The ballroom scene between Romeo and Juliet echoes a ballroom scene between young Oxford and Elizabeth we see in flashback, 'confirming' that the play originated in Oxford's personal experience rather than, as scholars have long known, in Arthur Brooke's *Tragical History of Romeus and Juliet*.[2] The killing of Julius Caesar occasions a declaration of social revolution; nowhere are the play's myriad political ambiguities acknowledged. The witches' scene from *Macbeth*, a nighttime special-effects extravaganza, visually aligns the play with the Gothic. This 'greatest hits' montage culminates with Hamlet's 'to be or not to be', moved so that it follows his confrontation with Gertrude and thus becomes the play's climactic speech. Shakespeare's Hamlet epitomizes the film's image of Oxford the Romantic genius, an isolated, noble figure of artistic, intellectual temperament, beleaguered by oppressive forces and making exquisite poetry of his tragic circumstance. Just to drive the image home, Emmerich pictures the groundlings suffering along with Hamlet as he delivers his lines in the rain; watching the play at court, Elizabeth, to the horror of her ladies-in-waiting, starts to unbutton her bodice, as if involuntarily drawn into empathy with the suffering prince.[3]

Notably, the film returns several times to the 'O for a muse of fire' prologue from *Henry V*, turning it into a definitive statement of Romantic artistic principles: the poet's desire for a transcendent mode of authorship which stands aloof from the inadequacy of vulgar stage production (underlined by Mark Rylance's jumping on the stage at 'this unworthy scaffold' and comic miming at 'when we talk of horses') and endorsement of the power of imagination and its service to a grand political cause (underlined by a closeup of Rylance and a groundling at ''tis your thoughts that now must deck our kings'). Crucially for the film's cultural politics, this speech imagines an aristocratic arena of theatrical production and reception – 'princes to act', 'monarchs to behold the swelling scene', and, by implication, an upper-class poet to match. Commitment to the Romantic principle that art proceeds from the artist's biography also accounts for one of the film's more glaring historical errors. *Anonymous* imagines that it is *Richard III* that Oxford writes and has performed to support the Essex rebellion, not *Richard II*, as the historical record indicates. This is not just because *Richard III* is more familiar to the film's target mass audience.[4] More importantly, the film's presentation of the hunchback king as a caricature of Robert Cecil imagines that *Richard III* was written out of Oxford's jaundiced experience of his political rival, the allusion central to the author's original conception and political plans.

Imagining that Shakespeare's plays have biographical origins typifies how popular culture has long formulated Shakespearian authorship, from as early as Widgey R. Newman's *Immortal Gentleman* (1935) which portrays Shakespeare as fashioning literary characters from the ordinary people he meets at Bankside, to as recently as *Shakespeare in Love* (1999).[5] In part, this conceptualization of authorship springs from narrative necessity, since it is difficult to imagine how one might make an interesting film from a writer seated at his book-laden desk scribbling scripts. Even more important, however, is popular culture's commitment to the principle of authorial biographicality, the notion that the art is fundamentally expressive of, or at least deeply co-extensive with, the author's life. This principle is often positioned against rival models of authorship that the writer must reject to become 'authentic': a professional conception of writing as verbal or adaptational craft, a commercial conception of writing as genre-driven, profit-oriented entertainment for the masses, a high-cultural conception of writing as a learned dialogue with literary tradition. Popular accounts of Shakespearian authorship create fictional biography out of the plays so, in circular fashion, they can present the plays as if they were grounded in the author's life experience. *Shakespeare in Love*, a film with which *Anonymous* has close affiliations, offers a playful version of this principle, imagining that what the film bills as Shakespeare's greatest early success, *Romeo and Juliet*, springs directly from the playwright's torrid but doomed (and entirely fictional) affair with Viola de Lessups. As the film would have it, *Romeo and Juliet* succeeds with both the public and Queen Elizabeth because it manages to capture 'the very truth and nature of love' by being rooted in Will's love life and by being played by Will and Viola in its premiere performance. The principle of biographical verisimilitude, the continuity between art and life, enables the transcendence of Shakespeare's writing over stultifying theatrical convention (cross-dressed boys as women) and commercial artifice (the genre fiction Will tries to write).

In *Anonymous*, this principle is also pursued, though for different ends. It is at work in Hamlet's killing of Polonius which, we are shown, has its direct (fictional) source in an incident in young Oxford's life, where he kills William Cecil's servant-spy who hides behind an arras after pawing through Oxford's writings. Oxford, so the film suggests, takes this raw material and reshapes it in *Hamlet* for purposes of vicarious revenge. Laertes's leave-taking scene establishes that the pompous, moralistic Polonius stands for Cecil, so that when Hamlet kills him in the later scene, we understand that we are watching an expression of Oxford's hatred towards his tyrannical father-in-law.[6] A more complex case is that of *A Midsummer Night's Dream*, which parallels the developing attachment between Oxford and Elizabeth (and is, not incidentally, the first Shakespeare snippet in the film). We first see Bottom and Titania's initial meeting performed before old Elizabeth, the exiled Oxford looking on from the wings to see the Queen's response. In a flashback, we are whisked back to an earlier performance before the young Elizabeth, where the boy Oxford, playing Puck, asks 'give me your hands, if we be friends' as if directly of the Queen. This is young Elizabeth and young Oxford's first contact, memories of which the older Oxford has conjured up for the ageing queen through the performance of *A Midsummer Night's Dream*. Backstage, the boy Oxford charms Elizabeth with his literary precocity[7] and his cheeky bid for royal service. Here Oxford first asserts himself as an author, and the spark between boy and Queen establishes that his poetry has awakened Elizabeth's interest, just as Bottom's song awakens Titania. Later, after the two have consummated their relationship, we see Elizabeth lounging on a fur-covered bed, an image reminiscent of Titania's boudoir-bower in the play. Taken together, these scenes suggest that *A Midsummer Night's Dream* proleptically depicts the forbidden, erotically intense relationship between Oxford and Elizabeth.[8] It is the biographical underpinnings of the plays that, so the film suggests, give them such affective power.

This drive to locate authorship in the life experiences of the author, the predisposition to affirm in one's responses to artworks 'the continuity between art and life', is an essentially Romantic predisposition that, Bourdieu argues, remains a foundational premise for much of popular culture's understanding of art.[9] What Richard Burt argues of *Shakespeare in Love* and Erika Jong's novel *Serenissima* also holds true of *Anonymous*: these post-modern pop biofictions provide 'not so much a critique of the Romantic account of literary authorship but instead [enable] its reinvention',[10] an extension of the popular aesthetic to Shakespeare's work, and, conversely, a use of Shakespeare's authority to perpetuate popular conceptions of authorship. At bottom, then, *Anonymous* is rather conventional in its conception of Shakespearian authorship. This is not to say, however, that *Anonymous* is undistinctive in its approach to this enterprise. For one thing, the current fashion in popular fictionalizations of Shakespearian biography is, as in *Shakespeare in Love*, to foreground their status as playful, postmodern biographical fantasy. This *Anonymous* never does, instead presenting itself as earnestly historical. The theatrical frame for its cinematic story does less to reveal the fiction's constructedness than to interpellate the film viewer as a privileged insider with special backstage access, a fellow of the actors, a lover of theatre. The position 'we' occupies lies behind the 'our' in Jacobi's freighted lines, 'Our Shakespeare, rise! Our Shakespeare. For he is all of ours, is he not?', implicitly posits a threatening 'them', the Stratfordian establishment. Even more distinctive is how *Anonymous* conceptualizes Shakespearian authorship and cultural politics. Of special interest is the film's portrayal of the public theatre audience. What attracts Oxford to the public stage is the prospect of using what he calls 'the mob' to support his political agenda – the preservation of traditional aristocratic right – and to generate animus towards the Cecils. After attending the public theatre for the first time he muses, 'Ten thousand souls, all listening to the writings of one man, the ideas of one man. That's power, Essex.' Later, when offering Jonson a play for production at the Rose, he confirms that he intends to harness the power of the commons, observing 'all art, Jonson, is political, otherwise it would just be decoration'. That statement, interestingly enough, accords with one of the key premises of recent scholarship – that Shakespeare's plays intervene in rather than simply reflect history. The film's conceptualization of that premise, however, leaves out elements that have preoccupied scholars – the extent to which audiences do not respond as one to art; the ways in which Shakespeare's plays question or even overturn the discourses they engage; the notion that performances involve performers' agendas that may not correspond to the author's.

These complications, however, do not concern Oxford. As the film conceives it, the groundlings find the populist and patriotic strains of Oxford's plays instantly compelling, galvanizing them into a unified political force. *Henry V*, the first of Oxford's plays to appear on the public stage, establishes the pattern. At the Crispin Crispian speech the groundlings spontaneously reach out their hands en masse to touch Henry, as if he were some rock star or faith healer commanding the adoration of the masses. Above it all in the lords' box, Oxford mouths the words 'band of brothers' as the actor says them, in effect functioning as the ventriloquist for it all. When the battle of Agincourt finally begins in the performance, the crowd sponta-neously erupts 'down with the French!' which Oxford, delighted, joins in. Exhilarated by this response, Oxford later exclaims to his wife, 'Ann, you should have seen them, the mob! They didn't just sit there like the reptilian of court, faces motionless, fangs momentarily retracted. No, they climbed the stage, they fought the French.' Other performances demonstrate the effect of Oxford's populist rhetoric with the groundlings. Following Cae-sar's assassination in *Julius Caesar*, the crowd roars approval at the line 'Tyranny is dead!'; when Hamlet slays Polonius, his resemblance to Cecil prompts one spectator to shout 'Not a day too soon for Cecil!', at which the audience breaks into sudden applause. This sequence of scenes culminates with *Richard III*, which Oxford uses to stir up the mob Essex needs to bolster his rebellion, a strategy which succeeds spectacularly well with the crowd but ends in political failure.[11] The commons' adoring response to the plays certainly affirms their poetic power, but what motivates Oxford's writing is not populist resistance to tyranny at all but rather the preservation of traditional aristocratic privilege – Oxford tells Elizabeth that his fellow conspirators 'only wanted a voice in government equal to their birth' – and the destruction of the bourgeois upstart Cecils. For all Oxford's initial dismay at the prospect of puppets, *Anonymous* conceives of Oxford the author as an aristocratic puppet-master, manipulating the (heart)strings of the commons with populist sentiments so that he can use 'the mob' for his own interests, all while maintaining the pretence that the plays issue from a man of the people, Shakespeare, a contemptible front-man. This scenario bears troubling resemblance to current American political practice – the creation of 'astroturf' organizations, pseudo-populist political front groups backed by behind-the-scenes power-brokers who use the zeal their rhetoric whips up to serve their own protection of economic privilege. If the Oxfordian case seems to rest upon classist assumptions, *Anonymous* seems to double down on them, depicting the playwright approvingly as an aristocratic puppeteer and his mass audience as enthusiastic if unwitting pawns.

Aside from the groundlings, *Anonymous* provides one other, equally revealing site of reception: Ben Jonson, the film's protagonist. In Shake-spearian biofictions, Jonson, typically portrayed as egotistical, pedantic, classically learned and well-connected, serves as foil for Shakespeare, his status as a professional wordsmith and courtly insider highlighting the more 'authentic' qualities of Shakespeare the author-genius. In *Anonymous*

Jonson too serves in this fashion, though Oxford, not Shakespeare, occupies the place of heroic author. Jonson is the one spectator (other than oily Marlowe) with sufficient literary taste to appreciate the exceptional quality of Oxford's work, and he is also the only one (other than Shakespeare) who knows the plays originate with Oxford. The playhouse scenes repeatedly feature closeups of Jonson set apart from the crowd, alone cognizant of sheer literary greatness. He glances at Oxford in amazed admiration and Oxford responds with an imperious nod, a secret exchange of recognition between the artistic elite. If Oxford is the heroic author pursuing grand political ends, Jonson is at first a cowardly one, unwilling to acknowledge that his comedy-writing is political, succumbing to envy when he exposes Oxford's caricature of Cecil and undermines the Essex rebellion. Jonson's 'sin' sets up a culminating scene of redemption and artistic legitimation, the inaugural moment of Oxfordianism. After the rebellion is crushed, Jonson visits Oxford on his death-bed, where the dying poet craves one thing: Jonson's acknowledgment of his writings' literary greatness, an acknowledgment Jonson tearfully offers. For Oxford, Jonson's imprimatur is the consolation for his political losses, losses which, Cecil has earlier revealed, include the throne itself. Tragic though they may be, those losses confirm Oxford as a genuine Romantic author-hero, brought low by his devotion to poetry, a figure, as Cecil himself declares, 'right out of a Greek tragedy'. Jonson here emerges as a stand-in for the modern Oxfordian, the one who alone knows the full biographical story and alone can appreciate the plays' value, the one who himself stands apart from his peers in his willingness to suffer for art – the spectatorial counterpart of Oxford the hero-author. To Jonson Oxford entrusts preservation of his works, threatened as they are by a conspiracy that, in the film's final moments, Jonson manages to circumvent. *Anonymous* amplifies the element of bardolatry – Jonson tells Oxford that 'I find your words the most wondrous heard on the stage, on any stage, ever' – so that Jonson, and those he stands for, can serve as the 'true', heroically isolated bardolater, set against 'the mob' who too willingly accept Shakespeare as an author.

For all its iconoclasm *Anonymous* is of a piece with much of popular culture's portrayal of Shakespearian authorship. Like many other fictional biographies of Shakespeare, it proceeds from a faith that his works express their author's life experience, and on that basis it creates a biographical tale retrofitted to those works, in order to bolster that faith. Other recent works of this sort have acknowledged their fictiveness through irony or their patently fantastic nature, and at first *Anonymous* presents itself as just an alternative biographical fiction, 'a different story, a darker story of quills and swords, of power and betrayal, of a stage conquered and a throne lost', a tale of authorship melded with elements of Shakespearian tragedy and thus somehow more appropriately 'Shakespearian'. But the film cannot resist the siren song of historical authenticity for its alternative version of events, and so it seeks to establish its veracity by turning, ironically enough, to cinematic allusion and magnificent computer graphics. However, what is most troubling about *Anonymous* is not its postmodern truthiness but its re-instantiation of an elitist Shakespeare. At the heart of the Shakespeare film boom of the last two decades has been a faith that Shakespeare's cultural future lies with screen media and the mass audiences they address. The film's many shots of rapt spectators watching Shakespeare's plays in the Rose and Oxford's delight in imagining 'ten thousand souls, all listening to the writings of one man', partake of the bardolatrous fantasy of Shakespeare having an irresistible appeal for the commons. And yet at the same time *Anonymous* seems uncomfortable with what mass appeal might imply – that Shakespeare was himself not of elite stock but a man of the people – and so it re-imagines scenes of reception in a troubling way: the author of Shakespeare's plays as an aristocratic pseudo-populist, his popular audience as puppets useful to his schemes. Even so, the film reserves a small, special space for an elite spectator not of the masses, one uniquely capable of perceiving the plays' and their author's greatness, one to whom the sacred texts and secret subtexts have been consigned for safekeeping. What is most noteworthy about *Anonymous*, in short, is not so much its tale of heroic authorship as its conceptualization of Shakespearian spectatorship, a tale that reveals the troubling cultural politics of the Oxfordian case.

CHAPTER 19

'The Shakespeare establishment' and the Shakespeare authorship discussion

Paul Edmondson

Shakespeare has enemies. Wherever one starts from, the questions and discussions about authorship are basically antagonistic. 'Kill Will: Hollywood and Rhys Ifans plunge a dagger into Shakespeare' a headline trumpeted.[1] But the antagonism comes in many shapes and guises.

The statement 'I have a right to question things with an open mind', is a perfectly reasonable-sounding starting point until one starts to wonder how there might be any room for doubt given the positive historical evidence in Shakespeare's favour. This is outlined throughout section two of this book and critiqued in Andrew Hadfield's essay. Absence of evidence is not the same as evidence of absence. Claiming to have a mind 'open' to the possibility that apparent certainties may not be quite as settled as they seem to be is no more than a rhetorical manoeuvre in this context and should be allowable only after the positive evidence for Shakespeare's authorship has been disproven (rather than merely ignored). I could say I have a mind 'open' to the possibility that the world is flat, but would need to disprove that it is not spherical (more or less) before I started to try to convince anyone else.

There is, too, the loaded assumption that even though one may lack the necessary knowledge and expertise, it is always acceptable to challenge or contradict a knowledgeable and expert authority. It is not. (If the focus of this volume were about a specialized area of nuclear physics those last two sentences would not even have been necessary.) But one characteristic of the Shakespeare authorship discussion is its apparent generosity of scope in which everyone can have their say, ignore the evidence for Shakespeare, propose alternative nominees, contradict authorities and feel empowered.

For many years the antagonism towards Shakespeare came from outside the academy. Now, however, a growing number of voices are claiming an academic right to question Shakespeare's authorship. Their kind of antagonism sounds like this: 'Shakespeare Studies is an industry in denial'; 'there are other ways of approaching knowledge'; 'let's hear from real historians

rather than from scholars of Shakespeare and other literature'; and 'Shakespearians have too much of a vested interest in the discussion.' In 2012, *Who
Wrote Shakespeare's Plays?* appeared by William D. Rubinstein, a professor
of twentieth-century history at the University of Aberystwyth. In it he per-
petuates the attitude that 'there is little in the way of direct unambiguous
evidence' for Shakespeare's authorship and encourages readers 'openly and
objectively' to 'make up their own minds', believing that the alternative
nominees 'all have pluses' and that 'the case for Sir Henry Neville plainly
appears to be both the strongest', 'and that with the fewest weaknesses'.[2]
These kinds of attitudes are enshrined in university courses in England
at Brunel University and in America at Concordia University (Portland,
Oregon). But the antagonism they perpetrate is no better informed, and
has no more claim to authority, than any of the other expressions of
anti-Shakespearianism. At Concordia University you can pay $125 a year
to become an Associate Scholar of the Shakespeare Authorship Research
Centre; $10,000 makes you a Life Scholar. In order to qualify you need to
'possess at least a B.A. and/or be a student or faculty member at the high
school, college or university level in America or Europe'.[3] There is clearly
no real advantage in having a degree; anyone from high school age upwards
is qualified enough, but you do need to supply up to 250 words outlining
your interests in the authorship discussion. For anyone with a first degree,
Brunel University offers an MA in Shakespeare Authorship Studies for
(2011) £4,400 for British students and £11,500 for overseas students. Mod-
ules include 'The Making of Shakespeare', 'Shakespeare the Collaborator'
(so far so legitimate) and 'The Shakespeare Authorship Question'. The
latter is described thus:

This module will examine and consider the suggested alternatives to Shakespeare
as author with a completely open mind. Outside speakers will be invited to put
their case to the student group. Students will examine the history and cultural
relevance of this phenomenon and will assess its cultural *raison d'etre*.[4]

The problem here is that phrase 'completely open mind'. Brunel University has awarded honorary degrees to Sir Derek Jacobi (2007), Mark
Rylance (2009) and Vanessa Redgrave (2011). These are among the finest
Shakespeare actors of the age, but Jacobi and Rylance have repeatedly and
consistently denied that William Shakespeare wrote the works attributed to
him. Redgrave plays the older Elizabeth I in *Anonymous*, in which Rylance
and Jacobi also star. Brunel's MA course is promoted on the website of the
anti-Shakespearian organization, The Shakespearean Authorship Trust.[5]

In an article in *The Times Higher*, William Leahy (himself both a trustee of The Shakespearean Authorship Trust and convenor of the Brunel MA course) made it clear that he is sceptical about Shakespeare's authorship and prefers to think of Shakespeare as 'an amalgamation of authors'. He describes the Brunel MA as 'a fully approved academic programme being run (in good faith) at a fellow UK higher education institution'.[6] There would be no need to criticize Brunel's MA if it were straightforwardly about authorship attribution studies and collaborative playwriting in the Renaissance period. But it does not seem to be.

The antagonism in the Shakespeare authorship discussion, then, expresses itself between those who participate in the focused enjoyment and understanding of Shakespeare and those who want to prevent Shakespeare of Stratford-upon-Avon from playing a major part in that equation, or to remove him from it altogether. Another perspective on the discussion shows a clash between the professional Shakespeare scholar and the anti-Shakespearian amateur. The former employs often highly specialized knowledge; the latter denies it, choosing to act on instinct rather than on evidence (which might be a belief in any alternative nominee, so long as it is not in Shakespeare of Stratford). The difficulty here is that the anti-Shakespearians, whose cause is parasitic, need always to oppose something, so 'the Shakespeare establishment' is construed as an edifice for them to contradict and challenge. When anti-Shakespearians are labelled as conspiracy theorists, they see their accusers as part of that conspiracy. Shakespearians are then forced into a position of taking the moral highground, often an unenviable and unpopular place. The fact is that the onus is on the anti-Shakespearians to disprove the evidence in favour of Shakespeare, rather than merely to express unsupported opinions about that evidence.

One way of dealing with antagonism, as with the school bully, is to ignore it. The problem then is that the antagonism continues. The bully becomes more and more frustrated and the bullying more intense. Shakespearians have too often ignored the antagonism generated by the anti-Shakespearians. In part this is because Shakespearians often find it difficult to know how to respond to a form of antagonism so disingenuous that expressions of it can quite literally leave them speechless. Some hold the view that Shakespearians should not engage in discussion with anti-Shakespearians because to do so gives the discussion inappropriate air-time. Others however believe that failing to engage in discussion might be wilfully misconstrued as oblique corroboration, like listening to something with which one disagrees and then failing to contradict it by choosing to

remain silent. This problem is sometimes compounded by Shakespearians who accuse their colleagues and counterparts who engage with anti-
Shakespearians of wasting their scholarly time and energy. In the end this
kind of suppression leads to indifference: 'What does it matter who wrote
the work, we still have the plays, and besides our accepted orthodoxy tells
us that a writer's biography shouldn't get in the way of analysing the work.'
Meanwhile, though, while some Shakespearians seem content simply to
ignore the proliferation of articles, books and websites devoted to trying to
disprove Shakespeare's authorship, the antagonism continues.

   Doubts about Shakespeare's authorship have long taken root in our
culture and are likely to remain. How may they best be countered? – for
countered they should be. James Shapiro has suggested one way in his book
Contested Will: Who Wrote Shakespeare? (2010). Shapiro believes that anti-
Shakespearians follow the methodology of Shakespearians who often make
deductions about Shakespeare's life from what he wrote (most conspicu-
ously by reading the Sonnets autobiographically). The anti-Shakespearians
can therefore offer a whole host of alternative nominees for the authorship
by telling the story of their preferred nominee through Shakespeare's work.
Shapiro would like to see this methodology fall out of use in Shakespeare
studies so that the underlying assumptions of the anti-Shakespearians
would then cease to be energized by it. Although the biography of any writer
will need to address the work, there needs always to be a critical awareness
of the temptation to find the life in the work and the work in the life.

The rest of this chapter will be focused on my own engagement with
the antagonism I have just outlined starting in June 2011 when I led The
Shakespeare Birthplace Trust's Authorship Campaign, a series of counter-
attacks against the anti-Shakespearians.

   Anyone who identifies Shakespeare as one of their main interests, let
alone those of us who engage with Shakespeare professionally, will know
how often casual questions about Shakespeare's authorship are raised by
many different kinds of people. The question is often raised in Stratford-
upon-Avon by visitors to the Shakespeare Houses or by school, college
and university groups on courses at The Shakespeare Centre. Information
about the authorship discussion has long been available on the Trust's
website, but we wanted to do more. Shapiro's important book appeared
a year before Roland Emmerich's anti-Shakespearian film *Anonymous* was
released. The Trust could have ignored it entirely, but the film, however
ridiculous it seemed likely to be, coupled with Emmerich's insinuating the
authorship discussion further into popular culture was poised to strike at

the heart of all we stood for. Anti-Shakespearians sometimes use the 'slur technique': 'Well, of course, you would defend Shakespeare because you are making money from his reputation.' In fact, the Trust is not doing so. As an independent charity with no endowment it is dependent on the many visitors to Shakespeare's Birthplace to fund its Library, Archive and collections (freely available to all) and its educational work. None of the other major Shakespeare organizations (The Folger Shakespeare Library, The Royal Shakespeare Company, Shakespeare's Globe) or Shakespeare societies seemed to wish to do anything in response to Emmerich's film, so the time seemed ripe for the Trust to step into the centre of the discussion. We decided to lead the Shakespeare Authorship Campaign because we thought more questions would be asked by our visitors and students in light of *Anonymous*, because we saw, and continue to see, something very wrong with the way doubts about Shakespeare's authorship are being given academic credibility by the Universities of Concordia and Brunel, and because we felt that merely ignoring the anti-Shakespearians was inappropriate at a time when their popular voice was likely to be gaining more ground.

On Monday 6 June 2011 at Dartmouth House, the London headquarters of The English-Speaking Union, the Trust and Sony Pictures organized what was called a public 'debate'. The motion was: 'This House believes that William Shakespeare of Stratford-upon-Avon wrote the plays and poems attributed to him.' Speaking for the motion were Stanley Wells, Michael Dobson (Director of The Shakespeare Institute, University of Birmingham) and I. On the opposing team were Roland Emmerich, Charles Beauclerk (a collateral descendant of Edward de Vere, the seventeenth Earl of Oxford) and William Leahy (Head of Brunel University's School of Arts). The Trust had been allowed to invite twenty guests in a room which held 120 people. It was packed. The event was live-streamed and filmed and is available to watch online.[7] The evening did not follow the strict format of a debate. Roland Emmerich, unusually as first speaker for the opposition, was allowed to speak first (he showed us the film trailer for *Anonymous* and spoke a little about why he wanted to direct it); the six speeches did not engage with each other in the way normally expected from debating teams. Moreover, for Shakespearians there can be no actual debate unless all the evidence for Shakespeare's authorship can be properly brought forward and discussed (rather than only being argued against by alternative narratives).

It was an exciting event in which strong views and passions made themselves felt. William Leahy argued that since Shakespeare's morals are questionable (on the grounds that he was guilty of money-lending, litigation, plagiarism, share-holding, tax evasion and grain hoarding) there is ample room to doubt that he is the author of the works attributed to him. Leahy said furthermore that Shakespeare's surviving signatures look as if they were 'written in a hand unlike that of someone who has made their living by writing. They look like they were written by a chimpanzee wearing oven-gloves.' He went on to say:

William Shakespeare is not an author. William Shakespeare is an amalgamation of authors . . . His is a complex and multi-faceted identity. . . . [He] paid playwrights to write plays for him. These eventually became attributed to him. William Shakespeare stole the work of some around him and passed it off as his own.[8]

Leahy's position at once admitted the complexity of Shakespeare's authorship (that he was a collaborator, as John Jowett's essay in this volume demonstrates, has become firmly established as an academic orthodoxy in Shakespearian studies over the last forty years) and eschewed easy explanations (the concept of 'genius'), but he did academia a public disservice by endorsing the slippery, unsubstantiated and impressionistic narratives of the anti-Shakespearians. One of my abiding memories of the evening is the way in which the dozen or so Shakespeare scholars present in the audience seemed to find it too incredible to engage in questions from the floor. Anti-Shakespearian arguments can often overwhelm the established intellectual methodologies of their audience, creating the effect of a vacuum in which the anti-Shakespearian can go on speaking, while the Shakespearian is left gasping in incredulity at the folly of what is being said. The motion before the House succeeded, but only just (or so it seemed), after the voting by acclamation.

It was decided fairly early on that the main expression for the Trust's Authorship Campaign would be the web. Put the search term 'Shakespeare Authorship' into Google and top of the list is 'The Shakespeare Authorship Page', presented by David Kathman (a contributor to this volume) and Terry Ross, which puts over the evidence for Shakespeare's authorship.[9] After this come many hundreds of sites hosted by anti-Shakespearians trying to advance their respective causes. Digital media seemed the most appropriate world in which to air our campaign.

The Trust worked in partnership with a small social media company Misfit, Inc.[10] whose directors, A. J. and Melissa Leon, and I came up with the idea of *60 Minutes with Shakespeare*: sixty voices, sixty questions, sixty seconds each (www.60minuteswithShakespeare.com). We would raise sixty questions and invite answers to them. In the sound-bite world of social media visitors to the polyphonic site could choose to stay there for anything from a minute up to a full hour (approximately – some of the contributions are longer and shorter than a minute). Stanley Wells and I co-authored the questions, many of which were enquiries about Shakespeare's writing, intellectual formation, publications and reputation as well as being weighted towards the authorship discussion. Finding people to speak coincided with my asking them to use the social media site 'Audioboo' on which to upload their contribution. On the whole, the contributors were ready to try it out, and there was always the option of my going to visit them and to record them another way. Contributors were encouraged to read from their own focused script of around 160 words so that their answer would be as close as possible to one minute in length. The first recording I made was with Roland Emmerich while he was staying in London promoting *Anonymous* with Sony Pictures. His is the only anti-Shakespearian voice on the site. Initially Emmerich recorded without a script but after the site went live he asked us if he could rerecord and improve his contribution, which we allowed. Contributors included international Shakespeare scholars and specialists (including some of our trustees), writers (Dame Margaret Drabble, Sir Michael Holroyd), journalists, television celebrities (Stephen Fry, Michael Wood), actors (Simon Callow, Sir Antony Sher, Dame Janet Suzman, Dame Harriet Walter) and theatre directors (Gregory Doran, Tina Packer). HRH The Prince of Wales makes a guest appearance on the site talking about Shakespeare's associations with royalty. A selection of the questions asked is listed at the end of this essay.[11] Within three days of the site being launched it received the equivalent in time of eleven days of engagement around the world. Clearly there was an appetite for this kind of discussion which constituted phase one of the campaign and reached, with a combination of BBC television and radio interviews about the Trust's response to the film, an estimated audience of 10,000,000 people.

Phase two of the campaign involved a public relations stunt on 26 October, the day *Anonymous* was released in the UK. The SBT arranged for the statue of Shakespeare that forms part of the Gower Memorial in the Bancroft Gardens in Stratford-upon-Avon to be covered up with a white sheet. On that same day ninety pubs up and down the country called 'The Shakespeare' covered their signs in black. The road signs that tell drivers they are now entering 'Shakespeare's County' had a line of black tape struck through them. The message was clear and simple. If Shakespeare of Stratford-upon-Avon did not write the works attributed to him, then he should be removed from our national life and popular culture. The campaign created a media storm. A key highlight was the

Figure 19.1. 26 October 2011: The great Shakespeare cover-up. The Gower memorial statue of Shakespeare in Stratford-upon-Avon veiled as part of The Shakespeare Birthplace Trust's Authorship Campaign. Reproduced by permission of The Shakespeare Birthplace Trust.

Figure 19.2. 26 October 2011: Warwickshire is no longer 'Shakespeare's County', since anti-Shakespearians seek to erase Shakespeare of Stratford-upon-Avon from national and international life. Reproduced by permission of The Shakespeare Birthplace Trust.

live broadcast from Shakespeare's Birthplace throughout the morning on BBC breakfast-radio and television. The cast and director of the film gave interviews about their response to our campaign. Mark Rylance and Derek Jacobi told *The Independent* they were planning a response to *60 Minutes with Shakespeare*. Overseas coverage included CNN, *The Washington Post*, *New York Times*, Arab News, BBC Arabic, *China Post*, Russia NTV, Swiss national news, Austria.com, France 24, German Radio ARD, *New Zealand Herald on Sunday*, ABC Madrid, *The Hindu*, *Daily Nation* (Kenya) and *The Star* (Canada). In all, it is estimated that news about the PR stunt reached an audience of around 26,000,000 people.

By 21 November 2011, the anti-Shakespearians had formulated and published online their seventy-six-page rebuttal of *60 Minutes with Shakespeare*. Their text runs to around 44,000 words, since each of the sixty-second scripts is quoted in full before being thrown out of court, often in a derisive manner. It is edited by John M. Shahan, Chairman and CEO of the Shakespeare Authorship Coalition (Claremont, California). Actor Michael York produced the Foreword in which he says that *60 Minutes with Shakespeare*

clearly put the film [*Anonymous*] on the defensive, suppressing attendance despite favourable reviews for the overall quality of the production, its impressive cast, and for several outstanding performances.[12]

In other words, *Anonymous* was a box-office failure, for which York blames *60 Minutes with Shakespeare*, but by this time the effect of the PR exercise had completely overtaken any attempts at rebuttal of the kind being produced by the anti-Shakespearians. The Introduction launches an international petition against the SBT and lays down the following challenge:

We, the undersigned, hereby request that the Shakespeare Birthplace Trust in Stratford-upon-Avon write a single definitive declaration of the reasons why they claim that there is no room for doubt about the identity of the author of the plays and poems of William Shakespeare, and post it along with the names of those who have endorsed it. Yes, there is a case to be made for the traditional attribution to William of Stratford; but what about all of the anomalies that do not fit, and which have led so many highly credible people to express doubt? With all of the questions raised, the issue calls for a definitive treatment.[13]

What are these so-called 'anomalies', and why should everything fit together tidily like the denouement to a detective novel? So far the SBT has ignored this antagonistic invitation, but a further expression of the Authorship Campaign might well have provided what was being called for by the anti-Shakespearians. This is a 7,500-word essay (co-authored by

Stanley Wells and myself) published on 28 October 2011 as a free e-book, *Shakespeare Bites Back* (www.shakespearebitesback.com) and was downloaded 40,000 times in its first five months. It is polemical and accessible in tone and sets out the evidence for Shakespeare as well as ways of critiquing the anti-Shakespearian cause. In the essay we challenge the terms 'Stratfordian', 'the man from Stratford' and 'anti-Stratfordian' as being untenable when discussing Shakespeare's authorship. Instead, we prefer to use the phrase 'anti-Shakespearian'. Our rationale is that artists cannot truly be separated from the social, cultural, economic and political contexts which make them unique. Just as it would not be acceptable to separate Mozart from Vienna and Salzburg, Michelangelo from Florence and Rome, or Charles Dickens from London, so it should likewise seem unacceptable to separate Shakespeare from Stratford-upon-Avon. To remove Stratford-upon-Avon removes part of what made Shakespeare Shakespeare. It is in the end impossible to separate the artist from the work however complicated and nuanced and contingent on theoretical fashions the connection may be. The terms 'Stratfordian' and 'anti-Stratfordian' are themselves symptomatic of anti-Shakespearian rhetoric. The essay ends with a manifesto and summation of our main points and provides, we hope, a resource for people to use in the discussion. We end by calling upon the Dean and Chapter of Westminster Abbey to remove the question mark before the year of Christopher Marlowe's death in the memorial window in Poets' Corner. As discussed by Charles Nicholl in this volume, Marlowe's death is well-documented; his corpse was seen by sixteen jurors; he did not remain alive to write plays and poems under the name of 'Shakespeare'. The question mark in Westminster Abbey denies history and should be removed.[14]

The SBT's Shakespeare Authorship Campaign was augmented by blogs on another of SBT's digital platforms (www.bloggingshakespeare.com), as well as by a section of the SBT's first online course made at around the same time (www.gettingtoknowshakespeare.com). *60 Minutes with Shakespeare, Shakespeare Bites Back* and all of this other content was made available free of charge and in fulfilment of the SBT's charitable objectives.

Who then is being antagonistic to whom? Let us be clear. There never has been and there is not currently a 'Shakespeare establishment'. Rather, there are millions of individuals of different languages and cultures who enjoy and study and teach and perform Shakespeare's work. Some of these people are at school, college or university; some belong to Shakespeare societies; some attend conferences; some work for theatre companies dedicated regularly to producing and performing Shakespeare's plays; some work in specialist research libraries around the world whose collections and archives focus especially on Shakespeare-related material; some write books and articles; some give talks; others enjoy simply attending those talks occasionally. Whilst there is no integrated consensus among these individuals about what Shakespeare 'means', or how one should think about his life, times and authorship, many of them are likely to have encountered some form of anti-Shakespearianism. The Shakespeare Authorship Campaign shows clearly a division between the way in which knowledge starts and how that knowledge is informed by the contextualizing of historical evidence. The SBT tried to provide a bridge for discussion between the professional academic and popular opinion. In doing so it exposed afresh the absurdity of anti-Shakespearianism, ultimately a dangerous phenomenon which can lead to conspiratorial narratives fuelled by denials of historical evidence. One likes to think that if there were any actual evidence that Shakespeare did not write the plays and poems attributed to him, then it would be Shakespeare scholars themselves who would discover and propagate it in their quest to know as much as possible about him. Now that would be undeniable and truly astounding.

Afterword

James Shapiro

In September 2011, a friend who teaches at a small college in upstate New York shared with me free teaching materials he had been sent, designed 'for students in English literature, theater, and British history classes'. A quick glance showed that Sony Pictures had commissioned this guide from a company called 'Young Minds Inspired', timed to coincide with the release of the film *Anonymous*, directed by Roland Emmerich.[1] The teaching guide suggests that teachers ask their students 'Are Shakespeare's plays the work of a highly educated writer with firsthand experience of aristocracy?' After posing another cleverly worded question hinting at pseudonymous authorship – 'what do we really know about this man named Shakespeare?' – the guide then urges teachers to 'Divide your class into two teams, the Upstart Crows and the Reasonable Doubters', to debate yet another leading question: 'Was William Shakespeare really an improbable genius, or just a front man for someone with real ability?' Only a class dunce would, by now, have missed the point: the glover's son from Shakespeare of Stratford could not have had 'real ability' since he lacked the education, breeding and firsthand experience to have written the plays and sonnets.

Not content to release their film in the tradition of *Shakespeare in Love* – a fantasy, a romp, a $30,000,000 Hollywood costume drama – Sony and Emmerich chose to pitch the film (which depicts the Earl of Oxford as the true author of Shakespeare's plays as well as Queen Elizabeth's son and lover) as a version of the truth, to be promulgated onscreen and in classrooms. To this end, the teaching guide declares that Elizabethan England was an 'era filled with political intrigue' which served as 'the perfect setting for a subterfuge that may have led to William Shakespeare taking credit for a series of masterpieces that were actually penned by a far more sophisticated author'. I was beginning to enjoy the syntax of the guide: was it a given that these masterpieces were actually penned by a more sophisticated writer and the subterfuge merely what led Shakespeare to take credit for them? It was hard to tell. My friend did not teach this lesson plan, nor did I. But

I imagine that somewhere in the United States a tired and unimaginative teacher, after asking which students preferred to be in which camp ('No, Katie, you have to sit with the Upstart Crows, too many already want to be Reasonable Doubters!'), may well have proceeded with this numbingly dull lesson. Had the film not been such a box-office disaster, such a scene might have been repeated in classrooms across the land.

This collection of expert essays edited by Stanley Wells and Paul Edmondson is written for Upstart Crows everywhere. Surprisingly, given how much is published on Shakespeare, until now no book has provided the comprehensive evidence necessary to satisfy those 'Reasonable Doubters', and in the process (as Stuart Hampton-Reeves shows) expose what it really means to call oneself a 'Reasonable Doubter'. I'm only sorry that the information set forth in this collection was not yet available to students asked to debate the authorship question in high school classrooms when *Anonymous* came out, or for that matter, before I wrote my own contribution to this subject, *Contested Will*. For I have learned a great deal from these pages – and I suspect that anyone who teaches Shakespeare or is interested in the authorship question will too.

This book will surely be recommended by scholars tired of being asked by strangers: 'Did Shakespeare write Shakespeare?' Yet it would be unfortunate if those same scholars – who because they have no doubts about Shakespeare's authorship find the entire subject a numbing bore and ancillary to their own interests and teaching – don't read it themselves. That's because many of the essays collected here do double duty, exposing what is wrongheaded about rival claimants while at the same time advancing scholarly claims that extend well beyond the question of authorship. Read together, for example, the essays on alternative candidates by Graham Holderness, Alan Stewart, Charles Nicholl, Alan H. Nelson and Matt Kubus offer a rich cultural history of prevailing attitudes in the late nineteenth and early twentieth centuries, invaluable for anyone interested in how Shakespeare and authorship were imagined at that time. The complementary essays by Andrew Hadfield and Stanley Wells remind us not only of how little documentary evidence survives about some of the greatest writers of early modern England, but also, comparatively, and surprisingly, how much survives about Shakespeare.

One of the few salutary things about the challenge to Shakespeare's authorship is that it has forced scholars to look much harder at some of their own underexamined claims. These include the dating of Shakespeare's plays, the extent to which these plays were written by someone immersed in the theatre, and the ways in which their author grappled with the challenges of writing for particular actors. The controversy also invites us to examine anew to what degree the plays reveal themselves to be written by someone who was a product of an Elizabethan grammar school and a native of Warwickshire. The contributions of James Mardock and Eric Rasmussen, Carol Chillington Rutter and David Kathman cover these issues expertly, and I know that I'll be drawing on their insights in my own teaching and scholarship (not least of all the fascinating account of how the author of the third part of *Henry VI* managed to write sixty-seven roles whose dizzying entrances and exits could be handled by only twenty-one actors, a task demanding the kind of technical skill and hands-on knowledge an aristocrat writing the play in a study is unlikely to have possessed).

But it is probably the essays of John Jowett and MacDonald P. Jackson that most profoundly affect mainstream Shakespeare scholarship that has nothing to do with refuting claims for Francis Bacon or the Earl of Oxford. The convincing arguments they make in their essays about attribution, style and co-authorship deepen our understanding of Shakespeare as a collaborative writer from the beginning to the end of his career. The list of likely collaborations is staggering to anyone who had been taught (as I was in the 1970s) that the plays were almost entirely solo-authored: the first part of *Henry the Sixth*, *Titus Andronicus*, *Sir Thomas More*, *Timon of Athens*, *Pericles*, *Henry VIII*, *The Two Noble Kinsmen*, the lost *Cardenio* and arguably a few others as well. Once you concede, say, that five of Shakespeare's last ten plays were written in active collaboration it makes it a great deal harder to insist that the Earl of Oxford – who died in 1604 before any of these plays were written – could have had anything to do with them. It also renders suspect the practice of reading the life out of the works (is the preoccupation with incest in *Pericles* Shakespeare's or Wilkins's? Is Timon's bitterness a reflection of Middleton's state of mind or Shakespeare's?).

Since no shred of documentary evidence has ever been found that suggests that anyone other than Shakespeare (and his collaborators Peele, Wilkins, Middleton and Fletcher) wrote the plays, the sole grounds on which rival claims ultimately rest are biographical: that what occurs in the plays and poems more closely corresponds to the events in another writer's life than they do to Shakespeare's. As Douglas M. Lanier astutely observes in his essay on Emmerich's film, *Anonymous* is built on just this premise: like 'many other fictional biographies of Shakespeare, it proceeds from a faith that his works express their author's life experience, and on that basis it creates a biographical tale retrofitted to those works, in order to bolster that faith' (Chapter 18). It is important to recall that it was Shakespeare scholars, beginning with Edmond Malone in the late eighteenth century, who first embraced reading the life from the works and the works through the life, and they who thus provided a road map subsequently followed by those making similar claims for Bacon, Marlowe, Oxford and seventy or so others. Paul Franssen's illuminating account of fictional treatments of alternative candidates for the authorship of the plays reminds us that these are predated by Shakespearian 'biofictions', dating back to 1804 and Alexandre Duval's short comedy, *Shakespeare amoureux*. It is easier to mock *Anonymous* than to recognize some of our own Romantic assumptions about artistic creativity recycled in Emmerich's film.

So it is not enough to deride anti-Stratfordians. As satisfying as it is to read *Hamlet* as the personal story of Shakespeare's grief over the loss of his son (two years earlier) or the anticipated death of his father (two years after he drafted the play), the temptation to speculate beyond what is corroborated by documentary evidence must be resisted. So too, must the desire to tell our students that *The Tempest* was Shakespeare's farewell to the stage, and the playwright a barely veiled Prospero, an old man heading into retirement and abandoning his rough magic. For we have no idea what Shakespeare felt about his son or father or how such feelings might have shaped his rewriting of an old play, also called *Hamlet*. And Shakespeare, after all, was only in his late forties when he wrote *The Tempest* and would collaborate on at least three other plays (and for all we know, and we do not for sure, perhaps wrote *Cymbeline* and *The Winter's Tale* after this as well). As exciting as it is to speculate about these or other autobiographical revelations in the plays, or claim to identify who the Dark Lady or Young Man of the Sonnets were, there is a steep price paid, to my mind, too steep a price, for speculatively reading Shakespeare's life out of the works: for it is this, more than anything else, that continues to legitimate the methodology undergirding all anti-Stratfordian claims.

The greatest problem with reading the life out of the works, whether done by believers or sceptics in Shakespeare's authorship, is how selective it is. Mainstream Shakespearians never argue that Shakespeare had the mind and heart of a serial killer, though by the same logic who else but a psychopath could have written the parts of Aaron, Richard III or Iago? Oxfordians like to claim that since their candidate had been captured by pirates and had three daughters, he has a better claim, on biographical grounds, to have written *Hamlet* and *King Lear*. Yet you never hear a supporter of Oxford's authorship of *Richard III* quote Charles Arundel's contemporary report that Oxford 'wold often tell my Lord Harrye, my selfe and Sowthewell that he had abused a mare' and then point to Richard's famous line about 'My kingdom for a horse' as evidence of a deeper and long overlooked romantic attachment.[2] The sooner that those of us who teach or write about Shakespeare for a living abandon making selective autobiographical connections, the faster the anti-Stratfordian movement will wither.

But it is unlikely that this movement will disappear any time soon – and even this outstanding collection of essays is unlikely to change the minds of any of those committed to toppling Shakespeare. The effort to unseat Shakespeare will continue, though in the wake of *Anonymous*, the focus of those committed to doing so will probably shift to influencing the sites where students and general readers first turn to for their information, especially the Wikipedia page for the Shakespeare Authorship Question.[3] If you want to see this struggle from the perspective of the trenches, I recommend looking at that site and at its discussion section, where various changes to the entry are raised (and to my considerable relief, invariably dismissed). Those who believe in Shakespeare's authorship owe a considerable debt to unsung heroes like Tom Reedy, who is not a professional scholar yet spends countless hours ensuring that the site remains fact rather than faith based, and draws on current scholarship to blunt the efforts of anti-Stratfordians to bend those facts.

The ultimate reason why arguments such as those advanced in these pages will not persuade those who want to deny Shakespeare's authorship has to do with the context in which they view historical evidence. What Stuart Hampton-Reeves writes about the 'Declaration of Reasonable Doubt' holds true of the anti-Stratfordian position in general: 'the Declaration is not just a declaration of doubt, it is also a declaration of faith, akin to the spiritual testament that Shakespeare's father kept to affirm his secret Catholicism' (p. 202). Hampton-Reeves's essay also shows that the number of anti-Stratfordians appears to be quite small, though quite vocal and determined. The dismal box-office showing of *Anonymous* has undoubtedly been a setback for them; and Emmerich's own admission that The Shakespeare Birthplace Trust shares the blame for his film's rapid demise is an indication that an organized response (detailed in his essay by Paul Edmondson) contributed to that end, and was a much better strategy than the one for too long adopted by Shakespearians, which was to ignore the problem and hope that it would go away.[4] The facts and analysis presented in this volume will make responding to the next film, or the next campaign, or the next question posed about Shakespeare's authorship by a student or a stranger or even a teacher that much easier.

A selected reading list

Hardy M. Cook

FOR SHAKESPEARE'S AUTHORSHIP

Chambers, E. K. *William Shakespeare: A Study of Facts and Problems*, 2 vols. (Oxford: Clarendon Press, 1930).

The starting places for those who use records to support the case for Shakespeare are Chambers and Schoenbaum (see below). In his monumental study, Chambers analyses the 'biographical *data* from records and traditions' and evaluates 'the results of biographical and historical study in relation to the canon of the plays', forming 'a considered opinion upon the nature of the texts in which Shakespeare's work is preserved to us'. Volume I provides a narrative of Shakespeare's life, stage and works; Volume II provides reprints of the records, contemporary allusions, the Shakespeare mythos, performances to 1642 and more, including fabrications. An excellent online copy of Volume I can be found in the Internet Archive at www.archive.org/details/williamshakespea005375mbp.

Elliott, Ward E. Y. and Robert J. Valenza. 'And Then There Were None: Winnowing the Shakespeare Claimants', *Computers and the Humanities* 30 (1996–7), pp. 191–245. www.claremontmckenna.edu/pages/faculty/welliott/ ATTWNrev.pdf

'Oxford by the Numbers: What are the Odds That the Earl of Oxford could have Written Shakespeare's Poems and Plays', *Tennessee Law Review* 72:1 (2004), pp. 323–453. www.claremontmckenna.edu/pages/faculty/ welliott/UTConference/Oxford_by_Numbers.pdf

In 1987, Ward Elliott, the son of an anti-Shakespearian, with a team of eight undergraduates from the Claremont Colleges, established the Shakespeare Clinic (www.cmc.edu/pages/faculty/welliott/shakes.htm) to address two questions: who was the 'True Shakespeare' and what did Shakespeare, whoever he was, write? With Robert Valenza, the Clinic performs stylometric analysis based on computerized tests of a library of electronic texts of early modern plays to determine authorship. Elliott and Valenza are two of the most prominent scholars performing stylometric analysis with computers to verify Shakespeare's authorship. Both of these essays can be obtained as pdf files from the web addresses cited above.

Kathman, David and Terry Ross. 'The Shakespeare Authorship Page: Dedicated to the Proposition That Shakespeare Wrote Shakespeare'. http://shakespeareauthorship.com/

'The Shakespeare Authorship Page' is the best online site refuting the claims of Oxfordians. Kathman and Ross explain that their website is for the intelligent non-specialist 'who doesn't know what to make of these challenges to Shakespeare's authorship'. Their aim is to 'provide context where needed, expose misinformation passed off by Oxfordians as fact, and . . . show . . . why professional Shakespeare scholars have so little regard for Oxfordian claims'. Of particular interest is Tom Reedy's and David Kathman's 'How We Know That Shakespeare Wrote Shakespeare: The Historical Facts'. Alan Nelson's 'Shakespeare Authorship Pages' is another excellent internet site supporting orthodox claims and refuting those of Oxfordians: http://socrates.berkeley.edu/~ahnelson/authorsh.html.

Matus, Irvin Leigh. *Shakespeare, in Fact* (New York: Continuum, 1994).

One of the best print studies that support the contention that Shakespeare of Stratford-upon-Avon is the author of the works of Shakespeare. Matus, using 'documents of Shakespeare, his colleagues, and of English Renaissance theater', convincingly refutes anti-Shakespearian claims. He addresses four areas at the heart of the authorship discussion: 'the contemporary record of and about Shakespeare' (man and dramatist); 'the contemporary materials that associate Shakespeare with popular theater' (especially in comparison with others in the theatre); Shakespeare's 'reputation in his own time'; and an evaluation of the 'qualifications' and 'circumstantial evidence' attributed to the current favourite alternative, the Earl of Oxford. Other noteworthy arguments in print for Shakespeare are F. W. Wadsworth, *The Poacher from Stratford* (Berkeley and Los Angeles: University of California Press, 1958), John Michell, *Who Wrote Shakespeare?* (London: Thames and Hudson, 1996) and Scott McCrea, *The Case for Shakespeare* (Westport, CT: Greenwood Press, 2005).

Schoenbaum, S. *Shakespeare's Lives* (London: Oxford University Press, 1970; new, revised edn, Oxford: Clarendon Press, 1991).

Schoenbaum, after being told that scholarship on Shakespeare's biography had been exhausted, dedicated the rest of his life to proving otherwise. In *Shakespeare's Lives* he addresses various myths and legends that have arisen. The second edition's new chapter, updates and added materials are welcome but the condensed and omitted materials are still worthy of attention. Other of Schoenbaum's significant studies related to issues of authorship include *William Shakespeare: A Documentary Life* (London: Scolar Press, 1975), *A Compact Documentary Life* (Oxford University Press, 1987, revised and updated from the *Documentary Life*) and *William Shakespeare: Records and Images* (London: Scolar Press, 1981).

AUTHORSHIP AS A CULTURAL PHENOMENON

Churchill, Reginald Charles. *Shakespeare and His Betters: A History and Criticism of the Attempts Which Have Been Made to Prove Shakespeare's Works Were Written by Others* (London: Max Reinhardt, 1958).

In his introduction, Churchill elucidates the scope of his study: 'The present book is the only one, I believe, which tries to cover the entire field, past and present' (p. 16). Churchill divides the question into two parts. He begins with a 'history of the subject, from the seventeenth century to the time of writing', and then he subjects the theories to a literary and cultural analysis. Churchill concludes, 'the plays required the poetic genius of the Sonnets intimately bound up with a professional knowledge of dramatic art. The combination is naturally rare, but then Shakespeares are only common in a book like this' (p. 223). An online copy is available at Questia, a paid subscription online library service: www.questia.com/PM.qst?a=o&d=191688.

Friedman, William F. and Elizebeth S. *The Shakespearean Ciphers Examined: An Analysis of Cryptographic Systems Used as Evidence that Some Author other than William Shakespeare Wrote the Plays Commonly Attributed to him* (Cambridge University Press, 1957).

The manuscript that became *The Shakespearean Ciphers Examined* was the winner of a Folger Shakespeare Library Literary Prize in 1955. It was condensed and then published in 1957. Elizebeth (sic) Smith Friedman was a noted cryptanalyst, whose naval unit solved the Enigma Code used by the Germans during the Second World War. She introduced her husband William to the field, and together in retirement they collaborated on *The Shakespearean Ciphers Examined*. They write: 'Shakespearean scholars have often had to deal with arguments that Shakespeare did not have the birth, breeding or education necessary to write the plays. The evidence brought forward by both sides in this particular argument is necessarily conjectural, and must therefore always be inconclusive. On the other hand, claims based on cryptography can be scientifically examined, and proved or disproved. In this book we examine the cryptographic evidence used to support the thesis that someone other than Shakespeare wrote the plays' (p. xv). To this end, the study disproves all claims of the arguments that the works of Shakespeare contain hidden ciphers pointing to other authors. Questia: www.questia.com/PM.qst?a=o&d=11853542/.

Gibson, Harry Norman. *The Shakespeare Claimants: A Critical Survey of the Four Principal Theories Concerning the Authorship of the Shakespearean Plays* (London: Methuen; New York: Barnes and Noble, 1962).

Gibson justifies his work in his introduction: 'The Great Shakespeare Controversy . . . is a subject that goes on expanding. New generations of theorists are constantly putting forward new claimants for the authorship of the immortal plays, and orthodox scholars are constantly discovering new details about the life and background of the Stratford actor, which they beat into weapons to repel the new invaders or use to make fresh raids into the domains of the older schools of thought' (p. 9). After keeping 'an open mind on the subject' and being ready 'to consider any new evidence' (p. 301), Gibson concludes that the theorists have 'given us an additional and very strong reason for the belief that William Shakspere of Stratford is the true author of the Shakespearean plays, namely that there is no one else who could be put in his place' (p. 306): Questia: www.questia.com/PM.qst?a=o&d=5820012.

Shapiro, James. *Contested Will: Who Wrote Shakespeare?* (London: Faber and Faber, 2010).

At the heart of Shapiro's even-handed and judicious *Contested Will* is the contention that 'Malone helped institutionalize a methodology that would prove crucial to those who would subsequently deny Shakespeare's authorship of the plays. That methodology presupposes that in writing his plays Shakespeare mined his own emotional life in transparent ways.' Shapiro further claims that Delia Bacon, who published her theories in the 1857 *The Philosophy of the Plays of Shakspere Unfolded*, 'more than anyone before or after, was responsible for triggering what would come to be known as the Shakespeare authorship controversy'. Shapiro concludes his study with a particularly useful 'Biographical Essay', a guide limited to the specific sources he used 'in print, manuscript, and electronic form, so that anyone interested can retrace or follow up' on his research.

AUTHORSHIP AND COLLABORATION

Hope, Jonathan. 'Applied Historical Linguistics: Socio-Historical Linguistic Evidence for the Authorship of Renaissance Plays', *Transactions of the Philological Society* 88 (1990), pp. 201–26.

The Authorship of Shakespeare's Plays: A Socio-Linguistic Study (Cambridge University Press, 1994).

Jonathan Hope describes his current work as 'Literary Linguistics (the application of linguistic techniques and theories to literary texts), with a strong emphasis on the analysis of Early Modern English, and Shakespeare's language in particular'. These two early works grew out of his doctoral work at Cambridge. The essay, 'Applied Historical Linguistics', studies differing rates of usage of grammatical variables to identify Shakespeare's collaborators in *Henry VIII*. In *The Authorship of Shakespeare's Plays*, Hope uses socio-historical linguistic evidence to compare the grammatical/linguistic usages of certain writers to resolve authorship debates surrounding disputed Elizabethan and Jacobean plays. The study is divided into three parts: methodology, studies of individual plays and groups of plays (Shakespeare-Fletcher collaborations; Shakespeare-Middleton collaborations; 1664 folio play additions; and diverse apocryphal plays) and distillation of findings.

Jackson, MacDonald P. 'Determining Authorship: A New Technique', *Research Opportunities in Renaissance Drama* 41 (2002), pp. 1–14.

Defining Shakespeare: 'Pericles' as Test Case (Oxford University Press, 2003).

'A Lover's Complaint Revisited', *Shakespeare Studies* 32 (2004), pp. 267–94.

Vickers, Brian. *Shakespeare, A Lover's Complaint, and John Davies of Hereford* (Cambridge University Press, 2007).

Jackson, MacDonald P. '"A Lover's Complaint", *Cymbeline*, and the Shakespeare Canon: Interpreting Shared Vocabulary', *Modern Language Review* 103.3 (2008), pp. 621–38.

'The Authorship of "A Lover's Complaint": A New Approach to the Problem', *Papers of the Bibliographical Society of America* 102 (2008), pp. 285–313.

An Appendix to 'The Authorship of "A Lover's Complaint": A New Approach to the Problem": A Control Test'. BibSite: www.bibsocamer.org/BibSite/ Jackson/Jackson.pdf.

'Shakespeare or Davies? A Clue to the Authorship of "A Lover's Complaint"', *Notes and Queries* 56.1 (2009), pp. 62–3.

MacDonald P. Jackson has been a tireless advocate for computer-assisted analysis for determining authorship. In his 2002 essay, he deploys the Literature Online (LION) database to trace parallels in words, phrases and collocations of several playwrights to examine the possible authorship of *Titus Andronicus*. In his 2003 book, he continues his work with LION to match individual peculiarities in usage in phrases and collocations to suggest George Wilkins as Shakespeare's collaborator in *Pericles*.

The individual work generating the most authorship attention in the past decade is 'A Lover's Complaint', and the leading combatants have been Jackson and Brian Vickers. In 2004, Jackson argues for Shakespeare's authorship using LION to analyse rare words, phrases, imagery, wordplay, style and content. In his 2007 book, Vickers considers 'A Lover's Complaint' un-Shakespearian in its 'moralizing and misogynistic' attitude and language and attributes the poem to John Davies of Hereford. Jackson counters in two 2008 essays and a 2009 *Notes and Queries* piece by noting discrepancies in variant spelling frequencies and variant word forms between Davies and Shakespeare, concluding that 'A Lover's Complaint' shares 'far more rare spellings with the Shakespeare canon than with the canon of any other poet or playwright of the relevant period'. Jackson also cites Shakespeare's habit of using the article 'a' before words beginning with 'h'.

Vickers, Brian. *Shakespeare, Co-Author: A Historical Study of Five Collaborative Plays* (Oxford University Press, 2002).

'Coauthors and Closed Minds', *Shakespeare Studies* 36 (2008), pp. 101–13.

One of the most forceful advocates for the collaborative authorship of a number of Shakespeare's plays has been Brian Vickers. *Shakespeare, Co-Author* asks 'How much do we know about Shakespeare's collaborations with other dramatists?' and attempts to extend that knowledge. Vickers labels those 'determined to cling at all costs to the post-Romantic image of [Shakespeare] as a solitary genius having no need of aid from lesser mortals' as the Shakespeare *conservators*. Vickers discusses the accepted Elizabethan activity of collaboration as 'reconstructed from the plays themselves and from documents connected with the Elizabethan stage'. The majority of the hefty 550-page-plus book consists of a detailed evaluation of the claims made for Shakespeare's co-authorship of *Titus Andronicus, Timon of Athens, Pericles, Henry VIII* and *The Two Noble Kinsmen*. Vickers finds that co-authorship is evident in the treatment of character and motive as well as in language and style. In his 2008 essay, Vickers argues that those 'who deny the very idea of Shakespeare as coauthor have opted out of the process by which knowledge grows'.

ANTI-SHAKESPEARIAN STUDIES

Bacon, Delia Salter. *The Philosophy of the Plays of Shakspere Unfolded* (London: Groombridge and Sons, 1857).

To all intents and purpose, Delia Bacon initiated the Shakespeare authorship controversy. In the 1840s, after her close reading for the underlying philosophy of some of the plays, she began doubting Shakespeare's authorship, eventually believing that Sir Francis Bacon was the author. Delia Bacon first expressed her theories in an article in *Putnam's Monthly Magazine* (1856), which she expanded into *The Philosophy of the Plays of Shakspere Unfolded* (1857). It is interesting that she never mentioned Bacon in the work. Shortly before her *Putman's* articles appeared, William Smith privately printed *Was Lord Bacon the Author of Shakespeare's Plays? A Letter to Lord Ellesmere*, which he expanded into *Bacon and Shakespeare: An Inquiry Touching Players, Playhouses, and Play-Writers in the Days of Elizabeth* in 1857. Bacon's *The Philosophy of the Plays of Shakspere Unfolded* can be downloaded from Google Books.

Donnelly, Ignatius. *The Great Cryptogram: Francis Bacon's Cipher in the So-Called Shakespeare Plays* (Chicago, New York and London: R. S. Peale & Company, 1888).

Inspired by Morse Code, ciphers and acrostics have been and remain one of the most popular methods employed by the supporters of Bacon to argue for his authorship of Shakespeare's works. Ignatius Donnelly's *The Great Cryptogram* was the first of these. Other cipher studies include Orville Ward Owen's *Sir Francis Bacon's Cipher Story* (1893), Booth's and Booth's *Some Acrostic Signatures of Francis Bacon* (1909), Bokenham's *A Brief History of the Bacon-Shakespeare Controversy with Some Cipher Evidence* (1982) and, most recently, Leary's *The Cryptographic Shakespeare* (1987). Baconian internet sites include Gerald Lawrence's 'Sir Francis Bacon's New Advancement of Learning': www.Sirbacon.Org/ and Francis Carr's 'Shakespeare Authorship Information Centre: Who Wrote Shakespeare': www.shakespeareauthorship.org.uk/.

Looney, J. Thomas. *'Shakespeare' Identified in Edward de Vere the Seventeenth Earl of Oxford* (New York: Frederick A. Stokes Company, 1920).

The first notable claim that Edward de Vere, the Seventeenth Earl of Oxford, authored the plays attributed to Shakespeare appeared in Thomas Looney's *'Shakespeare' Identified*. Looney categorizes the main arguments of the anti-Stratfordians against Shakespeare's authorship. Then he elucidates the qualities of the man who could have written the plays: matured man of genius, eccentric and mysterious, intense sensibility as a man apart; unconventional, unappreciated; pronounced literary tastes, enthusiast of drama, lyric poet of talent, superior classical education and associate of educated people. The person who fits all of these characteristics, according to Looney, is Edward de Vere. *'Shakespeare' Identified* can be downloaded from Google Books. Other studies advocating Oxford are by Charlton Ogburn (*The Mysterious William Shakespeare*, 1984), Richard F. Whalen (*Shakespeare – Who Was He?*, 1994), Joseph Sobran (*Alias Shakespeare*, 1997), Diana Price (*Shakespeare's Unorthodox Biography*, 2001) and Charles Beauclerk (*Shakespeare's Lost Kingdom*, 2010). The Shakespeare Oxford Society publishes 'The Oxfordian' and has a web presence at www.shakespeare-oxford.com/. Other Oxfordian internet sites include the 'Shakespeare Authorship Research Centre at Concordia University': www.authorshipstudies.org, 'The Shakespeare Fellowship': www.shakespearefellowship.org, 'Shakespeare Authorship Sourcebook': www.sourcetext.com/sourcebook, 'Shakespeare Authorship Coalition': http://doubtaboutwill.org and 'The Oxford Authorship Site': www.oxford-shakespeare.com.

Zeigler, Wilbur Gleason. *It Was Marlowe: A Story of the Secret of Three Centuries* (Chicago: Donohue, Henneberry, and Co., 1895).

Wilbur Gleason Zeigler contends in his novel *It Was Marlowe* that Marlowe did not die in 1593 but survived and went on to write the plays of Shakespeare. Marlowe is the most popular candidate after Bacon and Oxford. Advocates for Marlowe include J. M. Robertson (*The State of Shakespeare Study*, 1931), Calvin Hoffman (*The Murder of the Man Who Was Shakespeare*, 1955), David Rhys Williams (*Shakespeare, Thy Name Is Marlowe*, 1966), Peter Zenner (*The Shakespeare Invention*, 1999), Samuel Blumenfeld (*The Marlowe-Shakespeare Question*, 2008) and the websites of the International Marlowe-Shakespeare Society: www.marloweshakespeare.org and The Marlowe Society: www.marlowe-society.org.

OTHER CANDIDATES

An article in Wikipedia, 'List of Shakespeare authorship candidates', at the time of writing identifies seventy-nine persons who have been suggested as the author of Shakespeare's works. Alden Brooks proposed Edward Dyer in *Will Shakspere and the Dyer's Hand* (1943); Franz Maximilian Saalbach advocates John Florio (*William Shakespeare, Alias Mercutio Florio*, 1954) as does Lamberto Tassinari (*John Florio, the Man Who Was Shakespeare*, 2008); A. W. L. Saunders proposes Fulke Greville in *The Master of Shakespeare* (2007); Brenda James and William Rubinstein argue on behalf of Henry Neville in *The Truth Will Out: Unmasking the Real Shakespeare* (2005); Robin Williams (*Sweet Swan of Avon*, 2006), Penny McCarthy (*Pseudonymous Shakespeare*, 2006) and the 'Mary Sidney Society' website www.marysidneysociety.org maintain that Mary Sidney was the author; Karl Bleibtreu (*Die Lösung Der Shakespeare-Frage*, 1909), Abel Lefranc (*Sous Le Masque De 'William*

Shakespeare', 1918), Bruno Biedrins ('On the Problem of William Shake-speare's Authorship', *Latvijas Zinatnu Akademijas Vestis*, 1994), Ilya Gililov (*The Shakespeare Game*, 2003) and Brian Dutton (*Let Shakspere Die!*, 2007) put forward Roger Manners, Earl of Rutland, as Shakespeare; Basil Iske champions William Nugent (*The Green Cockatrice*, 1978); the case for William Stanley, sixth Earl of Derby, has been advocated by Jacques Boulenger (*L'Affaire Shakespeare*, 1919), Abel Lefranc (*A La Découverte de Shakespeare*, 1945), Claud Walter Sykes (*Alias William Shakespeare?*, 1947) and Arthur Walsh Titherley (*Shakespeare's Identity*, 1952).

Notes

GENERAL INTRODUCTION

1 S. Schoenbaum, *Shakespeare's Lives*, new edn (Oxford: Clarendon Press, 1991), p. 392.
2 Joseph C. Hart, *The Romance of Yachting* (New York: Harper and Brothers; unpaginated, 1848).
3 Dionysius Lardner, ed., *The Cabinet Cyclopaedia* (London: Longman, Rees, Orme, Brown and Green, 1830–49), vol. II, p. 100.

PART I: SCEPTICS

1 James Shapiro, *Contested Will: Who Wrote Shakespeare?* (London: Faber and Faber, 2010), pp. 14, 3.

1 THE UNREADABLE DELIA BACON

1 Delia Bacon, *The Philosophy of the Plays of Shakspere Unfolded* (London: Groombridge and Sons, 1857; Kila, MT: Kessinger Publishing, 2004). The book is described as 'unreadable then, and unreadable now' by Nina Baym in 'Delia Bacon, History's Odd Woman Out', *New England Quarterly* 69:2 (June 1996), pp. 223–49. James Shapiro calls it 'almost unreadable' in *Contested Will: Who Wrote Shakespeare?* (London: Faber and Faber, 2010), p. 120. Even Martin Pares, President of the Bacon Society from 1956 to 1962, states that '*The Philosophy of the Shakespeare Plays Unfolded* is one of the most extraordinary and most unreadable books.' See Martin Pares, 'Pioneer: In Memory of Delia Bacon', at www.sirbacon.org/apimdbmp.htm.
2 Delia Bacon, Preface to *The Bride of Fort Edward, Founded on an Incident of the Revolution* (New York: Samuel Colman, 1839), frontispiece.
3 [Delia Bacon], 'William Shakespeare and His Plays: An Inquiry Concerning Them', *Putnam's Monthly Magazine* 7 (January 1856), pp. 1–19.
4 Delia Bacon, 'William Shakespeare and His Plays', from Theodore Bacon, *Delia Bacon: A Biographical Sketch* (Boston and New York: Houghton, Mifflin and Co., 1888), p. 134. All quotations from this article are taken from Theodore Bacon's reprint.

5 Ibid., p. 141.
6 Ibid., pp. 136–7.
7 William Henry Smith, *Was Lord Bacon the Author of Shakespeare's Plays? A Letter to Lord Ellesmere* (London: William Skeffington, 1856), and *Bacon and Shakespeare: An Inquiry Touching Players, Playhouses, and Play-Writers in the Days of Elizabeth* (London: John Russell Smith, 1857).
8 John Donne, *An Anatomy of the World* ([W. S.] for S. Macham, 1611).
9 Shapiro, *Contested Will*, p. 108.
10 Ibid., p. 109.
11 Nathaniel Hawthorne, 'Preface' to Delia Bacon, *The Philosophy of the Plays of Shakspere Unfolded*, p. 10.
12 See Nina Baym's discussion in 'Delia Bacon, History's Odd Woman Out', *New England Quarterly* 69:2 (June 1996), pp. 223–49.
13 See Nancy Glazener, 'Print Culture as an Archive of Dissent: Or, Delia Bacon and the Case of the Missing Hamlet', *American Literary History* 16:2 (2007), pp. 329–49.
14 See the collection William Leahy, ed., *Shakespeare and his Authors* (London: Continuum, 2011).
15 Quoted in Shapiro, *Contested Will*, p. 119.

2 THE CASE FOR BACON

1 Invitation letter from Thomas Carlyle to Delia Bacon, 8 June 1853. Kenneth J. Fielding, ed., *The Collected Letters of Thomas and Jane Welsh Carlyle* (Durham NC: Duke University Press, 1970–), vol. XXVIII, pp. 165–6.
2 Emerson to Carlyle, 12 May 1853: 'Have you not a friend – Mr Spedding, who writes, or was writing Lord Bacon's Life? If he is near you, & accessible, can you not obtain for Miss Bacon an interview with him?' Quoted in Theodore Bacon, *Delia Bacon: A Biographical Sketch* (London: Sampson Low, Marston, Searle & Rivington, 1888), p. 58.
3 On Spedding, see Lisa Jardine and Alan Stewart, 'Editing a Hero of Modern Science', in Marina Frasca-Spada and Nick Jardine, eds., *Books and the Sciences in History* (Cambridge University Press, 2000), pp. 354–68.
4 On Delia Bacon, see Bacon, *Delia Bacon*; Vivian C. Hopkins, *Prodigal Puritan: A Life of Delia Bacon* (Cambridge, MA: Belknap Press of Harvard University Press, 1959); James Shapiro, *Contested Will: Who Wrote Shakespeare?* (London: Faber and Faber, 2010), pp. 83–110.
5 Bacon to his uncle, William Cecil, Lord Burghley, 1592. William Rawley, ed., *Resuscitatio or, bringing into publick light severall pieces, of the works* (London: William Lee, 1657), 3N2v (supplement, p. 96).
6 Delia Bacon to Julia Woodruff, [late July? 1853]. Quoted in Bacon, *Delia Bacon*, pp. 62–3.
7 Spedding to Nathaniel Holmes, January 1867 [copy]. Folger MS M.a.259, fo. 3v.

8 Spedding, 'Who wrote Shakespeare's *Henry VIII?*', *Gentleman's Magazine* (August 1850), pp. 115–24; (October 1850), pp. 351–2.

9 For earlier treatments of the case for Bacon, see Ignatius L. Donnelly, *The Great Cryptogram: Francis Bacon's Cipher in the So-Called Shakespeare Plays* (Chicago: R. S. Peale, 1888); S. Schoenbaum, *Shakespeare's Lives*, rev. edn (Oxford: Clarendon Press, 1991), pp. 385–430; Shapiro, *Contested Will*, pp. 83–149.

10 [Delia Bacon], 'William Shakespeare and His Plays: An Inquiry Concerning Them', *Putnam's Monthly Magazine* 7 (January 1856), pp. 1–19. See Shapiro, *Contested Will*, pp. 102–05.

11 'Our Weekly Gossip', *Athenaeum* 1430 (24 March 1855), p. 351.

12 William Henry Smith, *Was Lord Bacon the Author of Shakespeare's Plays? A Letter to Lord Ellesmere* (London: William Skeffington, 1856). On Smith, 'a Harley Street recluse', see Schoenbaum, *Shakespeare's Lives*, pp. 401–04.

13 William Henry Smith, *Bacon and Shakespeare: An Inquiry Touching Players, Playhouses, and Play-Writers in the Days of Elizabeth* (London: John Russell Smith, 1857).

14 Smith, *Was Lord Bacon*, p. 15.

15 Smith to John Russell Smith, 1 May 1857. Folger MS Y.c.2371. For the accusations, see Shapiro, *Contested Will*, p. 106.

16 Delia Bacon, *The Philosophy of the Plays of Shakspere Unfolded* (London: Groom-bridge and Sons, 1856).

17 Bacon to Messrs Phillips and Sampson (publishers), 5 July 1855, London. Folger MS Y.c.64 (2a).

18 Bacon, quoted in Nathaniel Hawthorne, 'Preface', *Philosophy*, p. xx.

19 Francis Bacon, *The twoo bookes . . . of the proficiencie and aduancement of learning* (London: Henrie Tomes, 1605), 2Q1r.

20 Francis Bacon, *Of the advancement and proficience* [sic] *of learning or the partitions of sciences IX Bookes*, trans. Gilbert Watts (Oxford: Robert Young and Edward Forrest, 1640), 2L1r–v (pp. 265–6). See Alan Stewart, 'Francis Bacon's Bi-Literal Cipher and the Materiality of Early Modern Diplomatic Writing', in Robyn Adams and Rosanna Cox, eds., *Diplomacy and Early Modern Culture* (Houndmills: Palgrave Macmillan, 2011), pp. 120–37.

21 Hopkins, *Prodigal Puritan*, pp. 56–7.

22 Bacon, *Philosophy*, pp. 98–9, 189.

23 Spedding to Nathaniel Holmes, January 1867 [copy]. Folger MS M.a.259, fo. 3v.

24 On Holmes, see Z[echariah] C[haffee], Jr., 'Holmes, Nathaniel', *Dictionary of American Biography*, vol. IX, ed. Dumas Malone (New York: Charles Scribner's Sons, 1932), pp. 168–9.

25 Holmes to Spedding, 16 November 1866, St Louis, Missouri [copy]. Folger MS M.a.259, fo. 3r. The American edition of the Spedding-Ellis-Heath *Works* was published in fourteen volumes by Taggard and Thompson in Boston, from 1860 to 1864.

26 Nathaniel Holmes, *The Authorship of Shakespeare* (New York: Hurd and Houghton, 1866).

27 Holmes to Spedding, 16 November 1866. Folger MS M.a.259, fo. 3r.

28 Spedding to Holmes, 15 February 1867, London. Nathaniel Holmes, *The Authorship of Shakespeare*, 3rd edn (New York: Hurd and Houghton, 1875), pp. 612–18, at 612–13, 613, 616.

29 Smith to Spedding, 22 April 1867, Highgate. Holmes, *Authorship*, 3rd edn, pp. 625, 626. In another letter he wrote 'Having been in the front of the fight for a decade of years, now that the American contingent has taken the field I think I may creditably retire to the rear.' Smith to Spedding, 1 May 1867, Highgate. Holmes, *Authorship*, 3rd edn, p. 626.

30 Ingleby's copy-book containing the letters is now Folger MS M.a.259.

31 C. M. Ingleby, LL.D., 'On Some Traces of the Authorship of the Works Attributed to Shakespeare' [London, 1869], p. 20.

32 Ingleby, 'On Some Traces', p. 19.

33 [C. M. Ingleby], *Shakespeare's Century of Prayse* (London: Trübner, 1874), where Ingleby mentions Smith's work (pp. 171–2); see also *The Shakspere Allusion-Book*, ed. Ingleby et al., rev. edn, 2 vols. (London: Humphrey Milford/Oxford University Press, 1932).

34 This discussion draws on materials in my 'Introduction' to *The Oxford Francis Bacon*, vol. I, *Early Writings 1584–1596* (Oxford University Press, 2012), pp. xxxix–xlii.

35 Bruce to Spedding, 14 August 1869, quoted in James Spedding, ed., *A Conference of Pleasure, Composed for Some Festive Occasion About the Year 1592* (London: Longmans, Green, Reader and Dyer, 1870), pp. xxvii–xxix. The volume is now at Alnwick Castle, shelfmark MS 525 (Safe 4).

36 Spedding, *Conference*. For a facsimile edition and transcript see Frank J. Burgoyne, ed., *Northumberland Manuscripts: Collotype facsimile & type transcript of an Elizabethan manuscript preserved at Alnwick Castle, Northumberland* (London: Longmans, Green, and Co., 1904). Some text visible in the facsimile has now disappeared in the manuscript itself.

37 Spedding, *Conference*, p. xix.

38 The Folger's copy of Holmes, *Authorship*, 3rd edn (Folger MS W.a.204) is Holmes's annotated copy: see p. 662 marginal note: 'Mr. Spedding (in his letter to me of the 11. Aug. 1872) esp. says, speaking of this volume, – "for the contents were not transcribed at the same time or by the same hand" (N.H. 1881.).'

39 Holmes, *Authorship*, 3rd edn, pp. 657–82.

40 Erasmus, *Adages*, trans. and ed. R. A. B. Mynors, *Complete Works of Erasmus*, vol. XLIII (University of Toronto Press, 1982), p. 401. See also James Hutton, 'Honorificabilitudinatibus', *Modern Language Notes* 46 (1931), pp. 392–5.

41 The next major discoveries were by Peter Beal and Graham Rees in the 1970s and 1980s.

42 British Library, Harley MS 7017, fos. 83r–129v. The word 'Promus' heads fo. 85r and the phrase 'A late promus of formularies and elegancies' is at fo. 106v.

43 For Spedding's discussion, see Bacon, *Works*, vol. VII (1859), pp. 189–95, quoted at 194, 195. The extracts are printed in ibid., pp. 197–211.

44 [Mrs Henry Pott], *Did Francis Bacon Write 'Shakespeare'? 32 Reasons for Believing that He Did* (London: W. H. Guest, 1884), p. 22.

45 Mrs Henry Pott, *The Promus of Formularies and Elegancies... by Francis Bacon Illustrated and Elucidated by Passages from Shakespeare* (London: Longmans, Green, and Co., 1883), pp. 2–3.

46 Ibid., 91.

47 Edwin A. Abbott, 'Preface' to Pott, *Promus*, pp. vii–xiv. On Abbott, see L. R. Farnell, 'Abbott, Edwin Abbott (1838–1926)', rev. Rosemary Jann, *Oxford Dictionary of National Biography* (Oxford University Press, 2004).

48 Abbott, 'Preface', pp. vii–viii.

49 The correct transcription was made in a second attempt, by noted Baconian Sir Edwin Durning-Lawrence: *Bacon is Shake-speare: Together with a Reprint of Bacon's Promus of Formularies and Elegancies* (London: Gay & Hancock, 1910). On Durning-Lawrence, see K. E. Attar, 'Sir Edwin Durning-Lawrence: A Baconian and his Books', *The Library* n.s. 5 (2004), pp. 294–315.

50 *The workes of Iohn Heiwood newly imprinted* (London: Thomas Marsh, 1587); Desiderius Erasmus, *Adagiorum... epitome* (Cologne: Johann Gymnich, 1581); John Florio, *Florios second frutes... To which is annexed his Gardine of recreation yeelding six thousand Italian prouerbs* (London: Thomas Woodcock, 1591).

51 See Bacon, *Early Writings 1584–1596*, pp. 516–22.

52 Details in *Journal of the Bacon Society* 1 (1886), pp. 5–7.

53 Donnelly, *Great Cryptogram*.

54 Orville Ward Owen, *Sir Francis Bacon's Cipher Story*, 4 vols. (Detroit: Howard Publishing, 1893–5).

55 Elizabeth Wells Gallup, *The Bi-Literal Cypher of Sir Francis Bacon Discovered in his Works and Deciphered* (Detroit: Howard Publishing, 1899).

56 W. C. Arensberg, *The Cryptography of Shakespeare*, Part 1 (Los Angeles: H. Bowen, 1922).

57 F. Friedman and E. S. Friedman, *The Shakespearean Ciphers Examined* (Cambridge University Press, 1957). On the Friedmans, see William H. Sherman, 'How to Make Anything Signify Anything', *Cabinet* 40 (Winter 2010/11), www.cabinetmagazine.org/issues/40/sherman.php.

58 Graham Rees, 'Introduction' to Francis Bacon, *Instauratio magna Part II: Novum Organum*, ed. Rees and Maria Wakely (Oxford University Press, 2004), pp. xxxi–xxxii.

3 THE CASE FOR MARLOWE

1 J. Thomas Looney, *'Shakespeare' Identified in the Seventeenth Earl of Oxford* (New York: Frederick A. Stokes Company, 1920), p. 121.

2 Henry Chettle, *Kind-Heart's Dream* (1592), sig. A4; Sir Robert Sidney, letter to Lord Burghley, 26 January 1592, TNA: PRO, SP 84/44, fol. 60; Robert Greene [attrib.], *Greene's Groatsworth of Wit* (1592), sig. E4v.

3 Wilbur Zeigler, *It was Marlowe* (Chicago: Donohue, Henneberry and Co., 1895), p. v.

4 Algernon Swinburne, *A Study of Shakespeare* (London: Chatto and Windus, 1880), p. 15.

5 Francis Meres, *Palladis Tamia* (London, 1598), sig. O06.

6 Anthony à Wood, *Athenae Oxonienses* [1691], ed. Philip Bliss, 4 vols. (London and Oxford: Rivington, 1815), vol. II, column 5.

7 John Aubrey, *Brief Lives*, ed. Oliver Lawson Dick (London: Secker and Warburg, 1950), p. 178.

8 T. C. Mendenhall, 'A Mechanical Solution to a Literary Problem', *Popular Science Monthly* 60:7 (December 1901), pp. 97–105; cf. John Michell, *Who Wrote Shakespeare?* (London: Thames and Hudson, 1996), pp. 228–30.

9 C. B. Williams, 'Mendenhall's Studies of Word-Length Distribution in the Works of Shakespeare and Bacon', *Biometrika* 62:1 (1975), pp. 207–12.

10 TNA: PRO, C 260/174, no. 27; J. Leslie Hotson, *The Death of Christopher Marlowe* (Cambridge, MA, 1925), pp. 28–34.

11 TNA: PRO, patent rolls 1401.

12 Calvin Hoffman, *The Man Who Was Shakespeare* (London: Max Parrish, 1955), pp. 9–10.

13 J. R. Dasent, ed., *Acts of the Privy Council, 1542–1604* (London: HMSO, 1890–1949), vol. XXIV, p. 244.

14 Hoffman, *The Man Who Was Shakespeare*, p. 126.

15 Ibid., pp. 139–40.

16 Fredson Bowers, ed., *The Complete Works of Christopher Marlowe*, Vol. II (Cambridge, 1981), p. 279; Hoffman, *The Man Who Was Shakespeare*, pp. 191–5; A. D. Wraight, *The Story that the Sonnets Tell* (Chichester: Adam Hart, 1994), p. 418.

17 I. M., 'To the Memory of Mr W. Shakespeare', in the unpaginated preliminary sheet of the First Folio (1623); Hoffman, *The Man Who Was Shakespeare*, pp. 220–1.

18 N. W. Bawcutt, ed., *The Jew of Malta*, The Revels Plays (Manchester, 1978; repr. 1997), Prologue, lines 1–2, 5–11, 14–17; Hoffman, *The Man Who Was Shakespeare*, pp. 164–6.

19 Hoffman, *The Man Who Was Shakespeare*, pp. 166–70.

20 David A. More, 'Drunken Sailor or Imprisoned Writer?', *The Marlovian* 8 (1996).

21 Peter Farey, 'Marlowe's Sudden and Fearful End', Appendix 1, and 'Was Marlowe's Inquest Void?', Parts 1 and 2; http://www2.prestel.co.uk/rey.

22 Louis Ule, *Christopher Marlowe, 1564–1607: A Biography* (New York: Carlton Press, 1994), pp. 265–84.

23 Wording from the Trust Deed drawn up between Hoffman and King's School, Canterbury, 1 May 1984.

4 THE LIFE AND THEATRICAL INTERESTS OF EDWARD DE VERE, SEVENTEENTH EARL OF OXFORD

1 The 'old' *Dictionary of National Biography* was completed in 63 volumes (London: Smith, Elder, and Co., 1885–1900). It is often found on library shelves in a later, 21-volume edition (Oxford University Press, 1921–2).

2 Percy Allen's medium was Hester Dowden: see Wikipedia, under 'Prince Tudor theory' (accessed 2 September 2011).

3 See Warren Hope, *The Shakespeare Controversy: An Analysis of the Claimants to Authorship, and their Champions and Detractors* (Jefferson, NC: McFarland and Co., 1992), *passim*.

4 Unless otherwise cited, all facts and quotations are taken from A. H. Nelson, *Monstrous Adversary: The Life of Edward de Vere, 17th Earl of Oxford* (Liverpool University Press, 2003). See also my 'Stratford Si! Essex No! (An Open-and-Shut Case)', *Tennessee Law Review* 72 (2004), pp. 149–69; my entry on Edward de Vere in the *Oxford Dictionary of National Biography*, 60 vols. (Oxford University Press, 2004), vol. LVI; and my article cited in note 10 below.

5 Letter of 11 May 1573, in Edmund Lodge, *Illustrations of British History, Biography, and Manners in the Reigns of Henry VIII, Edward VI, Mary, Elizabeth, & James I* (London: John Chidley, 1838), vol. II.

6 Steven W. May, ed., 'The Poems of Edward de Vere, Seventeenth Earl of Oxford, and of Robert Devereux, Second Earl of Essex', *Studies in Philology* 77:5 (1980).

7 N. W. Bawcutt, *The Control and Censorship of Caroline Drama: The Records of Sir Henry Herbert, Master of the Revels 1623–73* (Oxford: Clarendon Press, 1996), item no. 43.

8 Edmund K. Chambers, *The Elizabethan Theatre*, 4 vols. (Oxford, 1930), vol. II, pp. 338–9.

9 J. T. Looney, *'Shakespeare' Identified in Edward de Vere the Seventeenth Earl of Oxford* (New York: Frederick A. Stokes Company, 1920), pp. 503–30.

10 Wikipedia, under 'Anonymous' and 'Prince Tudor theory' (consulted 2 September 2011).

11 Alan H. Nelson, 'Calling All (Shakespeare) Biographers! or, A Plea for Documentary Discipline', in Ronnie Mulryne, ed., *Shakespeare, Marlowe, Jonson* (Aldershot: Ashgate, 2006), pp. 55–6.

12 Chambers, *Elizabethan Theatre*, vol. IV, pp. 334–5.

5 THE UNUSUAL SUSPECTS

1 Lillian Schwartz, 'The Art Historian's Computer', *Scientific American*, April 1995, pp. 106–11.

2 Ibid.

3 Paul Edmondson and Stanley Wells, *Shakespeare Bites Back: Not So Anonymous*, e-book. www.shakespearebitesback.com (accessed 12 January 2012).

4 Ralph Waldo Emerson, 'Shakespeare; or, the Poet', from *Representative Men* (Boston: Phillips, Sampson and Co., 1850). *Shakespeare; or, the Poet*, www.emersoncentral.com/shak.htm (accessed 5 September 2011).

5 30 June 1599, London. George Fenner to his partner Baltazar Gybels, Antwerp: 'Therle of Darby is busyed only in penning comedies for the commoun players' (State Papers, Domestic, Elizabeth, vol. 271, No. 34).

6 For a lengthy discussion of the trouble with the case for Derby, see R. C. Churchill, *Shakespeare and His Betters* (London: Max Reinhardt, 1958), pp. 170–82.

7 Leo Daugherty, 'Stanley, William, sixth earl of Derby (bap. 1561, d. 1642)', in H. C. G. Matthew and Brian Harrison, eds., *Oxford Dictionary of National Biography* (Oxford University Press, 2004), online edn, Lawrence Goldman, ed. (October 2009). www.oxforddnb.com/view/article/72296 (accessed 30 October 2011).

8 Brenda James, *Henry Neville and the Shakespeare Code* (West Sussex: Music for Strings, 2008), p. 16.

9 Ibid., p. 13.

10 Robert Nield, *Breaking the Shakespeare Codes: The Sensational Discovery of the Bard's True Identity* (Chester: C. C. Publishing, 2007), p. 218.

11 Ibid., pp. 137–8.

12 Robin P. Williams, *Sweet Swan of Avon: Did a Woman Write Shakespeare?* (Berkeley, CA: Wilton Circle Press, 2006), p. 45.

13 'Cervantes is Shakespeare!', Merovee. http://merovee.wordpress.com/2010/03/18/cervantes-is-shakespeare/ (accessed 12 January 2012).

14 'Memorabilia, Literary Antiquarian, Scientific, and Artistic', *Illustrated London News*, 10 January 1857, p. 19. Accessed online 26 December 2011.

15 Woody Allen, 'But Soft. Real Soft', in *Without Feathers* (New York: Random House, 1975).

16 George Elliott Sweet, *Shake-speare: The Mystery* (London: Neville Spearman, 1963), p. 93.

17 Ibid., pp. 152–3.

6 THEORIZING SHAKESPEARE'S AUTHORSHIP

1 Posted 1 October 2011: www.timeshighereducation.co.uk/comments.asp?storycode=417586 (accessed 6 October 2011).

2 N. W. Bawcutt, 'Was Middleton a Puritan Dramatist?', *MLR* 94 (1999), pp. 925–39.

3 Tracey Hill, *Anthony Munday and Civic Culture: Theatre, History and Power in Early Modern London, 1580–1633* (Manchester University Press, 2004); Donna B. Hamilton, *Anthony Munday and the Catholics, 1560–1633* (Aldershot: Ashgate, 2005).

4 David Wootton, 'John Donne's Religion of Love', in John Brooke and Ian Maclean, eds., *Heterodoxy in Early Modern Science and Religion* (Oxford University Press, 2005), pp. 31–58.

5 *ODNB* entries on Dekker by John Twyning, Munday by David M. Bergeron and Chettle by Emma Smith.

6 Alan Pritchard, *English Biography in the Seventeenth Century: A Critical Survey* (University of Toronto Press, 2005), pp. 7, 181.

7 Nicholas Von Maltzahn, 'John Milton: The Later Life (1641–1674)', in Nicholas McDowell and Nigel Smith, eds., *The Oxford Handbook of Milton* (Oxford University Press, 2009), pp. 26–47, at p. 26.

8 Roger Wilkes, *Scandal! A Scurrilous History of Gossip, 1700–2000* (London: Atlantic Books, 2002); T. H. White, *The Age of Scandal: An Excursion through a Minor Period* (London: Cape, 1950); Keith Thomas, *The Ends of Life: Roads to Fulfilment in Early Modern England* (Oxford University Press, 2009), pp. 98–9, 220–2, *passim*. Michael Mascuch makes the analogous point that the use of private notebooks appears to have been a new phenomenon after 1600: *Origins of the Individualist Self: Autobiography and Self-Identity in England, 1591–1791* (Cambridge: Polity, 1997), p. 72.

9 Charles Nicholl, *A Cup of News: The Life of Thomas Nashe* (London: Routledge, 1984), pp. 269–70.

10 Virginia Stern, *Gabriel Harvey: A Study of his Life, Marginalia and Library* (Oxford University Press, 1979), ch. 7.

11 MacDonald P. Jackson, 'Early Modern Authorship: Canons and Chronologies', in Gary Taylor and John Lavagnino, eds., *Thomas Middleton and Early Modern Textual Culture: A Companion to the Collected Works* (Oxford: Clarendon Press, 2007), pp. 80–97.

12 Thomas Middleton, *The Collected Works*, ed. Gary Taylor and John Lavagnino, 2 vols. (Oxford: Clarendon Press, 2007). On *The Family of Love*, see Gary Taylor, Paul Mulholland and MacDonald P. Jackson, 'Thomas Middleton, Lording Barry, and The Family of Love', *PBSA* 93 (1999), pp. 213–42.

13 See the *ODNB* entry by David Gunby.

14 It is a great loss that Mark Eccles never completed his projected biographical dictionary of Elizabethan authors: see 'A Biographical Dictionary of Elizabethan Authors', *HLQ* 5 (1942), pp. 281–302.

15 Katherine Duncan-Jones, *Ungentle Shakespeare: Scenes from his Life* (London: Arden Shakespeare, 2001); Charles Nicholl, *The Lodger: Shakespeare on Silver Street* (London: Penguin, 2007).

16 See Germaine Greer, *Shakespeare's Wife* (London: Bloomsbury, 2007), ch. 19. For different interpretations, see Duncan-Jones, *Ungentle Shakespeare*, pp. 272–5; Peter Ackroyd, *Shakespeare: The Biography* (London: Chatto & Windus, 2005), pp. 485–6.

17 David Bevington, *Shakespeare and Biography* (Oxford University Press, 2010), pp. 34–9.

18 This is the problem identified by James Shapiro in *Contested Will: Who Wrote Shakespeare?* (London: Faber and Faber, 2010), pp. 299–318.

19 Lukas Erne, *Shakespeare as Literary Dramatist* (Cambridge University Press, 2003).

20 See, for example, Jonathan Hope, *The Authorship of Shakespeare's Plays: A Sociolinguistic Study* (Cambridge University Press, 1994); Brian Vickers, *Shakespeare, Co-Author: A Historical Study of Five Collaborative Plays* (Oxford University Press, 2002).

21 Hope, *Authorship*, p. 12.

22 Vickers, *Shakespeare, Co-Author*, ch. 3.

23 The best-known attempt is A. D. Wraight and Virginia F. Stern, *In Search of Christopher Marlowe: A Pictorial Biography* (Chichester: Adam Hart, 1993, reprinted 1965). Statements such as 'Marlowe alone of his contemporaries exerted any deep and lasting influence on Shakespeare' (p. 68), are not true.

24 Not everyone would accept the view that *Macbeth* was written by Shakespeare and adapted by Middleton: Middleton, *The Collected Works*, pp. 1165–201.

25 For an overview of the arguments, see Patrick Cheney, '*Colin Clouts Come Home Againe, Astrophel*, and *The Doleful Lay of Clorinda* (1595)', in Richard A. McCabe, ed., *The Oxford Handbook of Edmund Spenser* (Oxford University Press, 2010), pp. 237–55, at pp. 250–1.

26 Interested parties should consult the one case against Spenser's authorship of the works attributed to him: Edward George Harman, *Edmund Spenser and the Impersonations of Francis Bacon* (London: Constable, 1914).

27 http://doubtaboutwill.org/declaration (accessed 17 October 2011); 'So Who Did Write *Hamlet*?', *The Guardian*, 15 October 2011, pp. 44–5.

28 Brenda James and William D. Rubinstein, *The Truth Will Out: Unmasking the Real Shakespeare* (Harlow: Longman, 2005), p. 212. See also Charles Beauclerk, *Shakespeare's Lost Kingdom: The True History of Shakespeare and Elizabeth* (New York: Grove, 2010), pp. 17–21.

29 See the *ODNB* entry by Anthony Parr; Lambert Ennis, 'Anthony Nixon: Jacobean Plagiarist and Hack', *Huntington Library Quarterly* 3 (1939–40), pp. 377–401.

30 Joseph L. Black, ed., *The Martin Marprelate Tracts: A Modernized and Annotated Edition* (Cambridge University Press, 2008), introduction, p. lxiii.

31 *King Edward III*, ed. Giorgio Melchiori (Cambridge University Press, 1998); Eric Sams, *The Real Shakespeare: Retrieving the Early Years, 1564–1594* (New Haven: Yale University Press, 1995), pp. 116–17.

32 Jeffrey Masten, 'Playwrighting: Authorship and Collaboration', in John D. Cox and David Scott Kastan, eds., *A New History of Early English Drama* (New York: Columbia University Press, 1997), pp. 357–82; Douglas A. Brooks, *From Playhouse to Printing House: Drama and Authorship in Early Modern England* (Cambridge University Press, 2000).

33 *ODNB* entry by Ian Gadd; Jason Lawrence, '*Who the Devil Taught Thee So Much Italian?*': *Italian Language Learning and Literary Imitation in Early Modern England* (Manchester University Press, 2005), 'Appendix: John Wolfe's Italian Publications', pp. 187–97.

34 STC 20569.

35 Sig. c3r.

36 John D. Staines, *The Tragic Histories of Mary Queen of Scots, 1560–1690* (Aldershot: Ashgate, 2009), ch. 1.
37 Louise Schleiner, 'Spenser's "E. K." as Edmund Kent (Kenned / of Kent: Kyth (Couth), Kissed, and Kunning-Coning', *ELR* 20 (2008), pp. 374–407.

7 ALLUSIONS TO SHAKESPEARE TO 1642

1 See John Jowett's essay, Chapter 8 below.
2 The best recent account of the allusions is given in *The Shakespeare Authorship Page* by David Kathman and Terry Ross: http://shakespeareauthorship.com/. *The Shakspere Allusion-Book: A Collection of Allusions to Shakspere From 1591 to 1700*, 2 vols. (1932), originally compiled by C. M. Ingleby, Miss L. Toulmin Smith and by Dr F. J. Furnivall, with the assistance of the New Shakspere Society: re-edited, revised and re-arranged, with An Introduction, by John Munro (1909), and now re-issued with a Preface by Sir Edmund Chambers (London: Oxford University Press, 1932) is badly out of date but still useful. It includes references to many unascribed allusions to the works. More reliable is the section on 'Contemporary Allusions' in E. K. Chambers, *William Shakespeare: A Study of Facts and Problems*, 2 vols. (Oxford: Clarendon Press, 1930).
3 John Jowett, 'Johannes Factotum: Henry Chettle and *Greene's Groatsworth of Wit*', *Papers of the Bibliographical Society of America* 87:4 (December 1993), pp. 453–86.
4 S. Schoenbaum, *William Shakespeare: Records and Images* (London, Scolar Press, 1981), p. 131.
5 'You rogue, here's lime in this sack too. There is nothing but roguery to be found in villainous man' (2.5.123–5).
6 *The Shakspere Allusion-Book* mistakenly assumes an edition of 1595.
7 Oddly Weever is not mentioned in the index of S. Schoenbaum's *William Shakespeare: A Documentary Life* (London: Scolar Press, 1974) or his *Records and Images*. There is however a reference to this poem in his *Shakespeare's Lives* (Oxford: Clarendon Press, 1970; 2nd edn, 1991), p. 26.
8 'black-browed' is first recorded by OED in *A Midsummer Night's Dream* (3.3.388).
9 Shakespeare is spoken of respectfully as 'Mr' (i.e. Master) because he is the only one of these poets still to be alive.
10 Stanley Wells and Gary Taylor with John Jowett and William Montgomery, *William Shakespeare: A Textual Companion* (Oxford University Press, 1987), p. 163.
11 *Shakespeare Survey 59* (Cambridge University Press, 2006), pp. 267–84.
12 Anne Shakespeare's gravestone, with a brass plate memorializing her, lies immediately under the monument even though she died seven years after her husband. The stone bearing the epitaph beginning 'Good friend for Jesus' sake forbear' is next to hers. If that really is the Shakespeare stone, its placing might support a hypothesis that Shakespeare was buried before there was any reason to place his stone where Anne's is placed.

13 Centerwall does not give the titles of those versions that he adds.
14 Chambers, *William Shakespeare: A Study of Facts and Problems*, vol. II, pp. 220–1.
15 Gordon Campbell, 'Shakespeare and the Youth of Milton', *Milton Quarterly* 33:4 (1999), pp. 95–105.
16 Hallett Smith, '"No Cloudy Stuffe to Puzzell Intellect": A Misplaced Testimonial to Shakespeare', *Shakespeare Quarterly* 1 (1950), pp. 18–21.

8 SHAKESPEARE AS COLLABORATOR

1 *Guardian*, 15 October 2011, p. 45.
2 The most useful recent single study is Hugh Craig and Arthur F. Kinney, eds., *Shakespeare, Computers, and the Mysteries of Authorship* (Cambridge University Press, 2009); see also Gary Taylor, 'The Canon and Chronology of Shakespeare's Plays', in Stanley Wells and Gary Taylor, with John Jowett and William Montgomery, *William Shakespeare: A Textual Companion* (Oxford University Press, 1987), pp. 69–144. For *Titus, Timon, Pericles, All Is True* and *Two Noble Kinsmen*, see also Brian Vickers, *Shakespeare, Co-Author: A Historical Study of Five Collaborative Plays* (Oxford University Press, 2002), which digests scholarship by MacDonald P. Jackson, Gary Taylor, R. V. Holdsworth, Ward E. Y. Elliott and Robert J. Valenza, Jonathan Hope, David Lake, as well as earlier work by Caroline F. E. Spurgeon, E. K. Chambers and others. For a review of attribution scholarship and especially Elliott and Valenza's work, see Jackson's chapter in this volume.
3 See Taylor and the relevant essays in Craig and Kinney, eds., *Shakespeare, Computers*; also MacDonald P. Jackson, 'Shakespeare and the Quarrel Scene in *Arden of Faversham*', *Shakespeare Quarterly* 57 (2006), pp. 249–93; and Warren Stevenson, *Shakespeare's Additions to Thomas Kyd's The Spanish Tragedy: A Fresh Look at the Evidence Regarding the 1602 Additions* (Lewiston, Queenston and Lampeter: Mellen, 2008).
4 Brean Hammond, ed., *Double Falsehood: Or, The Distressed Lovers* (London: Arden Shakespeare, 2010).
5 Gary Taylor and John Lavagnino, eds., *Thomas Middleton and Early Modern Textual Culture: A Companion to the Collected Works* (Oxford University Press, 2007), pp. 383–97 and 417–21.
6 See D. Allen Carroll, ed., *Greene's Groatsworth of Wit* (Binghamton: Medieval and Renaissance Texts and Studies, 1994), pp. 1–31.
7 For a review of scholarship, see ibid., pp. 131–45. See also the biographies: S. Schoenbaum, *William Shakespeare: A Compact Documentary Life* (Oxford: Clarendon Press, 1977, revised 1987), pp. 149–54; Stanley Wells, *Shakespeare: A Dramatic Life* (London: Sinclair-Stevenson, 1994), p. 24; Park Honan, *Shakespeare: A Life* (Oxford University Press, 1999), p. 160; Katherine Duncan-Jones, *Ungentle Shakespeare: Scenes from his Life* (London: Arden Shakespeare, 2001), pp. 46–8; Stephen Greenblatt, *Will in the World: How Shakespeare became Shakespeare* (London: Jonathan Cape, 2004).

8 Gerald Eades Bentley, *The Profession of Dramatist in Shakespeare's Time* (Princeton University Press, 1971); M. C. Bradbrook, 'Beasts and Gods: Greene's *Groats-worth of Witte* and the Social Purpose of *Venus and Adonis*', in *Shakespeare Survey 15* (Cambridge University Press, 1962), pp. 62–72.

9 Hugh Craig, 'The Three Parts of *Henry VI*', in Craig and Kinney, eds., *Shakespeare, Computers*, pp. 40–77.

10 Arthur F. Kinney, 'Authoring *Arden of Faversham*', in Craig and Kinney, eds., *Shakespeare, Computers*, pp. 78–99.

11 Giorgio Melchiori, ed., *King Edward III* (Cambridge University Press, 1998), Introduction, pp. 15–16.

12 For elaboration on this outline, and consideration of alternatives, see John Jowett, ed., *Sir Thomas More* (London: Methuen Drama, 2011), pp. 344–94.

13 Ibid., pp. 437–53.

14 These paragraphs summarize John Jowett, ed., *The Life of Timon of Athens* (Oxford University Press, 2004), especially pp. 132–55.

15 Francis Beaumont and John Fletcher, *Philaster, or, Love Lies a-Bleeding*, ed. Suzanne Gossett (London: Methuen Drama, 2009), pp. 4–7.

16 See, in addition to Hammond's edition as cited above, the collection of essays on *Cardenio* edited by Gary Taylor (Oxford University Press, 2012).

17 'The Shakespeare Authorship Question – A Suitable Subject for Academia?', http://bura.brunel.ac.uk/bitstream/2438/3919/3/Fulltext.pdf

9 AUTHORSHIP AND THE EVIDENCE OF STYLOMETRICS

1 Claimants are listed by Ward E. Y. Elliott and Robert J. Valenza, 'Oxford by the Numbers: What Are the Odds that the Earl of Oxford Could have Written Shakespeare's Poems and Plays?', *Tennessee Law Review* 72:1 (2004), pp. 323–453, at pp. 330–1; also in the same authors' 'A Touchstone for the Bard', *Computers and the Humanities* 25 (1991), pp. 199–209, at p. 200.

2 Calvin Hoffman, *The Man Who Was Shakespeare* (London: Max Parrish, 1955); also published as *The Murder of the Man Who Was 'Shakespeare'* (New York: Julian Messner, 1955).

3 James Spedding et al., eds., *The Works of Francis Bacon*, 14 vols. (London: Longman, 1857–74).

4 Ibid., vol. VII, pp. 265–86. 'The man of life upright', which Spedding doubtfully attributes to Bacon, is by Thomas Campion.

5 Caroline F. E. Spurgeon, *Shakespeare's Imagery and What it Tells Us* (Cambridge University Press, 1935), especially ch. 2, 'Shakespeare's Imagery Compared with That of Marlowe and Bacon', pp. 12–29 and Charts following p. 408.

6 Most readily available at www.sirbacon.org/NMANUSCR.HTM (accessed 25 November 2011); see also Bacon, *Works*, vol. VIII, pp. 325–43, 374–86.

7 Steven W. May, ed., 'The Poems of Edward de Vere, Seventeenth Earl of Oxford, and of Robert Devereux, Second Earl of Essex', *Studies in Philology* 77:5 (1980); reprinted in May's *The Elizabethan Courtier Poets* (Columbia: University of Missouri Press, 1991).

8 Steven W. May, 'The Seventh Earl of Oxford as Poet and Playwright', *Tennessee Law Review* 72:1 (2004), pp. 221–54, p. 227.

9 C. S. Lewis, *English Literature in the Sixteenth Century, Excluding Drama* (Oxford: Clarendon Press, 1954), *passim*.

10 George Puttenham, *The Arte of English Poesie* (London, 1589), sig. 2r. In his *Palladis Tamia* (1598) Francis Meres also named Oxford as among the 'best for comedy', along with writers who were not known to public theatre audiences and, later in the list, several who were, including Shakespeare, whom he evidently considered to be distinct from Oxford. See E. K. Chambers, *William Shakespeare: A Study of Facts and Problems*, 2 vols. (Oxford: Clarendon Press, 1930), vol. ii, pp. 193–5.

11 Spurgeon, *Shakespeare's Imagery*, pp. 12–15 and Charts.

12 David Bevington and Eric Rasmussen, eds., *Doctor Faustus A- and B-texts (1604, 1616)* (Manchester University Press, 1993), A-text, 5.1.104–5.

13 Chambers, *William Shakespeare*, vol. i, pp. 270–1. Compare Stanley Wells and Gary Taylor with John Jowett and William Montgomery, *William Shakespeare: A Textual Companion* (Oxford: Clarendon Press, 1987), pp. 89–134.

14 Chambers included metrical tables in *William Shakespeare*, vol. ii, pp. 397–408. Further metrical and other chronological indicators are described in Wells and Taylor, *Textual Companion*, pp. 93–134, 141–4 and MacDonald P. Jackson, *Defining Shakespeare: 'Pericles' as Test Case* (Oxford University Press, 2003), pp. 40–5, 59–70, 75–6. See also works cited in those volumes by Brainerd, Langworthy, Oras, Slater, Tarlinskaja and Waller, to which may be added MacDonald P. Jackson, 'Pause Patterns in Shakespeare's Verse: Canon and Chronology', *Literary and Linguistic Computing* 17 (2002), pp. 37–46 and 'A New Chronological Indicator for Shakespeare's Plays and for Hand D of *Sir Thomas More*', *Notes and Queries* 252 (2007), pp. 304–7.

15 Aspects of the evolution of Shakespeare's style less amenable to counting are discussed by Wolfgang Clemen, *The Development of Shakespeare's Imagery*, 2nd edn (London: Methuen, 1977) and Frank Kermode, *Shakespeare's Language* (New York: Farrar, Straus and Giroux, 2000).

16 W. Ron Hess, 'Shakespeare's Dates: Their Effects on Stylistic Analysis', *The Oxfordian* 2 (1999), pp. 25–59. This and older Oxfordian chronologies are examined by Elliott and Valenza, 'Oxford by the Numbers', pp. 376–89.

17 James Shapiro, *Contested Will: Who Wrote Shakespeare?* (London: Faber and Faber, 2010), pp. 244–54.

18 Wells and Taylor, *Textual Companion*, pp. 126–34.

19 Alden T. Vaughan, 'William Strachey's "True Reportory" and Shakespeare: A Closer Look at the Evidence', *Shakespeare Quarterly* 59 (2008), pp. 245–73.

20 Elliott and Valenza, 'Oxford by the Numbers'. A book is near completion. Among earlier key articles by Elliott and Valenza is 'And Then There Were None: Winnowing the Shakespeare Claimants', *Computers and the Humanities* 30 (1996), pp. 191–245.

21 First described in Elliott and Valenza, 'A Touchstone for the Bard' and in 'Was the Earl of Oxford the True Shakespeare? A Computer-Aided Analysis', *Notes and Queries* 236 (1991), pp. 501–6.
22 Elliott and Valenza, 'Touchstone', p. 207.
23 The standard deviation is a measure of dispersal around the mean. The set of values five, six and seven has the same mean (namely six) as the set one, three and fourteen, but the standard deviation is much larger in the second case than the first. Given a sufficiently large number of values, ninety-nine per cent may be expected to fall within two standard deviations of the mean.
24 Elliott and Valenza, 'Oxford by the Numbers', p. 374.
25 Gray Scott, 'Signifying Nothing? A Secondary Analysis of the Claremont Authorship Debates', *Early Modern Literary Studies* 12:2 (September 2006), 6.1–50: http://purl.oclc.org/emls/12-2/scotsig2.htm (accessed 25 November 2011); MacDonald P. Jackson, 'Is "Hand D" of *Sir Thomas More* Shakespeare's? Thomas Bayes and the Elliott–Valenza Authorship Tests', *Early Modern Literary Studies* 12:3 (January 2007), 1.1–36: http://purl.oclc.org.emls/12-3/jackbaye.htm (accessed 25 November 2011); Thomas Merriam, 'Untangling the Derivatives: Points for Clarification in the Findings of the Shakespeare Clinic', *Literary and Linguistic Computing* 24 (2009), pp. 403–16. Scott deals only with tests on full plays.
26 Ward E. Y. Elliott and Robert J. Valenza, 'Two Tough Nuts to Crack: Did Shakespeare Write the "Shakespeare" Portions of *Sir Thomas More* and *Edward III*? Part 1 and Part 2: Conclusion', *Literary and Linguistic Computing* 25 (2010), pp. 67–83, 167–77; Elliott and Valenza's latest results for *Arden of Faversham* allow scenes four to seven to be possibly Shakespearian (Elliott, 'Claremont Shakespeare Clinic Report, Sept 19, 2011', circulated by email).
27 Hugh Craig and Arthur F. Kinney, eds., *Shakespeare, Computers, and the Mystery of Authorship* (Cambridge University Press, 2009).
28 Their 'core Shakespeare' has two fewer plays than Elliott and Valenza's, because they exclude *Measure for Measure* and *Macbeth* as bearing signs of adaptation by Thomas Middleton and *The Taming of the Shrew* as having been considered collaborative by Chambers and others, but, unlike Elliott and Valenza, they include *Henry V*.
29 Hugh Craig's analysis of the poem is in 'George Chapman, John Davies of Hereford, William Shakespeare, and *A Lover's Complaint*', *Shakespeare Quarterly* 63:2 (2012), pp. 147–74.

10 WHAT DOES TEXTUAL EVIDENCE REVEAL ABOUT THE AUTHOR?

The authors wish to express their gratitude to Arthur Evenchik for suggestions on drafts of this essay.

1 Doubling charts for each play are a standard feature in the Arden Shakespeare Third Series.

2 See Eric Rasmussen, 'The Revision of Scripts', in John D. Cox and David Scott Kastan, eds., *A New History of Early English Drama* (New York: Columbia University Press, 1997), p. 448; Scott McMillin, *The Elizabethan Theatre and 'The Book of Sir Thomas More'* (Ithaca and London: Cornell University Press, 1987), p. 78.

3 David Bradley, *The Ignorant Elizabethan Author and Massinger's 'Believe as you List'* (Sydney University Press, 1992), p. 21; David Bevington, *From 'Mankind' to Marlowe: Growth and Structure in the Popular Drama of Tudor England* (Cambridge, MA: Harvard University Press, 1962), p. 91.

4 E. K. Chambers, *William Shakespeare: A Study of Facts and Problems*, 2 vols. (Oxford University Press, 1930), vol. i, p. 231.

5 Simon Palfrey and Tiffany Stern, *Shakespeare in Parts* (Oxford University Press, 2007), p. 2.

6 James J. Marino made this argument in 'Shakespeare After Editing', a paper given 9 April 2011 at the meeting of the Shakespeare Association of America in Bellevue, Washington.

7 Many textual aspects of Q1 have suggested error, corruption and piracy, of course, but the fact that Corambis also appeared in a later German adaptation of the play, *Der bestrafte Brudermord*, suggests that this change, at least, was intentional.

8 See James Marino, *Owning William Shakespeare* (Philadelphia: University of Pennsylvania Press, 2011), pp. 84–90.

11 SHAKESPEARE AND WARWICKSHIRE

1 Ignatius Donnelly, *The Great Cryptogram: Francis Bacon's Cypher in the So-Called Shakespeare Plays* (Chicago, New York and London: R. S. Peale & Company, 1888), pp. 28–9.

2 Thomas J. Looney, *'Shakespeare' Identified in Edward de Vere the Seventeenth Lord of Oxford* (New York: Frederick A. Stokes Company, 1920), p. 16.

3 Charlton Ogburn Jr., *The Mysterious William Shakespeare*, 2nd edn (McLean, VA: EPM Publications, 1991), p. 71.

4 For the early history of Stratford, see Robert Bearman, ed., *The History of an English Borough: Stratford-upon-Avon, 1196–1996* (Phoenix Mill: Sutton Publishing, 1997), especially pp. 43–79. For the school, see ibid. pp. 46, 48 and Nicholas Orme, *Medieval Schools: From Roman Britain to Renaissance England* (New Haven: Yale University Press, 2006), pp. 243, 367.

5 Mark Eccles, *Shakespeare in Warwickshire* (Madison: University of Wisconsin Press, 1963), p. 24.

6 S. Schoenbaum, *William Shakespeare: A Compact Documentary Life* (Oxford University Press, 1977), p. 321.

7 Edgar I. Fripp, *Shakespeare Studies: Biographical and Literary* (Oxford University Press, 1930), pp. 25–6; also see pp. 31–51 on John Brownswerd.

8 Alan H. Nelson, 'Shakespeare and the Bibliophiles: From the Earliest Years to 1616', in Robin Myers, Michael Harris and Giles Mandelbrote, eds., *Owners, Annotators, and the Signs of Reading* (London: British Library, 2005), pp. 49–73.

9 Schoenbaum, *Compact Documentary Life*, p. 38.

10 Eccles, *Shakespeare in Warwickshire*, pp. 80–3.

11 In a Chancery deposition given on 12 September 1588 (TNA c21/D22/4), Quiney described himself as a mercer of Stratford-upon-Avon, age thirty-five, implying that he was born in about 1553. His father Adrian also gave a deposition the same day, describing himself as a mercer of Stratford-upon-Avon, age sixty-eight.

12 Edgar I. Fripp, *Master Richard Quyny, Bailiff of Stratford-upon-Avon and Friend of William Shakespeare* (Oxford University Press, 1924), p. 16.

13 Ibid., p. 133.

14 Ibid., pp. 120–1, 154.

15 Ibid., p. 160.

16 Ibid., p. 189.

17 Ibid., p. 158.

18 The following biographical sketch is based mainly on Christopher Whitfield, 'Some of Shakespeare's Contemporaries at the Middle Temple (Part IV)', *Notes and Queries* 211 (1966), pp. 445–6.

19 E. K. Chambers, *William Shakespeare: A Study of Facts and Problems*, 2 vols. (Oxford: Clarendon Press, 1930), vol. II, pp. 96, 142–3.

20 The following biographical sketch is based primarily on Leslie Hotson, *I, William Shakespeare* (London: Jonathan Cape, 1937), esp. chapters 2, 4, 5 and 6, and Eccles, *Shakespeare in Warwickshire*, pp. 116–18.

21 T. S. Eliot, *Selected Essays, 1917–1932* (New York: Harcourt, Brace, 1932), p. 108.

22 For 'unwappered', see R. C. Churchill, *Shakespeare and His Betters* (London: Max Reinhardt, 1958), p. xiii; for the dialectal status of the other words, see C. T. Onions, *A Shakespeare Glossary* (Oxford University Press, 1911). See also Hilda M. Hulme's *Explorations in Shakespeare's Language* (London: Longmans, 1962).

23 Chambers, *William Shakespeare*, vol. II, p. 144.

24 Stanley Wells and Gary Taylor, with John Jowett and William Montgomery, *William Shakespeare: A Textual Companion* (Oxford University Press, 1987), pp. 163–4, list twenty-seven manuscript copies, and Brandon Centerwall adds seven more in 'Who Wrote William Basse's "Elegy on Shakespeare"?: Rediscovering a Poem Lost from the Donne Canon', in Peter Holland, ed., *Shakespeare Survey 59* (Cambridge University Press, 2006), pp. 267–84. The seven manuscript copies that mention Shakespeare's death date are B4, F7, R2, N, O4, O5 (in Wells and Taylor's notation), plus c (in Centerwall's notation), the copy in Basse's autograph. The copy mentioning Shakespeare's burial place is Y2.

25 M. H. Spielmann, 'Shakespeare's Portraiture', in *Studies in the First Folio* (Oxford University Press, 1924); Diana Price, 'Reconsidering Shakespeare's Monument', *Review of English Studies* 48 (1997), pp. 168–81.

26 Robert C. Evans, 'Whome None but Death Could Shake: An Unreported Epitaph on Shakespeare', *Shakespeare Quarterly* 39 (1988), p. 60.

27 Alan H. Nelson and Paul Altrocchi, 'William Shakespeare, "Our Roscius"', *Shakespeare Quarterly* 60 (2009), pp. 460–9.

28 Ogburn, *The Mysterious William Shakespeare*, p. 14.

12 SHAKESPEARE AND SCHOOL

1 This provision establishing the grammar school is contained in the Latin Borough Charter, in a translation transcribed in *Captain Saunders' Stratford Collections* held in The Shakespeare Birthplace Trust, Stratford-upon-Avon (see ER1/77). The original charter is held in the SBT archive. In fact, there had been teaching of some sort in the town since 1295. In 1427 permission was granted for the building of a 'Latin school'. Small, two storied, timber-framed, it remains the first recorded example of a purpose-built schoolhouse in England, and was in use until the time of the Dissolution. Stratford's town council, the pre-Reformation Guild of the Holy Cross, survived the reign of Henry VIII but was suppressed by Edward VI. The Charter of 1553 restored old Guild properties to the corporate hands of the town, in effect, re-naming an already old foundation and using confiscated property to endow it. See Richard Pearson, *King Edward VI School, Stratford-upon-Avon* (Tenterden: Gresham Books, 2008), pp. 5, 7, 10.

2 And the question has distracted the so-called 'anti-Stratfordians' since the middle of the nineteenth century. But as Robert Miola in *Shakespeare's Reading* (Oxford University Press, 2000) sanely observes, while for some people the 'temptation has proven irresistible' to imagine 'that Shakespeare's poetry and drama arose . . . from his life' (prompting, for them, an immediate question: how could such a life have produced such writing?), the surviving work itself 'gives more reliable witness to its genesis and origins. Shakespeare created much of his art from his reading', pp. 1–2.

3 G. B. Harrison, ed., *Greenes Groatsworth of Wit, Bought with a Million of Repentance*, 1592 (London: Bodley Head, 1923), pp. 46–7 (BM c.57.b.42, FIV). Not insignificantly, for those who think a university education was the essential equipment for an early modern playwright, Greene sees his life 'at the University of Cambridge' as his initiation into dissipation: 'I light amongst wags as lewd as my self, with whom I consumed the flower of my youth, who drew me to travel into Italy, and Spain, in which places I saw and practised such villainy as is abominable to declare.' See Harrison, ed., *Greenes Groatsworth of Wit*, pp. 19–20. See too Katherine Duncan-Jones's suggestion in *Ungentle Shakespeare: Scenes from his Life* (London: Arden Shakespeare, 2001), pp. 44–8 that either Thomas Nashe or Henry Chettle was the 'real' author of *Greenes Groatsworth of Wit*.

4 Quoted in T. W. Baldwin, *William Shakspere's Small Latine & Lesse Greeke*, 2 vols. (Urbana: University of Illinois Press, 1944), vol. 1, p. 15.

5 From the great ode to Shakespeare by Ben Jonson published in the First Folio of 1623, beginning: 'To the memory of my beloved, the author, Mr William Shakespeare, and what he hath left us.'

6 For a handlist of comparative curricula see Peter Mack, *Elizabethan Rhetoric: Theory and Practice* (Cambridge University Press, 2002), p. 13.

7 Ibid., p. 11.

8 M. H. Curtis, 'Education and Apprenticeship', in Kenneth Muir, ed., *Shakespeare Survey 17* (Cambridge University Press, 1964), p. 53.

9 See Mack in 'Rhetoric, Ethics and Reading in the Renaissance', *Renaissance Studies* 19:1 (2005), pp. 1–21.

10 Curtis, *Shakespeare Survey 17*, p. 53.

11 Ibid., p. 58.

12 In 'On the Method of Study', tr. Brian McGregor, in Craig R. Thompson, ed., *Collected Works of Erasmus*, vol. xxiv (University of Toronto Press, 1978), p. 667.

13 Throughout this section I am depending on Mack's *Elizabethan Rhetoric*, the core text for understanding how the Elizabethans were trained to read and write, and I am grateful to him for allowing me to use his work freely.

14 Miola, *Shakespeare's Reading*, p. 2.

15 Those phrases are Brian Vickers's, in 'Shakespeare's Use of Rhetoric', in Kenneth Muir and S. Schoenbaum, eds., *A New Companion to Shakespeare Studies* (Cambridge University Press, 1971), p. 91.

16 G. K. Hunter, in Peter Mack, ed., *A History of Renaissance Rhetoric 1380–1620* (Basingstoke: Macmillan, 1994), p. 103.

17 Peter Mack points out that pupils probably didn't read the whole of these books in class. Class reading perhaps stretched to a couple of books (or maybe even a few hundred lines). But that means that students had the ability to read the rest privately. R. R. Bolgar in 'Classical Reading in Renaissance Schools', *Durham Research Review* 6 (1955), pp. 18–26, writes about pupils not getting all the way through their texts (and that's how it looks from the marginalia too). The syllabus then, as today, was aspirational as well as actual. I'm grateful to Peter Mack for reading this piece and offering modifications.

18 Quoted in Katherine Duncan-Jones, *Sir Philip Sidney, Courtier Poet* (London: Hamish Hamilton, 1991), p. 31.

19 See Carol Chillington Rutter, 'The Alphabet of Memory in *Titus Andronicus*', in *Shakespeare and Child's Play* (London: Routledge, 2007), pp. 61–5 where I rely on the brilliant work done on medieval schooling by Marjorie Curry Woods.

20 This is St Augustine, remembering his own school exercise; quoted by Marjorie Curry Woods, 'Weeping for Dido', in Carol Dana Lanham, ed., *Latin Grammar and Rhetoric: From Classical Theory to Medieval Practice* (New York: Continuum, 2002), p. 284.

21 John Brinsley, *Ludus Literarius* (1612) (Menston: Scolar Press, 1968), pp. 210, 212–13.

22 Mack, *Elizabethan Rhetoric*, p. 12.

23 Miola, *Shakespeare's Reading*, pp. 2, 3.

24 Duncan-Jones, *Ungentle Shakespeare*, p. 15.

25 Miola, *Shakespeare's Reading*, p. 3. In any case, university training at Oxford and Cambridge was purely professional: in divinity, law or physic (that is, medicine). If university students read literature, it was extra-curricular. The 'only formal literary training provided by society' in Shakespeare's day, writes Baldwin, was the training had in the grammar schools (*Small Latine*, p. 662).

13 SHAKESPEARE TELLS LIES

1 All quotations from *The Tempest* refer to David Lindley, ed., *The Tempest*, New Cambridge Shakespeare (Cambridge University Press, 2002).
2 Harold Jenkins, ed., *Hamlet* (London: Methuen, 1982; repr. 1990), p. 122.
3 T. S. Eliot, 'Shakespeare and the Stoicism of Seneca', in *Selected Essays 1917–1932* (London: Faber and Faber, 1932).
4 F. R. Leavis, 'Diabolic Intellect and the Noble Hero', *Scrutiny* 6 (1937), an essay reprinted in *The Common Pursuit* (London: Chatto and Windus, 1952). William Empson on the word 'Honest' in *Othello* in his *Structure of Complex Words* (London: Chatto and Windus, 1951).
5 Helen Gardner, 'The Noble Moor', British Academy Lecture, 1956, reprinted in Anne Ridler, ed., *Shakespeare Criticism 1935–60* (London: Oxford University Press, 1963), pp. 348–70, at p. 358.

14 'THIS PALPABLE DEVICE': AUTHORSHIP AND CONSPIRACY IN SHAKESPEARE'S LIFE

1 Kathleen Hall Jamieson and Brook Jackson, 'Our Disinformed Electorate', www.factcheck.org/specialreports/our_disinformed_electorate.html (accessed 19 October 2011).
2 A notable exception to this tendency is James Shapiro's account of the controversy, *Contested Will: Who Wrote Shakespeare?* (London: Faber and Faber, 2010) that gives a full account of the complex life that led to Delia Bacon's breakdown.
3 The mass of evidence that demonstrates the case for Shakespeare's authorship is surveyed in Stanley Wells's chapter in this book (Chapter 7).
4 See Wendy Wall's discussion in *Staging Domesticity: Household Work and English Identity in Early Modern England* (Cambridge University Press, 2002) of the shift in Shakespeare's time between 'old wives' tales' and the demands of reason and revealed truth, and Shapiro's connection between the authorship debates and the intellectual work in biblical and classical studies.
5 As in the case of the controversy over the safety of the MMR vaccine.
6 See Marina Warner, *Managing Monsters: Six Myths of Our Time*, The Reith Lectures (London: Vintage, 1994).
7 See the comprehensive account of the play's production history in James Siemon, ed., *King Richard III*, The Arden Shakespeare (London: Methuen, 2009), pp. 79–124. The Saddam Hussein analogy appeared in Suleyman Al Bassam, *Richard III: An Arab Tragedy*, performed at the RSC Complete Works Festival in February 2007. Enemies change but the story remains.
8 Siemon, 'Introduction', p. 108.
9 As they were in the National Theatre 1992 production of *Richard III* starring Ian McKellen.

10 Bill Hicks, *Rant in E-Minor* (1997). Quoted in David Aaronovitch, *Voodoo Histories: How Conspiracy Theory has Shaped Modern History* (London: Vintage Books, 2010).

11 *A Midsummer Night's Dream*, 5.1.1–23. Other examples and their historical and theatrical context are discussed in Kathleen McLuskie, 'Your Imagination and Not Theirs', in Claire Gheeraert-Graffeuille and Nathalie Vienne-Guerin, eds., *Autour du Songe d'une nuit d'été* (Publications de l'Université de Rouen, 2003), pp. 31–43.

12 Aaronovitch, *Voodoo Histories*, p. 331.

13 Ibid., p. 81.

14 Siemon, 'Introduction', pp. 108–10.

15 Margaret R. Somers, 'The Privatisation of Citizenship: How to Unthink a Knowledge Culture', in Victoria E. Bonnell and Lynn Hunt, eds., *Beyond the Cultural Turn* (Berkeley: University of California Press, 1999), pp. 126, 129.

16 A phrase used by Robert Bearman, in 'Was William Shakespeare William Shakeshafte? Revisited', *Shakespeare Quarterly* 52 (2002), pp. 83–93; he was disputing Ernst Honigmann's influential view that Shakespeare spent the 'lost years' in the household of a recusant Lancashire gentleman. See Honigmann's response to Bearman, 'The Shakespeare/Shakeshafte Question Continued', *Shakespeare Quarterly* 54 (2003), pp. 83–6.

17 Analysed in Jerome de Groot, *Consuming History* (London: Routledge, 2008).

18 Samuel Schoenbaum, *Shakespeare's Lives* (London: Oxford University Press, 1970); Shapiro, *Contested Will*. See also the review of Shapiro's *Contested Will* that sarcastically congratulates him on having kept to an academic party line: www.truthaboutwill.org (accessed 19 October 2011).

19 Quoted in Shapiro, *Contested Will*, p. 232.

20 For an account of the development of the 'Watergate story' as a paradigm conspiracy see Aaronovitch, *Voodoo Histories*, p. 8.

21 Compare the visual effect created in Al Pacino's contrast between senior academic advisors and the street-wise populist enthusiasts in his docudrama, *Looking for Richard*.

22 The connection between this narrative and the rhetorics of twenty-first-century government policy for 'creativity' is analysed in Kathleen E. McLuskie, 'The Commercial Bard: Business Models for the Twenty-First Century', *Shakespeare Survey 64* (Cambridge University Press, 2012), pp. 1–12.

23 Quoted in Shapiro, *Contested Will*, p. 76.

24 Quoted and discussed in Schoenbaum, *Shakespeare's Lives*, pp. 53–9.

25 J. Leeds Barroll, 'Shakespeare without King James', in *Politics, Plague and Shakespeare's Theatre* (Ithaca: Cornell University Press, 1991) has shown that even Shakespeare's much discussed connection to the Royal Court via the King's Men playing company only gave him contact with court officials responsible for scheduling and paying for performances. The direct connection between James I and *Macbeth* via James's interest in demonology is imagined by Dr Johnson for his note on the play's opening stage-direction. See Samuel Johnson, *The Plays of William Shakespeare*, 8 vols. (London: J. and R. Tonson, 1765).

26 Charles Nicholl, *The Lodger: Shakespeare on Silver Street* (London: Penguin, 2007).

27 In particular he echoes the controversial account of the English Reformation offered in Eamon Duffy's *The Stripping of the Altars* (New Haven: Yale University Press, 1992) that analyses the limits of the Reformation project on the practice of early modern Christians. See also Germaine Greer's discussion of social history in her book *Shakespeare's Wife* (London: Bloomsbury, 2007).

28 In *Midnight in Paris*, Columbia Pictures, 2011.

29 The style has been a popular form of parodic biography, from *The Learned Pig* of 1786 (see Shapiro, *Contested Will*, p. 21) to Harry Rowe's learned puppet in the notes to his version of *Macbeth* (York: np, 1797) to the charming sequence of cockroach stories in Don Marquis's *Archy and Mehitabel* (London: Faber and Faber, 1934).

30 Henry Howard Furness, ed., *A New Variorum Edition of Shakespeare*, vol. x, *A Midsummer Nights Dreame* (Philadelphia; and London: J. Lippincott, 1895), p. 83.

31 In the case of the imagined connection between Shakespeare and the gentry Arden family that scepticism is supported by Robert Bearman's account of the complex archival history of Palmer's Farm in Wilmcote. See 'Discovering Mary Arden's house: Property and Society in Wilmcote, Warwickshire', *Shakespeare Quarterly* 52 (2002), pp. 53–83.

32 See the opening shots of *Anonymous*, Sony Pictures, 2011.

33 George Taylor, 'A New Shakespeare', www.stromata.typepad.com/stromata_blog/2005/09/a_new_shakespea.html (accessed 18 October 2011). This blog on authorship insists that records of Elizabeth's three children 'exist in archives in places like Madrid, Paris, Amsterdam and Venice'.

34 Aaronovitch, *Voodoo Histories*, p. 127.

35 William Ingram, *The Business of Playing: The Beginnings of Adult Professional Theatre in Elizabethan London* (Ithaca: Cornell University Press, 1992); Richard Dutton, *Mastering the Revels: The Regulation and Censorship of English Renaissance Drama* (London: Macmillan, 1991).

36 Virginia Woolf's description of biography as distinct from fiction in 'The Art of Biography', in *The Death of the Moth and Other Essays* (London: Hogarth Press, 1942), p. 123.

37 Compare Shapiro's thoughtful account of the modern view of the disconnection between biography and creativity, *Contested Will*, pp. 298–316.

38 De Groot, *Consuming History*, p. 249.

39 Jerome de Groot, 'Empathy and Enfranchisement, *Rethinking History* 10:3 (2006), p. 393.

40 See, for example, the Home Office decision, announced 18 October 2011, to release all the documents from the enquiry into the Hillsborough Football Stadium disaster from 1989: www.google.co.uk/search/hillsborough (accessed 18 October 2011).

41 www.doubtaboutwill.org (accessed 18 October 2011).

15 AMATEURS AND PROFESSIONALS: REGENDERING BACON

1 Edward Dowden, diary for 1883, entry for 14 March. Dowden papers, Trinity College Dublin, TCD MS 3116.

2 Delia Bacon, *The Philosophy of the Plays of Shakspere Unfolded* (London: Groombridge, 1857; quoted from Echo Library edition, 2005), p. 39. All further references are included parenthetically in the text of the chapter.

3 Edward Dowden, letter to A. E. Thiselton, dated 9 February 1903, National Library of Ireland, MS 5499.

4 Unless otherwise stated, all general details of Bacon's life – and of her family – are taken from Vivian C. Hopkins, *Prodigal Puritan: A Life of Delia Bacon* (Cambridge, MA: Belknap Press of Harvard University Press, 1959).

5 S. Schoenbaum, *Shakespeare's Lives*, 2nd edn (Oxford: Clarendon Press, 1991), p. 387.

6 Edward Dowden, letter to W. F. P. Stockley, dated 25 March 1910, in [Hilda M. Dowden (ed.)], *Letters of Edward Dowden and His Correspondents* (London: Dent, 1914), p. 364.

7 See Edward Dowden, *Shakspere: A Critical Study of his Mind and Art* (London: Henry S. King, 1875), pp. 47–9.

8 James Shapiro, *Contested Will: Who Wrote Shakespeare?* (London: Faber and Faber, 2010), p. 77.

9 See Hopkins, *Prodigal Puritan*, p. 177.

10 Gary Taylor, *Reinventing Shakespeare: A Cultural History, from the Restoration to the Present* (Oxford University Press, 1991), p. 220.

11 Josephine Guy, ed., *The Victorian Age: An Anthology of Sources and Documents* (London: Routledge, 2001), p. 201.

12 Harold Perkin, *The Rise of Professional Society: England since 1880* (London: Routledge, 1989), p. 2.

13 In *Printing Technology, Letters and Samuel Johnson* (Princeton University Press, 1987), Alvin Kernan argues for seeing Johnson as a decisive figure in serving to break the link between literary work and patronage.

14 There is one point of qualification that must be made here, however. While the resources available to Bacon were much narrower than those afforded to scholars within the academy, it is also the case that she did not take full advantage of all of the opportunities that were, in fact, at her disposal. Supporters such as Carlyle, Emerson and Hawthorne sought to facilitate contact with other scholars, together with access to institutions such as the British Museum library, but Bacon did not fully avail of this support, telling Emerson, for instance, that her theory about the plays relied on internal evidence from the texts alone and was 'independent of further historical collaboration' – see Hopkins, *Prodigal Puritan*, p. 188. In the *Philosophy* itself, Bacon writes: 'The facts which it contains . . . will not be dependent ultimately upon the mode of their dimensions of historical truth, and are accessible on more sides than one' (p. 419).

15 Nina Baym, 'Delia Bacon, History's Odd Woman Out', *New England Quarterly* 69:2 (June 1996), p. 224.

16 Ibid., p. 249.
17 Taylor, *Reinventing Shakespeare*, p. 220.
18 Edward Dowden, diary for 1882, entry for 3 February, TCD ms 3038.
19 See Edmund Bentley, *Far Horizon: A Biography of Hester Dowden, Medium and Psychic Investigator* (London: Rider, 1951), p. 16. Unless otherwise stated, all details of Hester Dowden's life are taken from this source. Edward Dowden's position seems genuinely to have been profoundly ambiguous. Christina Hunt Mahony provides an excellent account of the greater context in 'Women's Education, Edward Dowden and the University Curriculum in English Literature: An Unlikely Progression', in Margaret Kelleher and James H. Murphy, eds., *Gender Perspectives in Nineteenth-century Ireland: Public and Private Spheres* (Dublin: Irish Academic Press, 1997). Mahony notes that Dowden had taught at Alexandra College for Women before he joined the faculty at Trinity and that 'the choice and range of lecture material on offer at Alexandra . . . were considerably more modern and flexible than the syllabus Dowden was to create soon after at TCD' (p. 201). As Mahony notes, having strongly opposed the admission of women students, Dowden joked, when they finally were admitted to Trinity, 'I now have lasses as well as asses in my classes.' But it is worth also quoting the remainder of his comment: 'In all about 60, + have just got a sheaf of admirable essays from them' (letter to William McNeile Dixon, TCD MS 2259/18). In this, as in other matters, the position adopted by Dowden in private did not necessarily wholly accord with the position he adopted in public.
20 Hester Travers Smith, ed., *Psychic Messages from Oscar Wilde* (London: T. Werner Laurie, [1924]), p. 33.
21 Ibid., p. 35.
22 Percy Allen, *Talks with Elizabethans Revealing the Mystery of 'William Shakespeare'* (London: Rider, [1947]), p. 16.
23 Ibid., p. 40.
24 Shapiro, *Contested Will*, p. 228. By way of an example, I include one of the sonnets here. Of course, it falls far short of Shakespeare, and there are some jarring moments (drowned in sunlight, the internal rhyme of 'Here is no fear', etc.). But, viewed as an attempt at sonnet writing by someone who was not a practising poet, it is a creditable enough performance:

> When from the star-strewn heavens I gaze around,
> And mark the narrow compass of the Earth,
> Small as an atom in the sunlight drowned –
> I marvel how within such narrow girth
> My love for thee found sustenance and space;
> The wine too close was housed, too small the cup;
> My precious draught o'erflowed the narrow place,
> Lost all its perfumed flavour, soon dried up.
> Now has my love found her true path of grace;
> Deep in the soul she hides herself and me.

Here is no fear of time, of age no trace;
Forever of restraining fetters free –
So we enjoy the glory of the sun,
In sure affinity – for we are one.

(Allen, *Talks*, p. 196)

25 See Bentley, *Far Horizon*, p. 87.
26 G. D. Cummins, 'The Strange Case of Oscar Wilde', *Occult Review* 39:2 (February 1924), p. 110.
27 Taylor, *Reinventing Shakespeare*, p. 220.
28 Vivian C. Hopkins is adamant, in *Prodigal Puritan*, that Bacon was no feminist, but the point is made a number of times and with an insistence – for example, 'whatever idol blinded Delia's vision, it was never the idol of feminism' (p. 299) – that makes one wonder whether it might not be a case of protesting just a little too much.

16 FICTIONAL TREATMENTS OF SHAKESPEARE'S AUTHORSHIP

1 Arliss Ryan, *The Secret Confessions of Anne Shakespeare* (London: Penguin, 2010).
2 Farrukh Dhondy, *Black Swan* (London: Victor Gollancz, 1992).
3 Oscar Wilde, 'The Portrait of Mr. W. H.' (1889), in Ian Small, ed., *Oscar Wilde: Complete Short Fiction* (London: Penguin, 1994), pp. 49–79.
4 Delia Bacon, as quoted in J. Shapiro, *Contested Will: Who Wrote Shakespeare?* (London: Faber and Faber, 2010), p. 116.
5 Mark Twain, *1601* (1882; Project Gutenberg Etext, 2002), www.gutenberg.org/ebooks/3190 (accessed 3 January 2011).
6 J. Hirsh, 'Samuel Clemens and the Ghost of Shakespeare', *Studies in the Novel* 24 (1992), pp. 251–72.
7 George Moore, *The Making of an Immortal: A Play in One Act* (New York: Bowling Green Press, 1927).
8 William R. Leigh, *Clipt Wings: A Drama in Five Acts* (New York: Thornton W. Allen Company, 1930).
9 See Shapiro, *Contested Will*, pp. 136, 141–2.
10 Colin Wilson, *The Philosopher's Stone: A Prophetic Novel of the Future* (1969; New York: Warner Books, 1974).
11 Rhoda H. Messner, *Absent thee from Felicity: The Story of Edward de Vere Seventeenth Earl of Oxford* (Shaker Heights, OH: The Corinthian Press, 1975), p. 226.
12 Stephanie Caruana, 'Edward Oxenford: Spear-shaker' (1994). I am indebted to Stephanie Caruana for sending me a copy of her script.
13 L. Kositsky, *A Question of Will* (Montreal: Roussan Publishers, 2000).
14 Susan Cooper, *King of Shadows* (1999; Harmondsworth: Penguin, 2000).

15 Jaime Salom, *The Other William,* in *Three Comedies* (Boulder, CO: University of Colorado Press, 2004), pp. 169–227. Cf. Keith Gregor and Encarna Vidal Rodríguez, 'The "Other" William and the Question of Authority in Spanish Stage Depictions of Shakespeare', *Sederi* 12 (2001), pp. 237–46.

16 Rodney Bolt, *History Play: The Lives and Afterlives of Christopher Marlowe* (New York: Bloomsbury, 2005).

17 Sarah Smith, *Chasing Shakespeares* (New York: Washington Square Press, 2003).

18 Norma Howe, *The Blue Avenger Cracks the Code* (New York: Harper Collins, 2002).

19 Jennifer Lee Carrell, *Interred with their Bones* (New York: Dutton, 2007).

20 Mark Rylance, 'The Big Secret live! "I am Shakespeare" Webcam Daytime Chatroom Show!!' (2007). I am indebted to Mark Rylance for sending me a copy of the unpublished script.

21 Amy Freed, *The Beard of Avon* (2001; New York: Samuel French, 2004).

22 Vladimir Nabokov, *Bend Sinister* (1947; London: Corgi Books, 1962), pp. 79, 100–1.

23 Harry Mulisch, *De ontdekking van de hemel* (1992; Amsterdam: De Bezige Bij, 2003), pp. 246–9.

24 Luis Kutner, *The Trialle of William Shakespeare: Being a Playe in 3 Acts to be Rede and/or Performed* (Chicago: Bardian House, 1974).

25 C. Brahms and S. J. Simon, *No Bed for Bacon* (1941; London: The Hogarth Press, 1986).

26 Anthony Burgess, 'The Muse', in his *Enderby's Dark Lady: Or No End to Enderby* (New York: McGraw-Hill, 1984), pp. 142–60.

27 For a different reading, see Douglas Lanier, *Shakespeare and Modern Popular Culture* (Oxford University Press, 2002), p. 135. I am indebted to Douglas Lanier for suggesting many of the titles discussed in this chapter.

17 THE 'DECLARATION OF REASONABLE DOUBT'

1 James Shapiro, *Contested Will: Who Wrote Shakespeare?* (London: Faber and Faber, 2010), p. 218.

2 Michael Egan, ed., *The Tragedy of Richard II, Part One: A Newly Authenticated Play by William Shakespeare,* 3 vols. (Lampeter: Edwin Mellen Press, 2006).

3 See www.playshakespeare.com/shakespeare-news/3692-noted-shakespearean-egan-takes-over-the-oxfordian.

4 William Leahy, ed., *William Shakespeare and his Authors: Critical Perspectives on the Authorship Question* (London: Continuum, 2010).

5 Don Ostrowski, 'Three Criteria of Historical Study', 2003, see http://isites.harvard.edu/fs/docs/icb.topic957161.files/history.pdf (accessed 3 February 2012).

6 Mark Anderson, *'Shakespeare' by Another Name: The Life of Edward de Vere, Earl of Oxford, The Man Who Was Shakespeare* (New York: Penguin, 2005).

7 Shapiro, *Contested Will*, p. 209.

18 'THERE WON'T BE PUPPETS, WILL THERE?': 'HEROIC' AUTHORSHIP AND THE CULTURAL POLITICS OF *ANONYMOUS*

1 D. K. Hedrick, 'War is Mud: Branagh's Dirty Harry V and the Types of Political Ambiguity', in R. Burt and L. E. Boose, eds., *Shakespeare the Movie II* (London and New York: Routledge, 2003), pp. 413–30.

2 This technique of inventing a 'biographical' backstory for the ballroom scene is shamelessly lifted from *Shakespeare in Love*, which handles it with a lighter touch.

3 Christopher Measom, ed., *Anonymous: William Shakespeare Revealed*, A Newmarket Pictorial Moviebook (New York: Newmarket Press, 2011), p. 118, singles out Hamlet's sense of isolation and heroic affliction as the key sources of this speech's poetic power:

> A man sits alone on a stage. Is it better, he asks the audience before him, to suffer all the heartaches and the pain that the world throws at us or to end it all by taking one's own life, thus risking an eternity of suffering? In the court, Queen Elizabeth, lonely in her old age, sits silently bewitched by the power of Oxford's words. In the Rose Theatre, hundreds of groundlings stand, captivated, oblivious to the rain that drenches them as they listen.

What isn't engaged are any elements that might critically distance us from Hamlet – his penchant for delay and for over-intellectualizing and complicating his situation, his predilection for self-absorbed melancholy, his Oedipal self-loathing, his self-defeating demand for certainty.

4 Performance supervisor Tamara Harvey's note in Measom, ed., *Anonymous*, p. 122, acknowledges the historical inaccuracy of the change, stressing that it was necessitated by the film's target audience:

> Historically, it is the play *Richard II* that is linked to the Essex rebellion. However, without the benefit of a lengthy footnote, this is fairly tricky to convey to an audience that doesn't consist entirely of Shakespeare scholars.

The implicit attitude toward academic Shakespearians and historical fidelity is noteworthy. Elsewhere Measom, ed., *Anonymous* supplies a paragraph ('Switching Richards') which accurately lays out the basic historical narrative of the Essex rebellion and its relation to the Lord Chamberlain's Men's performance of *Richard II*, presenting it casually as 'an interesting footnote' rather than as a crucial detail. This note (p. 98) suggests that the change was made for different reasons:

> In the movie, the performance of *Richard II* was replaced with *Richard III* to suggest a connection between the villainous hunchbacked King Richard III and the ill-shaped Robert Cecil, the Queen's closest advisor.

Since the film so emphasizes Oxford's suffering at the hands of the oppressive Cecils, this change also helps preserve the thesis that the plays that bear

Shakespeare's name spring from Oxford's personal experience and are specifically targeted to those in power. Though this note is written by John Orloff, the film's scriptwriter, the fact that the admission is in passive voice makes the source of this controversial change difficult to trace – dare I say, strategically anonymous.

5 There is an alternative popular tradition, exemplified by Jacques Tourneur's film *Master Will Shakespeare* (1936), that imagines Shakespeare as a relatively ordinary working theatre professional, in this case a prompter who stumbles into a writing career when he supplies a line of his own for a forgetful actor. This tradition seeks to puncture the mythic stature of Shakespeare the author in an effort to bring his work into a pop cultural register; it is no accident that Tourneur's film was produced in conjunction with MGM's 1936 film of *Romeo and Juliet*. Even here, however, the other, dominant tradition makes its mark – in Tourneur's film the favourite play of its lovelorn Shakespeare is *Romeo and Juliet*.

6 The hypothesis that *Hamlet*, a central play for many Oxfordians, uses Polonius to burlesque William Cecil (and that Hamlet is to be identified with Oxford) stretches back as far as Thomas Looney in *Shakespeare Identified in Edward de Vere the Seventeenth Earl of Oxford* (New York: Frederick A. Stokes Company, 1920), pp. 457–86, and is developed at some length by Charlton Ogburn in *The Mysterious William Shakespeare: The Myth and the Reality* (New York: Dodd, Mead & Company, 1984), pp. 199–204. Ogburn explains away the lack of rancour between Oxford and Cecil in their correspondence by suggesting that 'neither could well afford to come to an open break with the other' and that the Cecils actively 'fram[ed] the historical record as it involved de Vere', p. 203.

7 Only here does Oxford utter lines indisputably his own: 'For truth is truth though never so old, and time cannot make that false which once was true.' These words come from Oxford's letter to Sir Robert Cecil dated 7 May 1603, where Oxford sought to capitalize on James's recent accession to beg for the restoration of dispossessed lands once part of the family estate. See William Plumer Fowler, *Shakespeare Revealed in Oxford's Letters: The Pre-Armada Letters, 1563–1585, and The Post-Armada Letters, 1590–1603, of Edward de Vere, Seventeenth Earl of Oxford* (Portsmouth, NH: Peter E. Randall, 1986), p. 771). In his commentary, Fowler makes much of this utterly conventional, poetically pedestrian sentence, linking it to the family name 'de Vere' and motto 'vero nihil verius' and charting for several pages similarities between it and passages from Shakespeare plays and poems (pp. 772–6); see also Joseph Sobran, *Alias Shakespeare: Solving the Greatest Literary Mystery of All Time* (New York: The Free Press, 1997), pp. 275–6.

By contrast, the film treats the passage simply as 'evidence' of the boy Oxford's gift for extemporaneous composition and, perhaps more importantly, as a metacinematic declaration of the moral basis for the film's Oxfordian thesis, provided by the man himself.

8 This parallel accords with the widespread scholarly argument that Titania's relationship with Bottom depicts Elizabeth's relationship with courtiers in comically degraded form, though few Shakespearians would identify Bottom specifically with Oxford. For a full discussion of the context of this reading, see Louis A.

Montrose, *The Purpose of Playing: Shakespeare and the Cultural Politics of the Elizabethan Theatre* (University of Chicago Press, 1996), pp. 152–69.

9 Pierre Bourdieu, *Distinction: A Social Critique of the Judgement of Taste*, trans. Richard Nice (Cambridge, MA: Harvard University Press, 1984), p. 14.

10 Richard Burt, '*Shakespeare in Love* and the End of the Shakespearean: Academic and Mass Culture Constructions of Literary Authorship', in Mark Thornton Burnett and Ramona Wray, eds., *Shakespeare, Film, Fin de Siècle* (London: Macmillan/New York: St Martin's Press, 2000), p. 221.

11 Even the witches' scene from *Macbeth* is prefaced by the comment, 'Macbeth was Scottish, wasn't he?', suggesting that Oxford intends the play to stir up anti-Scottish (and therefore anti-Jacobean) fervour with the mob.

19 'THE SHAKESPEARE ESTABLISHMENT' AND THE SHAKESPEARE AUTHORSHIP DISCUSSION

1 *The Sunday Times Magazine*, 16 October 2011 on the release of the film *Anonymous*.

2 William D. Rubinstein, *Who Wrote Shakespeare's Plays?* (Stroud: Amberley, 2012), p. 152.

3 www.authorshipstudies.org/databaseSubscriptions.cfm (accessed 20 March 2012).

4 www.shakespeareanauthorshiptrust.org.uk/pdf/macourse.pdf (accessed 20 March 2012).

5 www.shakespeareanauthorshiptrust.org.uk/pages/news.htm (accessed 20 March 2012).

6 www.timeshighereducation.co.uk/story.asp?storycode=417586 (accessed 20 March 2012). *Times Higher Educational Supplement*, 29 September 2011.

7 www.esu.org/news/2011/shakespeare-authorship-debate-monday-06-june (accessed 20 March 2012).

8 Ibid.

9 www.shakespeareauthorship.com

10 www.misfit-inc.com

11 In *60 Minutes with Shakespeare*, the kinds of questions which were raised and answered included:

How would Shakespeare have had access to books growing up in Stratford-upon-Avon? Did Shakespeare attend the King Edward VI grammar school in Stratford-upon-Avon? Is there anything in the works which requires their author to have been educated at a university? Are there any clear links to be made between Shakespeare's plays and the area around Stratford-upon-Avon? Were Shakespeare's plays published under his own name in his lifetime? If Shakespeare is a fraud, what about the historical evidence? Did Shakespeare become famous in his lifetime? Should we be concerned that there are gaps in the historical record?

The full list and sound recordings can be accessed at www.60minuteswithShakespeare.com

12 https://doubtaboutwill.org/pdfs/sbt_rebuttal.pdf, p. 2 (accessed 20 March 2012).

13 Ibid., p. 5.

14 Here is a letter to *The Times*, by Paul Edmondson and Stanley Wells published on 25 October 2011:

Sir,

In 2002, properly honouring Christopher Marlowe by installing a commemorative window in Poets' Corner, the Dean and Chapter of Westminster Abbey authorized the presence of a question-mark to precede the year of Marlowe's death. In doing so they flew in the face of a mass of unimpugnable evidence. Marlowe died on 30 May 1593 as a result of being stabbed in the eye by an identified criminal, Ingram Frizer. The coroner's report survives. It was witnessed by a jury of sixteen men who inspected the corpse. It is recorded that Marlowe was buried in the churchyard of St Nicholas at Deptford on the same day as the inquest (1 June 1593). Moreover there are numerous references to Marlowe's death and tributes to his genius in the years immediately following it. Most significantly Shakespeare himself alludes to Marlowe in *As You Like It* when Phoebe is swept off her feet on first seeing Rosalind disguised as Ganymede: 'Dead shepherd, now I find thy saw of might: / "Whoever loved that loved not at first sight"?' (3.5). The quotation is from Marlowe's famous erotic poem, *Hero and Leander* (published posthumously in 1598). In *As You Like It* (almost certainly written in 1599) Shakespeare paid a fine and public tribute to his dead colleague. If Marlowe wrote Shakespeare this means he is writing about himself as dead, and from beyond the grave. How good does the surviving evidence have to be before it can be refuted? The evidence of the coroner's report is unimpeachable. The question mark in Marlowe's memorial window should be removed.

Yours etc., Paul Edmondson and Stanley Wells.

AFTERWORD

1 See www.ymiteacher.com/pdf/AnonymousCollege.pdf. A similar version was also prepared for high school teachers: www.ymiteacher.com/pdf/AnonymousHS.pdf. There is also apparently a German version for use in classrooms in German-speaking countries: www.germany.info/Vertretung/usa/en/__pr/GKs/LOSA/2011/11/16Anonymous__Education.html(last accessed 7 April 2012). Subsequent quotations in my 'Afterword' are cited from the college guide.

2 Alan Nelson, *Monstrous Adversary: The Life of Edward de Vere, 17th Earl of Oxford* (Liverpool University Press, 2003), p. 214.

3 See http://en.wikipedia.org/wiki/Shakespeare_authorship_question.

4 For Emmerich's remarks, see: file:///Documents/FREELANCE/wells,%20ed.%20CUP%20authorship%20book/Roland%20Emmerich%20talks%20Shakespeare,%20Anonymous%20and%20being%20influenced%20by%20Steven%20Spielberg%20%7C%20Flix66.com.webarchive (accessed 7 April 2012).

Index

279